# Introduction

This book has been written to meet the needs of the practising mechanic, both professional and amateur, together with the increasing flow of student mechanics at further education colleges in the UK, and, in the US, in technical institutes running motorcycle mechanics courses. In the UK it will be of particular relevance to those following the City and Guilds of London Institute 3890 *'Repair and Servicing of Motorcycles'* course.

No previous knowledge of electricity is assumed and all terms are explained in a glossary at the end of the manual.

The reader will not find here a catalogue of electric circuits for all machines, but rather a book dealing with the principles of how and why things work. Armed with an understanding of fundamentals it will be easier to follow developments which will surely take place in electrical equipment design. There may be a description of components which do not at the moment figure in actual production machines but, in the opinion of the author, may appear in the future.

Modern motorcycles are remarkable examples of high technology and much of it is due to the electrical equipment designs of recent years. Electrical power requirements now demand generators of greatly increased output and because of the sensitivity of on-board electronic units, voltage regulators of high stability are needed. Not surprisingly these are also electronic!

The language of electronics is sometimes strange to beginners so a glossary of terminology is included as is emphasis on fault finding and testing.

Readers are introduced to the transistor, Zener diode and thyristor (silicon controlled rectifier) and other devices, for these vital rugged components lie at the heart of most electronic circuits found on the motorcycle. A basic understanding of the on-board computer, which finds so many applications in ignition, fuelling and chassis systems is now essential and is described in sufficient detail for most purposes.

For all this, it would be folly not to include an account of older electrical equipment for there are still many earlier motorcycles on the road; a description of dc dynamos and magnetos is therefore included.

Tony Tranter

Guildford 1998

---

**A word to those who think that electricity is too difficult to understand – start at the beginning with an open mind and it is surprising how simple it all is when taken a little at a time**

---

# About this manual

The text in each chapter is arranged in numbered section order and will correspond with the contents list at the beginning of the chapter. If a section in another chapter is referred to, a typical instruction 'see Chapter 4, Section 8' will be found.

All illustrations are keyed into the text with their section number and paragraph number, eg 3.2 refers to section three paragraph two in that Chapter.

**Whilst every attempt is made to ensure that the information in this manual is correct, no liability can be accepted by the authors or publishers for loss, damage or injury caused by any errors in, or omissions from, the information given.**

# Acknowledgements

Many people from the motorcycle world were consulted during the preparation of this third edition and much gratitude is expressed for their time given and interest shown. Companies which gave copyright permission to reproduce their material are acknowledged below; if a source has been unknowingly omitted, apologies are tendered.

Boyer Bransden Ltd; Roy Bacon (author and publisher); AO Services; BMW AG Ltd and the staff of the BMW Technical Institute, Bracknell; Honda Motor Europe Ltd and the staff of the Honda Technical Training department, Chiswick; Honda Motor Co Ltd, Tokyo; Old Bike Mart; Kawasaki Motors (UK) Ltd; Yamaha Motor Co. Ltd, Suzuki plc; Robert Bosch Ltd; British Standards Institution; Champion Sparking Plug Co Ltd; Gunson Ltd; NGK Spark Plugs Ltd; Joseph Lucas Ltd; Edward Arnold Ltd, for permission to reproduce illustrations from *Lamps and Lighting* by Hewitt and Vause; FKI Crypton Ltd; Rists Ltd; 'Radco' (Frank Farrington) for information on rotary magnetos; Drive Publications Ltd; Yuasa Battery Co Ltd, Japan; Feridax (1957) Ltd; 3M UK plc; Delta Press Ltd; Jerry Storr (Ex-Merton College Staff); Jeff Clew; the Draper Tool Company; Vehicle Wiring Products, Ilkeston; Phil Langdon of Shadowfax Engineering; Tippetts Motors, Surbiton; Denso Spark Plugs; Clarke International Ltd; Hodder and Stoughton and TecMate International S.A. (Belgium).

Professional mechanics are trained in safe working procedures. However enthusiastic you may be about getting on with the job at hand, take the time to ensure that your safety is not put at risk. A moment's lack of attention can result in an accident, as can failure to observe simple precautions.

There will always be new ways of having accidents, and the following is not a comprehensive list of all dangers; it is intended rather to make you aware of the risks and to encourage a safe approach to all work you carry out on your bike.

## Asbestos

● Certain friction, insulating, sealing and other products - such as brake pads, clutch linings, gaskets, etc. - contain asbestos. Extreme care must be taken to avoid inhalation of dust from such products since it is hazardous to health. If in doubt, assume that they do contain asbestos.

## Fire

● Remember at all times that petrol is highly flammable. Never smoke or have any kind of naked flame around, when working on the vehicle. But the risk does not end there - a spark caused by an electrical short-circuit, by two metal surfaces contacting each other, by careless use of tools, or even by static electricity built up in your body under certain conditions, can ignite petrol vapour, which in a confined space is highly explosive. Never use petrol as a cleaning solvent. Use an approved safety solvent.

● Always disconnect the battery earth terminal before working on any part of the fuel or electrical system, and never risk spilling fuel on to a hot engine or exhaust.

● It is recommended that a fire extinguisher of a type suitable for fuel and electrical fires is kept handy in the garage or workplace at all times. Never try to extinguish a fuel or electrical fire with water.

## Fumes

● Certain fumes are highly toxic and can quickly cause unconsciousness and even death if inhaled to any extent. Petrol vapour comes into this category, as do the vapours from certain solvents such as trichloro-ethylene. Any draining or pouring of such volatile fluids should be done in a well ventilated area.

● When using cleaning fluids and solvents, read the instructions carefully. Never use materials from unmarked containers - they may give off poisonous vapours.

● Never run the engine of a motor vehicle in an enclosed space such as a garage. Exhaust fumes contain carbon monoxide which is extremely poisonous; if you need to run the engine, always do so in the open air or at least have the rear of the vehicle outside the workplace.

## The battery

● Never cause a spark, or allow a naked light near the vehicle's battery. It will normally be giving off a certain amount of hydrogen gas, which is highly explosive.

● Always disconnect the battery ground (earth) terminal before working on the fuel or electrical systems (except where noted).

● If possible, loosen the filler plugs or cover when charging the battery from an external source. Do not charge at an excessive rate or the battery may burst.

● Take care when topping up, cleaning or carrying the battery. The acid electrolyte, evenwhen diluted, is very corrosive and should not be allowed to contact the eyes or skin. Always wear rubber gloves and goggles or a face shield. If you ever need to prepare electrolyte yourself, always add the acid slowly to the water; never add the water to the acid.

## Electricity

● When using an electric power tool, inspection light etc., always ensure that the appliance is correctly connected to its plug and that, where necessary, it is properly grounded (earthed). Do not use such appliances in damp conditions and, again, beware of creating a spark or applying excessive heat in the vicinity of fuel or fuel vapour. Also ensure that the appliances meet national safety standards.

● A severe electric shock can result from touching certain parts of the electrical system, such as the spark plug wires (HT leads), when the engine is running or being cranked, particularly if components are damp or the insulation is defective. Where an electronic ignition system is used, the secondary (HT) voltage is much higher and could prove fatal.

# Remember...

✗ **Don't** start the engine without first ascertaining that the transmission is in neutral.

✗ **Don't** suddenly remove the pressure cap from a hot cooling system - cover it with a cloth and release the pressure gradually first, or you may get scalded by escaping coolant.

✗ **Don't** attempt to drain oil until you are sure it has cooled sufficiently to avoid scalding you.

✗ **Don't** grasp any part of the engine or exhaust system without first ascertaining that it is cool enough not to burn you.

✗ **Don't** allow brake fluid or antifreeze to contact the machine's paintwork or plastic components.

✗ **Don't** siphon toxic liquids such as fuel, hydraulic fluid or antifreeze by mouth, or allow them to remain on your skin.

✗ **Don't** inhale dust - it may be injurious to health (see Asbestos heading).

✗ **Don't** allow any spilled oil or grease to remain on the floor - wipe it up right away, before someone slips on it.

✗ **Don't** use ill-fitting spanners or other tools which may slip and cause injury.

✗ **Don't** lift a heavy component which may be beyond your capability - get assistance.

✗ **Don't** rush to finish a job or take unverified short cuts.

✗ **Don't** allow children or animals in or around an unattended vehicle.

✗ **Don't** inflate a tyre above the recommended pressure. Apart from overstressing the carcass, in extreme cases the tyre may blow off forcibly.

✔ **Do** ensure that the machine is supported securely at all times. This is especially important when the machine is blocked up to aid wheel or fork removal.

✔ **Do** take care when attempting to loosen a stubborn nut or bolt. It is generally better to pull on a spanner, rather than push, so that if you slip, you fall away from the machine rather than onto it.

✔ **Do** wear eye protection when using power tools such as drill, sander, bench grinder etc.

✔ **Do** use a barrier cream on your hands prior to undertaking dirty jobs - it will protect your skin from infection as well as making the dirt easier to remove afterwards; but make sure your hands aren't left slippery. Note that long-term contact with used engine oil can be a health hazard.

✔ **Do** keep loose clothing (cuffs, ties etc. and long hair) well out of the way of moving mechanical parts.

✔ **Do** remove rings, wristwatch etc., before working on the vehicle - especially the electrical system.

✔ **Do** keep your work area tidy - it is only too easy to fall over articles left lying around.

✔ **Do** exercise caution when compressing springs for removal or installation. Ensure that the tension is applied and released in a controlled manner, using suitable tools which preclude the possibility of the spring escaping violently.

✔ **Do** ensure that any lifting tackle used has a safe working load rating adequate for the job.

✔ **Do** get someone to check periodically that all is well, when working alone on the vehicle.

✔ **Do** carry out work in a logical sequence and check that everything is correctly assembled and tightened afterwards.

✔ **Do** remember that your vehicle's safety affects that of yourself and others. If in doubt on any point, get professional advice.

● **If** in spite of following these precautions, you are unfortunate enough to injure yourself, seek medical attention as soon as possible.

THE BOOK

# Motorcycle Electrical Manual

## by Tony T

Please return
or

(3471-256)

ISBN 1 85960 471 4

**British Library Cataloguing in Publication Data**
A catalogue record for this book is available from the British Library

**Library of Congress Catalog Card Number 98-71630**

ABCDE
FGHIJ
KLMNO
PQRST

Printed by **J. H. Haynes & Co. Ltd., Sparkford, Nr Yeovil, Somerset, BA22 7JJ, England**

**Haynes Publishing**
Sparkford, Nr Yeovil, Somerset, BA22 7JJ, England

**Haynes North America, Inc**
861 Lawrence Drive, Newbury Park, California 91320, USA

**Editions Haynes SA**
Tour Aurore – La Défense 2, 18 Place des Reflets, 92975 Paris La Defense, Cedex, France

**Haynes Publishing Nordiska AB**
Box 1504, 751 45 UPPSALA, Sweden

# Contents

# Chapter 1
# The complete system

## Contents

### 1  An overall view

**1** In tackling the workings of motorcycle electrics, it is best to look first at the whole system and then to study the separate parts.

It is interesting to see that *the fuel provides the power to drive the motorcycle and also to run all the electrical system.* This is shown diagramatically below (see illustration 1.1).

**2** The generator provides power to the electrical components and also charges the battery so that the electrical circuits will work when the engine and generator are stopped. Essentially the generator must be of sufficient power output to run all electrical circuits simultaneously, with the exception of the starter motor – this being a job for the battery. Note that electrical power flows into the battery when charging and out of the battery when discharging.

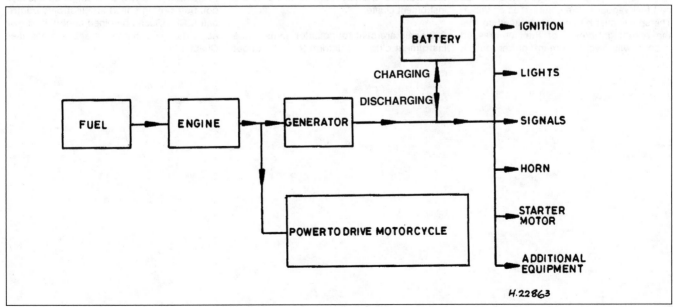

**1.1 Power conversion**

## 2 Charging and storage

**1** All road-going motorcycles will normally have a battery to store electrical energy. The battery will work only on direct current (dc) and the generator which charges it will need to provide a direct current for this purpose.

**2** A dynamo is a generator which produces a direct current output (see Chapter 11) and was used on older machines until about 1954 and in some East European types until recently. Most motorcycles however are fitted with an alternator, this producing alternating current (ac) which is converted into a form of direct current suitable for battery charging (see Chapter 12) by a rectifier.

**3** The direct current dynamo has a lower output than an alternator of the same physical size and it requires more maintenance. Additionally it has a maximum speed restriction due to the design. The alternator has the advantage of being able to charge the battery even when the motorcycle engine is at tickover, but the dynamo needs to run at a higher speed before it starts to charge. With the heavy city traffic of today, engines run at tickover speeds for significant periods. A dynamo-equipped machine would soon suffer a flat battery, whereas a machine with an alternator can keep the battery charged.

## 3 Ignition

**1** Petrol (gasoline) engines require a spark to ignite the compressed charge of turbulent air and fuel vapour in the combustion chamber. The spark must be accurately timed so that the resulting burning of the compressed vapour will give maximum power output consistent with economic fuel consumption. The spark jumps across the electrodes of a spark plug screwed into the cylinder head and the high voltage required is provided by either a magneto or a coil ignition circuit. How both work will be described in later Chapters.

**2 Magneto** – A magneto is an engine-driven generator designed to give a high voltage of up to 30,000 volts (30 kV) at the instant of ignition.

**3 Coil ignition** – An ignition coil is a transformer to step up the battery voltage to that needed to produce a spark at the plug gap. This is achieved by altering rapidly the current in the primary winding; traditionally this has been done by cutting off the current with an engine-driven switch (the contact breaker) but is today by electronic control. All such systems, however simple or complex, use an ignition coil at the final point where high voltage is applied to the spark plug.

## 4 Lighting and signalling

**1** The provision of front and rear lighting together with some form of horn is a legal requirement for road machines in most countries. Headlamps have a main beam and some means of beam dipping to avoid dazzle to oncoming road users. The taillight is most important for rider safety and usually it is housed with a brake stop light.

**2** Flashing turn signals are now almost universal on all modern motorcycles; in the UK and US the lens colour is amber. To warn the rider that the turn signals are working, a low wattage warning light is fitted in the instrument cluster.

**3** Signals are sent to indicator lights in the instrument cluster to inform the rider about the motorcycle condition such as low fuel, oil pressure, neutral position, headlamp main beam etc. Advanced motorcycles will have other signal devices which might include lean-over angle, ABS and slip condition etc.

## 5 Starting (engine cranking)

**1** Most motorcycles are equipped with a direct-current starter motor which has a high standstill-torque to turn the engine until it fires up. The current demand is high, and this necessitates a larger battery than would be needed on a machine without a starter motor. Battery design and condition are more than ever important and the wise rider does not use the starter for long if the engine is reluctant to fire.

## 6 Fuelling

**1** Fuel has traditionally been supplied via a carburettor to the engine cylinders in the form of an air/fuel vapour sucked in by the descending piston and it is likely that many motorcycles will continue to use this method. However, in some larger models, pumped fuel is injected in the form of a spray directly into the cylinder. Such *fuel injection systems* are electronically controlled and the fuel is fed by an electric fuel pump located in the tank (see Chapter 8).

**2** Since both the fuel injection and ignition are electronically controlled it was a logical step to combine the two by a single specialised computer often called an electronic control unit (ECU). Such combined control is known as an engine management system (see Chapter 9).

# Chapter 2
# Electrical basics

# Contents

## 1 Need you read this Chapter?

**1** If you are well experienced in electrical matters you may wish to skip this Chapter, but if you have never followed a course of instruction, or your knowledge is rusty, then time spent in reading it will be an investment.

**2** To read manufacturers' manuals, it is essential to have a clear understanding not only of electrical principles but also of the correct use of terminology; this is the reader's mental toolbox and is in every way as important as his or her practical toolkit.

**3** Even if you cannot see the relevance of some of the parts of this Chapter, be assured that all of it is important to understanding of the rest of the book!

## 2 The Atom – the source of electricity

**1** All material consists of atoms which are, in turn, made up of protons, electrons and neutrons. The atom has a centre (or nucleus) which consists of protons and neutrons. Around the nucleus, electrons orbit at definite

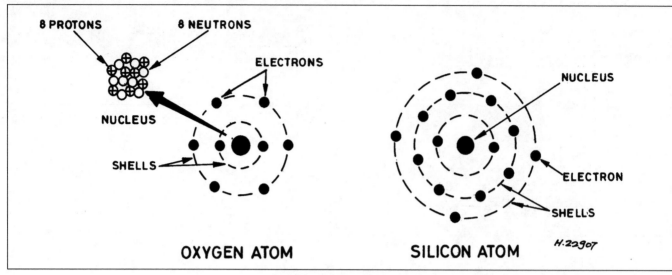

2.1 Simple atomic systems

distances from the centre and are grouped into orbits (called shells) each at a different radius. Illustration 2.1 shows two simple atoms both of which will figure later in this book.

2 The proton carries a positive electrical charge, the electron a negative charge and the neutron has no charge. Normally an atom is electrically neutral overall, meaning that the number of (positive) protons in the nucleus is matched by the number of (negative) electrons rotating in the orbital shells. In the table below note that in each case the numbers of protons and electrons are equal.

| Atom | Protons | Neutrons | Electrons |
|------|---------|----------|-----------|
| Hydrogen | 1 | 0 | 1 |
| Oxygen | 8 | 8 | 8 |
| Copper | 29 | 34 | 29 |
| Silicon | 14 | 14 | 14 |

Neutrons and protons are strongly attracted when close together in the atomic nucleus and when they are split apart huge amounts of energy are released, a phenomenon which is exploited in the nuclear reactor and the atomic bomb.

3 Because of the relatively large mass of the nucleus it may be regarded as fixed in place in solid materials. Electrons are held less firmly in the atom and in some circumstances may leave the parent atom. It is this feature which is the basis of electronics.

4 The atom is small, requiring millions to cover the width of a hairline, yet the internal dimensions are even more remarkable. To give some idea, if the nucleus were an apple then the overall size of the atom could be thought of as that of a concert hall and the electrons as flies buzzing around!

### 3 Free electrons (conduction)

1 An atom is, in practice, a complicated structure; the outermost orbital electrons are sometimes held very loosely to the nucleus like a distant planet may be to the sun. Collisions may occur, which result in some electrons being driven from their normal path and driving through the material lattice (see illustration 3.1). These are called **free electrons**. Some materials are rich in them, and others have few, or none at all. A material with many free electrons is a **conductor** and without free electrons is an **insulator**.

2 Imagine a copper wire as a mass of heavy copper atoms with swarms of free electrons in the spaces between them. These electrons are so small that there is plenty of room for them to fly about in all directions, but on the whole they do not progress very far in any one direction; their motion is random.

### 4 Electron flow (also known as current flow)

1 If a cell or a battery (a battery is merely a collection of cells) is connected to the ends of a copper wire, the free electrons drift along it, all in the same direction, just as when a pump is started, sending a flow of liquid along the pipes to which it is connected.

2 It is important to understand that a battery does not **make** the electricity any more than a pump makes a liquid. The battery and the pump are merely agencies to set in motion something which already exists.

3 Carrying the analogy further, it might be said that it is not the pump which moves the fluid, but the pressure difference which the pump creates that causes the motion. This is a valuable idea because, without stating the method used, it is the **pressure difference** alone which causes fluid flow. This also applies to electricity. Any device (eg battery,

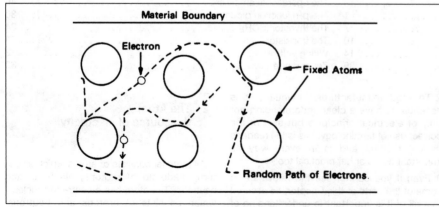

3.1 Free electron drift

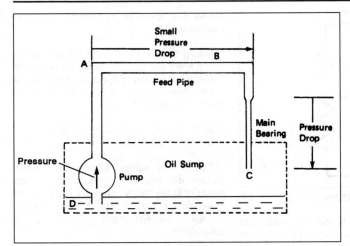

**5.2a  Oil pump and feed**

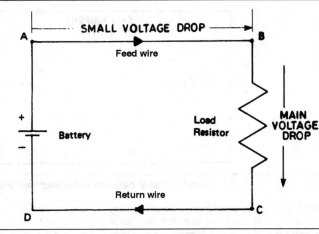

**5.2b  Battery and load**

alternator, dynamo) which will set up a **potential difference** (pd) in an electric circuit can give rise to electric current flow.

**4** As a pump produces a certain pressure, so a battery, alternator or dynamo produces an electromotive force **(emf)** measured in **VOLTS**. Potential difference **(pd)** is also measured in **VOLTS**.

**5** The idea of electron flow being the basis of electric current came long after a general convention that current flowed from the positive battery terminal, through the circuit back to the negative terminal.

Electrons, in fact, flow in the opposite direction and so care must be taken over which convention is used, particularly when working out electronic circuits.

In describing most electrical circuits, the current is assumed to flow from positive to negative unless otherwise indicated. (Note that the term **generator** is often used to mean either a dynamo or an alternator.)

## 5  The complete circuit

**1** A circuit, as the name implies, is a complete uninterrupted path round which current may flow. The battery or generator which pumps electrons round the circuit is similar in many ways to an oil pump working in a motorcycle engine. The oil flows continuously round the engine (primarily for lubricating bearing surfaces) and returns to the sump.

**2** It is helpful to compare the oil system shown in illustration 5.2a with the electrical system of illustration 5.2b.

**3** The oil pump produces a pressure difference between points A and D and this causes oil to flow through the feed pipe B to the main bearing where a large pressure drop occurs. This is because of the constriction between journal and bearing and most of the

pump energy is expended in forcing oil flow. Ideally, no energy is lost in the feed pipe, but in practice there will be a small pressure loss and with it a small energy loss. Compare this now with a corresponding electrical circuit:

**4** In the equivalent electrical circuit (see illustration 5.2b), the battery produces a potential difference (pd) between points A and D and this causes current to flow along the wire AB to the load resistor where a large voltage drop occurs. This is because the resistor is made of high resistance wire and most of the battery energy is expended in forcing current flow through the load resistor. Ideally no energy is lost in the connecting wires but in practice a small loss will occur.

**5** A practical realisation is shown in illustration 5.5a with a bulb load and a switch. To save wire, the motorcycle frame is used as the return conductor in illustration 5.5b and is referred to as 'earth' or 'ground'. Where the bulb connection is made directly to the motorcycle frame this is often a source of

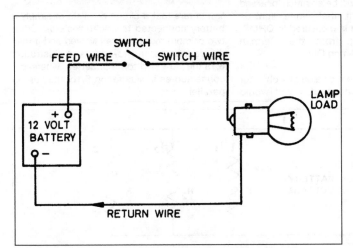

**5.5a  Simple practical circuit with insulated return**

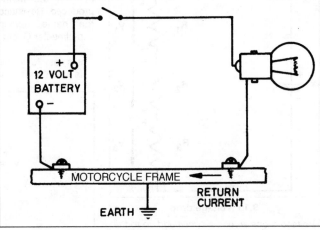

**5.5b  Use of motorcycle frame as earth return**

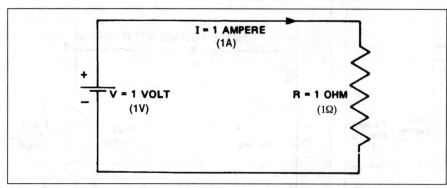

**7.2 The relationship between volts, amperes and ohms**

trouble in older machines. Corrosion may occur and this gives rise to a high resistance which robs the bulb of energy. When bulbs are dim or do not work at all, check the bulb first then make sure there is a good earth (ground) connection. It is surprising how many faults are due to bad connections!

**6** It is possible to connect the negative battery terminal to earth or the positive terminal and both ways round have been used in motorcycles. For some time now it has been standard practice worldwide to use negative earth (ground) systems, not the least reason being that it suits modern electronic components.

## 6  Fundamental quantities

**1** The number of electrons set in motion by a battery is astronomically large, so a convenient number (how many does not matter to us!) are lumped together and called a **COULOMB**.

**2** Again we are not often interested in the amount of electricity, but the *speed* of flow

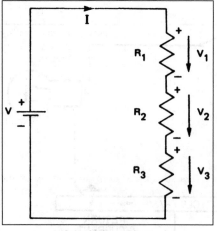

**8.1a  Voltage drop**

*Voltage drops around a circuit add up to the supply voltage*

round a circuit. The number of coulombs flowing past a point each second is the rate of flow and 1 coulomb per second is called an **AMPERE**.

| Name | Liquid system units | Electrical system units |
|---|---|---|
| Quantity | litres | coulombs |
| Pressure and pressure drop | Newtons per square metre | volts |
| Rate of flow | litres per second | amperes |

## 7  Ohm's law

**1** The load resistor is where the electricity will produce the desired effects. For example, an electric fire element consists of a spiral of wire with a resistance much higher than that of the connecting leads.

**2** The well known effect is that heat is produced, a phenomenon which will be considered later. Equally, the headlamp bulb of a motorcycle is a load resistor and the main effect of current flow will be so much localised heat in the filament that white light is produced. Resistance is measured in **OHMS**, the name deriving from the German experimenter Georg Simon Ohm.

It is easy to visualise the value of 1 ohm, for it is such that a voltage of 1 volt would

cause 1 ampere of current to flow (see illustration 7.2).

Georg Ohm is famous for his conclusion that current increases in direct proportion to the voltage applied to a constant resistance. For example, doubling the applied voltage will double the current flow.

ie     Voltage = current x resistance
or      V      = I x R

Today this seems elementary but its statement in 1826 cost Ohm his job because it did not fit the theory of the day. Note the use of symbols V, I and R for numerical values of voltage, current and resistance in calculations.

**3 Example:** A headlamp bulb working off a 12 volt battery takes a current of 3 amperes. What is the resistance of the bulb filament when taking this current?

         V = I x R
or      12 = 3 x R
so      R = 4 ohms

**4** It pays to learn the proper abbreviations for electrical quantities to save writing the full word every time. For example, write 12 volts as 12V, 3 amps as 3A, 4 ohms as 4Ω, and 36 watts as 36W. See Section 13 for more on this subject.

Note that a circuit may have a VOLTAGE, but never say or write AMPERAGE – the correct term is CURRENT. Thus, a component may have a voltage of 12 volts **across** it and a current of 5 amperes **through** it. Note also the symbol Ω (omega) is occasionally used for ohms so a resistance of 4Ω is read as 4 ohms.

## 8  Series and parallel circuits

**1** It is rare that a circuit consists of simply a battery connected to a load resistor. Often two or more resistors are involved and if they are connected end-to-end as in illustration 8.1a they are said to be in **series**, whereas if connected as in illustration 8.1b, they are in **parallel**.

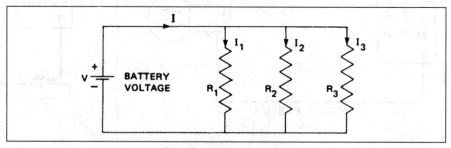

**8.1b  Resistors in parallel**

## 9  Series connection

**1** If, as in illustration 8.1a, the load consists of resistors $R_1$, $R_2$, $R_3$ with a supply voltage of V volts then by Ohm's Law:

$V = I \times (R_1 + R_2 + R_3)$ noting all the resistance values add up when in series.

Now Ohm's Law applies to each resistor and each will have its own voltage drop, namely:

$V_1 = IR_1$, $V_2 = IR_2$, $V_3 = IR_3$

The volt-drops $V_1$, $V_2$, $V_3$ always add up to the total supply voltage V, a point to remember when fault finding.

**2 Example:** To see how this equation might be used in practice, suppose $R_1 = 3.0W$, $R_2 = 1.0W$, and $R_3 = 2.0W$. How much current would be drawn from the battery if V = 12 volts?

$$12 = I \times (3 + 1 + 2)$$
$$\text{or } 12 = I \times 6$$
$$\text{so } I = 2 \text{ ampere (usually written 2A)}$$

**3** In practice, the internal resistance of the battery may be significant (especially if it is wearing out) and there may be unwanted resistance in the cables and connections. These undesired resistances would have to be taken into account for some purposes by using Ohm's Law as above.

## 10  Parallel connection

**1** Referring to illustration 8.1b it is clear that the battery must supply the current to all three branches and that the total current is the sum of the branch currents, that is: $I = I_1 + I_2 + I_3$

**2** Each branch has the full voltage V applied to it, so in this case the separate currents may be calculated and added.

**3** Note that this is the most frequent arrangement to be met in a motorcycle electrical system – for instance $R_1$ could be the lighting load, $R_2$ the horn, $R_3$ the ignition, and the current demand on the battery would be the sum of the separate currents.

**4 Example:** Suppose again the supply voltage to be 12 volts and the load resistors were $R_1 = 6\Omega$, $R_2 = 3\Omega$, and $R_3 = 4\Omega$, as in illustration 10.4.

$$I_1 = \frac{V}{R_1} = \frac{12}{6} = 2A$$
$$I_2 = \frac{V}{R_2} = \frac{12}{3} = 4A$$
$$I_3 = \frac{V}{R_3} = \frac{12}{4} = 3A$$

The total current drain from the battery is therefore I = 9A.

By using Ohm's Law again, it will be seen that if the equivalent resistance R of the 3 branches in parallel is worked out, it is given by:

$$V = I \times R$$
$$12 = 9 \times R$$
$$R = \frac{12}{9} = 1.33\Omega$$

The general case for resistors in parallel is:

$$\frac{1}{R} = \frac{1}{R_1} + \frac{1}{R_2} + \frac{1}{R_3}$$

Where R is the effective resistance of $R_1$ $R_2$ $R_3$ etc, connected in parallel.

Try this out on the above figures: with three resistors of 6 ohms, 3 ohms and 4 ohms in parallel, the combined resistance is:

$$\frac{1}{R} = \frac{1}{6} + \frac{1}{3} + \frac{1}{4} = \frac{2}{12} + \frac{4}{12} + \frac{3}{12} = \frac{9}{12}$$
$$\frac{1}{R} = \frac{9}{12} \text{ and inverting}$$
$$R = 1.33\Omega$$

## 11  Energy, work and power

**1** Words like energy, work and power are used in everyday speech but it is not always realised that they have precise meanings in engineering.

Suppose you have to carry 100 boxes up a flight of stairs; to do this involves a certain amount of work or expenditure of energy. You could do the task quickly or take a day over it but in both cases the work (energy) is the same. If you do the job quickly then the **rate of using energy** is high, that is to say the **power** is high. The power used is low if you do the job slowly. By definition therefore, power is the **rate of using energy**.

**2** Energy is measured in **JOULES**, where one joule is the energy expended when a pressure of one volt drives a current of one ampere through a load for one second.

So        joules = volts x amperes x seconds

or,        $J = V I t$

**Example:** If a 12 volt battery delivers 3 amperes of current to a headlamp bulb for 20 minutes, how much energy is used?

$$\begin{aligned}\text{Energy} &= V \times I \times t \\ &= 12 \times 3 \times 20 \times 60 \\ &= 43,200 \text{ joules}\end{aligned}$$

The joule is not used very much in routine electrical work but does occur in ignition systems. It is of interest to note that it is also the unit of energy in mechanical engineering, if SI (metric) units are used. It is the energy expended by a force of 1 Newton moving through a distance of 1 metre in the direction of the force, ie 1 metre-Newton = 1 Joule. For those brought up on Imperial units, the Newton is about ¼ pound force (lbf).

**3 Power** is the rate of utilising energy. The unit of power is the **WATT**.

$$\text{Watts} = \text{joules per second ie } \frac{\text{joules}}{\text{seconds}}$$

Remembering that
joules = volts x amperes x seconds

$$\text{Watts} = \frac{\text{joules}}{\text{seconds}} = \text{volts x amperes}$$

so   **Watts = volts x amperes** for a direct current circuit

In the example described, the battery delivering 3A at 12V is giving a power of
$W = V \times I = 12 \times 3 = 36$ watts

Two important derivations come from the formula $W = V \times I$

Remembering Ohm's Law which is $V = I \times R$ we can substitute for V in the power formula above and get:
$$W = I \times I \times R$$
$$W = I^2 R \text{ watts}$$

This shows that the power varies as the **square** of the current in a circuit; so if current goes up by 3 times the power goes up $3^2$ or 9 times.

By substituting for I in the power formula we arrive at $W = V^2 \div R$ watts, an equally important formula.

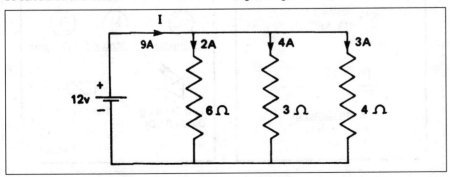

**10.4  An example of current drain by resistors in parallel**

## 12 Wiring volt-drop

**1** Examination of motorcycle wiring will show that the wires and cables are of different thicknesses, and that often the wire is not one solid strand, but made up of several strands twisted together.

The designer chooses a cable so that the current flowing from the source to the load does not produce an undue waste of energy in the wires carrying it.

It is important to remember that although the wires are made of copper, which is a good conductor, nevertheless there is some finite resistance in which heating loss and volt-drop will occur. This means less power to the load, and inefficiency. Remember from the previous section that power varies as the square of the voltage or current so a small loss of voltage to a bulb, for example, shows up as a more significant power loss. The battery shown connected to the bulb (see illustration 12.1) has a terminal pressure of 12 volts and ideally all this voltage should appear across the bulb; however, here the connecting wires have a resistance which gives a loss of 0.2 volt for both go and return, leaving only 11.6 volts to light the bulb filament. The voltage to the bulb has fallen by 3.33% and the power and illumination has fallen by 11% approximately.

**2** The result in this case is poor illumination due to the waste of power in the wires. Better results would be obtained by using thicker cables, but the limits to increasing diameter are determined by the cost of copper and undesirable stiffness of thick wires. We shall consider later how to select a suitable size of cable.

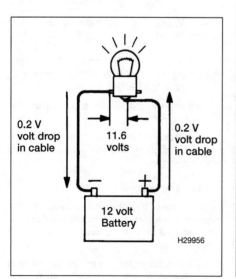

**12.1 Volt-drop in connecting cables**

## 13 Component symbols

**1** It is tedious and inconvenient to draw every component we meet in electrical work and so symbols are used extensively unless there is a special reason to depict the object. For example we often do not need to draw a battery in detail and a simple symbol will suffice. Ideally there would be a worldwide agreement on symbols, like a universal language for engineers, but unfortunately this is not so.

**2** The most common symbols in use are shown in illustration 13.2. In Chapter 16 we shall consider a wider range of symbols and how they occur in wiring diagrams of complete motorcycles.

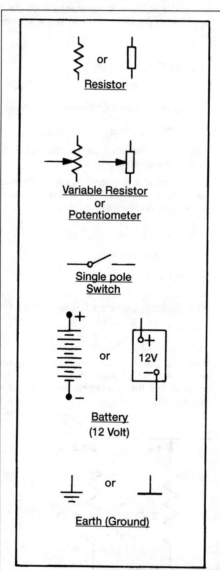

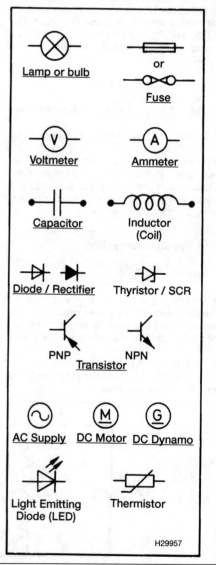

**13.2 Component symbols**

## 14 Permanent magnets

**1** A bar magnet free to pivot about its centre point will take up a position so that one end will point to the earth's magnetic north pole. That end of the magnet is referred to as its **north pole** and the opposite end the **south pole**.

**2** Around the magnet is a region to which iron will be attracted and this region is said to have a magnetic field; it is most concentrated at the N and S poles. The pattern of the **magnetic flux** in this region may be visualised by laying a piece of cardboard over the magnet and sprinkling iron filings on to the cardboard.

These take up a pattern and it helps visualisation if we think of magnetic lines of force going from N to S (see illustration 14.2). In reality, there are no individual lines but a magnetic flux which permeates the whole of the space involved.

**3** Magnetic flux is measured in **WEBERS** but rather more important is how concentrated is this flux in a given area through which the magnetic field is imagined to pass. The number of Webers passing through an area of 1 square metre (1 m²) is the MAGNETIC FLUX DENSITY (B) and the unit of flux density is the TESLA (T).

**4** It is found that if the N pole of one magnet is brought close to the S pole of another, a significant force of attraction from one to the other will be felt. Similarly, if two N (or two S) poles are brought close to each other then there is force of repulsion (see illustration 14.4).

Magnetic lines of force may be imagined as elastic threads which seek to shorten yet repel each other sideways, giving rise to patterns which help an understanding of magnetic attraction and repulsion.

**5** Electrical machines and some instruments which use permanent magnets need strong magnetic fields. The straight bar magnet gives a weak field but a much better **magnetic flux density** is obtained if the bar is bent so that the N and S poles are close (see illustration 14.5).

Magnet steel is expensive and is often made in rectangular blocks. Making a complex shape such as a horseshoe or a square out of magnet steel is not a good design because of cost. The solution is to use cheaper iron to make up part of the path for magnetic lines of force, thanks to the phenomenon of **magnetic induction**.

**6** Magnetic induction is an important effect. If a block of iron is brought into a magnetic field it will temporarily acquire N and S poles and behave like a magnet so long as the external

magnetic field is present. Such iron is referred to as soft iron because it loses virtually all of its magnetism when removed from the magnetic field (see illustration 14.6a). If soft iron is used to make up a **magnetic circuit** it in effect carries the magnetic field to where it will be used and butts up to the permanent magnet steel, the N and S poles of which are transferred to the ends of the soft iron (see illustration 14.6b).

**7** There is a relationship between current and magnetism, discovered in 1820 by the Danish experimenter Oersted, and this lies behind much of modern electrical equipment. He found that a wire carrying a current produced a surrounding magnetic field. Furthermore,

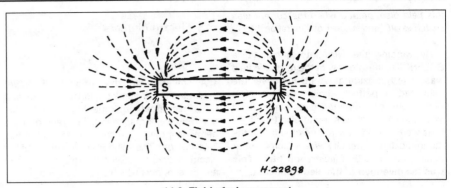

**14.2  Field of a bar magnet**

*Direction of arrowheads is agreed convention*

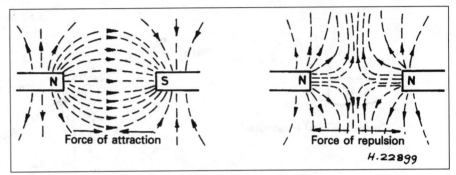

Force of attraction                    Force of repulsion

**14.4  Forces between magnetic poles**

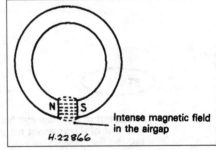

Intense magnetic field in the airgap

**14.5  A strong field is obtained by magnet shaping**

*By shaping the magnet so that the poles are close together, a stronger and more useful field is obtained*

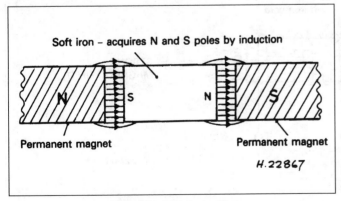

Soft iron – acquires N and S poles by induction

Permanent magnet                    Permanent magnet

**14.6a  Magnetic induction**

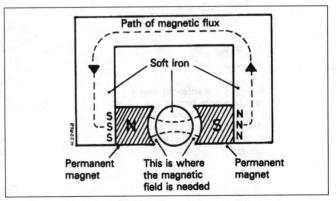

Path of magnetic flux

Soft iron

Permanent magnet          This is where the magnetic field is needed          Permanent magnet

**14.6b  Example of magnetic induction – soft iron used to carry magnetic flux around an iron circuit**

*this field disappeared when the current was switched off* (see stage 1 of illustration 14.7).

By winding the wire into a coil (ie a SOLENOID), the intensity of the magnetic field was raised considerably and moreover the field had a pattern similar to that of a permanent bar magnet (see stage 2 of illustration 14.7). It was found also that if the coils were wound over a core of soft iron the magnetic field intensity was much greater again (see stage 3 of illustration 14.7). **This was the invention of the electromagnet.**

## 15 Electromagnets

**1** A limitation to the amount of power generated in permanent magnet dynamos and other electrical equipment is due to the relatively weak magnetic field strength of the permanent magnet and lack of control of this field strength. The solution lies in the use of the electromagnet (or solenoid), which consists of an iron core over which a coil is wound.

**2** Passing direct current through the coil will induce a magnetic field in the iron, which may then bear a strong resemblance to an ordinary permanent magnet with the differences that:

(a) *The strength of the magnetic field can be controlled (within limits) by varying the current in the coil.*
(b) *The magnetic field virtually disappears when the current is switched off.*

**3** The arrangement of the electromagnet is shown in illustration 15.3, together with a

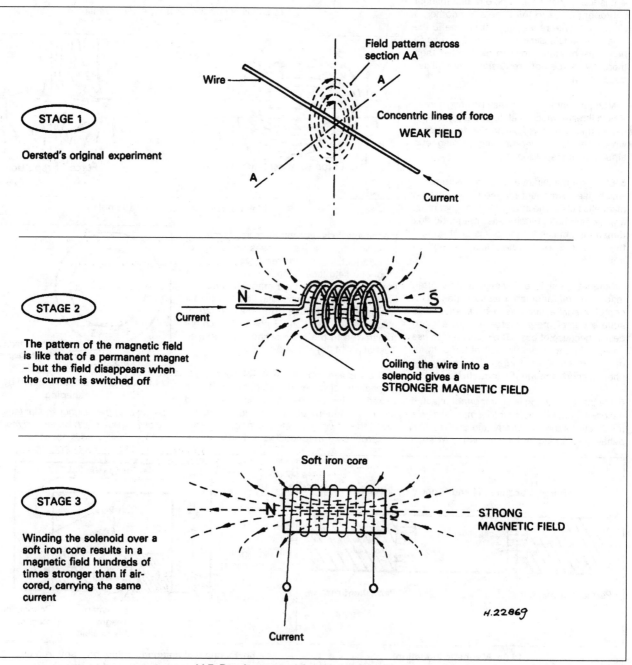

**STAGE 1**

Oersted's original experiment

**STAGE 2**

The pattern of the magnetic field is like that of a permanent magnet – but the field disappears when the current is switched off

**STAGE 3**

Winding the solenoid over a soft iron core results in a magnetic field hundreds of times stronger than if air-cored, carrying the same current

14.7 Development of the electromagnet

graph showing the way in which field strength varies with coil current. Note that beyond a certain current the magnetic flux density flattens off – the iron is then said to be **saturated**.

**4** The electromagnet finds many uses in electrical equipment for motorcycles; instead of a permanent magnet in a dynamo or alternator, for example, it is possible to use electromagnets with the advantage that the electrical output can be regulated by varying the current in the electromagnet windings. In motor and generator practice, the electromagnets producing magnetic flux are called field poles and the coils are field windings.

## 16 Relays and solenoids

**1** The relay is used to switch heavy current on, or off, by means of a much smaller control current (see illustration 16.1). A typical example is the starter motor, where the current may rise to more than a hundred amperes. In this particular instance, the heavy cable needed to carry this current from the battery must be short to avoid voltage loss, and could not conveniently be brought to a handlebar switch anyway because of the cable stiffness and bulk. The relay overcomes this problem since it is located in the short path between battery and starter and only a thin control cable need go to the starter button.

**2** It is well known that magnetic poles will exert a pull on nearby iron or steel. This effect

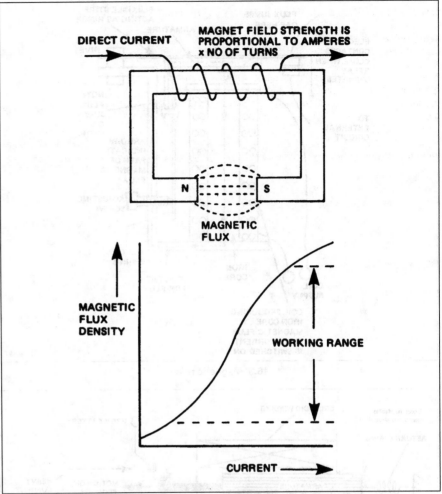

15.3  The electromagnet

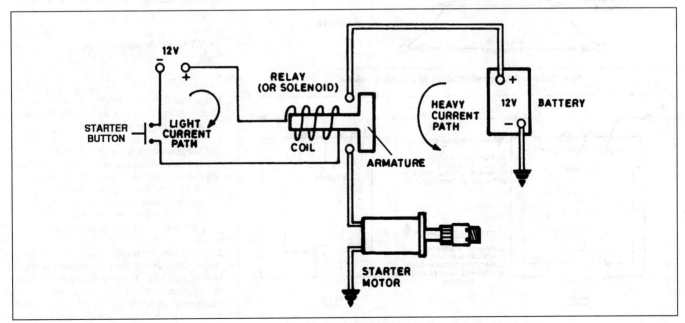

16.1  Principle of the relay

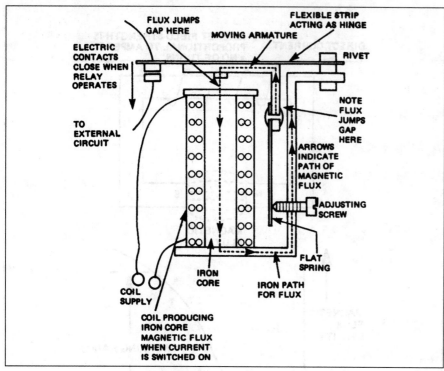

16.3 Magnetic relay

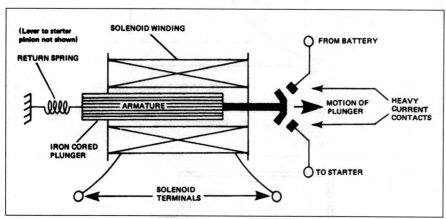

16.4 Schematic representation of a starter solenoid

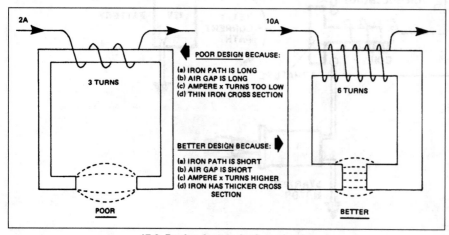

17.2 Design factors for iron circuits

is used in the relay in which a strip of iron is pulled by the magnetic field created when current is switched on. The movement of the iron strip, called an **armature**, can be made to open or close electrical contacts. The **relay is therefore an electrically operated switch** having a variety of uses, some of which will be described later in this book.

**3** A simple relay is shown in illustration 16.3 in which the armature is held in one position by the flat spring until the coil current is switched on. Then the magnetic flux set up by the coil causes the armature to be attracted to the central iron core and so closes the contacts. When the current is switched off the magnetic field disappears and the armature returns to the rest position, the contacts opening. This relay has contacts which are **normally open** (NO). Other arrangements have **normally closed** (NC) contacts and more involved types have combinations of both. This type of relay is widely used in motorcycle and automobile engineering.

**4** An application of the relay is the **solenoid**, used as a starter motor switch in some Moto Guzzi and BMW models. Illustration 16.4 shows a schematic for a starter solenoid (note the large crosses to symbolise a winding of copper wire). This relies on the fact that an iron core is attracted towards the mid point of a coil carrying current. The armature plunger carries a closing contact which switches on the main current to the starter motor. The pull exerted on the iron armature can be so great that, in the case of the pre-engaged starter motor, its movement may be powerful enough directly to engage the starter pinion into a flywheel gear ring in addition to switching on the heavy current of the starter motor. It will be seen that this is a specialised form of a relay.

## 17 The magnetic circuit

**1** It is found that the magnetic field in an iron circuit depends upon several factors over which the designer has control:

(a) The number of turns of wire on the coil N.
(b) The current flowing in the coil, I amperes.
(c) The iron path details which include the iron and airgap lengths L, the cross-sectional area of the flux path A and the property of the iron known as permeability μ (pronounced MEW).

**2** In general, magnetic flux will pass more readily through iron than air and so if a strong field is required, then an iron path of short length and large cross-sectional area is necessary, together with a coil designed to make the product of amperes x turns as large as possible (see illustration 17.2).

**3 Magnetomotive force** driving the flux through the iron path (sometimes called the iron circuit) is the amperes x number of coil turns, written NI. The factor limiting the passage of flux is the **reluctance** which depends upon iron and air path lengths, iron and airpath cross-sectional area and iron permeability μ.

**4** Similar to Ohm's Law, the relationship between the above is:

Magnetomotive Force = Flux x Reluctance
MMF = φ x Reluctance
or NI = φ x Reluctance . . . . . . . . . . . . (1)
(φ is pronounced FY)

Compare this with:
Electromotive Force = Current x Resistance

The importance of the equation (1) is that for a given iron path, the flux depends on the Ampere-Turns so the higher the current and the number of turns of wire it flows through, the higher will be the magnetic flux up to the point where the iron becomes magnetically saturated.

This formula is used in the design of many types of electrical equipment such as transformers, motors and generators and other electromagnetic devices. Here we look just at the main ideas but for further reading see the recommended books at the end of this Chapter.

## 18 Motors and generators

**1** Millions of motors, dynamos and alternators are in use in motorcycles and other vehicles, representing the greatest use of electrical machines in any branch of industry. It is a credit to designers that relatively few failures occur, for these machines are subject to heavy utilisation, need very little maintenance and work in a hostile environment, having to cope with wide temperature ranges, dust, damp and, in the case of generators, speed variations from a few hundred to thousands of revolutions per minute with high acceleration forces.

**2** The motor and generator (included in this term are dynamos and alternators) are not really separate for it is only a question of energy flow. In the case of the direct-current motor, electrical energy is put in and mechanical energy emerges at the shaft. The same machine could be driven by an external prime mover and electrical energy would be available at the terminals. The dc motor and the dc generator are, then, essentially the same device. A similar picture may be stated for the alternator which *could* be driven as a motor by connecting it correctly to an alternating current supply. The relationship between the dc motor and generator is particularly important here.

**3** Most electrical pointer (analogue) instruments are really a highly specialised form of direct-current electric motor operating over a limited angular range of about 120° only. Designers use the same form of calculations in designing both moving-coil instruments and dc motors.

**4** The details of dc generators, alternators and motors will be dealt with in the later Chapters of this book. Here the two important principles of motor and generator action are stated, and armed with this information, the way in which machines and instruments work will be readily understood.

## 19 The generator rule

**1** If a wire moves across a magnetic field it is found that a voltage is generated in it for so long as there is motion (see illustration 19.1). The voltage obtained is found to depend upon:

(a) *The length of wire in the magnetic field.*
(b) *The velocity of the wire at right angles to the magnetic field.*
(c) *The strength of the magnetic field.*

The actual value in volts is:
E = BLV volts
where:
B = strength of magnetic field measured in webers per square metre (or Tesla)
L = length of wire (metres)
V = velocity of wire at right angles to the magnetic field (metres per second)

There is no need to be concerned about any calculations to read further: all that is important is to remember the factors which fix the size of the generated voltage.

**2** In order to make a generator, the wire is formed into a rectangular coil and spun round inside the magnetic field (see illustration 19.2a). If we mentally cut through the coil

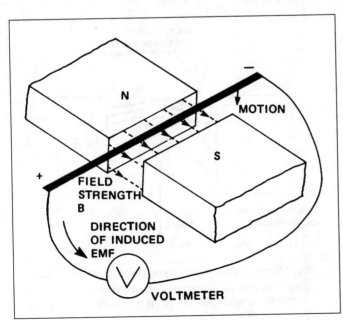

**19.1 Induced emf in moving conductor**

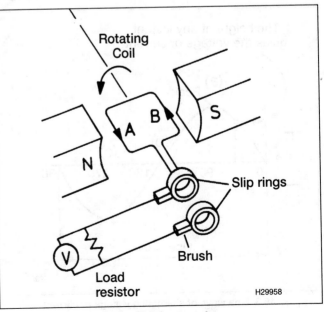

**19.2a Simple generator**

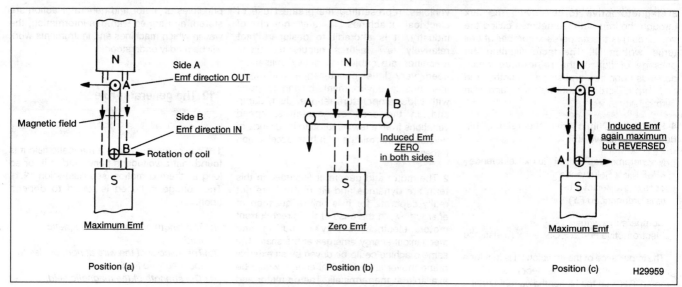

**19.2b Coil position and generated emf**

*see text for details of a, b, c positions*

sides (see illustration 19.2b) and see the emf in the coil as it rotates through a complete turn, then when the coil sides are cutting the magnetic field at right angles the maximum induced emf occurs (position a). Note that the dot is an arrow head showing voltage direction *out* of the page and the cross indicates voltage *into* the page. At right angles to the magnetic field (position b) the emf is zero because there is no cutting of the field. Finally, when the coil has spun through 180° (position c) there is again maximum emf but **in the opposite direction**.

**3** Plotting the emf out on a graph to a base of degrees of motion gives a sine wave (see illustration 19.3). It shows that the simple generator is producing an alternating voltage output. Connected to a load resistor it will produce an alternating current (ac) in it. The complete wave is a *cycle*, and the number of complete cycles per second is the *frequency*. Frequency is measured in **cycles per second** or **Hertz (Hz)**. We shall return to alternating current later.

## 20 The motor rule

**1** This is the converse of the generator situation. Electric current passed down a wire located in a magnetic field will experience a force at right angles to both current and field directions.

**2** Illustration 20.2a shows a wire carrying a current. The wire is situated in a magnetic field, the direction of which is conventionally agreed to be from N to S in the air path. The wire will create a magnetic field of its own and this field will interact with that of the motor field, giving rise to a force acting downwards. The numerical value of the force will depend upon:

(a) *The strength of the magnetic field, B webers per sq metre (Tesla).*
(b) *The amount of current flowing in the wire, I amperes.*

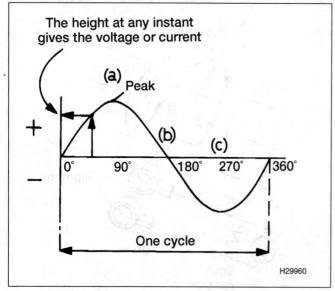

**19.3 Sine wave of alternating voltage or current**

*see text for details of a, b, c positions*

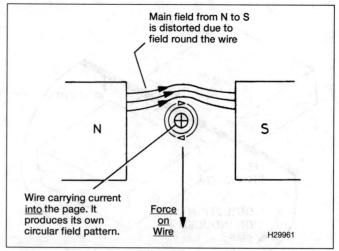

**20.2a Force on a current-carrying wire in a magnetic field**

- *Magnet lines of force spread away from each other*
- *The main field and the field due to the wire current react, giving a downward force*
- *This is how electric motors work!*

*(c) The length of wire inside the magnetic field, L metres.*

The force is:  **F = BIL Newtons**
(see illustration 20.2b)

**3** If now the wire is bent into a rectangular shape and located within the magnetic field again, the directions of current in the two sides are opposite and so will be the forces acting on them. It now remains only to pivot the rectangular coil on bearings for it to become a simple electric motor, for the two forces will give rise to rotation (see illustration 20.3).

This idea of motor operation will be particularly useful when reading Chapter 15 on starter motors, where the subject will be developed further.

**4** The turning capability of a motor shaft is of great importance. This is measured as **torque**. Torque occurs a great deal in engineering. As an example, in illustration 20.4, torque is applied to a nut by means of a spanner and is a measure of turning capability. It is simply the force and distance multiplied, but on the condition that the direction of force *is at right angles* to the direction to the nut centre.

**Note 1:** *Be careful to write torque as Newton-metres (Nm) not metre-Newton. The first is the unit of torque and the second is the unit of work or energy; it surprising how even some makers of torque spanners get it wrong in their leaflets!*

**Note 2:** *Note also that the hyphen (-) means 'multiply by', so when writing Newton-metres we mean Newtons x metres. Later in discussing batteries we use the term ampere-hours and this means amperes x hours.*

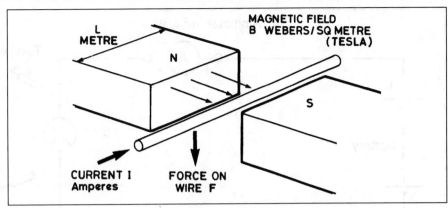

**20.2b  How to calculate motive force**

**Note 3:** *Many use the oblique ( / ) in error but this means divide by. So speed, for example, is written m/s meaning metres per second (metres divided by seconds). Remember that the oblique always reads 'per' and you will not get it wrong.*

**5** Looking again at the simple motor in illustration 20.3, the coil radius is R, and there are two operating sides each giving a force F, so:

Motor torque = 2 x F x R Newton-metres (Written Nm)

## 21 Test instruments and measurements

**1** The quantities most often met in electrical work are amperes, volts and ohms. Not surprisingly the meters (sometimes called instruments) used to measure them are ammeters, voltmeters and ohmmeters. There

are a few basic rules on their use which must always be remembered, because if a meter is misused it can be a very expensive mistake. First, the rules for using them and then a description of how they work:

### Ammeter

**2** The ammeter measures current **through** a circuit; it is connected so that this current flows through the ammeter (in **series** with the lamp load as shown in illustration 21.2). The instrument designer keeps the internal resistance of the ammeter as low as possible so as not to interfere with the measured circuit.

If by accident the ammeter were connected across the load instead of in series with it, this would be disastrous. Because of the low ammeter resistance a heavy current would flow, destroying the instrument and possibly melting the connecting wire insulation.

### Voltmeter

**3** The voltmeter measures electrical pressure (called voltage) and should be connected

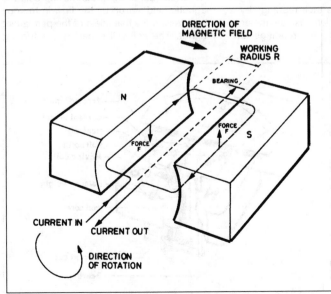

**20.3  Basic electric motor**

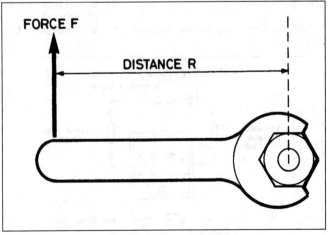

**20.4  Illustration of torque**

*Torque = F x R*
*In the Metric system torque is measured in Newton-metres (Nm), or less correctly as kilogram-metres (kgf m). In the Imperial system torque is measured in pounds-feet (lbf ft).*

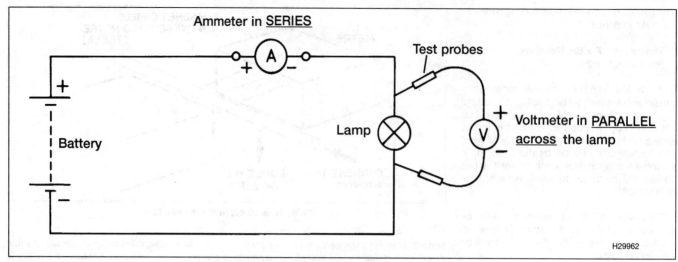

**21.2 How to use an ammeter and voltmeter**

*Both instruments may have terminals marked + and −, connect them as shown*

across the part of a circuit to be measured (in parallel, across the lamp as in illustration 21.2).

For the circuit not to be disturbed by the presence of the voltmeter, the internal resistance of the meter is high – ideally infinite, but never so in practice.

Think of the hydraulic pressure gauge. It measures oil pressure but no oil actually passes through it, and in the case of the voltmeter no current should ideally go through it.

## Ohmmeter

**4** An internal battery in series with the meter movement and a variable zero-setting resistor are the main components of the ohmmeter. The illustration 21.4 shows a simplified arrangement.

With the test prods shorted together the zero knob adjusts the internal resistor until the pointer reads full scale. Under the pointer the scale is marked 'zero' on the ohms scale. The prods may then be applied to the component to be tested and the pointer will read downscale due to the added resistance of the component.

The scale is calibrated against known standard resistors, is cramped at one end and is a non-linear scale.

There is one rule in using an ohmmeter – **never apply the test prods to a live circuit**. At the very least, the reading will be in error if the test circuit is live and probably the ohmmeter will be destroyed. *Always disconnect the motorcycle battery if you are testing a component in-situ on the bike.*

**5** Test meters may give their readings by a pointer on a scale, in which case the meter is an **analogue** type. If the readings are presented in figures then the meter is a **digital** type.

## Moving coil instruments

**6** This type of instrument is really a special form of electric motor with a limited motion. It is the usual form of instrument movement used in analogue meters and is found in ammeters, voltmeters and ohmmeters.

The movement has a permanent magnet with two shaped poles and between them is a soft iron cylindrical core. In the airgap between the poles and the core is pivoted a moving coil on jewelled bearings. This coil carries all or part of the current to be measured (see illustration 21.6). An indicating pointer is attached to the coil.

**7** When current flows in the moving coil, the magnetic field set up by the flow in the coil interacts with the main field of the permanent magnet. The coil will experience a turning

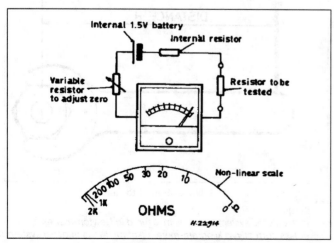

**21.4 The ohmmeter in use**

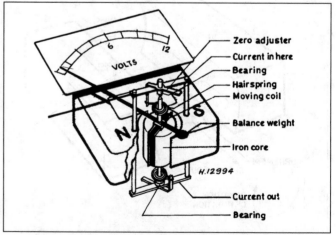

**21.6 Moving coil instrument of a typical analogue meter**

force dependent upon the amount of the current flowing in it and so is a basic ampere meter (always called an **ammeter**).

The action is exactly like the electric motor (see illustration 20.3) but with motion limited to the angle between the scale zero and full scale deflection.

**8** The coil is wound on a lightweight aluminium former. As the coil and former move through the magnetic field, a current (eddy current) is induced in it. The damping effect of the eddy current circulating in the former allows the pointer to give a steady reading without oscillations.

It is possible to design a moving coil meter with a full scale reading of 50 microamperes (50μA) or even lower, but more usually a cheaper and more robust construction is used with a full scale deflection of 1 to 10 milliamperes (mA).

**9** The moving coil instrument will read direct current only. If alternating current is passed through it there will be no deflection because the average of a complete alternating current cycle is zero.

It is possible to read alternating current and voltage with a moving coil instrument if a rectifier is used with it (see Chapter 12 Charging – Alternators).

**10** To make a voltmeter, the moving coil instrument has a series resistor of high value. If several ranges are required then different series resistors (called multipliers) are switched in. Using the same instrument as an ammeter, the movement would be bridged by low shunt resistors (see illustration 21.10).

## Moving iron meters

**11** These are attractive because they are cheaper and much more rugged than a moving coil type. Also the moving iron meter does something that the moving coil meter does not: it will read current whichever way it passes through. This means that it will read alternating current without the use of a rectifier.

Alternating current is usually measured in root-mean-square (rms) terms and this means, for example, that an alternating current of 3 amperes (rms) will produce as much heat in a headlight bulb as 3 amperes dc (direct current). Because of the way in which deflection occurs, the scale is not linear as is that of the moving coil instrument and tends to be cramped at one end.

**12** There are two types of moving iron meter, the first depends upon repulsion of two iron pieces, one of which is fixed and the other attached to the moving pointer (see illustration 21.12) and the second which has two irons

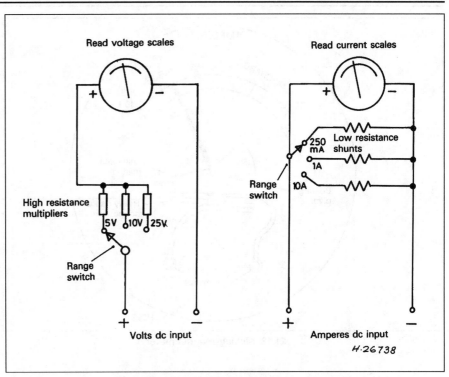

**21.10 Multirange testmeter for dc volts and amperes**

which attract each other. The repulsion meter is used more frequently and we need not be concerned with the attraction type here.

When current is sent through the coil the two irons shown in the repulsion instrument become magnetised with the same polarity and repel each other. One iron is fixed and the other will deflect the pointer to give a scale reading.

Whichever way the current flows the irons will acquire magnetic poles and will always

repel each other. This means that the moving iron meter will respond to an alternating current. In practice the irons are shaped to give a more linear scale but here we are looking at the principle of operation only.

## Moving magnet meters

**13** Used for many years as a charge/discharge ammeter in motorcycles, the simplest unit consists of a coil of heavy wire close to a permanent magnet which is mounted on bearings and attached to the pointer.

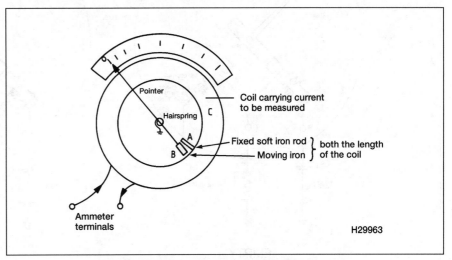

**21.12 Repulsion-type moving iron instrument**

When current flows through coil C, rods A and B are magnetised in the same direction. B moves away from fixed rod A because poles of the same polarity repel each other

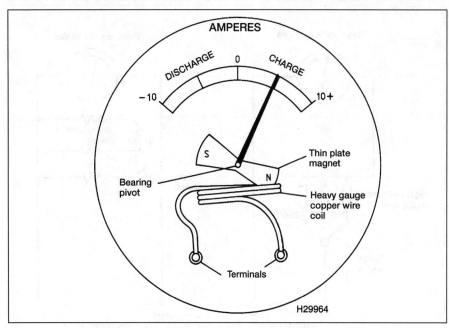

**21.13 Moving-magnet meter**

iron magnet to the empty position as shown in the illustration. Conversely when the tank is full the resistor takes less current and more is deflected to the deflecting coil.

### Bi-metal instruments

**15** The instrument consists of a bi-metal strip in the form of a 'U' with a heater coil wound on one leg. As the strip bends due to the unequal expansion of the two different metals used in the strip, a pointer moves across the scale to indicate fuel level in the application shown. The U shape as a whole compensates for any ambient temperature change so the instrument should always zero correctly. Due to thermal lag this instrument responds slowly and is not sensitive to fuel surges when braking or cornering (see illustration 21.15). One disadvantage is the need for a stabilised supply voltage but this is readily obtainable from a simple bi-metal instrument voltage stabiliser (IVS).

**16** Although not an instrument, the IVS is another example of a bi-metal strip application. The heated bi-metal strip opens contacts when it bends and these cut off the current supply to the heater wound over the strip. The strip cools and bends back to the original position and closes the contacts again. The result is an **average** voltage of 10 volts (some use 7 volts) to the instrument which is also a sluggish bi-metal type so the switching on and off has no effect (see illustration 21.16).

As current flows one way, the N pole will be pulled into the coil and when the current reverses the S pole will be pulled in. This is ideal as a cheap, rugged instrument for mounting on an instrument panel. It is not accurate but serves the purpose (see illustration 21.13).

**14** Another example of moving iron types is the fuel level gauge. The operating unit is a variable resistor attached to a float in the fuel tank (see illustration 21.14). As the fuel level drops, the resistor is progressively shorted out by the slider arm allowing more current to flow in the control coil. This pulls the moving

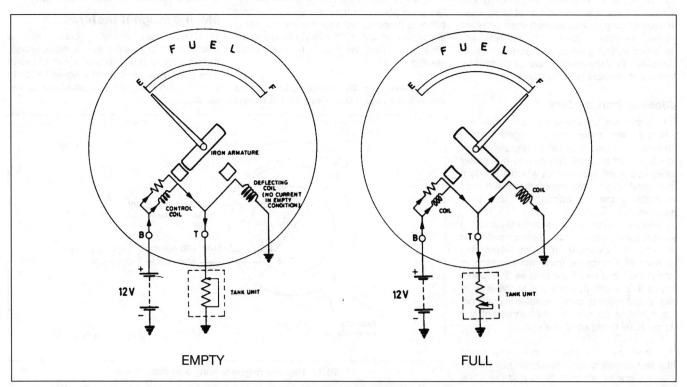

**21.14 Moving iron fuel gauge**

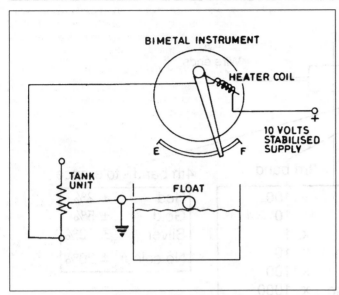

**21.15  Bi-metal fuel gauge**

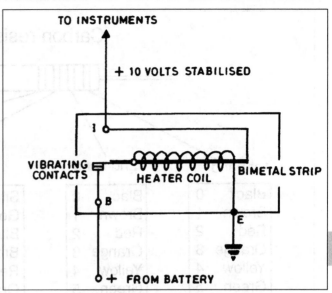

**21.16  Bi-metal voltage stabiliser (IVS)**

**2**

IVS units can become faulty giving rise to erratic instrument readings. The best way to check the unit is to disconnect it at terminal I. Now connect a good quality moving coil voltmeter between terminal I and earth (ground). The voltage should pulse with an average value of 10 volts (or 7 volts in some cases). If the reading is not correct or unstable the unit must be changed. We shall meet the bimetal strip again in Chapter 14.

**21.19a  General purpose analogue multimeter**

### Digital meters

**17**  All electrical quantities can be measured by instruments which display the result in figures. Such instruments are called digital meters and, in general, are more accurate than analogue meters.

We do not need to go into the design of them but in essence the input voltage or current is sampled several times per second and measured in terms of clock pulses. Most digital meters use seven segment liquid crystal displays, the seven segments being electronically switched to give any number from 0 to 9.

**18**  A valuable feature of the digital voltmeter is the high input resistance of the order of 10MΩ (ten megohms), which is much higher than that of an analogue meter. When a voltmeter has a high input resistance it disturbs the measured circuit less and so the reading will be more accurate.

### Multimeters

**19**  It is inconvenient to have separate meters for volts, amperes and ohms. Combined

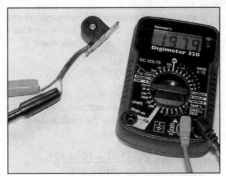

**21.19b  Digital multimeter measuring sensor resistance**

multipurpose meters are nearly always used in practice and can measure the three quantities A V and Ω plus other special features such as dwell angle. Such meters are known under various names and abbreviations including multimeter, VOM (Volt-Ohm-Milliampere), DMM (digital multimeter) and AVO (a trade name meaning amps, volts, ohms). Examples of analogue and digital multimeters are shown in illustrations 2.19a and 2.19b.

**20**  Analogue multimeters particularly need special care when switching from one range to another. The rotary switch may pass through current ranges (amperes) before reaching the desired voltage or other range. Remember that an ammeter has a very low resistance so if the test prods are left connected to a live circuit, this can mean the end of an expensive instrument. *Always disconnect the test meter before changing ranges*.

**21**  Digital meters have some protection against overload but it is safe practice to disconnect the meter whether it is digital or analogue. We shall consider test equipment including meters again in a later Chapter.

### 22 Resistance and Resistors

**1**  Resistors may be wire wound on a former, or for small current work of powdered carbon. Resistance wire is often of constantan or manganin and, for bulb filaments, tungsten which has a very high melting point of 3380°C. For most electronic circuits, carbon resistors are used but are capable of dissipating much less heat than wire wound types.

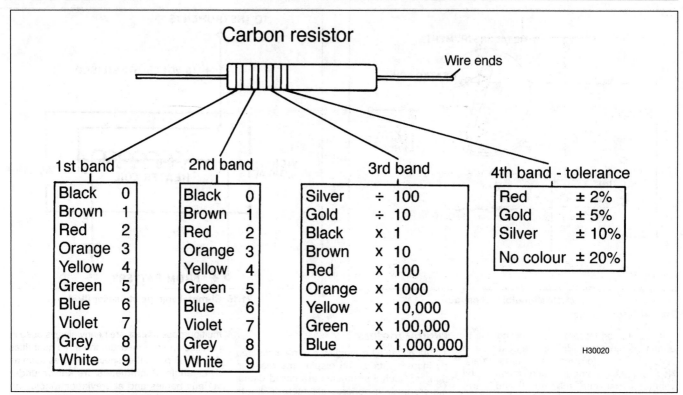

# Carbon resistor

Wire ends

| 1st band | | 2nd band | | 3rd band | | 4th band - tolerance | |
|---|---|---|---|---|---|---|---|
| Black | 0 | Black | 0 | Silver | ÷ 100 | Red | ± 2% |
| Brown | 1 | Brown | 1 | Gold | ÷ 10 | Gold | ± 5% |
| Red | 2 | Red | 2 | Black | x 1 | Silver | ± 10% |
| Orange | 3 | Orange | 3 | Brown | x 10 | No colour | ± 20% |
| Yellow | 4 | Yellow | 4 | Red | x 100 | | |
| Green | 5 | Green | 5 | Orange | x 1000 | | |
| Blue | 6 | Blue | 6 | Yellow | x 10,000 | | |
| Violet | 7 | Violet | 7 | Green | x 100,000 | | |
| Grey | 8 | Grey | 8 | Blue | x 1,000,000 | | |
| White | 9 | White | 9 | | | | |

H30020

**22.2 Resistor colour codes**

**2** To read the ohmic value of a carbon resistor, colour bands are painted on the body and are read as two figures and a multiplier. Using the table in illustration 22.2, a resistor with the first band yellow, the second band green and the third band red would have an ohmic value of 4500 ohms. A further band of colour say, gold, would give a tolerance of

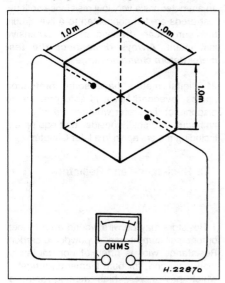

**22.3 Specific residence**

*The resistance between opposite faces of a 1 metre cube is the Specific Resistance of the metal*

5%. Like all measurements there will be some possible error and if there were no need for a precise value in the circuit then a 5% tolerance would be cheaper than a 1% tolerance resistor (see illustration 22.2).

**3** The resistance of a wire will depend on the length (L), cross-sectional area (A) and the specific resistance (ρ) which is the characteristic of the wire material. ρ is pronounced ROE.

Specific resistance ρ is that resistance measured between opposite faces of a cube of size 1 metre, made of the wire material (see illustration 22.3). This material is usually copper for most wiring purposes on a motorcycle. The value of ρ for copper is $1.72 \times 10^{-8}$ ohm-metres (Ω-m).

If we wish to calculate the resistance R of a coil of copper wire, length L metre and wire cross-sectional area A sq. metres, then:

$$R = \frac{\rho L}{A} \text{ ohms}$$

**Example:** A solenoid wound in copper wire of 0.657 sq. mm cross-sectional area uses 70 metres of wire. Calculate the resistance of the finished solenoid winding.

$$R = \frac{\rho L}{A} = \frac{1.72 \times 10^{-8} \times 70}{0.657 \times 10^{-6}}$$

$$R = 1.83 \text{ ohms}$$

Now try working out the resistance of a copper wire coil using 120 metres of wire 0.7112 mm in diameter, remembering that cross-sectional area (CSA) is given by:

$$CSA = \frac{\pi d^2}{4} \quad d = \text{wire diameter}$$

Answer: R = 5.196 ohms   or   R = 5.196Ω

**4** The **potential divider** or voltage divider consists of two resistors in series. The purpose is so that part of a supply voltage can be tapped off to give a fraction of it.

Consider the illustration 22.4 in which two resistors $R_1$ and $R_2$ are connected in series across a voltage of V volts. The current flowing is:

$$I = \frac{V}{R_1 + R_2} \text{ amperes}$$

The voltage $V_0$ dropped across $R_2$ is, by Ohm's Law:

$$V_0 = I \times R_2 = V \times \frac{R_2}{(R_1 + R_2)} \text{ volts}$$

From this we see that the fraction of the supply voltage which has been tapped off is proportional to the resistance $R_2$ as a fraction of the total resistance $(R_1 + R_2)$.

**5** Often, instead of fixed resistors, a resistive track with a tapping slider is used and occurs

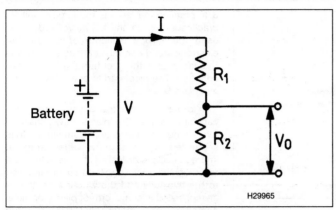

**22.4 Potential (voltage) divider**

**22.5a Potentiometer**

Wiper contact picks off zero to 12volts

2

frequently in motorcycle electronic equipment (see illustration 22.5a). The track may consist of a film of resistive carbon or less frequently be wire wound. The voltage divider is then called a **potentiometer**.

Potentiometers are used in many ways but could be found, for example, operated by the handlebar twistgrip where the voltage tapped off is proportional to the throttle opening. Such information is fed to an electronic control unit (ECU) which in turn controls the ignition and possibly also the fuel injection system The potentiometer is conveniently located on the carburettor throttle shaft (see illustration 22.5b).

**6 The Wheatstone Bridge.** This simple circuit, used for the measurement of resistance, comes from the early days of electrical experimental work and was invented by Sir Charles Wheatstone in 1834. Used for generations by engineers and physicists, it still has an application in modern engine technology (see illustration 22.6).

When the ratio of the resistors $P \div Q$ is equal to the ratio $R \div X$ the voltages at points A and C are equal and the meter will read zero.

Now we can use this idea to measure an unknown resistance value, say that of X, provided the other values are known. R, which is a precision variable resistor, is adjusted until the sensitive meter reads zero and the bridge becomes balanced.

then since $\dfrac{P}{Q} = \dfrac{R}{X}$

$$X = \dfrac{QR}{P} \text{ ohms}$$

When X is a hot wire located in the air intake of a fuel injection system, it is easy to see the practical application to our work in motorcycle engineering (see Chapter 8, Section 4).

Another method is to make X a thermistor and the bridge becomes a temperature sensing circuit. As the temperature rises the resistance of X decreases and unbalances the bridge.

The reading of the unbalance voltage registered on the voltmeter between points A and C could be scaled in degrees Celsius or the unbalance voltage could be routed to an electronic control unit for engine management.

## 23 Temperature coefficient of resistance

**1** Most metals increase in resistance as temperature rises and some semi-conductors fall in resistance with an increase in temperature. Both effects are important in motorcycle electrical systems.

Temperature coefficient $\alpha$ is defined as the *change of resistance per ohm per degree Celsius*. The value of the coefficient $\alpha$ is usually given at 20°C and for copper is + 0.0043. $\alpha$ is pronounced ALPHA.

**22.5b Throttle position sensor (two-track potentiometer) from the XJ900S**

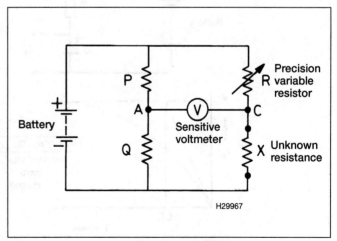

**22.6 Wheatstone bridge**

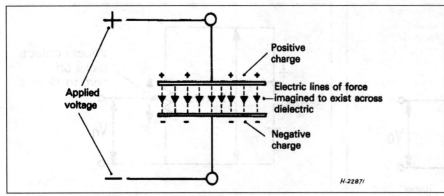

**24.2 Basic capacitor**

**2 Example:** If a solenoid of resistance 1.83Ω at 20°C were heated to 50°C in use, calculate the resistance at this temperature.

Resistance at 50°C = Resistance at 20°C + increase due to heating

Increase due to heating
= $R_{20}$ x 0.0043 x (50 – 20)
= 0.129 $R_{20}$

Resistance at 50°C = $R_{20}$ + 0.129 $R_{20}$
$R_{50}$ = 1.83 + (0.129 x 1.83)
$R_{50}$ = 2.07 ohms

## 24 Capacitance

**1** A capacitor (sometimes known as a condenser) is a component which will store charge and give it out again when required. It finds many applications in ignition systems and electronics.

**2** The most basic capacitor consists of two parallel metal plates as shown in illustration 24.2; applying a voltage V between the plates will result in a surge of current to charge the plates. The amount of charge (q coulombs) stored depends on:

(a) The area and spacing of the plates.
(b) The applied voltage.
(c) The type of insulator between the plates.

The *larger* the overlapping plate area, the larger the capacitance.
The *smaller* the spacing, the larger the capacitance.

**The charge q (coulombs) stored by applying 1 volt is called the CAPACITANCE,** the symbol for which is C. Capacitance is measured in farads and the relationship between voltage, capacitance and charge is: q = CV

**3** In practice the farad is too large a unit for practical purposes and the microfarad (µF) is used, being one millionth of a farad. In electronics and communications even this is too large and the picofarad (pF) is more common. The picofarad is one millionth of a microfarad.

In order to make the physical size of a capacitor smaller, the 'plates' may consist of two long rectangular aluminium foils separated by a slightly wider strip of impregnated paper (called the dielectric) and rolled up like a Swiss roll. Wires are attached to the two foils and the whole assembly is encapsulated in some form of plastic or metal container. The metal container is often connected internally to one of the foils and the case bolted down to earth (ground). Such metal cased capacitors are used in contact breaker units.

Capacitor design is highly developed and several other means of making a capacitor exist, but the basic idea of two separated plates is good for all types.

**4** Leakage may take place through the insulator (the dielectric) resulting in a fall of voltage between the plates. Serious leakage can cause malfunction of ignition, with misfiring, poor starting or total failure as a result. Workshop technicians will be certain to come across faulty capacitors at some time.

**5** The **Electrolytic Capacitor** is noted for its high capacitance per unit volume. The dielectric between the two aluminium plates is a very thin aluminium oxide layer and in order to preserve this layer the *applied voltage must always be in one direction*. The polarity is clearly shown, as is the maximum working voltage which may be anything from a few volts to several hundred. The polarity must never be reversed nor the working voltage exceeded or the electrolytic capacitor will be destroyed.

This type is often found in power units for smoothing out voltage variations and eliminating mains hum from audio equipment.

## 25 CR charge and discharge

**1** If a capacitor C is connected to a supply voltage V through a resistor R (see illustration 25.1) the voltage rise $V_O$ across the capacitor follows a curve (an *exponential* curve).

The time taken for the voltage to rise to 63% of the supply voltage V is the **time constant** of the circuit and equals CR seconds. Theoretically the voltage never quite reaches V but in practice after a period of 5 x time constant the final voltage is reached for all practical purposes.

**2** Similarly the time taken to discharge a charged capacitor C through resistance R is

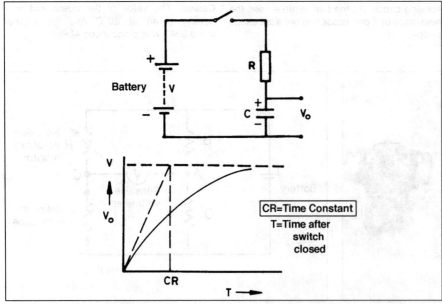

**25.1 Charging capacitor C through resistance R**

*Voltage across C reaches 63% of V in CR seconds*          CR = Time constant

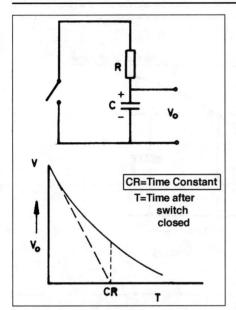

**25.2  Time of discharge of CR circuit**

*Capacitor C initially charged to V volts*
*Voltage across C falls to 37% of V in CR*
*seconds*
*CR = Time constant*

CR seconds where discharge is meant that the voltage falls to 37% of the initial voltage (see illustration 25.2).

  Both CR charge and discharge are widely used in electronic timing circuits.

**3 Example:** Calculate the time taken for a capacitor of 0.1 microfarad to reach 63% of final voltage if supplied through a 4.7 megohm resistor from a direct current supply as in illustration 25.1.

  Time constant = CR seconds = 0.1 x 10⁻⁶ x 4.7 x 10⁶ = 0.47 seconds.

## 26 Inductance

**1** Already we have seen that a coil carrying a direct current will set up a magnetic field around it. This is the steady state condition but of great importance is what happens when we attempt to **change** the current. Suppose a coil is switched on to a battery supply and the current begins to flow (see illustration 26.1). Magnetic lines of force spread out from the centre of the coil and in doing so pass through the coils of wire and generate an electromotive force, ie a voltage. This induced emf always acts so as to *oppose* the change of current (Lenz' Law) and the voltage depends on:

(a) *The rate of change of current.*
(b) *The coil design. This factor is the inductance of the coil and is measured in henrys.*

  Induced emf = Inductance x **rate** of change of current.

The symbol for inductance is L and the unit of inductance is the **henry**.

**DEFINITION:** A coil has an inductance of 1 henry when a current change rate of 1 ampere per second in it results in an induced emf of 1 volt.

**2** Opening a switch carrying current through an inductive coil will cause the current to fall very rapidly (see illustration 26.2). This results in the collapse of the surrounding magnetic field towards the coil centre and an induced emf will appear as shown. This can be a sharp pulse voltage and *may be much higher than the voltage supplying the coil current.*

  A sudden break of coil current is the foundation of ignition coil operation and will be met again later. Note that the direction of the emf is to try to maintain the current and it is sometimes called *back emf* – Lenz Law again!

  Remember – the back emf is not related to the supply voltage but depends only upon the inductance of the coil and the *rate* of change of current in it.

**3** A close analogy may be drawn between the inductor (ie a coil having the property of inductance) and the flywheel (see illustration 26.3). A sudden switch-on of current will produce a back emf so that for an instant, no current will flow and will then rise. A sudden application of torque to a flywheel does not produce immediate rotation but a gradual rise of rotational speed.

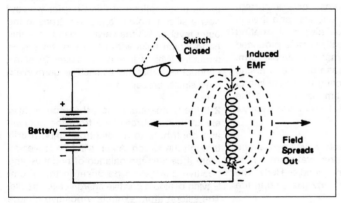

**26.1  Field build-up**

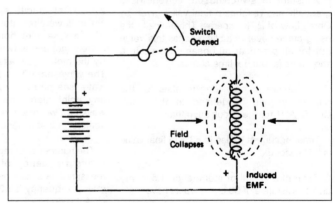

**26.2  Field collapse**

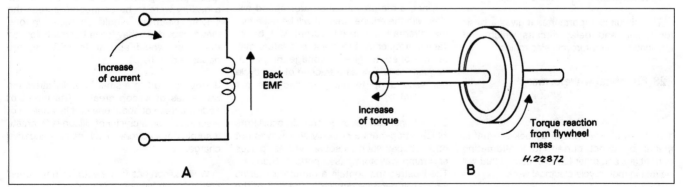

**26.3  An inductor (A) is like a flywheel (B)**

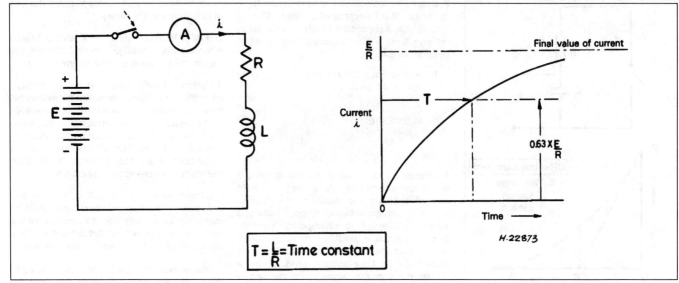

$$T = \frac{L}{R} = \text{Time constant}$$

**27.1 Current growth in an inductive coil on dc**

## 27 Inductance in a dc circuit

**1** Suppose an inductive coil of L henry of winding resistance R ohms is switched on to a dc supply of E volts (see illustration 27.1). At the instant of switching on, current rises gradually and reaches a final value given by Ohms Law of E/R amperes. Theoretically the rising curve never actually reaches this value but for all practical purposes does so in a short time (about 5 x time constant).

A measure of how long it takes for the current to rise is defined in the TIME CONSTANT for the circuit such that:

Time for current to rise to 63% of final value is L/R seconds.

**2 Example:** A coil of inductance 1.5 henry and a resistance of 50 ohms would have:

Time constant $= \frac{1.5}{50} = 0.03$ seconds

This circuit is important as it gives a basis for timing and delay circuits which find applications in motorcycle electronics.

## 28 Electrical waveforms

**1** At this point we pause to look at what is meant by direct current (dc), alternating current (ac) and other forms of current that will be met in motorcycle electrical work.

Most readers will know that direct current means a flow of current as produced by a battery. This ideal can be shown on a graph having a base of time (see illustration 28.1a, part 1). In many circuits however the flow may be altering with time but still be in the same general direction (see part 2) – it is still direct current dc because the **average** is still in one direction. This is a varying dc.

**2** Many electricity sources give a current which flows alternately one way and then in the reverse direction. This is alternating current (ac) and is typically what is produced by the motorcycle alternator in simple form. The waveshape to a base of time is a sine wave (see part 3). Erecting a vertical line at any point along the timebase to cut the waveform will give the value of the current (or voltage) at that instant.

The number of complete waves per second is the **frequency** of the waveform. It is measured as cycles per second or Hertz. The mains frequency is 50 Hertz (Hz) and in the USA it is 60 Hz.

Since a motorcycle alternator speed will alter with the engine speed it will be seen that the alternating current output will be of varying frequency. Electronic oscillators may be designed to give a voltage output at frequencies as low as a fraction of one cycle per second up to many megacycles per second (MHz).

**3** Electronic circuits often contain oscillators which can generate not only sine waves but other shapes such as square waves, pulses and ramp waveforms (see parts 4, 5 and 6). The illustrations contain a number of terms which will become familiar in the rest of the book.

## 29 Semi-conductors

**1** As the name suggests, a semi-conductor has a resistivity between that of a conductor and that of an insulator. However, this fact is not the important feature of semi-conductors. In the first sections of this Chapter we saw how a silicon atom has four electrons in the outer layer called the valence band. It is this band which links with others in the silicon structure. While silicon is much used for semi-conductors, other metals such as germanium have similar properties.

**2** If the temperature rises, these outer layer electrons may break free from the nucleus and contribute to an electron random drift through the silicon. As an electron leaves an atom it causes the balance of negative and positive charges to be upset in that atom, leaving behind a positive charge called a hole. The silicon atom exhibits a positive charge until it picks up another stray electron. If now a battery were to be connected across the silicon, electrons would all move in one direction and, as they leave behind holes, so the holes would appear to move in the opposite direction.

**3 Doping:** Adding a small impurity alters the properties of silicon greatly. The effect of adding a trace of about one part in a million of arsenic to a pure crystal of silicon is to create a surplus of electrons which carry a negative charge.

While silicon has four electrons in the outer ring (or shell), arsenic has five and so cannot bond with the nearby silicon atoms. The extra

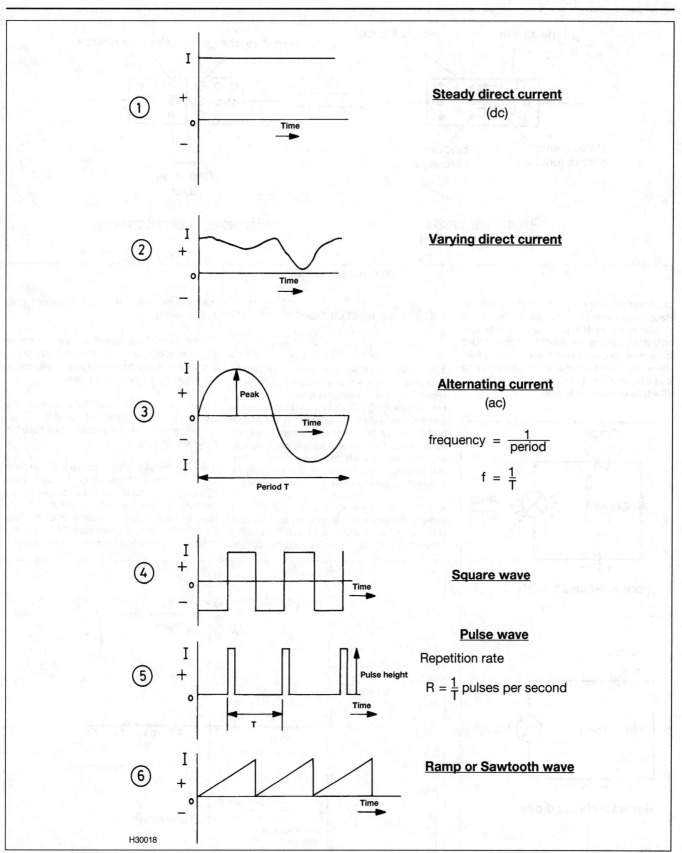

**28.1  Electrical waveforms**

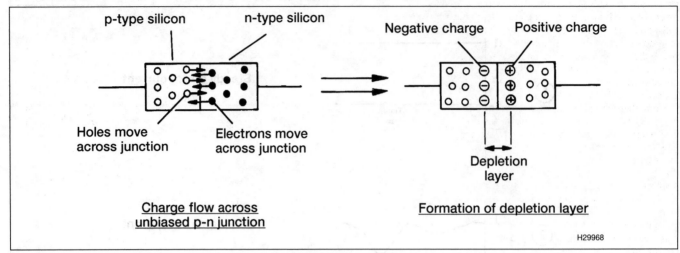

**30.1 The p-n junction**

electrons are free to drift through the crystal. Because of the excess of electrons, the silicon crystal is called **N type**. If an impurity with only three electrons in the outer shell is added to pure silicon, such as indium or boron, then there will be a shortage of electrons so positive charges (holes) exist in the silicon. This type of silicon is **P type**.

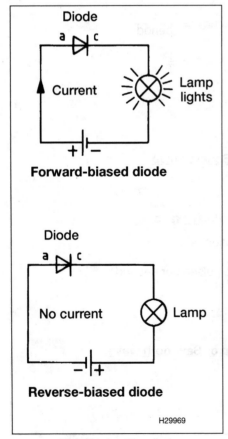

**30.2 The junction diode**

*a = anode     c = cathode*

## 30 The p-n junction diode

**1** If a junction is made between P type and N type silicon, the + holes migrate into the N region and the – electrons into the P region (see illustration 30.1). They can go only so far however because the electrons on the P side and the holes on the N side exert a pull on each other. They form a potential barrier as though there were a battery connected across the junction. The region at the junction is called the depletion layer.

**2** If this p-n junction is now connected to an external battery and a load such as a bulb, it is found that the bulb will light with the battery connected one way round but will not light if the battery connections are reversed (see illustration 30.2).

If we think of the depletion layer voltage as a battery, clearly it assists the external battery or opposes it depending on which way round the external battery is connected.

External current may flow across the junction in one direction but not in the other. In other words, **the p-n junction is a rectifier or diode.**

**3** If the external battery positive terminal goes to the P terminal of the p-n diode, current will flow easily and the diode is said to be *forward biased*. If the battery connections are reversed the diode is *reverse biased*. Note from the graph (see illustration 30.3) that the forward-direction volt drop across the diode is

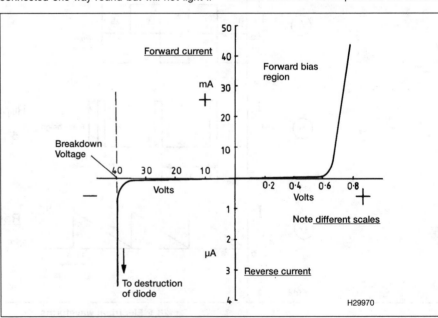

**30.3 Characteristic of p-n diode**

small, about 0.65 volt. When the diode is reverse-biased, much larger applied voltages will send only a very small current in the reverse direction until a point is reached where the diode breaks down and the reverse current rises sharply. At this point the diode is quickly destroyed.

From this we learn that the diode is not perfect in practice. Motorcycle rectifier testing involves checking for abnormal reverse currents for which nothing can be done but to replace the rectifier element or a complete assembly.

**4** Although the battery supplies direct current (dc) to the motorcycle, the charging generator in modern machines produces alternating current (ac) and this must be converted into some form of direct current (dc) in order to charge the battery. p-n junction diodes are used for this purpose and we shall be looking at their use in detail in Chapter 12.

In most electronic circuits the diode appears frequently and they are made with a wide range of current ratings according to whether they are for light current electronics or heavy rectification duty. Two types are shown in the illustration.

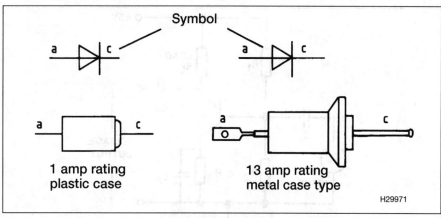

**30.4 Rectifier diodes**

## 31 The transistor

**1** The bipolar junction transistor (BJT) is a sandwich of p-n-p or n-p-n material, rather like two diodes back to back. If a current can be made to flow between the middle section of the sandwich and one outer layer, then a much greater current would be able to flow straight through between the outer layers (see illustrations 31.1a and 31.1b).

**2** Illustration 31.2 shows the action. Current into the base $I_b$ will permit a current flow $I_c$ between collector and emitter. The current flow from collector to emitter is much larger than the base current and is controlled by it. Switching $I_b$ on or off simultaneously switches

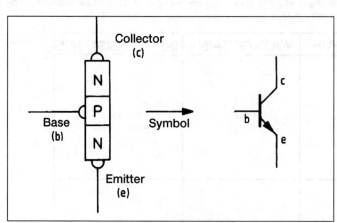

**31.1a  n-p-n transistor**

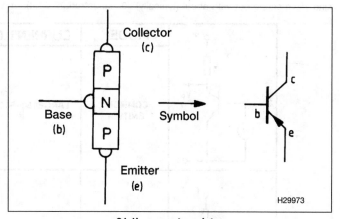

**31.1b  p-n-p transistor**

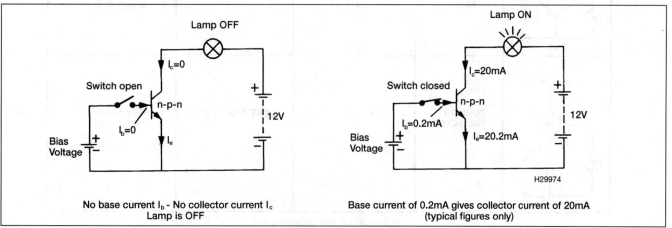

No base current $I_b$ - No collector current $I_c$
Lamp is OFF

Base current of 0.2mA gives collector current of 20mA
(typical figures only)

**31.2  The transistor as a switch**

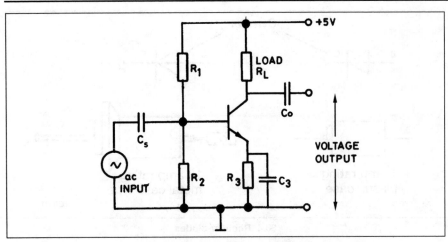

**31.4 Single stage common-emitter amplifier**

*Co and Cs block dc*        *$R_1$ and $R_2$ provide forward bias*
*$R_3$ acts as temperature compensator*

on or off the main collector current flow. Regarded this way the transistor is a **switch**. This action is used in ignition coils which are part of an electronic ignition system.

**3** If, instead of switching on or off, the base current $I_b$ is varied, say, in a sine wave fashion, the collector current will also vary in a sine wave shape but with about (typically) 50

to 100 times the amplitude. Used this way the transistor is a **current amplifier**.

**4** To obtain **voltage amplification** (or voltage gain) a load resistor $R_L$ in the collector circuit may be used. Current variations through $R_L$ produce voltage variations across it which can be much larger than the input voltage (see illustration 31.4). If the alternating output

voltage is larger than the alternating input voltage then we have a basic voltage amplifier!

To run the transistor properly, a bias voltage of about 650 millivolts (mV) must be provided between the emitter and base.

Here bias is obtained by resistors $R_1$ and $R_2$ to avoid the use of a bias battery. $R_3$ compensates for temperature effects; as temperature rises the emitter current will **rise**, but the extra volt-drop this causes in passing through $R_3$ is sensed by the base as a bias tending to **reduce** emitter current. Capacitor $C_3$ passes any alternating component to earth preventing ac feedback to the base. Note that *as far as ac* is concerned the +5 volt line is at earth potential, since the supply will have large electrolytic capacitors between the positive and earth (ground) for voltage smoothing purposes. The effective ac resistance (called reactance) to earth (ground) of large value capacitors is very small.

**5** The junction transistor can be operated in three different ways which are named according to which terminal is common to both the input and output. They are common-emitter (CE), common-base (CB), and common-collector (CC). Their characteristics are shown in illustration 31.5.

| | MODE | CURRENT GAIN | VOLTAGE GAIN | INPUT RESISTANCE |
|---|---|---|---|---|
| | COMMON EMITTER | LARGE 50-500 | HIGH | MEDIUM ABOUT 2kΩ |
| | COMMON BASE | LESS THAN 1.0 ABOUT 0·99 | HIGH | LOW ABOUT 50 Ω |
| | COMMON COLLECTOR | LARGE | LESS THAN 1.0 | VERY HIGH ABOUT 1MΩ |

**31.5 Transistor operation modes**

*Biasing not shown*

## 32 The Metal Oxide Field Effect Transistor (MOSFET)

**1** While the junction transistor is essentially a current operated device, the MOSFET has a much higher input resistance and is voltage-controlled. The immediate advantages over the basic junction transistor are the lower power demand and the very high input resistance.

**2** Illustration 32.2 shows an N-channel MOSFET which has an n-p-n silicon structure. There are three terminals, the *gate*, the *drain* and the *source*. The gate is insulated from the p section by a thin film of silicon oxide and acts rather like a capacitor plate.

**3** If no voltage is applied to the gate, the structure behaves like two p-n junctions back to back and no current can flow through from source to drain.

**4** The p section will have a *limited* number of free electrons although, being a p-doped section, it has predominantly more p holes. If a + voltage (relative to the source terminal) is applied to the gate, then the free electrons will be attracted toward the gate and form an effective n channel. Current can then flow through from source to drain since it is an n channel path all the way. The resistance between source and drain is low (see illustration 32.2).

**5** The MOSFET can be used as a switch and is *voltage controlled* as distinct from the junction transistor which is *current controlled*.

**6** Power versions of the MOSFET for controlling larger currents are increasingly replacing conventional bipolar junction transistors in many vehicle applications and extend to the integrated circuits (IC) also.

Smart power is a term used to describe power MOSFETs which have built-in temperature protection and possibly other functions.

## 33 Zener diode

**1** This diode is used as a voltage limiter, applications being in voltage stabilisers or peak voltage clipping.

Strangely, the useful range is in the *reverse* direction, unlike a normal diode. When the Zener type has a reverse voltage applied, it will allow very little current through until it reaches the **Zener voltage** at which point it will conduct, without self destruction, up to

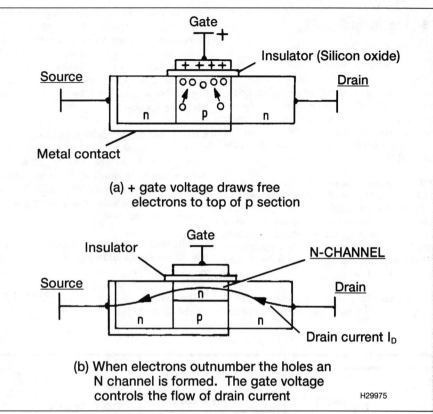

**(a) + gate voltage draws free electrons to top of p section**

**(b) When electrons outnumber the holes an N channel is formed. The gate voltage controls the flow of drain current**

H29975

**32.2 The n-channel MOSFET**

the maximum rating. The forward current characteristic is not normally used.

**2** Illustration 33.2 part A shows the Zener voltage which can be chosen by the designer and 33.2 part B gives a simple application as a voltage regulator. The current limiting resistor R will absorb the voltage variations of the supply voltage, leaving a constant (stabilised) output voltage. It should be noticed that the circuit will not work unless the supply voltage is higher than the Zener voltage.

**3** A problem with early alternators was the prevention of battery overcharging due to poor regulation. (Regulation here is a term meaning the variation of alternator voltage with engine speed.)

The Zener diode was used effectively for some years before more sophisticated electronic circuits were developed. Connected across the dc output from the alternator rectifier, the Zener diode drains off excess current once the desired charging voltage is attained (see Chapter 12).

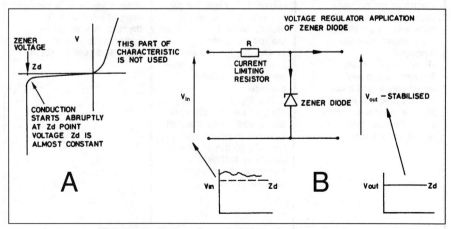

**33.2 Zener diode – characteristic and one application**

*The Zener diode conducts by reverse current*

## 34 The thyristor (SCR)

**1** This is a 4 layer p-n-p-n device which has the property of rapid current switching. Like a mechanical switch, it is either fully on or fully off but has no moving parts and is switched from the OFF to the ON state by a small current fed into the gate terminal.

**2** The operation is explained in illustration 34.2 in which the term avalanche breakdown is used. This is similar to the way in which the Zener diode breaks down when a reverse voltage above a certain threshold is applied. While the Zener process is scientifically different from avalanche breakdown, the effect is the same.

**3** The essential features are that when the gate current triggers the thyristor, current flows from anode to cathode and from this point on the gate has no further effect. Only by reducing the anode-cathode voltage to (near) zero can the device be switched off. This characteristic is ideally suited for capacitor discharge ignition (CDI) – see Chapter 6 – and also for several other electronic applications.

**4** If the anode is positive relative to the cathode, a triggering pulse of current at the gate switches on the device in a few microseconds. It will then have an almost constant voltage drop of about 1 volt independent of the amount of current flowing from anode to cathode.

A thyristor switching a 10A current might typically require a gate triggering current of 60mA at 3 volts.

The thyristor is alternatively known as a Silicon Controlled Rectifier (SCR).

## 35 Light emitting diodes (LED)

**1** A forward-biased p-n junction diode will emit light when carrying current, the colour depending upon the proportions of phosphorous and arsenic in the alloy used for the semi-conductor (see illustration 35.1). Colours may be red, yellow or green, but maximum optical efficiency is obtained using red light.

**2** A current limiting resistor must be used to set the current within the range 2mA to 25mA, the voltage drop across red diodes being 2.0V. LED life is very long; it is rugged and consumes very low power. The light output is not high and so they are confined to warning lights and nacelle indicator lights.

Bar charts are formed by using a series of LEDs or an alpha-numerical (letters and numbers) display may be utilised (see illustration 35.2).

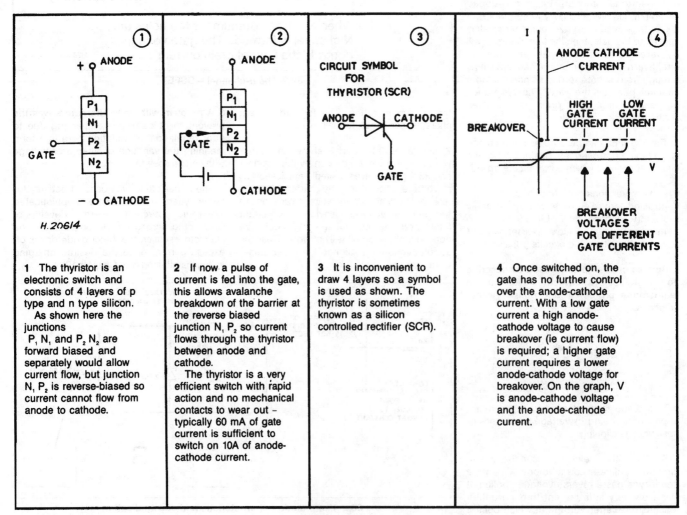

**1** The thyristor is an electronic switch and consists of 4 layers of p type and n type silicon.
As shown here the junctions $P_1 N_1$ and $P_2 N_2$ are forward biased and separately would allow current flow, but junction $N_1 P_2$ is reverse-biased so current cannot flow from anode to cathode.

**2** If now a pulse of current is fed into the gate, this allows avalanche breakdown of the barrier at the reverse biased junction $N_1 P_2$, so current flows through the thyristor between anode and cathode.
The thyristor is a very efficient switch with rapid action and no mechanical contacts to wear out – typically 60 mA of gate current is sufficient to switch on 10A of anode-cathode current.

**3** It is inconvenient to draw 4 layers so a symbol is used as shown. The thyristor is sometimes known as a silicon controlled rectifier (SCR).

**4** Once switched on, the gate has no further control over the anode-cathode current. With a low gate current a high anode-cathode voltage to cause breakover (ie current flow) is required; a higher gate current requires a lower anode-cathode voltage for breakover. On the graph, V is anode-cathode voltage and the anode-cathode current.

**34.2 The Thyristor**

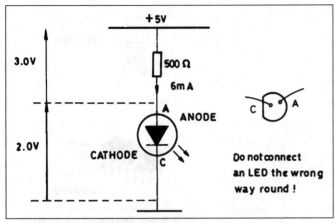

**35.1 LED and typical operation conditions**

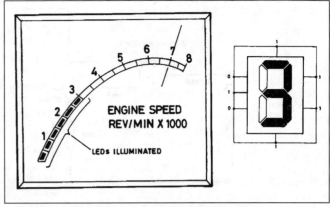

**35.2 Light emitting diode applications**

*LEDs are set in separate compartments on a printed circuit board (PCB) Each LED has a silvered reflector on the curved compartment wall*

## 36 Photo-diodes and photo-transistors

**1** A p-n junction fabricated from silicon with a high impurity layer is found to be sensitive to light. Electronic action at the junction under light stimulus will generate a voltage and will give current into a load circuit, the energy coming from the light falling on the photo sensitive junction. About 600 millivolts is a typical output voltage.

**2** If light falls on the base-collector junction of a transistor with similar impurity doping, then amplification will take place. The device is then a phototransistor and gives a larger output voltage than a diode. Both the diode and the phototransistor have transparent cases to allow light to reach the sensitive junctions.

**3** Such an opto-electronic transistor can be obtained to suit different light frequency bands. An example is the phototransistor used with a light emitting diode (LED) as a trigger in an opto-electronic ignition circuit (see illustration 36.3).

## 37 Light-dependent resistors (LDR)

**1** This is a resistor having a resistance which varies according to the amount of light falling upon it (see illustration 37.1). The dark resistance is very high (a few megohms) and falls to a low value (about 100 ohms) in sunlight.

**2** Response time is slow, of the order of 100 milliseconds, but the LDR is much more rugged than the photodiode or the phototransistor.

## 38 The Darlington Pair

**1** There are many circuit design arrangements of transistors but one in particular is worthy of note here. Transistors may be used for low level voltage or current amplification, in which case they are physically small and use low currents, or they may be required to deliver power to some form of load such as an ignition coil or an actuator. Then the transistor is designed to deal with larger currents and is physically bigger.

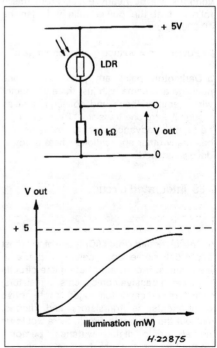

**37.1 LDR and light response curve**

**36.3 Opto-electric trigger**

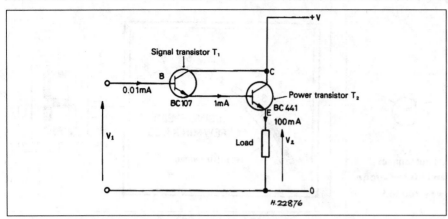

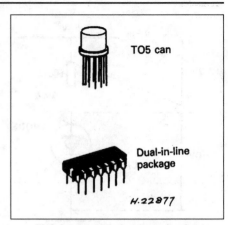

**38.2 The Darlington pair**

*T₁ and T₂ are housed in one package with three leads E, B, C*

**39.3 Integrated circuit packaging**

**2** The two may be combined in one device in which transistor $T_1$ amplifies the input signal $V_1$ (see illustration 38.2). Direct connection of the emitter of $T_1$ to the base of $T_2$ provides the base current for $T_2$ and this in turn controls a much larger current from collector to emitter of the power transistor $T_2$.

**3** The current amplification of $T_1$ (the gain) may be 100 and also for transistor $T_2$. Thus the overall current gain will be 100 x 100 = 10,000. An assumed input current of 0.01 mA to $T_1$ will produce a current of 100 mA in the load of transistor $T_2$ (see illustration 38.2).

**4** With the Darlington pair, the voltage gain is approximately unity; ie the input and output voltages will be nearly equal. From this it follows that the power gain will also be 10,000, since:

Power gain = voltage gain x current gain

**5** Darlington pairs are provided in one package and come with just three connector wires: emitter, base and collector, just as though it were one transistor. The circuit is to be found in advanced ignition systems and has many other applications where a power drive is required.

## 39 Integrated circuits

**1** The integrated circuit (IC) is one of the most important single advances ever made in electronics. It consists of complete circuits comprising **passive** components, ie resistors, inductors and capacitors together with **active** components, ie transistors and diodes. Without the integrated circuit, there would be no electronic digital watches, personal computers or the great achievements in space research, automation or in communication systems.

**2** Two types of IC are used, the hybrid and the monolithic. In one type of hybrid IC, the components are produced by deposition of a thin film (in vacuum) on a base of alumina. The active devices are added afterwards by bonding transistors and diodes on to the circuit by ultrasonic techniques. Thick film technology is based on printing thick films (about 25µm thick) on to an alumina substrate. The film makes up the passive circuit components using similar techniques to silk screen printing. The transistors (known as 'flip-chip' transistors) are added later and are transistor chips without the casing, being bonded into the circuit by welding.

**3** Most important is the monolithic IC, so called because the entire circuit is fabricated within a single block of silicon crystal. Complete circuits including the transistors, cover clocks, timers, logic systems, etc., and can be bought in a single package. These packages are containers either in the form of a small can (the TO5) or the dual-in-line (DIL) type (see illustration 39.3).

**4** DIL ICs consist of a plastic base into which the integrated circuits are embedded.

Fourteen or sixteen leads are brought out along the two sides of the bar which is typically 20 mm long by 5 mm wide and 2.5 mm deep. Larger units with more output leads are common for circuits of greater complexity such as clocks and calculator chips.

## 40 The operational amplifier

**1** The operational amplifier (known as an 'op-amp') is an integrated circuit (IC) that is so useful as to merit special note. The IC chip contains about 25 internal transistors which give a very high voltage gain (ie, the ratio of output voltage to input voltage). The actual gain does not matter, so long as it is very high, and is typically in the range 500,000 to one million.

**2** Op-amps usually come in the dual-in-line 8 pin package. In the op-amp shown, there are two input terminals, numbered 2 and 3 (see illustrations 40.2a, b and c) and an output

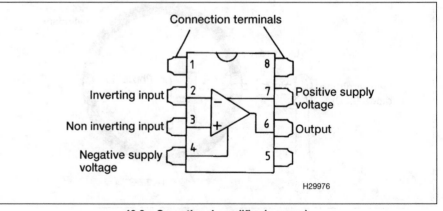

**40.2a Operational amplifier (op-amp)**

*8-pin DIL (dual in line) package*

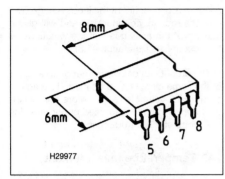

**40.2b Op-amp package**

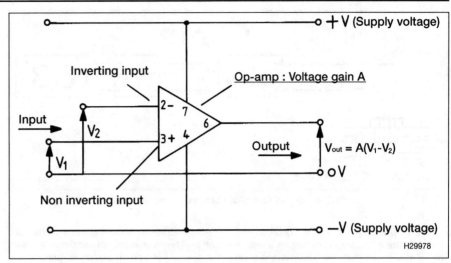

**40.2c Op-amp connections**

terminal 6. With an input signal to pin 2 the output voltage is much higher and inverted, that is to say, if the input voltage rises, the output voltage falls and vice versa. If an input signal is applied to pin 3 the output voltage is again much higher than the input but is of the same shape ie, non inverting.

**3** This op-amp works as a *differential* amplifier which means that it takes the difference of the voltages between terminals 2 and 3 as the input. If the same signal voltage were to be applied to 2 and 3 the output voltage would be zero at terminal 6 because one input is trying to drive the output positively and the other negatively. There are several ways to connect this versatile IC but in vehicle electronics perhaps the most useful is as a comparator.

**4** The comparator, as the name suggests, compares two input voltages and provides a binary output signal for further processing. When the non-inverting voltage is greater than the inverting voltage, the output of an op-amp is approximately equal to the supply voltage.

If however the non-inverting voltage is less than the inverting voltage the op-amp output is very low, just above zero. These two

conditions are a form of the binary 0 or 1 or put another way OFF or ON (see Section 41 below)

An example is shown where a twistgrip throttle control has a potentiometer (remember! a tapped sliding resistor) built in. When the potentiometer is in the low position, there may be a slight output from it due to manufacturing tolerances but what is really needed is a **definite** signal to the ECU that the engine is at idle.

**5** When the output from the throttle potentiometer is below a set figure say 0.4 volt, the comparator output is high (1 or ON). If the throttle is opened above the threshold of 0.4 volt this switches the comparator to the low condition (0 or OFF) (see illustration 40.5).

Such output information tells the ECU whether to apply slow running control. This type of comparator is the Schmitt Trigger and we shall meet it again in Chapter 7 dealing with Transistor and Digital Ignition.

## 41 Analogue and digital signals

**1 Analogue** quantities are those which are continuously present, the most common example being the reading of a pointer on an instrument. The difficulty with analogue measurement is low accuracy, where for example, the pointer reading at the low end of a scale could be comparable with the pointer thickness and so liable to be misread.

**2 Digital** quantities are expressed in numbers and moreover only two numbers (0 and 1) are used. Any number in the conventional **denary** scale in use in everyday arithmetic (ie to base 10) can be converted into **digital binary** form (ie to base 2) and vice versa. The number then can be written in binary form as a set of 0 and 1 figures.

Electronic circuits are easily devised where the voltage or current in them can be fully OFF

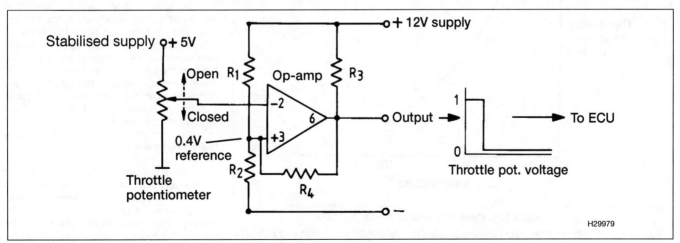

**40.5 Op-amp comparator for idle condition detection**

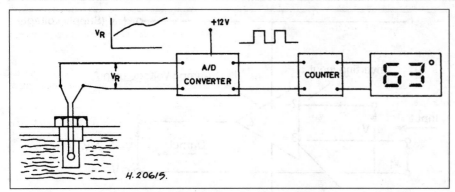

**41.3  Analogue to digital conversion requirement**

or ON. By assigning 1 to the ON condition and 0 to OFF the manipulation of numbers will be free of the errors that can occur in analogue representation.

**3** Many quantities that need to be measured for engine operation come in analogue form. These could be, for example, engine and coolant temperatures, air intake volume and battery voltage. For presentation to the electronic control unit ECU (a specialised computer) these need to be converted to digital form since computers work in digital mode only.

Examples where analogue/digital conversions are used will be found later in this book, particularly in relation to ignition and fuel injection systems. An instrument example is shown in illustration 41.3 where the temperature of an engine coolant is sensed by a temperature-dependent resistor (schematic only). The variation of resistance with temperature will be an analogue quantity and before it is usable in a computing device it will need to be converted into digital form.

**4** The principle of AD conversion uses again the comparator. The analogue signal is applied to one input terminal and to the other a **ramp** voltage (see illustration 28.1). This is the shape of a sawtooth, that is, it rises linearly from zero and drops back to zero abruptly at a certain point. When the ramp voltage is less than the analogue voltage, an electronic pulse generator (called a clock) sends pulses to a digital counter.

At the point where the analogue voltage equals that of the ramp, the counter switches off by the snap action of the op-amp comparator. The number of pulses it has counted is a measure of the input voltage. The process repeats continuously and will give a reading of the analogue voltage variations as they occur (see illustration 41.3).

The output could now be sent on to an ECU or the same circuit could be made to read out on a digital voltmeter scale. More complex A to D convertors are also used but are outside the scope of this introduction.

## 42 Temperature measurement

**1** Knowledge of temperature is a common requirement in vehicle engineering. The principal methods of measurement are by the thermistor and the thermocouple.

**2 Thermistors** are semi-conductor resistors which change their resistance value with temperature. When the resistance *decreases* with an increase in temperature it has a *negative temperature coefficient* (NTC) and vice versa (see illustration 42.2a).

In motorcycles and automobiles the negative temperature coefficient type (NTC) thermistor is used in measuring engine temperature and for sensing air intake temperature in engine management systems. In electronics generally the NTC thermistor is used to compensate for other components which rise in resistance with temperature. The thermistor is useful for temperature measurement up to 200°C but beyond that the thermocouple is used. Often the thermistor is encapsulated in a brass sleeve for mechanical protection (see illustration 42.2b).

**3 Thermocouples** consist of two dissimilar wires joined together and connected to a sensitive moving coil instrument. The first experimenter (Seebeck) found that current would flow round the two wire circuit provided there was a *temperature difference* between the junctions. The voltage is more often measured and this is known as the thermal emf. The thermal emf is of the order of millivolts and will increase up to a certain maximum as the temperature difference between the junctions rises. By calibrating the thermal emf against temperature, the instrument can then be scaled in degrees Celsius (see illustration 42.3) and so we have an electrical thermometer. The thermocouple is more accurate than the thermistor as a measuring device.

**4** In practice we do not bother with a cold junction and connect the meter so that it is, in effect, the cold junction (see illustration 42.4). In engine control systems the output of the thermocouple, located in the exhaust, may be fed into the electronic control unit ECU) and there are many other applications in industry

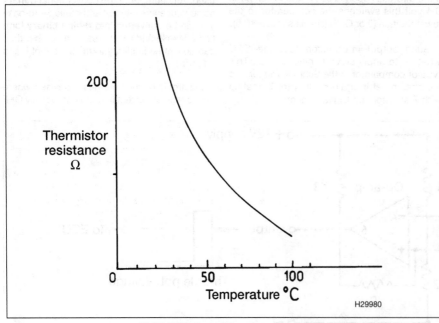

**42.2a  NTC thermistor characteristic**

*Typical characteristic for engine temperature gauge. Other ranges for electronics and ECU use higher values eg 35 kΩ at 20°C to 150Ω at 100°C*

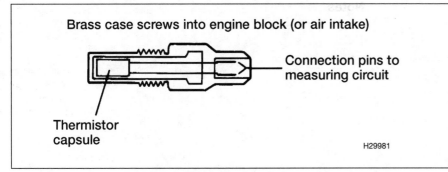

**42.2b NTC thermistor and capsule**

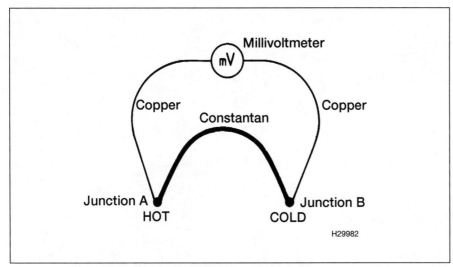

**42.3 Principle of the thermocouple**

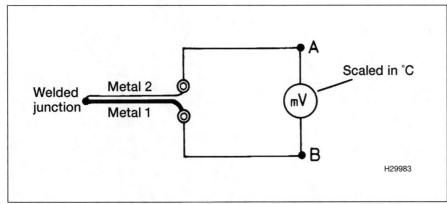

**42.4 Practical thermocouple thermometer**

such as furnace temperature measurement. Several metal combinations may be used and the combination of copper/constantan shown is good up to 400°C.

Modern thermocouple wires are of nickel alloys or platinum/rhodium and are capable of measuring up to 1200°C.

Note that both the thermistor and the thermocouple give an analogue output which may have to be converted to digital form if intended for feeding to an ECU.

## 43 Sensors

**1** A sensor is any device which detects or measures a quantity, usually in electrical form, so that it may be used in measurement or control. It is also sometimes called a transducer; an older name still is a pick-up.

Modern vehicles, whether motorcycle or automobile, use sensors more and more and the study of them is becoming a subject in its own right. Probably the most common early sensor was the gramophone pick-up which used a stylus to convert record surface groove variations into music, but now all manner of physical quantities can be changed by a sensor into an electrical signal.

**2** In vehicle engineering, the quantities often measured or detected are temperature, air flow, engine knock, pressure, speed, fuel levels and position, just to list a few. In this book, sensors will be described as they arise in the following Chapters since it is better to see them in context rather than deal with them in detail at this stage.

## 44 Further reading

**1** Only a simple survey of electrical principles has been possible in this Chapter, but all topics are directly relevant to the motorcycle. For further reading on electrical work see 'Principles of Electricity' by Morley and Hughes (Addison-Wesley Longman). For information on electronics see 'Electronics' by Malcolm Plant (Hodder and Stoughton, Teach Yourself Series).

**Notes**

# Chapter 3
## Ignition and combustion

## Contents

### 1 The petrol (gasoline) engine

**1** The purpose of an engine is to convert fuel energy into mechanical energy (work). To do this the fuel is burnt inside the engine having first been mixed with air.

**2** A mixture of fuel and air in the approximate ratio of 1:15 is compressed inside a cylinder by a moving piston and, at the correct moment, ignited by a spark. The spark is produced by the motorcycle ignition system and how it is done will form much of the rest of this book.

**3** The mixture burns very quickly and, in so doing, creates a high gas pressure which pushes the piston down the cylinder bore. The piston is connected to a crankshaft by a connecting rod and the up and down (reciprocating) motion is converted at the crankshaft into rotary motion. It is this crankshaft rotation which drives the rear wheel after transmission via the clutch and gearbox.

**4** Attempts have been made to produce a rotary motion directly in the form of the Wankel engine. The Suzuki RE5 was a technical masterpiece but was not well accepted by riders because of reliability problems and it had a short production life, as did models by Hercules and Van Veen. Norton also made a rotary-engined motorcycle which was in production from 1987 to 1993. For these reasons we will be concerned only with the reciprocating engine.

**5** Two forms of reciprocating engine are in common use; they work on the two-stroke and the four-stroke cycles (the term 'cycle' means a sequence of operation). Both have advantages and disadvantages.

**6** The two-stroke engine is of simpler construction than the four-stroke and is cheaper to manufacture. In the simple form it is less efficient, has poorer fuel economy and is a greater noise and pollution producer than the four-stroke. However, in recent years, it has become much more sophisticated and the modern two-stroke is used primarily in the interests of light weight and power output.

**7** Four-stroke engines were employed in larger motorcycles because of the superior fuel economy and spread of power over the engine speed range. They are, however, more complicated in design, but developments in both types have led to a blurring of the differences. Now small four-strokes and large two-strokes are used widely also.

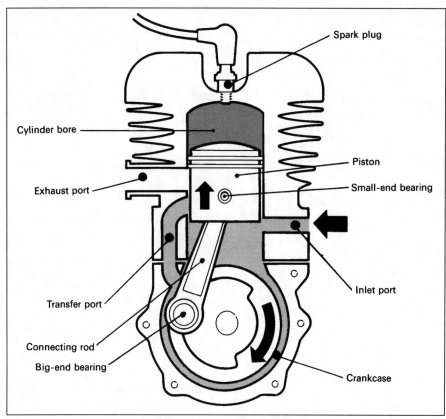

Spark plug

Cylinder bore

Piston

Small-end bearing

Exhaust port

Inlet port

Transfer port

Connecting rod

Big-end bearing

Crankcase

**2.1 The two-stroke engine**

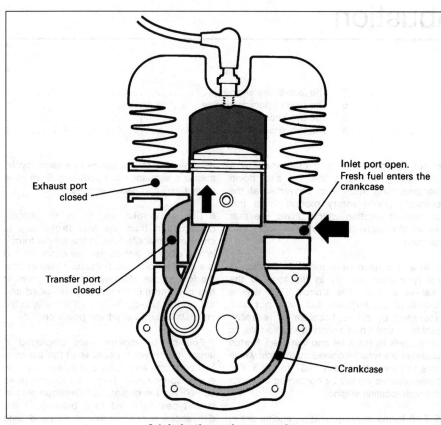

Exhaust port closed

Inlet port open. Fresh fuel enters the crankcase

Transfer port closed

Crankcase

**3.1 Induction and compression**

## 2 The two-stroke engine

**1** Illustration 2.1 shows a simple piston-ported two-stroke engine which we will use to follow the two-stroke cycle of operations.

**2** Ports are holes in the side of the cylinder which allow the air/fuel mixture to enter (the inlet port) and the exhaust port is for discharging the spent gases. In addition there are transfer ports for passing the incoming charge to the top of the cylinder where it undergoes compression due to the rising piston.

**3** Note that the crankcase has an important secondary role acting as a form of pump for the air/fuel mixture. It is a closed chamber, closed at the top by the piston and clearly of varying volume as the piston rises and descends. The crankshaft passes through the crankcase and it is necessary to use seals to prevent loss of pressure or vacuum. Seals often need to be replaced when overhauling a two-stroke engine since seal leakage will result in poor starting and running.

## 3 The two-stroke cycle

**1** Reference to illustration 3.1 shows the induction of air/fuel vapour and compression: the piston is nearing the top of its stroke, and the shaded area above it indicates that the air/fuel mixture is being compressed ready for combustion. As the piston has been rising the crankcase volume has been increasing, but since it is sealed a partial vacuum has been created. The piston has now passed the inlet port and a fresh charge is drawn into the crankcase from the carburettor, indicated by the arrows.

**2** Illustration 3.2 shows the spark plug igniting the compressed mixture and the expanding gases forcing the piston downwards. The piston has now covered the inlet port and has begun to compress the fresh mixture trapped below it. At about the same time, the top of the piston passes the exhaust port and transfer port. Though most of the useful power has been extracted, the gases in the combustion chamber are still under pressure and rush out through the exhaust port.

The fresh mixture charge is now able to escape from the crankcase into the combustion chamber. Note that the transfer port directs the incoming mixture upwards, where it helps to displace the burnt gases. If this were not done, the incoming mixture would tend to rush straight out of the exhaust port, wasting fuel and leaving some of the

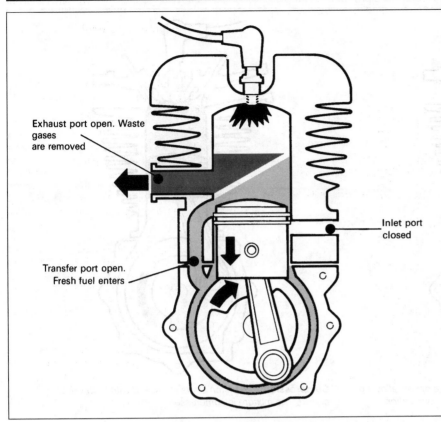

Exhaust port open. Waste gases are removed

Inlet port closed

Transfer port open. Fresh fuel enters

**3.2 Ignition and exhaust**

spent mixture from the last power stroke in the cylinder.

The piston has now passed the bottom of its stroke and begins to ascend. The exhaust and transfer ports are closed and the mixture in the combustion chamber is compressed. As the piston continues to rise, the inlet port is uncovered and so the cycle is completed.

**3** The engine described is a 'piston ported' two-stroke and is the simplest form. Today piston-ported engines are to be found mainly on mopeds where a high power output is not necessary.

Improvements on the basic design may involve the use of deflector pistons to help gas flow, reed valves or disc valves to prevent blow back of mixture through the inlet port and power valves to change port timing. For more detail readers should consult the 'Motorcycle Basics Manual' which is a companion book in this series.

**4** The important point to note from the description of operation is that there must be **one spark per engine revolution**. This is in contrast to the four-stroke engine where there is **one spark per two revolutions** of the engine (see next Section).

## 4  The four-stroke engine

**1** While the two-stroke engine is simple in principle, the need to burn carefully calculated amounts of fuel at the right time and disposing of the burnt gases poses more of a problem.

A different approach is to allow four-stokes of the piston to complete the cycle of operation and this gives the name to the engine. The first successful engine working on this idea was the horizontal gas engine designed by the German engineer N.A. Otto in 1876 and some 50,000 of them were sold in the first seventeen years of production.

The four-stroke operating cycle employed is sometimes known as the Otto cycle and most internal combustion engines built since its introduction have worked on the same principles.

**2** The combustion chamber of the basic four-stroke engine now has no cylinder ports but instead has poppet valves (see illustration 5.1), one for air/fuel intake and one for exhausting the spent gases. Despite the increased mechanical complexity and the fact

that there is only one power stroke per two revolutions, the induction and exhaust stages can now be more carefully controlled and the engine is relatively more efficient.

**3** The many designs for valve operation have occupied engineers for many decades and today the four-stroke mechanical design has reached an efficiency peak which is increasingly difficult to improve.

## 5  The four-stroke cycle

**1** The four parts to the cycle are shown in illustration 5.1 overleaf:

**Induction** of the air/fuel mixture occurs as the piston descends. The cam operated inlet valve (shown in black) opens to allow the vapour to be sucked into the cylinder.

**Compression** of the fuel charge occurs next as the piston rises and the valves are both closed.

**Ignition** of the compressed air/fuel mixture by a spark at the spark plug occurs just before the piston reaches the top dead centre. In a few milliseconds the fuel has burnt causing a large build up of pressure which is timed to give the maximum downward thrust on to the piston. **This is the power stroke**.

**Exhaust:** the piston rises again and the exhaust valve opens. The piston pushes the spent gases out to the atmosphere via the exhaust system.

## 6  Spark requirements for combustion

**1** Petrol (gasoline) engines require an electric spark at the spark plug electrodes in order to ignite the compressed air/fuel vapour. This spark must occur at a precise point in the cycle of engine operation so that maximum downward pressure on the piston occurs shortly after top dead centre.

The plug voltage requirements may be anywhere within the range 5000 to 30,000 volts and depend upon several factors, including the mixture strength, the shape of the combustion chamber, the compression rate, the temperature, and the condition of the plug and its gap dimension.

**2** Once the air/fuel vapour breaks down under the electric stress of the plug voltage, a high intensity spark travels from the negative centre electrode to the positive earth (ground)

**3**

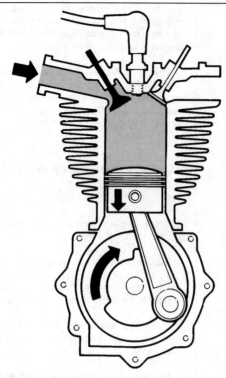

***Induction:*** *As the piston descends the inlet valve opens, allowing the fuel/air mixture to be drawn directly into the combustion chamber*

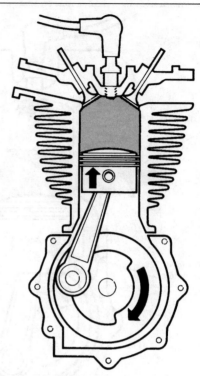

***Compression:*** *The piston starts to ascend with both valves closed. The mixture is compressed*

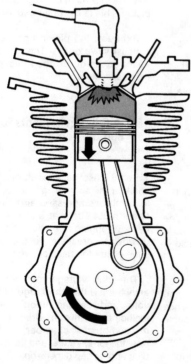

***Ignition:*** *The spark plug ignites the compressed mixture, forcing the piston down the bore*

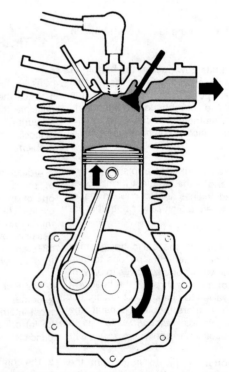

***Exhaust:*** *The exhaust valve opens to allow the burnt gases to be expelled through the exhaust port*

**5.1 The four-stroke cycle**

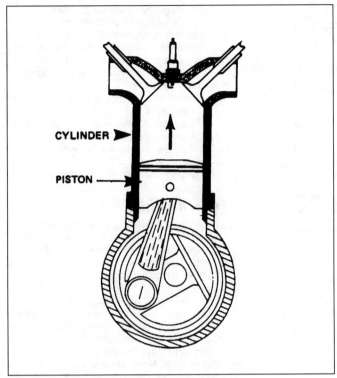

6.3a Compression of fuel vapour

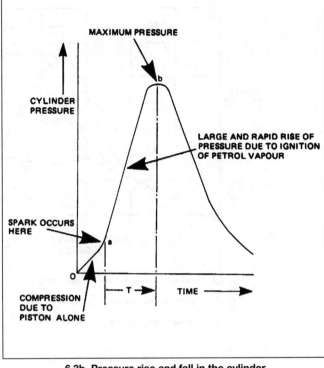

6.3b Pressure rise and fall in the cylinder

**3**

electrode. The spark temperature of several thousand degrees Celsius is sufficient to ignite the fuel vapour in the vicinity which then continues to burn by itself by the process of a travelling wave flame.

**3** In normal conditions, the spark will occur before the piston has reached TDC (Top Dead Centre). Emanating from the spark region a flame front will travel across the vapour-filled space and, although combustion is completed in a fraction of a second, the gas pressure increases steadily, rises to a maximum and then falls away (see illustrations 6.3a and 6.3b). The time from the point of ignition to the completion of combustion is about 2 milliseconds, so the spark will be timed to allow for the delay in pressure build-up. At cruising speeds a typical angle of advance (ie before TDC) is 30 to 40°, but it will be seen that a particular angle of advance suits one speed only and it is essential to incorporate a form of control to vary the ignition advance angle with speed.

**4** Manufacturers' tests will determine the optimum ignition advance angle for all speeds and loads. The factors which have to be considered are:

(a) Pollution levels of exhaust.
(b) Absence of engine knock or detonation.
(c) Good fuel economy.
(d) Maximum engine power output.

**5** The energy contained in the spark discharge must be sufficient to ignite the air/fuel mixture and for an air:fuel ratio of 14.7:1 the minimum energy requirement is 0.2 millijoule (for a definition of the joule see Chapter 2).

This figure rises to 3 mJ or more if the mixture is weaker or richer and allowing for adverse conditions, a practical energy level of each spark must be about 30 mJ for reliable operation. If an ignition system cannot supply this level of energy to the spark plugs whether by design shortcomings or by electrical losses, then misfiring will occur.

## 7  Combustion factors

**1** The air:fuel ratio ($\lambda$) required in theory for complete combustion is 14.7:1. At this ratio, $\lambda = 1.0$. $\lambda$ is pronounced LAMBDA.

In practice an air deficiency of about 10% ($\lambda = 0.9$) gives maximum engine power and corresponds to fastest flame travel across the cylinder head space, but unfortunately unacceptable pollution by hydrocarbons and carbon monoxide is the result. Where excess air is supplied, that is, a weaker mixture, power falls off due to a slower flame speed.

The optimum ratio for producing the cleanest exhaust is when $\lambda = 1.1$ approximately. Pollution is a subject of major interest due to regulations by governments world-wide and will be discussed at various points within this book.

**2** Power and economy are linked to the speed of the flame in the cylinder after ignition. The flame speed in turn depends upon many factors including:

**Cylinder design:** If the compression ratio is high then, because of the greater density of the inhaled fuel charge, the flame speed is high. The location of the spark plug and the length of the spark gap come under the cylinder design. In general, the better the exposure of the cloud of fuel vapour to the igniting spark, the better the combustion performance.

**Ignition timing:** Spark timing is crucial and must be such that gas pressure reaches a maximum to give downward piston thrust at about 12° ATDC (after top dead centre). If the spark is made to occur too early (over advanced) flame speed is so high that the charge is virtually exploded, an effect known as detonation (see later). This will damage the engine and must be avoided. Conversely, if the spark occurs too late (retarded), burning is slow and the gas pressure maximises too late. Low power and

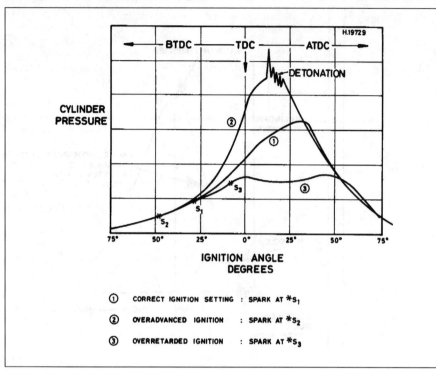

7.2 Effects of ignition angle

poor fuel consumption are the results (see illustration 7.2).

**Fuel charge turbulence:** In practice, the vapour cloud is not stationary when the spark occurs but is a swirling mass. Flame propagation is helped by such turbulence and cylinder heads are designed to give good fuel charge turbulence.

**Exhaust gas presence:** Any exhaust gas that remains in the cylinder and mixes with the incoming fresh charge will lower the flame speed and result in reducing the maximum temperature reached. From the pollution standpoint this is advantageous since the generation of undesirable oxides of nitrogen rises very rapidly with an increase in maximum combustion temperature. In fact, in some engines it is practice to pass back to the cylinder a proportion of the exhaust gases, a process that is known as Exhaust Gas Recirculation (EGR). There are limits to the amount which may be fed back, however, beyond which fuel consumption rises rapidly.

## Detonation

**3** From the previous paragraphs it would appear that the highest possible flame front speed should be obtained in order to achieve best engine power. There is a limit, however; reached when the flame speed becomes supersonic. Under these conditions the flame does not travel across the cylinder head space steadily but the fuel charge explodes.

This is known as **detonation** and can cause serious engine damage. Detonation occurs at a particular pressure level, this being determined by fuel grade, design of cylinder head and other factors.

## Knock

**4** Before the onset of detonation another form of fuel ignition malfunction may occur. Remote from the point where the flame starts, namely at the spark plug electrodes, a volume of gas (the end gas) will be heating due to the approaching flame front. The combination of compression due to the upward piston motion and flame front heating can cause spontaneous ignition and a rapid increase in pressure. This is called **knock** and is often regarded as a combined effect with detonation but in fact the two effects are different although similar in results.

## Effects of knock and detonation

**5** At the onset of these phenomena, a light rattling noise known as pinking occurs and is often first noticed when the engine is heavily loaded. Because energy is expended in unwanted noise and heat, reduced power to the road wheel will occur. In serious cases and where the effect has been present for some time, the power will be markedly reduced and blue exhaust smoke given off. Eventually the piston crown may actually melt. Factors which may contribute to knock and detonation include:

(a) Poor cylinder head design. Modern designs allow for efficient cooling of the cylinder head, particularly the region remote from the plug where the 'end gas' is located. Attention is given to the desirable turbulence of the induced fuel vapour charge.
(b) Air:fuel ratio. A weak mixture is more likely to detonate.
(c) Fuel grade. Compression ratio and grade of fuel are related – a low compression ratio engine can use a fuel with a lower octane number.
(d) Ignition timing. Over-advanced timing may result in detonation.

### Knock sensing

**6** For best efficiency an engine should be tuned to run up to the limit where knock occurs. This may be achieved with the aid of electronic controls found in an increasing number of modern engine designs.

At the onset of knock, high frequency vibrations are set up in the end-gas region. It is possible to pick up these structure-borne vibrations by a sensor which gives an electrical signal voltage proportional to the knock level. Many other vibrations are also present in a running engine but these can be filtered out, leaving the sensor knock voltage alone to be sent on to an on-board electronic control unit (ECU).

When knock signals occur, the ECU retards the ignition to reduce the knock level. Such arrangements are often part of a more comprehensive system of engine management, at present restricted to only a few advanced motorcycle engine designs.

### Pre-ignition

**7** A local hot point within the cylinder head volume may give rise to spontaneous fuel combustion, producing a pinking sound and a substantial loss of power. This is known as **pre-ignition**.

The cause is frequently a deposit of carbon which heats to the incandescent point and causes the fuel to ignite before the spark occurs at the plug. Older engines needed frequent decarbonising to remove such unwanted carbon residues but modern engines and fuels have reduced the need considerably.

A linked effect is that of 'running on' in which the engine continues to run after the ignition has been switched off. This is due to the hot carbon spot firing the incoming fuel charge spontaneously.

Modern anti-pollution requirements have resulted in 'lean burn' engine design in which the air:fuel ratio is high (ie the mixture is weak). Weak mixture gives hotter combustion chamber temperatures than in earlier designs so measures are taken to shut off fuel supply when the ignition is switched off. This is achieved either by switching the incoming air into the manifold (and not going through the carburettor) or to block off the slow running jet in the carburettor.

## Combustion and pollutants

**8** When air and fuel are mixed into a vapour and ignited inside the engine cylinder, combustion drives the engine and produces power at the rear wheel. There are, in addition, products of combustion which are passed out via the exhaust system.

If the proportions of air and fuel are correct at about 14.7:1 by mass (the Stoichiometric ratio) then the exhaust produces carbon dioxide, water and nitrogen, all being harmless. In practice, because perfect mixing cannot be achieved, there will also be carbon monoxide (CO) and oxygen present.

Perfect combustion is never achieved and some of the products from incomplete burning are harmful and pollute the atmosphere. About 1% of the exhaust gas is harmful, this proportion being made up of carbon monoxide (CO), oxides of nitrogen ($NO_x$) and hydrocarbons (HC). All three are dependent upon the air-to-fuel ratio; the problem being that if the proportion of CO and HC increases that of $NO_x$ decreases and **vice versa**.

**Oxides of nitrogen ($NO_x$)** have no smell and are tasteless but as they emerge and mix with atmospheric oxygen they produce red-brown nitrogen dioxide ($NO_2$) which, if breathed in, causes irritation of the lungs. Oxides of nitrogen combine with water to produce nitric acid which precipitates as acid rain. The gas components of nitrogen oxide (NO) and nitrogen dioxide ($NO_2$) are classified together as $NO_x$.

**Hydrocarbons (HC):** Exhaust gas hydrocarbons are present in various forms and all are dangerous. They emerge from parts of the cylinder volume where full combustion has not taken place and, on four-stroke engines, also from blow-by past the piston and into the crankcase, where they are ventilated back to the air filter for recombustion. It has also been found that hydrocarbon emissions take place by evaporation from the fuel tank and the carburettor. Some California models have sealed tanks and an evaporative emission control system which ensures no leakage of fumes.

**Carbon monoxide (CO)** prevents the body from absorbing oxygen into the blood stream and is highly dangerous, especially as it has no smell. It is known that as little as 0.3% of carbon monoxide in the air can cause death within 30 minutes.

**Lead:** Lead compounds deposited by motorcycles as a result of combustion, act as cellular poisons in blood, bone marrow and the nervous system. Lead is not a naturally occurring component of the fuel but an additive to prevent engine knock. About 75% of added lead is blown out of the exhaust and the remainder is absorbed in the engine oil.

## 8  The catalytic converter

**1** The toxic components of exhaust gas can be reduced substantially by the use of a catalytic converter built into the exhaust system. Catalytic converters are not widely used on motorcycles, but are appearing on models sold in certain world markets.

Several designs have been evolved, but the type which is now mostly used is the three-way catalytic converter since it will degrade CO, HC and $NO_x$ simultaneously. The two characteristics of the converter are:

(a) The after-burning of CO and HC is promoted reducing them to carbon dioxide ($CO_2$) and water ($H_2O$) both of which are harmless.
(b) The device converts the nitrogen oxides ($NO_x$) into neutral nitrogen (N) which is a harmless constituent of air.

**2** The catalytic converter will reduce more than 90% of the exhaust gas toxic substances to harmless alternative substances but in order to achieve this, two conditions apply:

(a) Unleaded petrol must be used exclusively because lead would destroy the catalytic properties of the noble metals used in the converter.
(b) The air:fuel ratio must be held at the Stoichiometric Ratio 14.7:1 precisely (Lambda $\lambda = 1.0$) and this implies the use of a Lambda closed-loop control system (see illustration 8.2).

Note that in illustration 8.2 the term single-bed here means only one box in the exhaust system; early versions used more than one.

The use of converters without a Lambda closed-loop control system is possible, but the best result in elimination of toxic products will not normally exceed 50%. Lambda closed loops are explained further in Chapter 9.

**3** The converter has to be located at a point in the exhaust system so that the temperature range will be within 400°C to 800°C (750 to 1470°F). Useful conversion takes place only above 250°C (480°F). Above 800°C (1470°F) thermal ageing of the substrate and the sintering of the noble metals used to coat the substrate will occur. Improvements in the usable temperature range are likely so that the converter positioning will not be so critical (see illustration 8.3).

**4** The converter is shown in illustration 8.3 consists of one or more ceramic blocks made

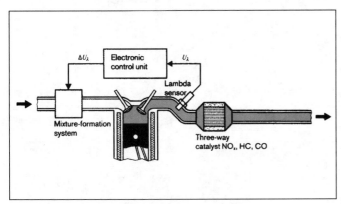

**8.2 Single-bed three-way catalyst**

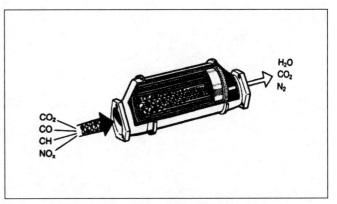

**8.3 The location of the catalyst box is important**

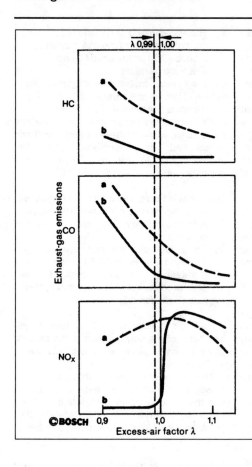

### 8.5 Results achievable by a three-way converter

CH   Hydrocarbons
CO   Carbon monoxide
NOx  Oxides of nitrogen
a    Without aftertreatment
b    With aftertreatment

*The exhaust gas emissions are influenced by the air/fuel mixture and by the aftertreatment. The absolute necessity for a high degree of control accuracy is shown by the pronounced increase of the noxious carbon monoxide (CO) just below the λ = 1.0 point, as well as by the sudden jump in the noxious oxides of nitrogen (NOx) just above the λ = 1.0 point*

of magnesium-aluminium silicate, perforated by several thousand small through-holes which carry the exhaust gases.

The ceramic is, in manufacture, first washed with a coating of aluminium oxide, effectively increasing the surface area of the catalyst by several thousand times. This coating then has a surface layer deposit of the precious (noble) metals rhodium and platinum.

Platinum and palladium cause oxidisation of the hydrocarbons (HC) and carbon monoxide (CO) and rhodium reduces the oxides of nitrogen ($NO_x$). The total weight of precious metals used in a converter is approximately 3 grammes.

**5** Results achievable by a 3-way converter are shown graphically in illustration 8.5 where the need for keeping the air:fuel ratio at λ = 1.0 is seen to be vital. A small rise in λ towards a weaker mixture will produce a substantial rise in the oxides of nitrogen ($NO_x$).

# Chapter 4
# Ignition – coil and battery

## Contents

**4**

 *Warning: Ignition systems produce high voltages. At the least, a shock can be painful but also lethal for those with a cardiac problem. Do not touch the high tension parts with bare hands unless the ignition is off. When a working HT lead has to be handled, use insulated pliers or special high voltage grips. The low voltage side of a contact breaker circuit can give voltages of some 300 volts when the points open.*

*Warning: Do not turn the engine over by hand when the ignition is on.*

### 1 Coil ignition

**1** Up to 1930 petrol-driven (gasoline-driven) vehicles usually employed the magneto for spark production. This was a high voltage generator driven by the engine which required no battery, but as the advent of electric lighting involved the use of a storage battery, the alternative system of coil-ignition took over. This had been patented as early as 1908 by C F Kettering of the Dayton Engineering Laboratories Company (DELCO) and his sketch (see illustration 1.1a) compared to that in illustration 1.1b shows that the method has changed little in 90 plus years.

**2** The development in electronics has brought about the end of the Kettering coil and battery ignition monopoly and in the last three decades more changes have been introduced in the design of ignition systems than in the previous 90 years.

**3** The coil and battery system is still to be found on motorcycles and a knowledge of its

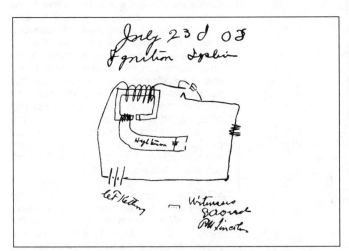

**1.1a  Coil and battery ignition system – patent sketch 1908**

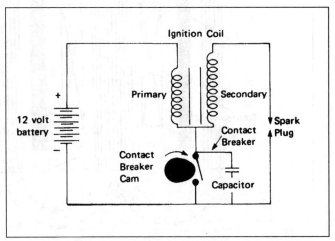

**1.1b  Present day form of coil and battery system**

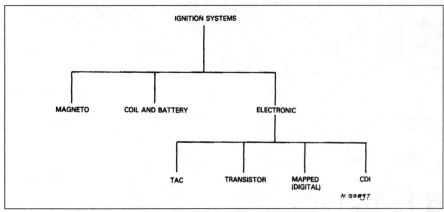

**1.3 Classification of ignition systems**

*TAC Transistor-assisted contacts (obsolete)      CDI Capacitor discharge ignition*

operation is essential, but it now forms part of a group of other systems shown diagrammatically in illustration 1.3. For all the advances in design, the ignition coil remains. It is how it is supplied with ignition energy that has changed.

## 2   The Ignition coil

**1** Ignition coils depend upon electromagnetic induction for their operation and are today efficient and reliable because of long development and lack of moving parts. When current is switched on through a coil of wire, a magnetic field is developed and appears to come from the coil centre (see illustration 26.1 Chapter 2).

Clearly, as the current increases, the magnetic field spreads out and the individual turns are cut by the field. Similarly, if the current is switched off (see illustration 26.2 Chapter 2), the magnetic field collapses in towards the centre and again the turns of wire are cut by the field.

It is important to note that once the coil current settles down to its final value, determined only by the wire resistance, the surrounding fields become stationary.

**2** Also in Chapter 2 it is explained that a voltage is induced in a wire passing through a magnetic field. It is of no importance whether the field or the wire is moving, so long as there is **relative** movement, and in the case described, the field is passing through the wires simply by increasing and decreasing the

strength of the field. So, when the current in the coils is switched on or off there will be an induced emf, but since the voltage depends on the **rate** at which the current is changed, it is usual to **break** the current rather than **make** it, the exception to this being the energy transfer system described in Chapter 5.

**3** During the very short period of time over which the magnetic field reduces to zero, the induced voltage which may be measured across the coil reaches up to 300 volts. Note that this induced emf is not directly related to the 12 volt supply; the battery has simply been a means of creating the magnetic field. The switch is the means of rapidly altering the magnetic field so the coils are cut by magnetic force lines as the field either builds up or collapses.

## 3   Primary and secondary windings

**1** The voltage required to produce a spark across the plug electrodes cannot be obtained from the simple coil shown in illustrations 26.1 and 26.2 in Chapter 2, because increasing the number of turns of wire would raise the resistance so high that the battery could not force through the necessary current.

**2** One solution is to use two coils wound concentrically, the primary with about 300 turns through which the battery current flows, and a secondary which has a large number of turns, perhaps 20,000. When the current is broken (or closed) by a contact breaker, the change of magnetic flux affects each turn of wire **in both primary and secondary windings**. The secondary voltage is high enough to produce the required spark.

**3** Wound on a laminated iron core to increase the flux density, and enclosed in a metal case or by resin encapsulation, the device is called an ignition coil, a specialised example of a transformer used in several branches of electrical engineering (see illustration 3.3a). Most common on motorcycles is the moulded open magnetic circuit ignition coil, especially because of its resistance to vibration. The windings and iron core are completely encapsulated in a synthetic resin. The centre core does not have such a complete magnetic path and consists of a bar of straight laminations, and is the earth (ground) connection (see illustration 3.3b).

**4** The secondary is wound on top of the primary winding in this type, to give maximum insulation from the steel core. Among the varieties of moulded ignition coils will sometimes be found a type with a closed iron path which shows outside the windings. The

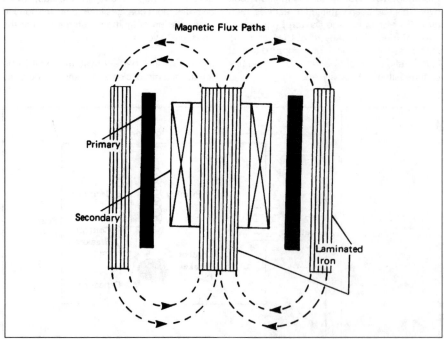

**3.3a  Ignition coil windings and magnetic paths**

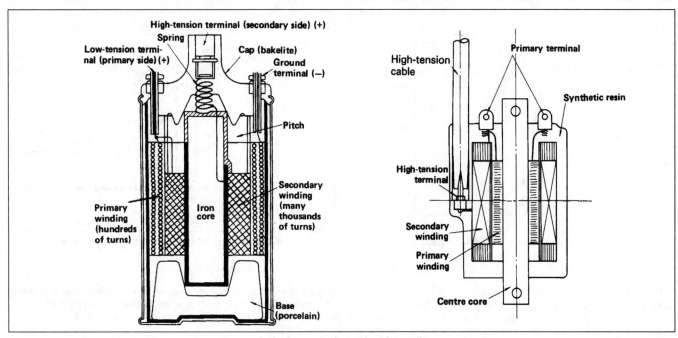

3.3b  Construction of ignition coils

operation and winding construction are, however, the same as the centre core types.

**5** Some twin cylinder engines use a single ignition coil with both secondary winding ends brought out, one end to each spark plug (see illustration 3.5). It can be seen that the secondary current flows through the plugs in series and there will be one wasted spark since only one cylinder will be ready to fire. A disadvantage of this method is that the current will flow through one plug in the normal manner but the reverse way in the other and means that for reliable sparking the plugs must be kept in good serviceable condition, since it takes a higher voltage to run a plug the reverse way. The real reason for this arrangement is to avoid a distributor.

The wasted spark idea is used also in multicylinder engines. In the case of a four cylinder engine, two coils are used, the ends of coil 1 going to cylinders 1 and 4 and the ends of coil 2 going to cylinders 2 and 3. On modern motorcycles the supply to the ignition coils is from an electronic control unit which will be specifically designed to drive two coils (see Chapter 7).

## 4  Spark energies

**1** When the contact breaker opens, the collapse of the magnetic field results in inductive energy passing round the secondary circuit as a component of the spark (see illustration 4.1).

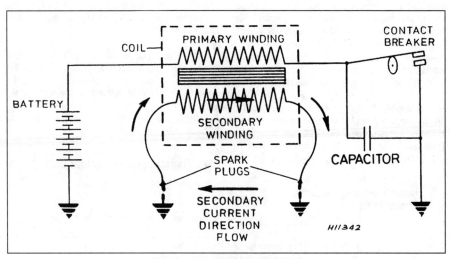

3.5  Double-ended ignition coil

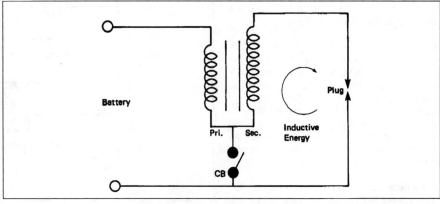

4.1  Inductive energy discharge

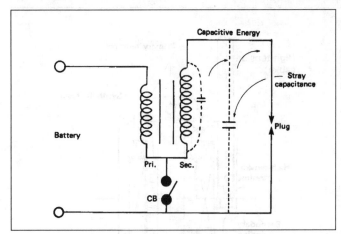

**4.2 Capacitive energy discharge**

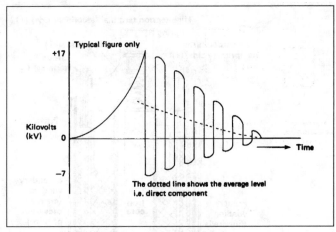

**4.3 Waveform of spark discharge at the plug**

**2** The coil and external high-tension wires also have a certain capacitance which is charged by the generated voltage in the secondary coil and which must discharge across the plug gap during the spark (see illustration 4.2). Of the two forms of energy, that due to the inductive effect is much larger than that due to capacitance, but both have an important effect on the voltage waveform. This waveform is examined using electronic diagnostic equipment and contains considerable information on the state of the engine and its auxiliary electrical circuits.

**3** The waveform of the inductive component is oscillatory, whilst that of the capacitive component is unidirectional. Combined, they give an oscillatory damped wave with a unidirectional (dc) property (see illustration 4.3).

## 5 How does the capacitor assist ignition?

**1** It is helpful to see what would happen in a coil ignition system which has no capacitor fitted. As the contacts open, the current flowing round the primary circuit will tend to continue and will therefore maintain the circuit momentarily as a spark across the contact points.

**2** The voltage induced in the secondary winding depends on the **rate** at which the primary current is reduced. A lingering spark across the points is therefore undesirable, since the current is obviously being cut off **slower** than if no spark occurred. Additionally, the mating surfaces of the two contacts would become rough and pitted due to metallic transfer via the spark, thus creating increased contact resistance.

**3** If a capacitor of about 0.2 μF (microfarads) were connected across the contacts, then at the point of opening, the current would flow

into the capacitor, leaving none to establish a spark across the contact breaker points. In addition, the current flowing into the capacitor will charge the plates, so developing a capacitor terminal voltage in opposition to the battery supply voltage. This effect helps rapidly to reduce the primary coil current and boosts the secondary induced voltage (see illustration 5.3).

**4** Thus the rapid reduction of current flow during the points' opening phase enables the magnetic field to collapse suddenly, producing a higher voltage in the secondary winding than if no capacitor were connected. Contact breaker point erosion is also substantially reduced.

## 6 The Capacitor (condenser)

**1** The basic properties of a capacitor have

been covered in Chapter 2, but it is worth looking again at how initial current flow into the capacitor charges up the plates.

When the voltage due to charge on the plates is equal and opposite to the supply voltage, the current ceases. This is the feature explained in the previous Section and shown in illustration 6.1.

**2** Capacitors are made in a variety of forms. The type shown in illustration 6.2 being typical of an ignition capacitor with one terminal internally connected to an enclosing metal can which is earthed (grounded) to the motorcycle engine/frame. It is important that the capacitor should be located as close to the contact breaker as possible. A long wire would possess some inductance (even though it is not in a coil form) and in conjunction with the capacitor could give rise to electromagnetic radiation.

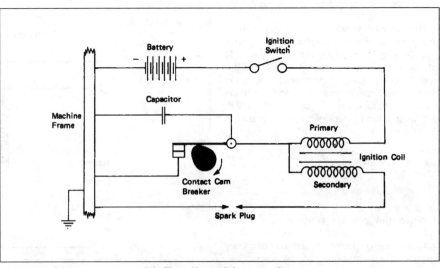

**5.3 The effect of the capacitor**

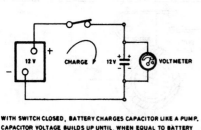

WITH SWITCH CLOSED, BATTERY CHARGES CAPACITOR LIKE A PUMP. CAPACITOR VOLTAGE BUILDS UP UNTIL, WHEN EQUAL TO BATTERY VOLTAGE, NO FURTHER CHARGE WILL FLOW.

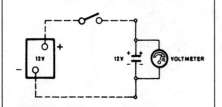

WHEN BATTERY IS DISCONNECTED BY OPENING SWITCH **CHARGE** AND **VOLTAGE** ARE RETAINED.

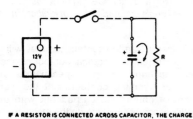

IF A RESISTOR IS CONNECTED ACROSS CAPACITOR, THE CHARGE DRAINS AWAY AND VOLTAGE FALLS. IF RESISTANCE IS HIGH, VOLTAGE FALLS SLOWLY AND VICE VERSA.

**6.1  Charge and voltage retention of a capacitor**

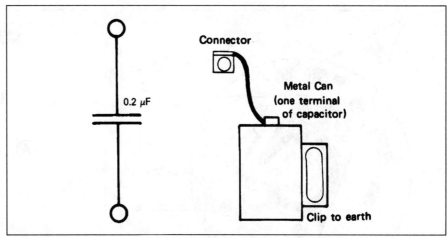

**6.2  Ignition capacitor**

## 7  Faulty capacitor symptoms

**1** If the internal connections of the capacitor break it is said to be open-circuit (OC) although this is not a very frequent fault. The effects would be severe sparking and burning of the contact breaker points, difficult starting and poor running.

**2** Another possible failure is short circuiting (SC) internally, having the effect of permanently bridging the contacts. Under these circumstances, there is no primary current interruption and no spark at the plug.

**3** The third possible fault is a condition between OC and SC, where the insulation resistance between the capacitor lead and its case falls to a low value, say much less than 1 megohm. Starting and slow running may be acceptable but the performance falls off at high speeds.

## 8  The Contact breaker

**1** The purpose of the contact breaker is to interrupt primary current flow to the ignition coil; it is essentially an engine driven switch. It is located often on the end of the crankshaft and is operated by a rotating cam and a heel which follows the cam contour under light pressure from a flat spring (see illustration 8.1).

**2** When the heel touches the cam over the low radius sector, the contacts are closed; the heel is forced outwards as the cam lobe comes under it and the contacts are opened.

**4**

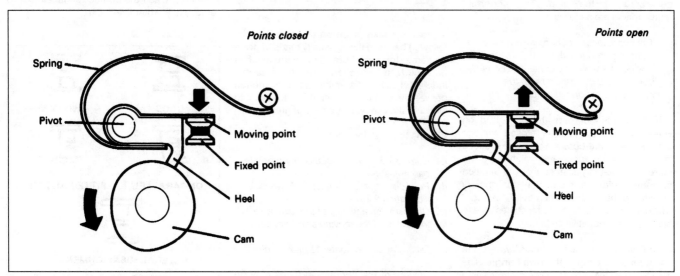

**8.1  Contact breaker operation**

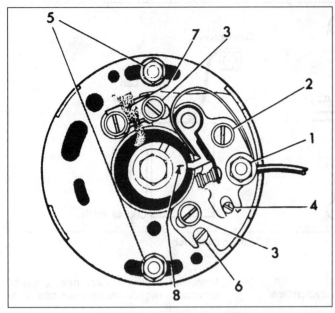

**8.2 Contact breaker assembly**

| 1 | Lead terminal | 6 | Baseplate eccentric adjuster |
| 2 | Points gap adjuster screw | | screw |
| 3 | Baseplate securing screw | 7 | Lubrication wiper |
| 4 | Eccentric gap adjuster screw | 8 | Cam lobe peak |
| 5 | Timing plate securing screw | | |

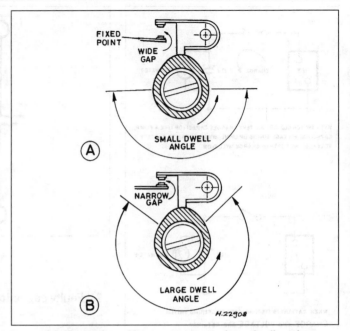

**8.5 Illustration of how contact gap alters dwell angle**

A  A wide gap gives later closing and earlier opening of points. Results in a reduction of dwell angle and advancing of ignition timing

B  A narrow gap gives earlier closing and later opening of points. Results in an increase of dwell angle and retardation of ignition timing

In illustration 8.2 only one cam lobe and contact set is shown but it is common practice to use two sets of contacts with one cam lobe for twin and four cylinder machines. In some cases, more than one cam lobe will be found. The contact breaker assembly illustrated shows the baseplate on which the contact breaker set is mounted together with the cam heel, spring and adjustment screws.

**3** When the cam opens the contacts, current is interrupted in the ignition coil and a spark is generated at the plug. The important requirements are as follows.

(a) The contacts must open at the correct point of piston travel.
(b) The gap between the contacts when fully open should correspond with the manufacturer's specification.

**4** If the gap is incorrect, the angle through which the points will be closed will be incorrect with the possible result of reduced ignition performance and misfiring. The correct gap setting ensures that the duration of contact closure is sufficient for primary current to build up; remember Chapter 2 which showed that direct current takes time to build up in an inductive coil.

**5** The angle of cam rotation when the contacts are closed is the **dwell angle**. The illustration shows that too wide a gap gives a small dwell angle and too small a gap gives a

large dwell angle. Notice the effects on ignition timing.

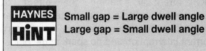

**HAYNES HINT** Small gap = Large dwell angle
Large gap = Small dwell angle

## 9  Contact breaker service

**1** Wear will take place on the cam heel (or follower) because this is usually made of nylon or some form of fibre. The cam itself is hardened and so should retain its profile indefinitely, but to minimise the friction between the cam and heel, it is necessary to lubricate the cam with a smear of grease.

**2** Items to check include:

(a) Cam follower wear, necessitating points gap adjustment.
(b) Poor condition of contact surfaces (see illustration 9.2).
(c) Corrosion on any part of the assembly.
(d) Insulation of the moving arm from earth (ground).
(e) Oil or dirt on the contact breaker points.

**3** Dressing of the contact surfaces may be carried out with a strip of fine (400 grit)

sandpaper. Clean the contact surfaces with a suitable solvent or electrical contact cleaner. Some mechanics keep a special dressing stone for trimming contacts but the work cannot of course, be carried out with the breaker assembly in place on the machine.

**4** Most mechanics however, rarely dress contacts, renewing them in preference. This is the best course of action in view of the low cost of a new set and the care necessary to achieve a perfect finish. When fitting a new assembly, clean the contact surfaces first to remove any protective finish.

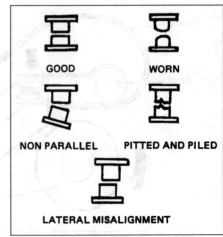

**9.2 Contact conditions**

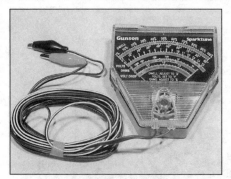

**9.11 Sparktune meter**

## Setting the contact breaker gap

**5** Start by removing the spark plug(s) so that the engine may be turned over easily. Note that motorcycles have one, two or three sets of points, but the method of adjustment is the same for each.

**6** To check the gap the engine must be rotated by one of the following means:

(a) *Apply hand pressure on the kickstart (where fitted).*
(b) *Use a spanner on the engine turning hexagon on the end of the crankshaft or alternator rotor.*
(c) *With the motorcycle on its main stand, turn the rear wheel by hand with the engine in a high gear.*

**7** Turn the engine until the contacts open to the maximum and insert a feeler gauge which corresponds to the recommended gap between them. If no information is available, try a gap of 0.3 – 0.4 mm (0.012 – 0.016 in). The feeler gauge should *just* slide through the gap between the contacts with a slight drag. If too tight or too loose, slacken the baseplate screw so that the fixed contact may be moved to give the correct gap. This is done with either a flat-bladed screwdriver twist in a slot or by turning an eccentric screw. When the gap is correct tighten the baseplate screw.

**8** If the engine has more than one set of contacts, repeat the process. It is worth rechecking the gaps after the engine has been turned by hand a few times.

**9** Setting the gap by feeler gauge can give satisfactory results if done carefully, but accurate setting is vital, particularly on high performance engines. A better method is to use a dwell meter.

## Using a dwell meter

**10** The real purpose of setting the gap correctly is to ensure that the contacts are closed long enough during an engine cycle for current to build up in the ignition coil primary winding.

**11** With the engine running slowly, a dwell meter connected to the contacts will read the angle of rotation during which the contacts are closed and give the reading in degrees or percentage dwell. The correct figure can be found in the workshop manual. An inexpensive meter is the Gunson Sparktune (see paragraph 14) which will read dwell accurately, check contact resistance and act as a useful voltmeter (see illustration 9.11).

**12** The gap should be adjusted until the correct dwell angle is registered on the meter. This usually means stopping the engine to carry out the adjustment although experienced mechanics have been known to do it with the engine running!

**13** Having set the contact breaker gap(s), the next step is to set the ignition timing.

**14** The Sparktune is an inexpensive instrument especially good for motorcycles with contact breaker ignition. It is really a voltmeter with an ingenious circuit arrangement so that volts, HT cable ohmic resistance, dwell, points condition, engine timing and battery condition can be measured.

Dwell measurement using this instrument is based on the average voltage between the ignition feed wire and the contact breaker as the points open and close. The instrument is not able to follow rapid variations and the pointer takes up a position on the scale which is an average of the square pulse of voltage at the input terminals (see illustrations 9.14a and 9.14b). When the points are open the instrument tries to read the battery voltage and when they are closed it tries to read zero. The actual reading depends on what proportion of the time the contacts are closed which is by definition dwell. The figures used are for demonstration only and the actual dwell setting must be taken from the manufacturer's handbook.

**4**

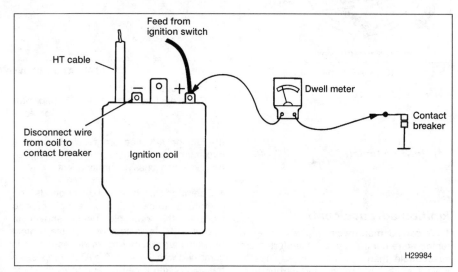

**9.14a Measurement of dwell**

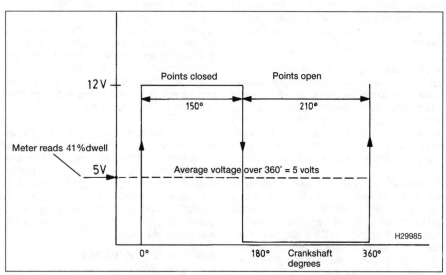

**9.14b How the dwell meter works for a single cylinder engine**

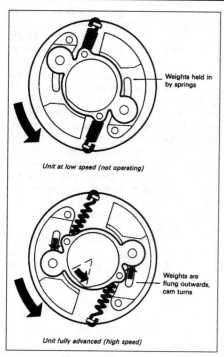

Unit at low speed (not operating)

Weights held in by springs

Weights are flung outwards, cam turns

Unit fully advanced (high speed)

**10.4a ATU operation**

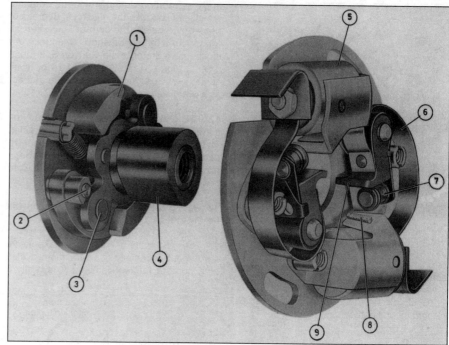

**10.4b ATU with twin contact breaker unit**

1  Centrifugal weights
2  Centrifugal weight pivot
3  Cam pivot
4  Cam
5  Capacitor
6  Contact leaf spring
7  Contacts
8  Cam lubrication pad
9  Cam follower (or heel)

## 10 Ignition timing

### Ignition advance control

**1** Air-cooled motorcycle engines have no temperature control and are therefore more susceptible than liquid-cooled engines to maladjustment of ignition and carburation, which can lead to overheating. Whether air or liquid-cooled, accurate ignition timing is of high importance and the instructions stated by the manufacturer must be adhered to exactly.

**2** While some small 2-strokes have fixed ignition advance, the 4-stroke engine requires some means of increasing ignition advance as the engine speed rises. In the early days of motorcycling, a handlebar control was fitted to permit the rider to advance the timing as the speed rose, but this was a poor compromise (see Chapter 5 on Magnetos).

**3** Automatic advance has been achieved by mechanical means until the arrival of electronic ignition systems. The mechanical automatic advance unit, sometimes known as the automatic timing unit (ATU) is attached to the contact breaker assembly and causes the contacts to open earlier as the engine speed increases. At rest and low speeds the ATU has no effect, but above a certain speed increases

the ignition advance progressively up to a maximum amount (fixed by the designer) beyond which it has no further effect.

**4** Operation of the ATU depends on centrifugal force acting on a pair of bob weights, the principle being shown in illustration 10.4a. Instead of fixing the contact breaker cam directly to its driveshaft, it is combined with the ATU. The ATU comprises a baseplate with a central support pin which carries the cam. The cam can turn on the pin but its movement is controlled by two spring-loaded bob weights. At rest and at low speeds, the springs hold the cam in the retarded position but as engine speed rises, the weights are flung outwards, turning the cam relative to the baseplate and thus advancing the ignition point. A twin set complete with contact points and capacitors is shown in illustration 10.4b.

**5** The correct operation of the ATU can be checked using a stroboscope (timing light) as described under the dynamic timing check heading below. Failure is often due to broken or weak springs, or the weights sticking on the pivots due to rust. The unit requires no regular maintenance other than to see if it has free movement; if necessary apply lubricant to the bob weight pivots.

### Ignition timing check

**6** The ignition timing is set so that the contacts open at a particular point of the crankshaft

revolution. The workshop manual will state whether the timing must be carried out with the automatic advance unit fully advanced or fully retarded. For those tests where the timing is to be set at fully advanced, the cam must be locked in the full advance position by any one of various methods, from jamming the weights with a matchstick to fixing a special washer to lock the cam solid. On later engines the manufacturers did not advise jamming the ATU weights out to the fully advanced position, but instead specified that the full advance markings were checked dynamically at a speficied engine speed (see below).

**7** The equipment required to check the timing will depend on the form in which the motorcycle manufacturer has expressed the timing specification. There is also a choice of whether the timing is checked statically (engine stopped) or dynamically (engine running), the latter is necessary for checking the operation of the ATU.

**8** For all the static methods of checking the timing, some means will be necessary for determining the exact point at which the contact breaker points separate – it is not sufficient to do this visually. Methods include connecting a bulb across the contacts or a multimeter on the VOLTS range, or best of all, a buzzer.

**9** When the contacts are closed the voltage across them will be zero (or very low) but when

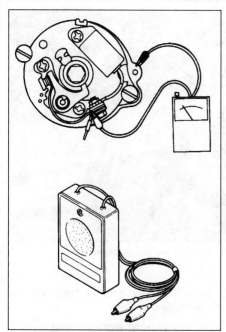

**10.9 Multimeter/buzzer shown connected across points**

they open full battery voltage will appear. At this point the bulb will light, the meter will read or the buzzer will sound, according to the method chosen (see illustration 10.9). It follows that for all the methods given, the ignition must be switched on.

**10** On multi-cylinder engines, ensure that the correct set of contacts is checked for a particular cylinder; ie contacts might be marked 1.4 to correspond with F 1.4 on the ATU of a four cylinder engine, meaning cylinders 1 and 4. Timing marks are sometimes used for ignition timing as described below and on almost all machines are found on the flywheel or alternator rotor periphery.

**Note:** *Before commencing a check of the timing, the points gap(s) must first be checked and if necessary adjusted.*

### Static – dial gauge method

**11** A static check is made where the timing is expressed in terms of piston position (eg 1.87 mm before top dead centre – BTDC). This will require the use of a dial gauge with a spark plug hole adapter (see illustration 10.11). The tip of the gauge touches the piston crown and registers any up or down movement. When it reaches the maximum point as the engine is slowly turned this is TDC (Top Dead Centre). The dial is set to read zero at this point and then the engine is turned until the specified distance BTDC is reached.

**12** At this point, the contact breaker should just be on the verge of separation. Note that it is possible to be on the wrong part of a

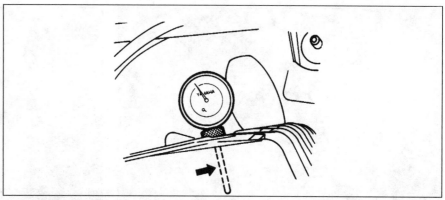

**10.11 Dial gauge and adapter (arrowed) shown in position**

4-stroke cycle – the piston must be on the compression stroke – the best way of ensuring this is to check that the inlet valve has just closed as the piston begins to rise in the cylinder.

### Static – degree disc method

**13** If the timing setting is expressed in terms of crankshaft position (eg 20° BTDC) a degree disc will be required and a means will have to be found of attaching it to the crankshaft end (or camshaft end on older machines) (see illustration 10.13). A pointer will also need to be attached to the casing so that the disc can

be read accurately. Clamp the disc so that it reads zero at TDC and then turn the engine slowly until the specified number of degrees BTDC is reached. At this point the points should just be on the verge of separation.

**14** TDC can be found by using a dial gauge in the spark plug hole. Another method is to use a short rod glued to an old spark plug centre. This is laid in the spark plug hole and the degree disc reading noted when the piston just touches the rod. Turn the engine backwards until the piston touches the rod again; TDC is midway between the degree disc readings.

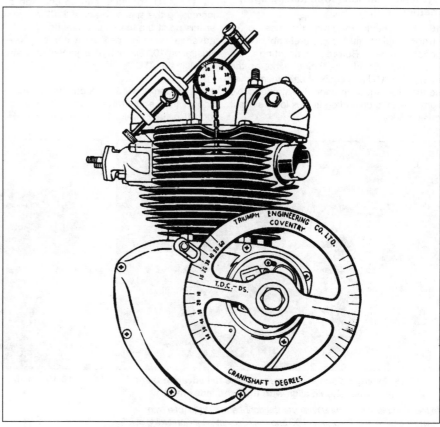

**10.13 Degree disc shown attached to the camshaft**

**10.15 ATU timing mark for cylinders 1 and 4 shown aligned with index mark**

**10.17 Stroboscope in operation**

### Static – flywheel or ATU reference mark alignment method

15 If the flywheel or ATU has suitable marks (a scribed line or F is common) it is possible to check that when they align the points are on the point of separation (see illustration 10.15). This method is quite satisfactory, but there have been instances where there have been inaccuracies in manufacture.

### Dynamic – stroboscope (timing light) method

16 This check requires the use of a stroboscopic timing lamp, preferably of the xenon type. Before connecting the equipment, identify the timing marks on the flywheel or ATU and chalk or paint them white so that they show up under the stroboscopic light. (Typist's correction fluid is ideal since it dries quickly!)

17 The stroboscope should be connected as directed by its manufacturer and shone at the timing marks with the engine running at idle; the marks will appear frozen in position, and it will be possible to see any misalignment between fixed and moving marks (see illustration 10.17). If the marks do not align, stop the engine and make adjustment, repeating the test until the marks are accurately aligned.

18 The ATU operation can be checked by increasing the speed to about 3500 rev/min; at this point the marks corresponding to full advance should be in alignment (see illustration 10.18). Lack of alignment indicates a fault in the ATU.

19 A modern low cost Xenon strobe lamp is shown in the illustration. This features an inductive clamp which is clipped round the HT

lead and the unit also has the facility for measuring engine speed.

### Ignition timing adjustment

20 If a check of the timing indicates inaccuracy, adjustment should be made. In almost all cases timing adjustment is made by rotating the baseplate on which the contact breaker is mounted after slackening the securing screws. Slots are usually provided to allow adjustment in small increments. Note that in cases where the baseplate is hidden behind the flywheel, removal of the flywheel may well be necessary for access.

21 On multi-cylinder engines, which have two or three sets of points, checking and adjustment will be necessary for each set. The order of adjustment is important because the first set of points is usually mounted directly on the baseplate, whereas the others have individual movement.

**10.18 As engine speed is increased, the full advance mark (arrowed) should align with the fixed index mark**

*In the example shown the R relates to the right-hand cylinder of a twin cylinder engine, the T indicates TDC and the F indicates ignition timing at idle. On some engines, the full advance mark is represented by two scribed lines*

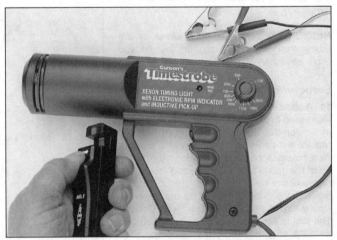

**10.19 Stroboscope with HT clamp and speed indicator**

**22** Often on small 2-stroke singles there is no provision for setting the timing other than by contact breaker adjustment. If a satisfactory gap cannot be obtained after timing adjustment, a new set of points is needed.

**23** After all adjustments, recheck the ignition timing.

## 11 Ignition high voltage path

**1** The high voltage generated by the ignition coil is applied to the spark plug which is screwed into the cylinder head (see illustration 2.1 Chapter 10).

The spark plug consists of an outer steel body with a ceramic insulator, through the centre of which is an electrode spaced accurately from the earth (ground) electrode. The gap is typically between 0.6 mm and 1.0 mm. The spark plug is subjected to hostile conditions such as pressure of up to 70 bar at the point of ignition and must produce a spark at a pressure of about 10 bar. The voltage can be anything up to 30 kilovolts (kV) and the electrode temperature can be between 350 – 900°C for long periods. (The bar is a pressure of 14.5 lbf per square inch, psi)

From this one can see that the apparently simple spark plug is a highly technical component and much research has gone into the present day range. For further details see Chapter 10.

**2** The secondary terminal of the ignition coil is connected to the insulated terminal of the spark plug by a high voltage cable.

Early HT cable consisted of multistrand wire with rubber insulation but modern cables have a graphited conductor of several thousand ohms resistance to reduce ignition interference in electronic and radio equipment. The outer is now of tough plastic with very high insulation resistance.

This part of the circuit carries the spark voltage averaging 10 to 20 kV and in motorcycles is often exposed to rain and damp. Note the use of separate plug top ignition coils for each cylinder used in newer Triumph models; this reduces the HT path length to the absolute minimum.

Not surprisingly, a high number of fault conditions arise from the high tension (HT) part of the electrical system.

Poor starting on a damp or wet morning can often be corrected by drying off the HT cable and the spark plug cap.

The ignition coil can sometimes benefit from a wipe down, particularly the older metal-cased type. A damp start aerosol spray will also help since it will act as a damp repellent.

For all this the ignition system on the motorcycle is remarkably efficient and modern components have reduced trouble to a large extent.

## 12 Service work and fault finding

**1** Maintenance of coil ignition equipment is important because of the high voltages involved and the adverse weather effects on exposed components. Simple regular attention to the vulnerable parts of the system will be repaid with dependable performance. Essential maintenance includes:
(a) *Check the condition of the spark plug(s). Clean, regap and renew regularly (see Chapter 10).*
(b) *Keep all HT leads clean. They are often exposed to road dirt and rain and must be in good condition with no surface cracks. Replace all suspect HT cable without delay and always uses cable of the correct resistance and quality.*
(c) *Check contact breaker points for both correct gap and low contact resistance. Use an ohmmeter across closed points with the ignition switched off. The resistance must be only a fraction of an ohm, ideally zero. Alternatively use the Gunson Sparktune to measure the volt drop across the contacts when they are closed with the ignition switched on.*
(d) *Lubricate the automatic timing unit but sparingly since excess lubricant will be flung out centrifugally.*

**2** This Chapter has explained the way in which the coil and battery ignition system works. Inevitably in all vehicle equipment servicing has to be carried out and faults traced and corrected. Please refer to Chapter 18 for further information on ignition problems.

**4**

**Notes**

# Chapter 5
# Ignition – magnetos

## Contents

**5**

### 1  The Magneto

**1** By 1920, most four-stroke motorcycles used a magneto for ignition and they were still in use into the 1960s. Even today, one special type, the flywheel magneto, remains in use for small engines. The magneto is an engine-driven generator designed to produce pulse voltages at specific times during rotation. The pulse voltage is sufficient to provide ignition sparks at one or more spark plugs.

**2** All magnetos depend upon speed of rotation for spark voltage production since the internal coils will be subject to a magnetic flux change as the rotor turns. It is the rate of change of magnetic flux through a coil which fixes the voltage generated, as explained in Chapter 2, and this is a disadvantage for ease of starting. It is essential that the magneto and external connections to the plug(s) are in good condition. The rival ignition coil and battery system does not depend on how fast the engine can be kickstarted and has as a result, won the supremacy battle. However, the coil and battery system needs a good charged battery, whereas the magneto is an independent generator.

**3** Magnetos divide into the three following groups:

*(a) Rotating-armature.*
*(b) Rotating-magnet.*
*(c) Flywheel.*

Of these, many variations appeared and some incorporated a battery charging facility. Very popular was the Lucas Magdyno in which a rotating armature magneto carried a dynamo on top of the frame, the dynamo being gear driven by the magneto (see illustration 1.3a). Another type widely used was the Lucas twin-cylinder magneto which did not have a charging facility (see illustration 1.3b).

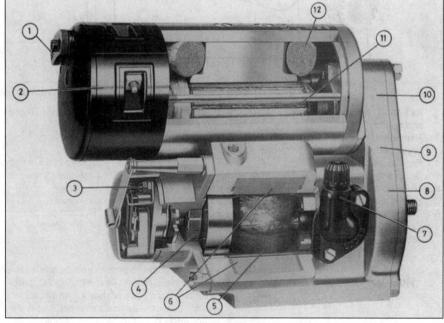

**1.3a  Lucas Magdyno**

| | | |
|---|---|---|
| 1  Dynamo output leads | 5  Armature | 9  Magneto drive |
| 2  Dynamo commutator and brushes (beneath cover) | 6  Magnets | 10  Dynamo gear |
| 3  Contact breaker | 7  HT pickup | 11  Dynamo armature |
| 4  Insulation washer | 8  Main drive gear | 12  Dynamo field winding |

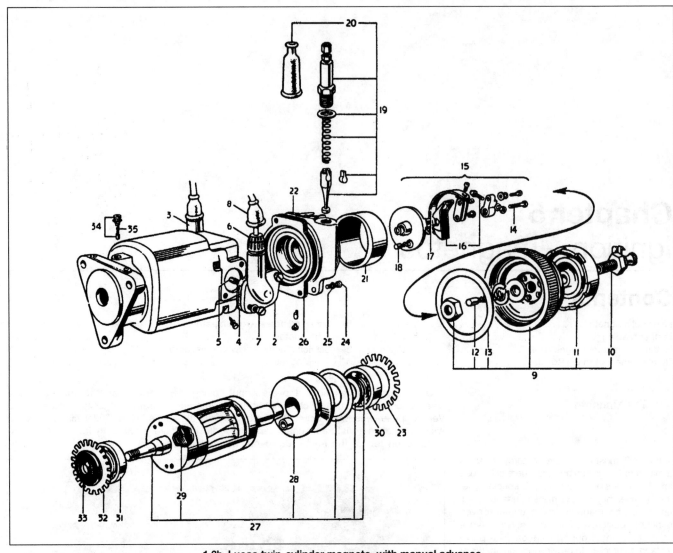

**1.3b Lucas twin-cylinder magneto, with manual advance**

| | | | |
|---|---|---|---|
| 2 | Left-hand pick-up with brush and spring | 19 | Manual advance control assembly | 28 | Slip ring |

2 Left-hand pick-up with brush and spring
3 Right-hand pick-up with brush and spring
4 Pick-up seating washer
5 Brush and spring
6 Moulded nut
7 Screw
8 Rubber cap
9 Contact breaker cover assembly

10 Terminal assembly
11 Moulded breather cap
12 Brush and spring
13 Rubber gasket
14 Screw
15 Contact breaker assembly
16 Contact set
17 Contact spring
18 Contact earthing (grounding) brush and spring

19 Manual advance control assembly
20 Rubber cap
21 Cam
22 End plate with bearing ring
23 Bearing insulating cup
24 Screw
25 Washer
26 Shim
27 Armature

28 Slip ring
29 Condenser
30 Contact breaker end bearing
31 Drive end bearing
32 Bearing insulating cup
33 Oil seal
34 Earth (ground) brush spring and holder
35 Earth (ground) brush

## 2  Rotating-armature magneto

**1** The essential components in this type are a rotating armature with primary and secondary windings, a contact breaker with a capacitor, a high voltage slip-ring and a strong permanent magnet (see illustration 2.1a). The electric circuit is shown in illustration 2.1b.

**2** As the rotating armature (rotor) passes under the magnetic poles (see illustration 2.2, part A) a strong flux passes through the rotor and coils. Follow the motion to the point where the rotor edge is just leaving the N pole tip (see illustration 2.2, part B): the magnetic flux is now passing across to the rotor tip $t_1$ which is fast moving away anticlockwise (counterclockwise). At or about this point the flux coming out of the N pole into the rotor 'sees' an alternative path through the advancing rotor tip $t_2$ and suddenly jumps over to it (see illustration 2.2, part C). *Note that as far as the rotor and coils are concerned, the flux is now passing through it in the opposite direction. The flux change in the rotor is* **twice** *the flux of the magnet, since it has reversed its direction.*

The **rate of** change of magnetic flux is very rapid and generates a maximum current in the primary winding, via the closed contact breaker.

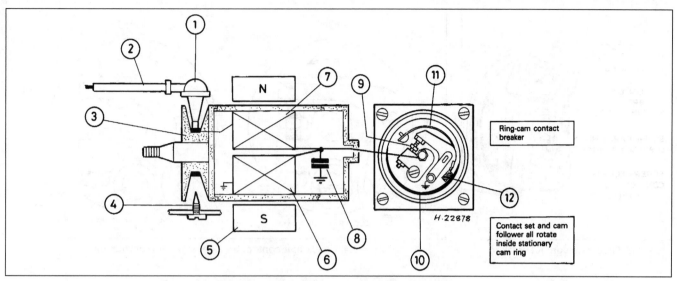

**2.1a Essentials of the rotating-armature magneto**

1 HT pickup
2 HT lead to spark plug
3 Brass slip ring in bakelite moulding
4 Safety spark gap screw
5 Strong permanent magnet
6 Primary winding
7 Secondary winding
8 Capacitor
9 Contacts
10 Cam profile
11 Leaf spring to keep cam heel in contact with cam profile
12 Cam heel

At or near this point, the contact breaker points open and the high primary current is interrupted. The induced voltage in the rotor secondary winding is picked up by the slip ring brush and connected to the spark plug by the high tension (HT) cable. The ignition spark has occurs. (Note that an electrical 'brush' is a shaped carbon rod which slides on the rotating slip ring but has good electrical contact with it.)

**3** The contact breaker unit may be of the ring cam or face cam type. The former has a stationary ring with a contour such that the rotating cam heel opens and closes the contact at the correct point, as in illustration 2.1a, whereas the face cam unit has a contoured cam shape which is mounted at

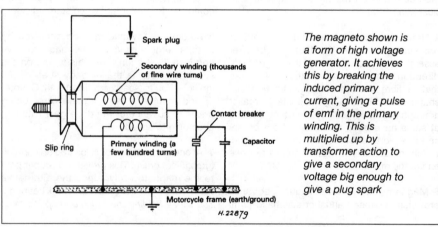

**2.1b Electric circuit of rotating-armature magneto**

The magneto shown is a form of high voltage generator. It achieves this by breaking the induced primary current, giving a pulse of emf in the primary winding. This is multiplied up by transformer action to give a secondary voltage big enough to give a plug spark

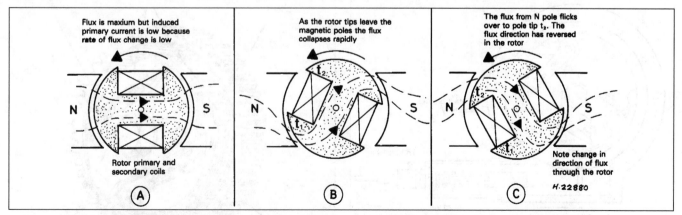

**2.2 The highest rate of flux change produces best the best spark – the contact breaker must open near this point**

Stage A   Induced current in primary is low
Stage B   Flux collapsing – induced primary current rises rapidly
Stage C   Flux in rotor reverses – high primary current. Contact breaker opens between stage B and C, giving best spark

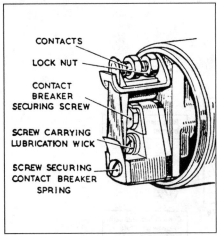

**2.3 Face-cam contact breaker**

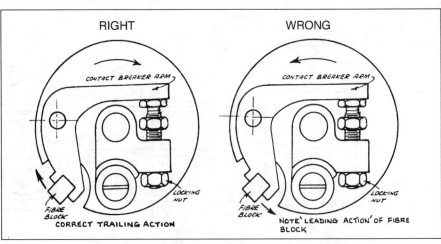

**2.4 Check that contact breaker is for correct rotation**

right angles to the driveshaft, like a large washer of varying thickness (see illustration 2.3). A cam heel running on this contour controls the opening and closure of contacts by a black bakelite push rod. See also the face cam unit on the Lucas Magdyno (see illustration 1.3a).

**4** Note in the case of the ring cam contact breaker, it is essential that the breaker assembly matches the rest of the magneto for direction of rotation. Illustration 2.4 shows that the fibre block which follows the ring cam shape should be trailing the contact breaker arm and not leading it. Often magnetos found at sales have been assembled from others and it is worth checking for correct rotation, which incidentally is viewed from the drive end of the magneto.

**5** Magnetos may have ignition advance provision in either manual or automatic form.

Manual advance is by a cable attached to the contact breaker (stationary) plate (see illustration 2.5) which is operated by the rider from a handlebar control. Many a rider remembers being whacked by the kickstart lever because he forgot to set the advance control to 'fully retarded' when starting!

**6** Automatic advance may be achieved by using a centrifugal unit at the magneto drive end (see illustration 2.6). This works on the same principle as that already seen in coil ignition circuits (see illustration 10.4a, Chapter 4) and results in the magneto rotor being driven in advance of the drive gear rotation, according to speed.

**7** At one end of the rotor is located an earthing (grounding) brush. This provides a proper path to the magneto body, since the alternative route would be via grease-packed bearings. *The screw holding the brush and spring must*

*be removed before taking the magneto apart.* Sometimes the earthing (grounding) screw head is hidden under the serial number plate. In mentioning dismantling, it is also vital to take out the safety spark gap screw, for failure to do so will result in a fractured Bakelite slip ring (see illustration 2.1a).

## 3 Rotating-magnet magneto

**1** The disadvantages of the rotating-armature magneto lay in the problems of rotating at high speed. Armature windings were under increasing stress as speeds were raised. Centrifugal loads tended to throw the windings outwards, so causing coil fractures; contact breaker surge or bounce could also occur causing unwanted operation of the contact breaker.

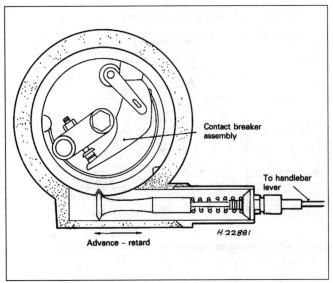

**2.5 Manual ignition advance and retard mechanism**

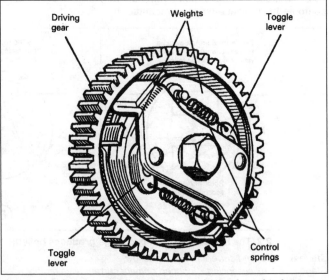

**2.6 Automatic ignition advance and retard mechanism**

Later magneto developments brought the rotating-magnet magneto in which the primary and secondary coils were stationary on an armature. The rotor consisted of an Alnico (Aluminium-nickel-cobalt) magnet which ran between the stator laminations on which the coils are wound. Sudden flux reversal in the stator occurred as the poles passed under the stator laminations. Of small diameter, the rotational inertia was low, reducing the loading on the driving gear (see illustrations 3.1a and 3.1b).

**2** Ball bearings carry the rotor shaft at both ends and on a shaft extension is the contact breaker, which is stationary, being operated by a shaft-mounted cam. There is no complication of the slip-ring and pick-up because the coils are stationary. HT spark current is picked up by a spring blade which is moulded into the end cover and makes contact with a round HT pickup.

Originally designed for racing, the rotating-magnet magneto came into use in road machines as the Lucas SR1 for single cylinder engines up to the SR4 for four cylinder models (see illustration 3.2).

### 4 Servicing notes – rotating-armature and rotating-magnet magnetos

**1** Many magnetos can be made to work again simply by giving them a good clean, then dressing and setting the contact breaker points. Contacts may be cleaned by passing a strip of solvent-dampened rag through them. With no manufacturer's information available try setting the contact breaker to 0.012 in (0.3 mm).

**2** Clean the slip ring with a solvent-damped rag and check that the HT pick-up carbon brush is in good condition.

**3** Old horseshoe magnets made before circa 1935 tended to lose magnetism with time and use. Magdynos and magnetos later than this date do not normally suffer loss of magnetism. A weak spark can result from a weak magnet; turn over the magneto by hand and if there are two points per revolution where resistance to turning is felt, the magnets are good. If not, the magnets should be re-magnetised by a specialist.

**4** Stripping down should be carried out with care; remember to remove the spark gap screw and the earthing (grounding) brush on rotating-armature types. Take care of shims for these are vital in setting end-play in the shaft; face-cam magnets are particularly fussy and the shims should be fitted to give zero end-play. Remove the Bakelite pickup complete; this may be screwed to the body or clipped in place. On flange fitting types (as

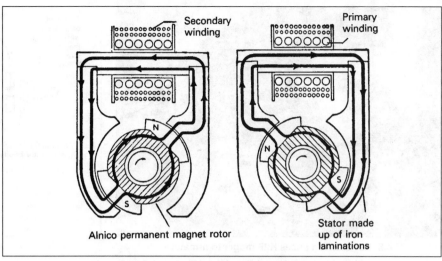

3.1a **Principle of rotating-magnet magnetos**

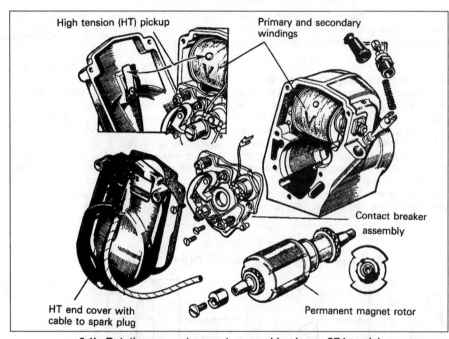

3.1b **Rotating-magnet magneto assembly – Lucas SR1 model**

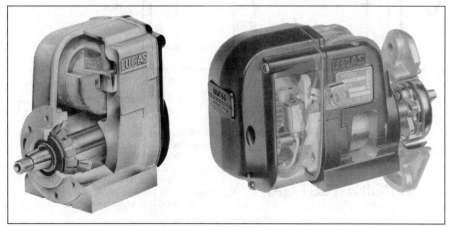

3.2 **Lucas SR1 (left) and SR4 (right) rotating-magnet magnetos**

**5**

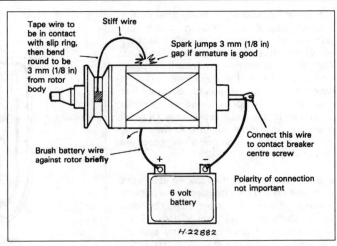

**4.6 Rewinding a Lucas K2F magneto armature**

*(Photograph courtesy of Dave Lindsley)*

**4.7 Rotating-armature winding test**

with the Lucas Magdyno) a paper or cork gasket is used – do not use gasket cement on reassembly since subsequent removal will be difficult.

5 The contact breaker should be removed after taking out the centre screw, noting which way the components are positioned, eg the flat spring on face-cam types. Look at the contacts (points) and if they are blackened this is an indication of capacitor problems. Usually it is better to send the magneto to a specialist for a new capacitor but the more adventurous may try replacing the faulty capacitor with a modern type of 0.2 µF (microfarad) size (see references at the end of

this Chapter). Sometimes a flat capacitor from a motor lawnmower engine might be persuaded to fit.

6 After carefully withdrawing the armature, inspect the windings visually and if the insulation is spongy there is the chance that after a hot run the shellac may jam the rotating armature – a rewind is essential. A broken slip ring side is not an uncommon fault and specialists will supply a replacement, but in general it pays to send a magneto with a faulty armature or slip ring assembly to a magneto repairer. Bearings require special extractors without which replacement is again best carried out professionally.

Rewinding a magneto is a job for the specialist mainly because the wire used for the secondary winding is very thin and prone to break in the hands of the inexperienced. Illustration 4.6 shows the armature of a Lucas K2F magneto being wound on a professional coil winding machine. The primary winding will be of the order of 200 – 250 turns of 0.71 or 0.85 mm enamelled wire and the secondary between 8000 and 12,000 turns of 0.071 mm wire. Lucky is the amateur winder who can get to the finish without breaking such fine wire!

7 A simple test for armature windings is shown in illustration 4.7. If a 6 volt battery is connected to the contact breaker centre bolt and the other battery lead flicked against the armature body, a spark should jump across the improvised spark gap. If the spark is good it is an indicator that all is well but even so, misfiring could occur at high speed because of internal sparking (tracking). No spark, however, does confirm that the windings are faulty and that the armature should be rewound.

8 The ideal way of checking the magneto is to run it on a bench test so that it drives sparks across a 5 to 6 mm gap. A belt drive can be rigged up from a lathe or using a separate motor of about $\frac{1}{4}$ horse power. The standard three point test rig shown in illustration 4.8 ensures even sparking from a good magneto. The third point, although not connected to anything, will simulate the ionizing conditions that normally are present round a spark plug.

## 5 Flywheel magneto

1 Used mainly on small engines, the flywheel magneto is a rotating-magnet type usually found on two-strokes and on some competition four-stroke machines. It is also

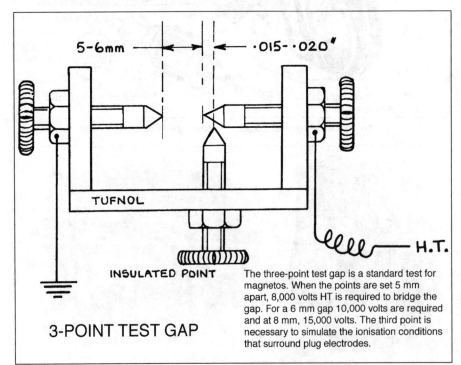

The three-point test gap is a standard test for magnetos. When the points are set 5 mm apart, 8,000 volts HT is required to bridge the gap. For a 6 mm gap 10,000 volts are required and at 8 mm, 15,000 volts. The third point is necessary to simulate the ionisation conditions that surround plug electrodes.

**4.8 Standard test gap for magneto testing**

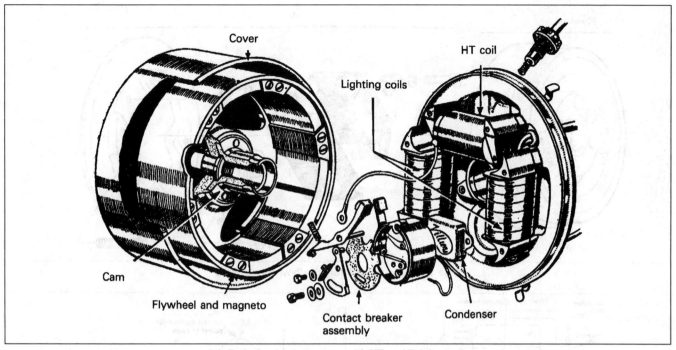

**5.2  Early flywheel magneto with HT and lighting coils**

widely used on two-stroke lawnmowers and in other non-motorcycle applications. The essential difference between it and the rotating-magnet magneto described in Section 3 is that the magnets revolve around the stator windings and not inside them. Additionally the flywheel into which the magnets are cast has sufficient mass as to act as the main engine flywheel to carry the crankshaft over the compression resistance. (There is always an exception to the rule: one or two early models did have the stator outboard of the magnets!)

**2** Early flywheel magnetos had a coil for lighting (or battery charging) and an ignition coil plus contact breaker and capacitor (see illustration 5.2). This type was a complete unit with two outputs, one for charging (or lighting) and the other an HT cable going straight to the plug. Because it was self contained, it was supplied as a bolt-on package for engine manufacturers by such well known companies as Villiers, BTH, Wipac, Miller and others.

**3** Later flywheel magnetos for motorcycles have an external ignition coil and work on the principle of energy transfer (see later). Internally the magneto has a coil for lighting (or charging), an ignition source coil for supplying the external ignition coil, plus a contact breaker and capacitor (see illustration 5.3). The rotating magnets are cast into a flywheel of sufficient mass to act as a crankshaft flywheel for small engines.

Developments have led to the CDI system which dispenses with the contact breaker and capacitor (see Chapter 6).

*Operation*

**4** The unit shown in illustrations 5.4a and 5.4b is a simple flywheel magneto for a small Yamaha motorcycle. Cast into the flywheel is a set of permanent magnets which pass over the stationary coils, generating an alternating voltage in them. Refer to illustration 5.3 and

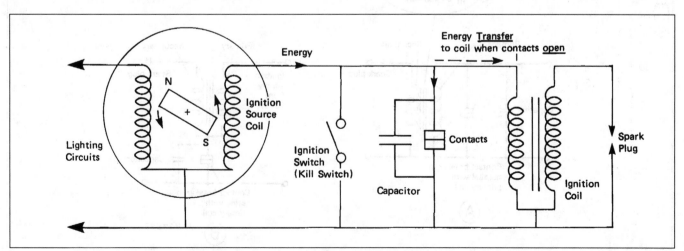

**5.3  Alternating current (ac) ignition circuit of flywheel magneto**

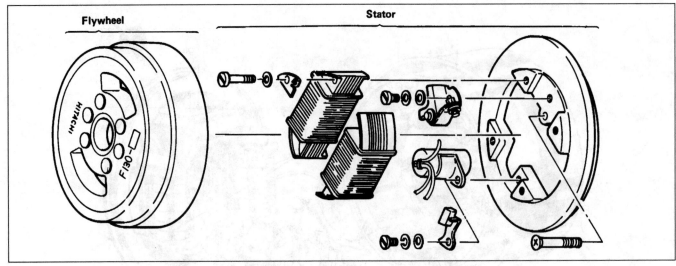

5.4a  Exploded view of Yamaha flywheel magneto

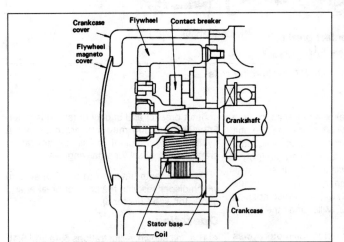

5.4b  Assembly of Yamaha flywheel magneto

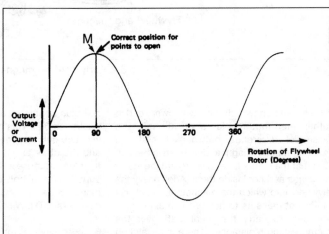

5.4c  Waveform of magneto source coil output

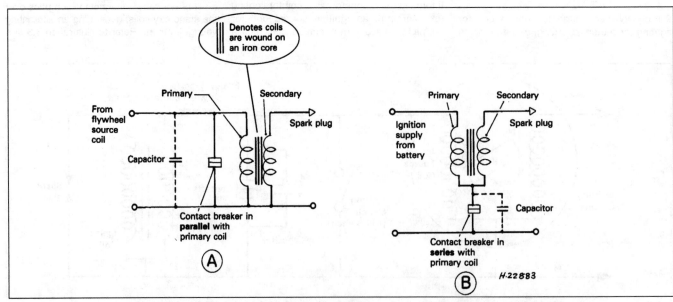

5.5  Showing difference between Energy Transfer (A) and usual coil and battery ignition (B)

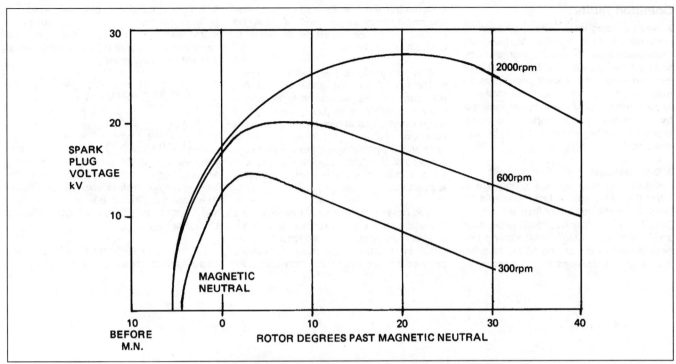

**5.6 The effect of magnetic timing on plug voltage at various speeds**

note that the source coil is connected to a pair of contacts which, when closed, short circuit the alternating current to earth (ground).

At or near the point of maximum current flow (point M in illustration 5.4c) the contacts open. The current is abruptly transferred to the ignition coil primary winding, the voltage across it being stepped up by transformer action. This gives a secondary voltage sufficient for a good spark at the plug providing the contact breaker opening coincides with maximum source coil current or approximately so. It is because the energy from the source coil is **transferred** at the moment of contact breaker opening to the ignition coil primary winding, that the method is known as **Energy Transfer**.

**5** Note the essential difference between Energy Transfer (ET) and conventional coil ignition. With ET the contact breaker is in parallel with the ignition coil primary; in conventional coil ignition it is in series (see illustration 5.5).

### *Timing*

**6** The magnet rotor is keyed to the crankshaft and as it turns the energy pulse generated in the stationary coils will occur over several degrees of rotation. In general, about +10° makes not more than a 30% difference in plug voltage, this depending on the design. However, the fall off in plug voltage is not symmetrical around the magnetic neutral (the centre line between the magnetic poles) and drops away rapidly before magnetic neutral

(see illustration 5.6). It should be clear that the maximum spark voltage available does not occur at a fixed setting for all speeds and so a compromise is found by the manufacturer. It is important that the recommended timing point is used to maintain optimum performance and for many machines this is determined only by the correct setting of the contact breaker gap. A small error in the contact breaker gap is more serious in energy transfer than in conventional coil ignition systems.

### *ET Automatic advance for four-strokes*

**7** Four-stroke engines mostly require ignition timing control which will progressively advance the spark from somewhere around 200 rev/min up to about 3000 rev/min at the crankshaft. Automatic advance is achieved by a pair of bob weights which fly outwards by centrifugal force against spring tension as described in Chapter 4. As the weights move outwards the contact breaker is made to open earlier; the spring strength is all important and service manuals show that regular checks must be made on them.

Because the spark intensity falls off so rapidly in ET systems only a limited amount of advance is possible and is substantially less than in coil and battery ignition. For this reason, automatic advance mechanisms are not interchangeable between ET and coil and battery machines. It is common for an ET automatic advance to be within the range 5° – 10° at the contact breaker, this

corresponding to 10° – 20° at the crankshaft for a four-stroke engine.

### 6 Servicing notes – flywheel magneto

### *Servicing notes*

**1** Little needs to be done to a flywheel magneto apart from checking the contact breaker gap which averages out between the various makes from 0.010 – 0.015 in (0.25 – 0.38 mm). If the manufacturer's specification is not available it is best to try variations for best spark and performance. Older designs require removal of the flywheel rotor for which a puller will probably be required. When the flywheel is removed, bridge the magnetic poles with a keeper which can be any large chunks of ferrous metal such as spanners or even a strip cut up for the job; these replace temporarily the magnetic path provided by the iron laminations of the stator assembly. Modern magnets do not require keepers according to manufacturers but habit dies hard and the advice is to use them anyway.

 *When a flywheel is taken off it seems that ferrous filings appear as if from nowhere and stick to the poles – be careful to get rid of them before reassembly.*

**5**

## Common faults

**2 Weak magnets:** Poor sparking performance may be due to slow self demagnetisation of older magnets. Low turning resistance when the flywheel is turned by hand when on the shaft shows that the magnetic pole strength is low. The solution is to have the flywheel magnets remagnetised by a specialist in this work. Performance improvement after remagnetising can be quite dramatic!

**3 Coil leakage:** High voltage coils may eventually develop leakage giving rise to internal tracking so in effect the sparks are occurring in the coil rather than at the spark plug. The effects may be difficult to pin down and may show up as difficult starting or a petering out of the engine as the magneto warms up. A professional rewind is essential.

**4 Capacitor trouble:** As with most ignition equipment, the capacitor (condenser) may fail in one of three ways – short circuit, leaking or open circuit (see below).

With a short circuit there will be no spark and a test meter may show zero or low resistance from the live terminal to the case. A leaking capacitor gives rise to misfiring and rough running, first at high speed then as the fault worsens also at low speed. If the capacitor is open circuit there will be heavy sparking at the contact breaker points with signs of burning such as a white powdery appearance.

In all cases a replacement is essential. If a manufacturer's service replacement is not available an alternative capacitor may be fitted in another position if necessary, provided it is proofed against the weather. An automobile capacitor may be used, or perhaps one from another source such as a motor lawnmower engine, providing it has a capacitance of about 0.2 µF (microfarad) at 400 volt rating minimum.

## 7  Further reading

Readers interested in going further into magneto work are referred to *Restoring Motorcycles: Electrics* by Roy Bacon, *The Vintage Motorcyclists' Workshop* by 'Radco' (Haynes), and *Classic Bike magazine,* April 1992, article by Frank Farrington 'Classic Craftsmanship'.

For specialist repairers of magnetos see *'Old Bike Mart'* magazine.

# Chapter 6
# Ignition – Capacitor Discharge Ignition (CDI)

## Contents

**Warning: Capacitor Discharge systems are dangerous. There is high spark energy at high voltage and a shock can be lethal.**

**Warning: Do not touch the high tension parts with bare hands unless the ignition is off. When a working HT lead has to be handled, use insulated pliers or special high voltage grips.**

**Warning: Do not turn the engine over by hand when the ignition is on.**

### 1 Deficiencies of the Kettering ignition system

**1** The development of Capacitor Discharge Ignition (CDI) is one simple way of achieving a reliable spark up to high speeds using electronics. However, before looking at CDI in detail it is worth considering why contact breaker ignition has now been superseded.

Although the contact breaker plus coil and battery system has been in use for nearly a century, its shortcomings in performance and maintenance costs have long been appreciated. Mechanically, it is difficult to manufacture a cam, heel follower and spring mechanism which provide and maintain the required accuracy. Every few thousand miles it is necessary to reset the contacts to allow for heel wear; in addition the breaking of the coil primary current produces the effect of 'pitting and piling' because of metal transference with the spark.

**2** It should be noted that to obtain enough energy for spark production (about 30 millijoules are required – for a definition of the joule see Chapter 2) the coil designer will allow as large a primary current as possible, consistent with reasonable life of the contact breaker points – but for long contact life the current should be small. The graph in illustration 1.2 shows the general effect of break current on the life of points.

At high speeds the centrifugal force acting on the moving parts of the contact breaker assembly may be sufficient to cause the gap to increase beyond the design gap, due to flinging out when the heel loses contact with the cam.

**3** These troubles have always been present but in recent times have become more undesirable due to engine design developments. Compression ratios have increased, demanding a higher spark voltage; additionally, higher maximum engine speeds are used needing a higher rate of sparking. All these limitations are best summarised as follows:

(a) *Plug fouling – For high compression ratios, petrol additives (lead salts) are used in the UK to prevent detonation. Unfortunately, these additives appear to contribute to fouling of plugs.*
(b) *Mechanical limitations of contact breakers are now severe.*
(c) *The time taken for 30 millijoules of electrical energy to build up between sparks limits the rate to about 400 sparks per second, or time per spark 0.0025 second. This may be too low a spark rate for high-speed multi-cylinder engines.*

(d) *To overcome plug fouling, and to produce reliable sparks in cylinders of higher compression rates, a higher spark voltage of 15 to 30 kilovolts (kV) is required. Another reason for higher ignition system voltage is to do with both economy and the achievement of low pollution emission; weaker mixtures are now used and in turn are more difficult to ignite by sparks.*
(e) *Contact breaker points pitting and burning due to the high coil primary currents used.*
(f) *Inaccuracy occurring at high speeds due to backlash and whip in the contact breaker drive mechanism.*

It is not surprising that ignition system designers have looked for alternative methods, and the arrival of the transistor and allied semiconductor devices has provided several solutions to the problem.

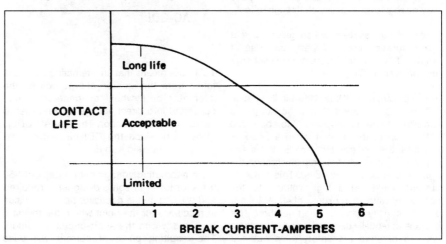

**1.2 Contact life versus break current**

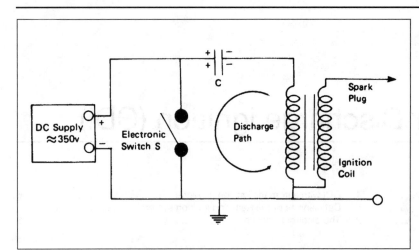

**2.3  Principle of Capacitor Discharge Ignition (CDI)**

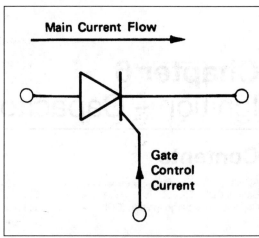

**3.2  Thyristor or Silicon Controlled Rectifier (SCR)**

## 2  Capacitor Discharge Ignition (CDI)

**1** Under ideal conditions less than 1 millijoule of energy will properly ignite the fuel:air mixture in the combustion chamber. The first part of the arc of perhaps only 1 microsecond duration ignites the mixture and the remainder of the spark contributes little or nothing. However, the practical condition is that the mixture may be wrong, or unevenly mixed, and it may be that the ignitable gas may not even have reached the plug electrodes at the time that the spark occurs. It is found in practice that if the spark duration is made to last about 300 microseconds then the probability is that ignition will occur satisfactorily for all normal cylinder conditions.

**2** A further desirable feature of the ideal spark in an engine is that the energy flow at the plug should reach a maximum in a very short period of time. This sudden rush of electrical energy will help to counteract plug fouling and may be regarded as a 'punch through' effect.

An ignition system which gives correct spark duration coupled with rapid rise of energy flow is the Capacitor Discharge Ignition system (CDI).

**3** The principle of CDI is shown in illustration 2.3. If it is assumed that a dc supply is available to charge capacitor C to about 350 volts, then at the instant when a spark is required, the electronic switch S closes and capacitor C is discharged rapidly through the ignition coil primary winding. This pulse of current results in a high voltage to the secondary winding in excess of 40 kV to give a high intensity spark of short duration. This spark is potentially dangerous and it would be wise to observe the safety rules outlined above.

## 3  The electronic switch

**1** Electronic switching is invariably by means of the thyristor, often called a Silicon Controlled Rectifier (SCR). Refer back to Chapter 2 for the basic principles of how the thyristor works, but in essence it is a switch which is either open circuit (that is, no current can flow through it) or short circuit – just like a mechanical on/off switch.

**2** To switch the thyristor ON, a very small current is fed into the gate terminal. This small current is derived from a sensor which detects the instant when a spark is required. Only when the capacitor has discharged itself fully through the thyristor and the ignition coil primary winding, does the thyristor resume the OFF position until the next gate signal arrives from the sensor. The symbol for the thyristor is shown in illustration 3.2.

## 4  AC-CDI

**1** AC-CDI means that an alternating voltage is taken from the ignition charge coil on the alternator or flywheel ac generator, then converted into direct voltage by a rectifier to charge up the capacitor. The title AC-CDI is misleading, since the CDI capacitor must always be supplied with dc.

An alternating voltage with a peak of 350 volts (or lower in some designs) is required and will charge the capacitor up to this value in readiness for the point where the thyristor breaks down to the short-circuit condition. The resulting pulse of current will pass round the ignition coil primary winding, generating a spark voltage in the secondary winding.

**2** In illustration 4.2, as the alternator rotor magnet passes under the pulse coil, a voltage pulse is generated which serves to trigger the thyristor (Another example of those basic principles in Chapter 2!)

The simple circuit shown has a movable pulse coil so that ignition timing can be adjusted; the pulse rectifier ensures that only positive pulses reach the thyristor gate. In practice the following two additions might be made:

(a) A pulse shaping circuit might be included in the path to the thyristor gate. This ensures a sharp-sided pulse with which to switch on the thyristor precisely.
(b) Some means of achieving ignition advance as the engine speed increases. This will be dealt with further on in this Chapter.

**3** Hitachi, Femsa, Motoplat and others have marketed a range of flywheel electronic ignition systems which have certain common features; sparking will begin at speeds from 200 – 500 rev/min, depending on the make, and all depend on good electrical connections between the engine, the electronic boxes (usually housing the ignition coil and CDI components) and the generator.

Most units should produce a spark of 5 – 6 mm long in air and it is important that the engine should never be stopped by pulling off the HT lead. Furthermore, the systems should not be run with sparks longer than 8 mm under test, or there may be trouble with internal insulation. With such high voltages available, the spark has to go somewhere so if it cannot get to the plug to discharge harmlessly it will probably break down insulation somewhere such as the HT cable or internally in the coil.

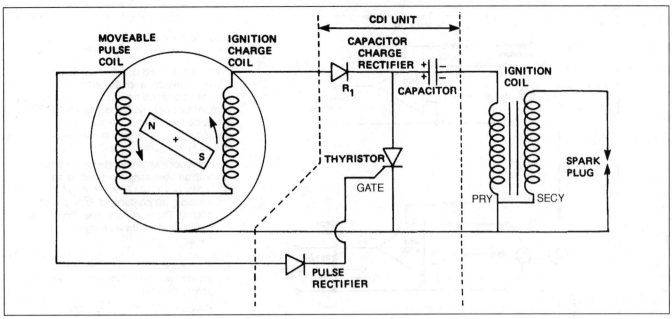

**4.2  Simplified CDI circuit using a flywheel generator**

Where the ignition is for twin cylinders it is important to test with both plugs connected. Finally, mechanics should again remember that CDI systems generate a lot of energy and are **DANGEROUS**.

## 5  Battery CDI

**1** An alternative method of supplying power to a CDI unit from the battery is now described.

The disadvantage of AC-CDI is that the starting-up spark voltage depends on how fast the engine can be turned over. At low rpm the battery-operated CDI gives a greater spark energy (see illustration 5.1).

Because the alternator does not now need an ignition charge coil, it can be designed to give a larger output for battery charging. Finally, the current demand for a battery CDI is lower than that of a transistorised ignition circuit at low rev/min. However, the starting success is dependent on having a well-charged battery!

**2** A method has been found to convert the 12 volts dc of the motorcycle battery up to the high dc voltage (200 – 350 volts) required to charge the capacitor.

First, the 12 volts is applied to a transistor circuit designed to oscillate, that is, to generate an alternating voltage. A built-in transformer then transforms the alternating voltage of this oscillator up and it is then rectified to produce the required direct voltage.

This circuit is known as an invertor and in high powered versions may be made to operate some household equipment off a 12 volt supply battery. The principle of the oscillator/ invertor is shown in illustration 5.2a, and a simplified practical circuit in illustration 5.2b.

**6**

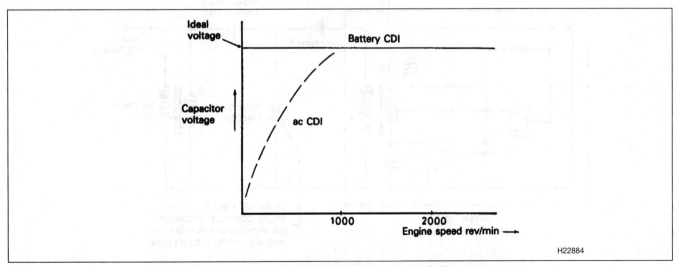

**5.1  Illustration of how battery CDI works better than AC-CDI at low speeds**

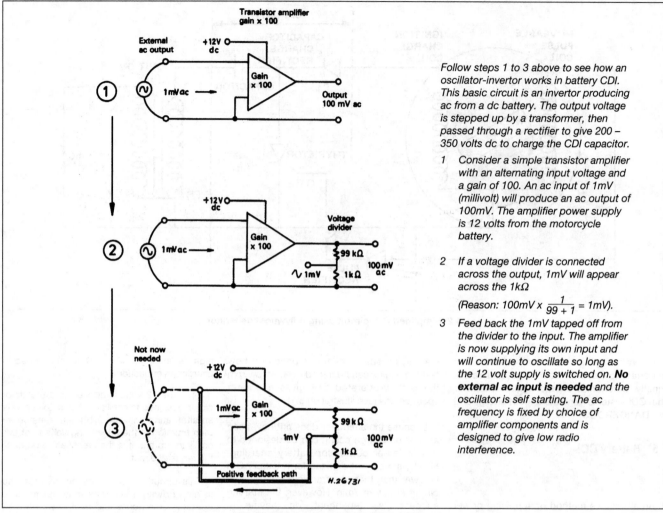

Follow steps 1 to 3 above to see how an oscillator-invertor works in battery CDI. This basic circuit is an invertor producing ac from a dc battery. The output voltage is stepped up by a transformer, then passed through a rectifier to give 200 – 350 volts dc to charge the CDI capacitor.

1   Consider a simple transistor amplifier with an alternating input voltage and a gain of 100. An ac input of 1mV (millivolt) will produce an ac output of 100mV. The amplifier power supply is 12 volts from the motorcycle battery.

2   If a voltage divider is connected across the output, 1mV will appear across the 1kΩ

(Reason: $100mV \times \frac{1}{99 + 1} = 1mV$).

3   Feed back the 1mV tapped off from the divider to the input. The amplifier is now supplying its own input and will continue to oscillate so long as the 12 volt supply is switched on. **No external ac input is needed** and the oscillator is self starting. The ac frequency is fixed by choice of amplifier components and is designed to give low radio interference.

**5.2a  Principle for an invertor for CDI**

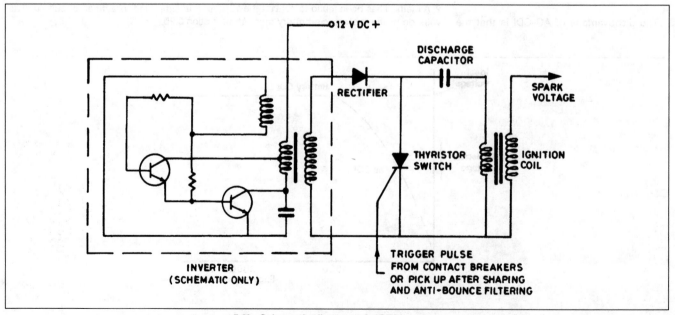

**5.2b  Schematic diagram of a CDI invertor**

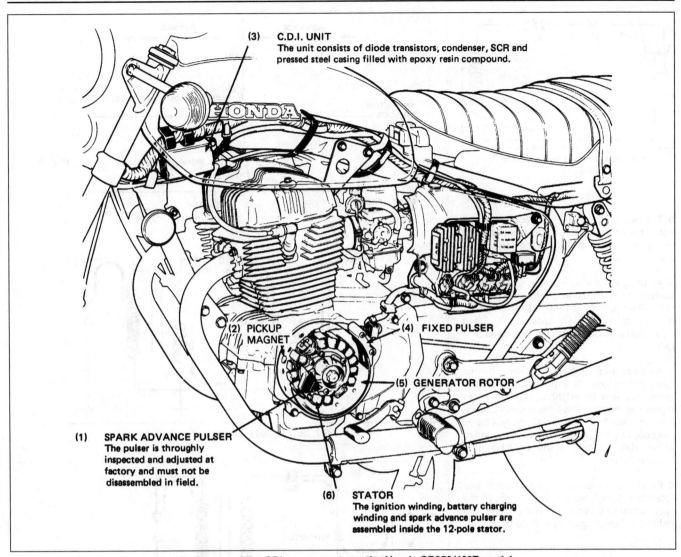

**(3) C.D.I. UNIT**
The unit consists of diode transistors, condenser, SCR and pressed steel casing filled with epoxy resin compound.

**(2) PICKUP MAGNET**

**(4) FIXED PULSER**

**(5) GENERATOR ROTOR**

**(1) SPARK ADVANCE PULSER**
The pulser is throughly inspected and adjusted at factory and must not be disassembled in field.

**(6) STATOR**
The ignition winding, battery charging winding and spark advance pulser are assembled inside the 12-pole stator.

**6.2a Layout of the CDI components on the Honda CB250/400T models**

6

## 6  CDI with automatic ignition advance

**1** The use of electronic ignition in no way lessens the need for automatic advancing of the spark over the lower speed range. Two methods are described below which are both ingenious and effective.

### CDI Advance – Method 1

**2** This is the older of the two methods and was used on Honda CB250T and 400T models. It gave the required advance with speed plus a means of limiting the maximum advance, all by a set of coils assembled within the generator. Illustration 6.2a shows the location of the CDI components on the machine and illustration 6.2b the electrical circuit. Referring to this diagram again, the operation is as follows.

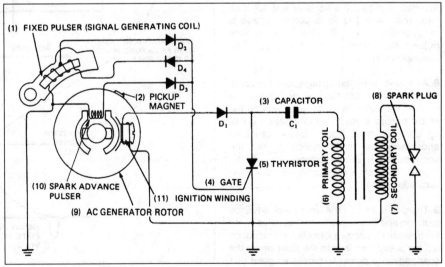

(1) FIXED PULSER (SIGNAL GENERATING COIL)
$D_2$
$D_4$
$D_3$
(2) PICKUP MAGNET
(3) CAPACITOR  $C_1$
(8) SPARK PLUG
$D_1$
(5) THYRISTOR
(10) SPARK ADVANCE PULSER
(4) GATE
(11) IGNITION WINDING
(6) PRIMARY COIL
(7) SECONDARY COIL
(9) AC GENERATOR ROTOR

**6.2b  Schematic diagram of the CDI system on the Honda CB250/400T models**

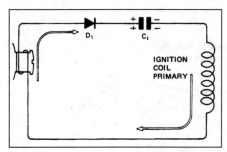

**6.4 Charging of the capacitor C₁**

**3** The pick-up magnet (2) is a button-magnet set in the rotor and this generates pulses of nearly constant magnitude in the fixed pulser coil (1).

**4** As the generator rotor turns, an alternating current is generated in the ignition winding (11). This current is rectified by diode $D_1$ and charges the CDI capacitor $C_1$ (see illustration 6.4). During this time the thyristor is OFF.

**5** As the pick-up magnet (2) passes under the fixed pulser coil (1) a pulse of current is generated and flows through diode $D_2$ to trigger the thyristor. The ignition spark occurs. Note that the fixed pulser coil has two parts, the second part generating a small **negative** pulse which is fed to the thyristor gate through diode $D_4$.

**6** Finally as the pick-up magnet continues rotation it generates a pulse voltage in the spark advance pulser coil (10) and this is also fed to the thyristor gate by a diode $D_3$.

**7** The characteristic of the spark advance pulser coil is that it gives a broad + pulse of voltage which rises steeply as the engine speed rises. A certain fixed voltage is required to trigger the thyristor and it will be seen that when the fixed pulser voltage is much greater than that of the spark advance pulser, the spark is fixed in time (see illustration 6.7).

**8** As speed rises, the voltage from the spark advance pulser cuts the thyristor trigger line before that from the fixed pulser and so the spark occurs earlier (see illustration 6.8a). Ignition advance has been obtained and increases with speed since the spark advancer pulser voltage skirt cuts the trigger line at ever earlier points (see illustration 6.8b).

**9** There is a limit to the amount of advance required and this is where the negative pulse from rectifier $D_4$ comes into play. In illustration 6.9 the speed has risen to the point where the spark advance pulser voltage is so great that the trigger point has advanced almost to the

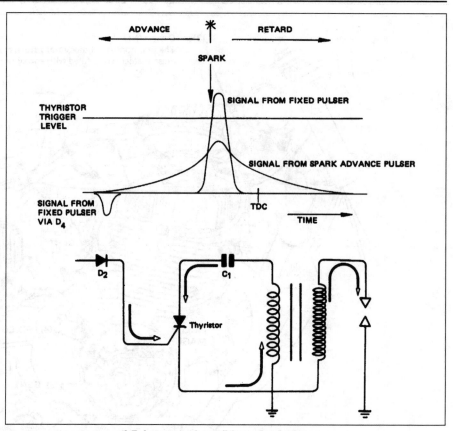

**6.7 Low speed condition – fixed advance**

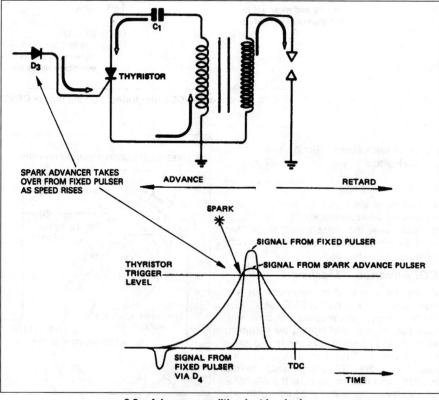

**6.8a Advance condition just beginning**

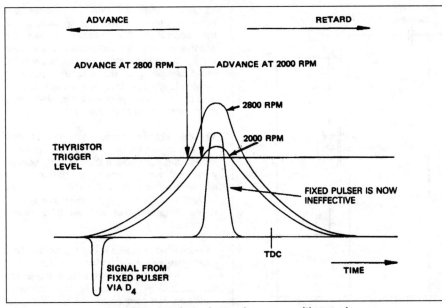

6.8b  **Showing that advance increases with speed**

fixed position of the negative pulse from $D_4$. Here the negative pulse balances out the positive output from the advance pulser rectifier $D_3$ and so further ignition advance is stopped.

## CDI Advance – Method 2

**10** The more recent method of obtaining ignition advance depends upon electronic circuitry.

**11** Illustration 6.11 shows a pulse generator and the waveshape of the voltage produced in it as the rotor reluctor passes. (A reluctor is a steel projection which passes close to the pulse coil iron core, raising the magnetic flux level and thus inducing voltage pulses in the coil.) It will be seen that as the reluctor approaches the pulse generator, the magnetic flux across the gap will be increasing and as it moves away, the magnetic flux will be decreasing. This gives rise to a positive then a negative voltage pulse.

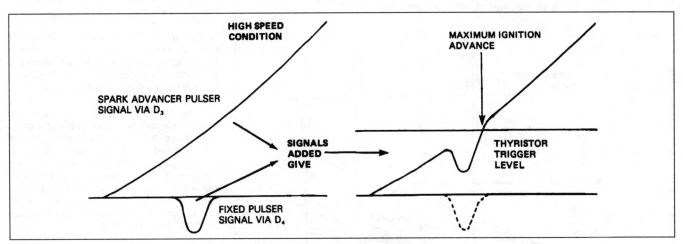

6.9  **Condition of maximum advance**

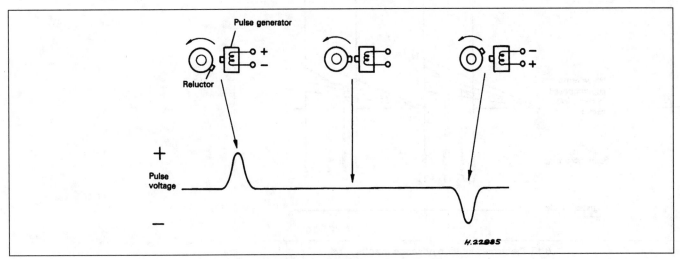

6.11  **Voltage pulses from pulse generator**

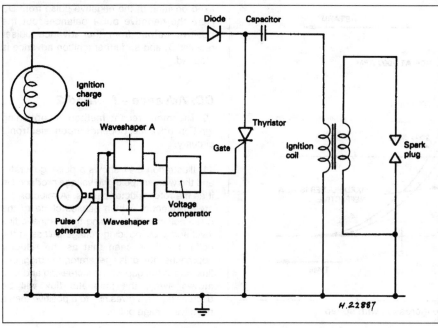

**6.12 Electronic ignition advance for CDI**

**12** Inside the CDI unit the pulses are connected to two wave shaping circuits (see illustration 6.12). Wave shaper A detects the positive going pulse and produces a voltage wave with an initial step, then a linearly rising ramp shape until the negative pulse is received. Wave A then drops back to zero until the next positive pulse is received. *Wave A remains constant for all speeds.*

**13** Wave shaper B takes the incoming pulses and is triggered when the negative pulse is received. It generates a linearly rising voltage waveform which continues until the next negative pulse arrives, but the slope of the waveshape B depends upon engine speed. *Wave B gets lower in height as speed increases.*

**14** Waveforms A and B are connected to a logic-gate voltage comparator circuit. This circuit produces an output pulse to trigger the thyristor (SCR) subject to the following condition. *The comparator will send the spark signal to the thyristor when waveform A is greater than waveform B or when the negative pulse is received.*

**15** Looking at the waveforms in illustration 6.15, waveform B is shown for speeds increasing from $N_1$ to $N_4$. At $N_1$, waveform B is greater than waveform A, so the thyristor is triggered by the negative pulse at time $T_1$.

At $N_2$ the engine speed has risen and waveform B cuts waveform A giving a spark signal earlier to the thyristor at time $T_2$. When engine speed is at $N_4$ or greater, no further advance is possible because waveform A is not inclined and is inoperative. The result is that ignition advance occurs progressively from point $T_1$ up to $T_4$ and no further. As an example, $T_1$ may correspond to about 10° BTDC and $T_4$ to 35° BTDC.

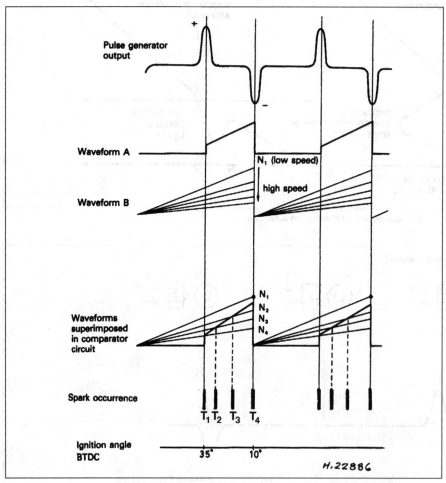

**6.15 Electronic ignition advance graphs**

# Chapter 7
# Ignition – Transistor and digital ignition

## Contents

**7**

### 1  Goodbye contact breakers!

**1** We have already seen in Chapter 6 why the contact breaker eventually gave way to other means of breaking the ignition coil primary current. However it did not happen suddenly for there was a transitional stage when the contact breaker remained but was used in conjunction with a transistor to break the ignition coil primary current. This phase of development did not last long and the contact breaker soon went into history.

However, now that it is possible to look back, it is realised that the contact breaker was a crude form of sensor because like all modern sensors it signalled the point in time when the coil primary current is to be cut off and the subsequent spark takes place.

The time-honoured contact breaker must take a place along with the modern sensors described in this and other Chapters.

### 2  Transistor ignition development

**1** The first appearance of transistor-driven ignition for motorcycles was in the form of aftermarket kits or designs for owner constructors.

Early circuits still employed the contact-breaker, but connected into a transistor circuit so that the current being broken at the contact breaker points was much smaller. Such circuit systems were known as TAC (Transistor Assisted Contacts).

**2** Using a mechanically operated contact breaker was really a compromise and soon circuit designers were using non-contacting sensors to pick up a signal indicating when sparking should occur. Circuits using transistors are prone to sharp pulse voltages (transients); ignition coils are a prime source of spike pulse voltages and protection has to

be given to the driving transistor(s) to avoid destruction. To some extent the development of modern sophisticated electronic systems proceeded in parallel with transistor devices which became less susceptible to transient failure.

**3** Circuit development began using analogue technology with designs to keep the energy at the coil constant and to produce an ignition advance curve to suit the engine. However more and more variables such as intake temperature, battery condition, engine load etc. resulted in a change to digital methods which could handle variables more quickly and efficiently using computer techniques.

**4** Today, the most advanced and precise ignition systems are digital. Sensor analogue signals are converted to digital form and then processed by a computer for control of voltage and timing of the spark pulse. These methods will now be looked at more closely.

## 3 Transistor-Assisted Contacts (TAC) coil ignition

**1** This was the first attempt to improve the shortcomings of the (then) conventional coil and battery system; it is obsolete but forms a good introduction to present day technology.

Use of a transistor as a switch to break and make the ignition coil primary current was a first step; it is still necessary to turn the transistor on and off, and to do this the contact breaker (S) is retained (see illustration 3.1). This simple circuit shows an n-p-n transistor connected into the ignition coil primary circuit. The load current flows from collector *c* to emitter *e* only so long as the emitter is negative relative to the base *b*. If the switch (S) is opened (this corresponds to the contact breaker) then the emitter-base current is cut off; this switches off the collector current which flows through the coil primary and the spark occurs at the plug.

With the figures shown as an illustration only, it will be seen that the controlling base current of 0.16A is only 2% of the controlled collector current of 8A. *So, the transistor can switch a large current in the collector circuit on or off by switching a much lower current in the base circuit.*

The circuit arrangement is not really practical because of the need for an additional battery to bias the emitter to be negative with respect to the base. However, it shows the basic requirements and there are ways of supplying the base/emitter bias without a battery by simple circuitry which we shall look at later.

Because the contacts now handle a low current, 0.16A in this case, their life is greatly

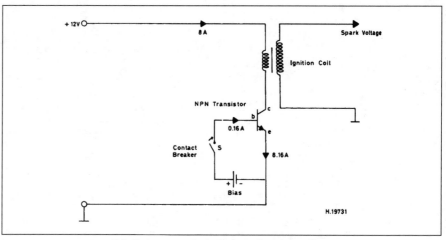

**3.1 Base current controls main current flow**

extended and, moreover, no capacitor is required since the contacts are partly isolated from the ignition coil primary. It is claimed that a set of TAC points had a life of 100,000 miles (160,000 km).

**2** A factor to be considered when designing an ignition coil suitable for TAC is that of the primary coil inductance L, measured in henrys (see Chapter 2); inductance L depends upon the number of turns of a coil, and the energy stored in the magnetic field around the coil is:

$$W = \frac{1}{2} LI^2 \text{ joules.}$$

*where* W = energy stored (joules)
I = coil current (amperes)
L = coil inductance (henrys)

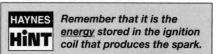

**HAYNES HiNT** *Remember that it is the energy stored in the ignition coil that produces the spark.*

**3** It is important to have the ignition coil primary current rise as quickly as possible when the contacts are closed, in order to build up energy ready for the next contact-break. Inductance in an electrical circuit is similar to the inertia of a flywheel. As a heavy flywheel takes time to accelerate, so current rise takes time in an inductive circuit (see illustration 3.3) (see Chapter 2).

**4** The primary current rise time is significantly reduced allowing a higher maximum rate of sparking (see illustrations 3.3 and 3.4). Designers have, therefore, taken the opportunity to set the value of the ignition coil current higher than that in earlier conventional coils – about 8 amperes instead of 3 amperes in one particular design. This allows the inductance (and therefore number of primary turns) to be reduced and results in a secondary-to-primary turns ratio of about 250:1 or even 400:1 compared with about 66:1 in an old 'conventional' coil. The low primary coil resistance will also reduce the

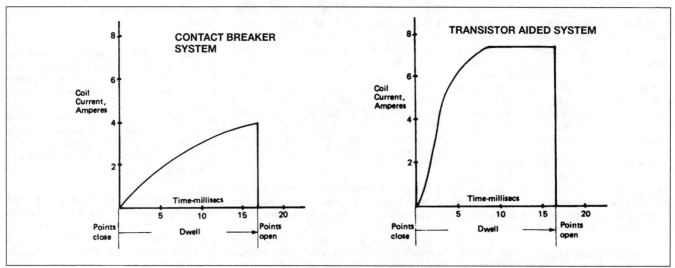

**3.3 Rise times of coil current comparison**

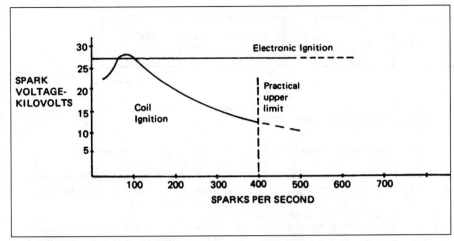

3.4  Performance comparison between conventional and electronic systems

but most now dispense with contacts and substitute a sensor. Sensors are looked at again further in this Chapter.

## 4  Basic TAC ignition circuit

**1** A drawback of the circuit shown in illustration 3.1 is the need for a separate battery in the base control path. In practice, the supply of current for both the base and collector branches is drawn from the same battery; all that is needed is a pair of resistors across the main battery supply, their resistance being calculated to make the centre tap correspond to the voltage required at the base. One way in which this might be done is shown in illustration 4.1.

**2** This is a simple two transistor circuit and note that the transistors are complementary, that is, one is p-n-p and the other is n-p-n. Transistor $T_1$ is an amplifier and passes an output signal to the base of transistor $T_2$ which drives the ignition coil primary.

The direction of the arrows on the emitters shows that $T_1$ is of the p-n-p type and $T_2$ is n-p-n. (It should be recalled that a p-n-p transistor is ON when the emitter voltage is positive relative to its base, and the n-p-n transistor is ON when the emitter voltage is negative relative to its base.)

**3** With the contact breaker closed, the current flow through $R_1$ and $R_2$ will produce volt-drops with polarities as shown. The volt-drop across $R_2$ is sufficient to switch $T_1$ to

resistive power loss in the coil so more energy is available for the spark.

**5** It might reasonably be asked what other advantage this gives. The answer is that if current is changed rapidly in an inductive circuit, transient voltages are generated across the inductive coil and these could be hazardous to electronic components elsewhere in the electrical system. It is therefore of advantage to keep the primary coil inductance *low*.

**6** This rise-time of coil current after the contacts have closed has been a limiting factor to the maximum possible spark rate, since at high engine speeds the next spark was due before the current could rise to its maximum value. The reduced primary

inductance of ignition coils driven by transistors has meant much improved performance, as shown by the typical graphs of illustrations 3.3 and 3.4. The retention of good sparking voltage at high engine speeds is required for efficiency and economy.

**7** Several advantages stem, therefore, from the use of transistor-assisted contact breaking, which include a higher maximum sparking rate, and less plug fouling and contact wear, leading to longer intervals between each service.

The disadvantage of retaining mechanical contacts remained, however, and no motorcycles are now fitted with TAC as original equipment. Aftermarket conversion kits are still popular with the owner market,

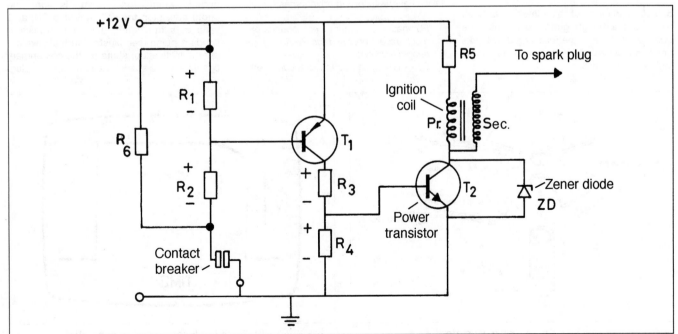

4.1  TAC circuit using complementary transistors

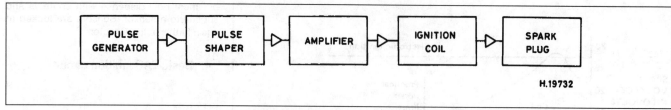

H.19732

5.3 Pulse-triggered electronic ignition

ON. $T_1$ collector current will give volt-drops on $R_3$ and $R_4$ The volt drop across $R_4$ will switch $T_2$ to ON.

When the contact breaker opens there is no forward bias to $T_1$ which shuts OFF. This removes the forward bias from $T_2$ which also switches OFF, so no collector current flows through the ignition coil primary winding. As a result of the sudden drop in primary current, the induced voltage in the secondary winding of the ignition coil provides the spark at the plugs.

**4** At the point when ignition occurs, there will be a high emf (voltage) generated in the ignition coil primary winding of the order of a few hundred volts, enough to destroy transistor $T_2$. The Zener diode ZD is chosen to conduct at about 100 volts and so protects $T_2$ from large voltage spikes.

The bias chain $R_1$ $R_2$ is made up of resistor values to give correct bias to transistor $T_1$. Resistor $R_6$ sets the contact breaker current to about 250 mA, sufficient to burn off dirt and corrosion. $R_5$ is a ballast resistor to limit primary coil current.

**5** Many variations of this circuit have been used, but although good results may be obtained with TAC, the following drawbacks of using mechanical contacts to generate the ignition signal remain:

(a) *Need for regular servicing due to cam-follower heel wear.*
(b) *Contact bounce at high speeds.*
(c) *Relatively high manufacturing cost.*

The next stage in solid state transistor ignition involved getting rid of mechanical contacts.

## 5 More about sensors

**1** A sensor is a conversion device which will measure or detect a quantity and produce a corresponding electrical signal. Quantities usually measured in motorcycles and automobiles are speed, position, temperature, pressure, liquid level, air flow and oxygen content of exhaust gases.

**2** For the purpose of ignition, to trigger the spark some form of sensor is required to produce an electrical signal at the instant when the spark is required. The contact breaker was a crude sensor which carried out this function, but a non-contacting trigger device has the following advantages:

(a) *Elimination of contact wear, bounce or mechanical freeplay; thus the timing will remain accurate.*
(b) *Spark timing can be made accurate over*

all speed and load conditions by electronic control.
(c) *The fall-off of spark energy with speed can be eliminated by electronic control of the dwell period.*

The trigger sensor is sometimes called a **pulse generator**, a **signal generator** or a **pickup**.

**3** Pulse generators fall usually into 3 types:

(a) Optical.
(b) Hall Effect.
(c) Variable reluctance.

In general, the pulse signals are too small for direct use and do not always have the optimum waveform, so circuits will **shape** the incoming signal and then **amplify** it as shown in the block diagram of illustration 5.3.

### Optical pulse generator

**4** An engine-driven segmented chopper disc breaks an infra-red beam normally focused onto a photo-transistor (see illustration 5.4a). The infra-red is produced by a gallium arsenide semiconductor diode when connected to a low voltage supply. During the period when the beam is on the photo-transistor, the coil current is ON; as a vane cuts the beam, the photo-transistor sends a pulse (see illustration 5.4b) which, after amplification, shuts off the coil primary current and the spark is generated at the plug.

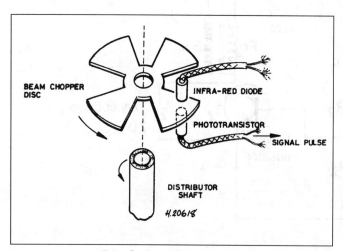

5.4a **Optical pulse generator**

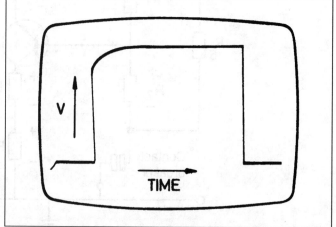

5.4b **Trace produced by optical generator**
*Courtesy FKI Crypton Ltd*

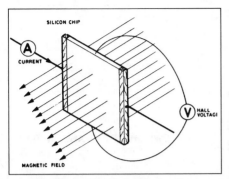

5.5a  Illustrating Hall-effect voltage

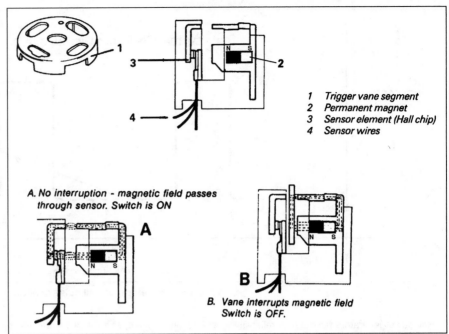

1  Trigger vane segment
2  Permanent magnet
3  Sensor element (Hall chip)
4  Sensor wires

A. No interruption - magnetic field passes through sensor. Switch is ON

B. Vane interrupts magnetic field Switch is OFF.

5.5b  Effect of trigger vane in Hall sender

Several variations of this arrangement exist; the pulse may be generated at the instant when the vane allows the beam to pass through to the photo-transistor; another possibility is the use of a light emitting diode (LED) instead of an infra-red diode.

## Hall-effect pulse generator

5 This device consists of a silicon chip through which a small current is passed between opposite edges. When a magnetic field passes through the major surface of the chip, a voltage appears between the other two edges (see illustration 5.5a). This is the Hall voltage and is used to trigger the ignition spark when the magnetic field is changed, this being achieved by a metallic trigger vane segment disc (see illustration 5.5b). The magnetic field is usually provided by a small permanent magnet on the opposite side of the gap from the Hall chip. Note that the vane will break the magnetic field as it passes in the gap between the permanent magnet and the Hall element.

6 Typically, the chip will take a current of about 30mA, delivering a 2mV Hall voltage signal with a positive temperature coefficient, that is, the Hall voltage increases with an increase of temperature. The chip is usually built into an integrated circuit, providing signal shaping and amplification.

The example shown in illustration 5.6 is a Siemens Hall-IC chip, the Hall generator being located in the centre of the chip; note the size – 1.5 x 1.6 mm!

7 Illustration 5.5b shows that at A the magnetic field crosses the air gap when the vane is not in between the gap faces and the Hall chip gives an output voltage; at B the vane is between the air gap faces and provides a path for the magnetic flux, shielding the Hall chip so the output voltage falls to a low level (see illustration 5.7). The voltage waveform is roughly rectangular and is processed by the integrated circuit to give a sharp ON-OFF output.

8 The rotor vane is shaped so as to give the required ratio of ON/OFF. This gives a pre-set dwell angle which can be varied by the electronic circuit into which the pulse signal is fed.

Finally, when the Hall voltage is switched ON (= high) the ignition coil current is switched OFF, generating a spark at the plug from which it follows that the spark occurs *as the vane passes out of the air gap.*

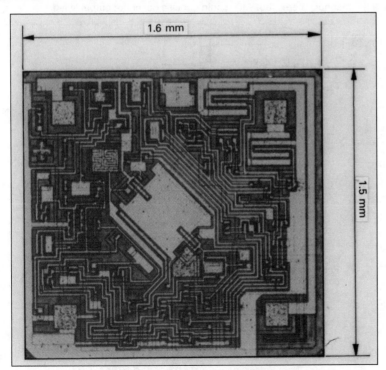

1.6 mm

1.5 mm

5.6  Hall integrated circuit chip (Siemens)

*The Hall generator is located in the centre*

**7**

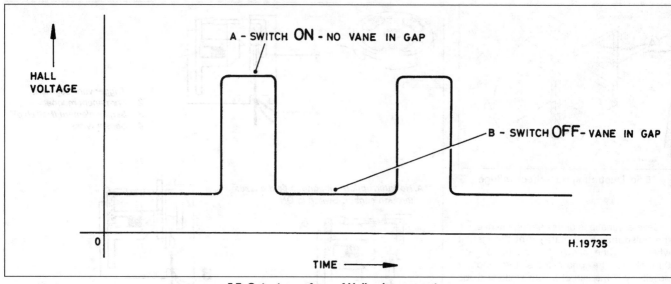

**5.7 Output waveform of Hall pulse generator**

Hall pulse generators have a high reliability and have the advantage over the optical type where dirt may affect the LED light or infra-red path.

 **Warning: It should be noted that it is possible to produce spark voltage when working on a Hall system even though the engine is stationary – the energy delivered is DANGEROUS.**

### Variable reluctance pulse generator

**9** This type of sensor is now common in many motorcycle and automobile ignition designs. It has already been described in Chapter 6 on CDI systems but it is worth looking at it again.

To remind you what the term 'reluctance' means; it is the magnetic equivalent to resistance in the electric circuit and is a measure of how easily magnetic flux can pass round a magnetic circuit.

**10** Going back now to the fundamentals of electromagnetism, it will be remembered that if a coil is subjected to a *change* of magnetic field, a voltage (emf) will be induced. The voltage generated will depend upon the following.

(a) *The rate at which the magnetic field changes.*
(b) *The number of turns of wire in the coil.*
(c) *The direction of flux change, that is, increase or decrease.*

This principle is used in a device to trigger an ignition spark. The magnetic field is varied by altering the reluctance of the magnetic circuit.

As a trigger wheel tooth approaches the iron core of the pick-up winding, the flux rises

rapidly only to fall as rapidly as the tooth moves away. The maximum voltage is generated just before and just after the teeth are opposite each other. The output is a form of alternating voltage which is passed through a pulse shaping circuit and on to the power transistor switch controlling the ignition coil current (see illustration 5.10). In practice the teeth on the trigger wheel may not be as big as shown and could be gear teeth (see below) or, in reverse form, be indentations in a solid disc. Note that the field is produced by a permanent magnet here but it could

alternatively be by a coil supplied with direct current.

The output voltage will vary in two ways with a speed increase:

(a) *The frequency will increase.*
(b) *The magnitude will increase from a fraction of a volt upwards.*

Both these changes can be sensed and used by the electronic module into which the pulse generator output is fed.

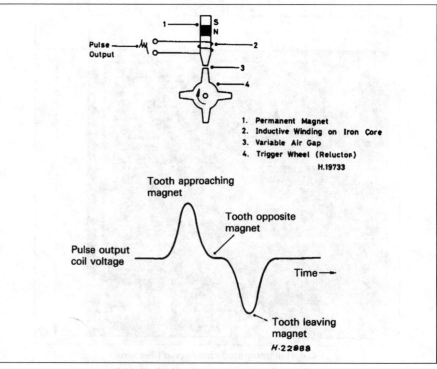

**5.10 Variable reluctance pulse generator**

**5.11a Crankshaft sensor (pick-up): note timing indentations**

**5.11b Sensor (pick-up) and shaped timing disc (Yamaha XJ900S)**

The idea of using the flywheel teeth occurs in certain models, in which a sensor counts the teeth as a series of impulses and can then pass this information to the computer module to read speed and estimate advance required.

11 The use of a pulse generator (sensor) working off the end of the crankshaft is shown in illustration 5.11a. Here the sensor picks up the indentations in the crankshaft flange. Another variation from the Yamaha XJ900S model (see illustration 5.11b) has the pulse generator pick-up coil mounted to sense the rotating plate bolted onto the end of the crankshaft.

The coils shown here have a resistance of 446 – 545 ohms indicating that they are wound with fine wire.

Note in illustration 5.11a that there must be an irregularity in the crankshaft indentations to indicate a set point such as top dead centre and this is provided by the semicircular cut-out shown.

## 6 Pulse shaping

1 The signals produced by sensors sometimes have a smooth change (see illustration 5.10) and are not sharp enough to produce a sudden clean cut-off of ignition coil current; additionally, the sensor voltage can vary with speed.

One solution is to pass the sensor voltage into a **Schmitt trigger** circuit which will produce a sharp square wave of constant peak voltage. The Schmitt trigger employs two transistors in which voltage signals from the second are sent back to the first (see illustration 6.1).

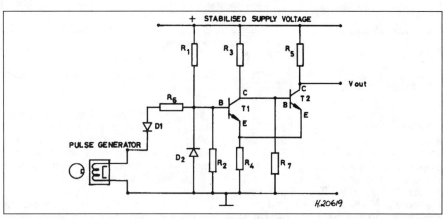

**6.1 Schmitt trigger**

2 This is known as feedback and results in an extremely rapid switching action from ON to OFF and vice versa (see illustration 6,2). As the pulse generator voltage reaches point A the Schmitt trigger circuit produces a sharp square wave which ends when the pulse generator voltage rises to the turn-on point B. This square wave gives a definite signal to the following circuits and is much more precise than the generated pulse wave.

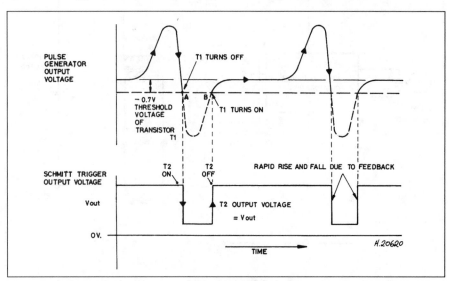

**6.2 Input/output of Schmitt trigger**

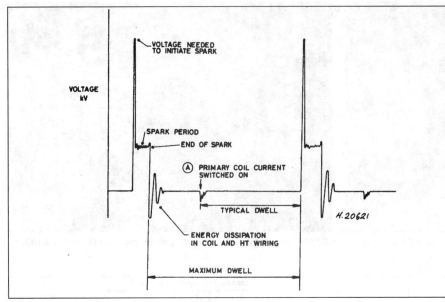

**7.2 Coil secondary voltage**

## 7 Dwell control

**1** In contact breaker ignition, the DWELL ANGLE (the angle over which the contacts are closed) is fixed by the shape of the lobe(s) and the gap setting of the contact points. The DWELL PERIOD (which is of course a *time*) is not fixed and will decrease as the engine speeds up and it is the dwell period in time that determines how far the ignition coil primary current can build up before the next spark. Electronic systems can ensure that the dwell period is much more precisely controlled.

**2** Illustration 7.2 shows a simplified waveform of coil secondary voltage. The high peak is the voltage provided by the ignition coil secondary winding; once the spark has begun, a lower, flat voltage plateau shows the voltage required to maintain the spark.

At point A the coil primary current is switched on and the typical dwell period begins. *Dwell control consists of moving point A back to the left as speed rises so that the coil primary current has time to rise.* The limit is the point of time when the spark ends. Circuit design to achieve this control need not concern us here but fuller detail is given in the Author's *'Automobile Electrical and Electronic Systems manual'* (Haynes). The important point is that *dwell can be controlled electronically*.

## 8 Constant energy ignition

**1** By monitoring the ignition primary current and feeding back the result as a voltage to the power transistors supplying the coil, control over the coil current is maintained over all engine conditions and variations of battery voltage. The results are as follows:

(a) *Primary current reaches a safe maximum value for a defined period and is limited to this value.*
(b) *Spark voltage is almost constant throughout the engine performance range.*

## 9 Electronic ignition

**1** Electronic ignition here means systems which incorporate some or all of the features of electronic control of sensor signal detection and processing, then producing correct ON OFF switching of primary current to one or more ignition coils.

Manufacturers' drawings generally show the sub-circuits described so far as one block diagram which may be labelled SPARK UNIT (for example), ECU (Electronic Control Unit) or IGNITER.

The spark units will each contain a pulse shaper, advance and dwell controls, an amplifier with a power stage for driving primary current into the ignition coils and a voltage stabiliser to ensure that a constant supply voltage is delivered to the electronic circuits irrespective of battery voltage variations.

**2** A basic block diagram (see illustration 9.2a) shows all this as an ignition timing control circuit and a Darlington-pair power drive (see Chapter 2). Note the technique of using two spark plugs in series with one double-ended ignition coil secondary winding; although both plugs will spark simultaneously, only one will fire a cylinder, the other spark being redundant in another cylinder not ready for combustion. This is called the wasted spark (see illustration 9.2b); note that in one plug the electrons jump from the centre electrode to the earth (ground) electrode and this is the 'correct' way. The electron current then

**9.2a Basic transistor ignition circuit**

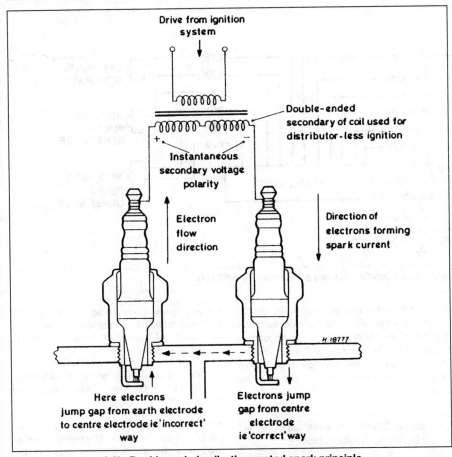

9.2b Double-ended coil – the wasted spark principle

*One plug fires in a cylinder under compression and produces a power stroke. The other plug spark occurs in another cylinder not ready for ignition – this is a **wasted spark**.*

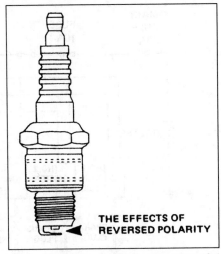

9.2c Electrode erosion due to reversed polarity

passes to the left-hand plug and jumps the 'wrong' way, remembering that ideally the plug centre electrode voltage should be negative so that erosion will take place from it

and not from the earth (ground) electrode. The effects of reversed polarity are shown in illustration 9.2c. Periodically changing over the two spark plugs will even out the wear.

Incidentally this is not a new idea and was used in Citroen 2CV cars among others.

Some early motorcycle twins used a rotating distributor to send the spark to two cylinders in correct order. This method suffered the disadvantages of mechanical wear and the loss of approximately 2kV of spark voltage at the distributor rotor arm.

**3** A Honda diagram (see illustration 9.3) shows a four cylinder arrangement as used on the CB750/900 and CBX750 models. Note that one ignition coil drives spark plugs in 1 and 3 cylinders, and the other coil drives 2 and 4 cylinders. To achieve this only two spark units and two pulse generators are needed.

**4** An interesting variation is the Honda ignition system used on the vee-four VFR750F

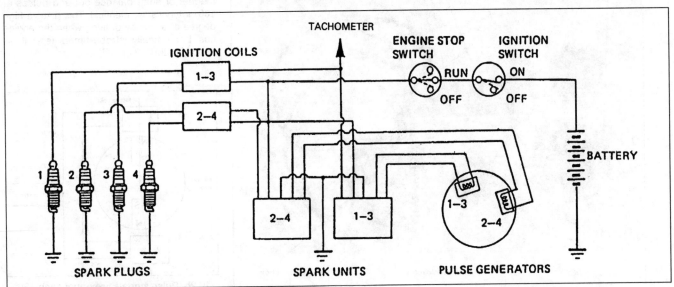

9.3 Four cylinder transistor ignition as used on the CB750/900 and CBX750 Honda models

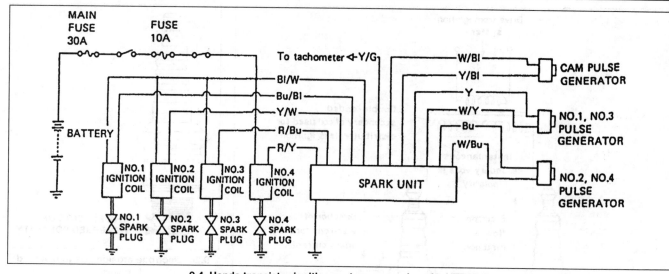

**9.4 Honda transistor ignition system as used on the VFR750F**

(see illustration 9.4). This uses one ignition coil per spark plug and a further pulse generator on the inlet front bank cam. Pulses from this sensor are used to indicate to the spark unit which coil to fire next in the ignition sequence. If the cam pulse generator fails, the engine will not run, so avoiding possible engine damage.

When the starter button is first pressed the engine turns over without firing until the spark unit receives its first signal from the cam pulse generator. Thus the ignition starts at the correct point in the cycle to match the engine rotation.

5 It is to be noted that some of these ignition circuits have provision for ignition advance with rise of engine speed only. No account is taken of load, ie how far the throttle is open and the result is an advance angle curve which is a good compromise but cannot be perfect.

## 10 Boyer Bransden aftermarket electronic ignition kits

1 Originally designed for Boyer's production racing 500 and 650 Triumph twins, this system gained deserved popularity for conversion of British machines from Lucas 4CA and 6CA contact breaker units to electronic ignition.

Today, units are supplied for a wide range of British, German and Japanese motorcycles.

2 The Mk III system converts a contact breaker twin into an electronic ignition machine with automatic speed advance. The camshaft-driven magnetic rotor turns beneath two sensor coils mounted at 180° to each other on a printed circuit board. These components replace the contact breaker mounting plate, the centrifugal advance unit and cam (see illustration 10.2a).

Any variation or misalignment of coils, magnet or shaft balance out and pulses at 180° intervals are identical. This gives a high degree of accuracy of firing when the engine has been finally strobe-timed (see illustration 10.2b).

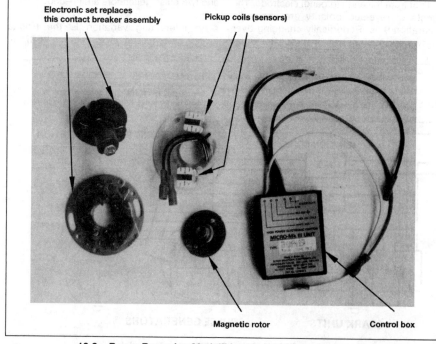

**10.2a Boyer-Bransden Mark III ignition system components**

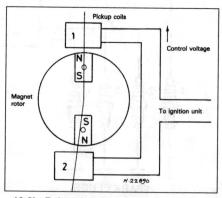

**10.2b Pulse signals are equal each 180° even with misalignment**

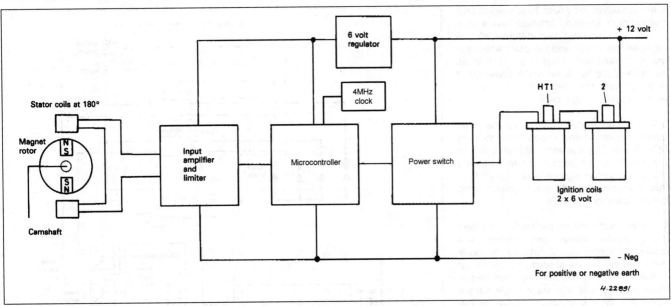

**10.4 Wiring diagram for Boyer-Bransden micro digital ignition system**

**3** There is now a 'Micro-digital' version which has several improvements and employs a miniature computing unit smaller than a postage stamp. The system samples engine speed every 50 rev/min and adjusts the advance to a pre-programmed advance/retard curve. It also regulates the energy to the coil(s) and a maximum rev/min limit can be set into the program. Starting speed and tickover stabilisation are also controlled by the unit.

**4** Illustration 10.4 shows the circuit elements. The power switch refers to the driver circuit which switches the coil primary current on or off. Two 6 volt coils in series are shown but a single 12 volt coil could be used.

## 11 Digital ignition

**1** The Boyer digital unit described in the previous section is an example of digital techniques which now are set to eliminate earlier methods entirely. Digital computers use on-off pulses for rapid calculation and control. Information is sent to the computer about the status of various factors on the motorcycle by one or more of the sensors which have been described earlier. Not all the sensor signals come in digital (ON/OFF) form and have to be converted into digital form before use.

**2** First generation computers control ignition advance by comparing the signal coming in from a speed and crankshaft position sensor with a program embedded in the computer. By interrogating the incoming signal at several

million times per second the computer is able to set the precise value of advance at all speeds and this yields a significant improvement in performance over earlier methods using centrifugal weights.

**3** The use of digital methods soon expanded so that other variables such as load were also measured and taken into account by the on-board computer.

Again, the key to this precision lies in the pre-programmed memory in the computer which has in store all correct ignition advance figures corresponding to engine speed and in some cases load and engine temperature among other possible parameters.

## 12 Ignition advance v engine design

**1** When an engine is first built, the manufacturer will run it over the speed range and find, experimentally, the best angle of ignition advance for each speed.

At every spot value of speed, the ignition advance required is noted and a graph (A) plotted like that shown in illustration 12.1. This procedure will then be repeated for a series of throttle opening positions giving rise to a family of ignition advance graphs.

**7**

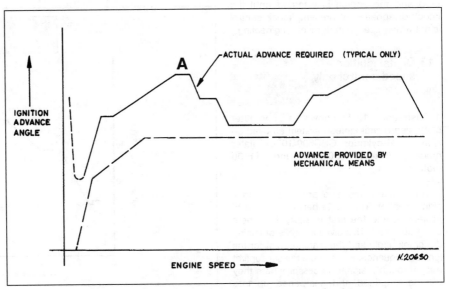

**12.1 A shortcoming of mechanical advance mechanisms**

**2** Ignition advance by centrifugal weights on a distributor or ignition camshaft gave a poor match, with at best two different slopes between low speed and the point where the graph flattens out. Illustration 12.1 is an example of the actual engine requirement at one load and the best that a mechanical advance system might provide.

**3** The digital system can store the ideal advance angle against speed in the memory ROM (Read Only Memory). Signals from the crankshaft speed sensor are fed into the microcomputer giving crankshaft speed; from this the computer will send ignition firing signals to the ignition coils.

**4** It is not sufficient for the sensor to inform the computer about speed alone. The crankshaft position is also required and this is measured either by a special position-sensor or using a rotating reluctor which has certain teeth missing to signal via a single sensor where the piston is located. This can be Top Dead Centre (TDC) or sometimes 90° BTDC.

The computer will provide an advance curve which matches closely the advance curve produced by the makers in their tests for maximum output. The advance set by the ECU however must not be greater than the ideal values because too much advance will produce **engine knock** (see Chapter 3).

**5** The working curve eventually placed in the computer (ECU) memory will closely mirror the ideal curve but with an allowance for error and wear. When an engine is too far advanced, knock occurs and this is highly undesirable (see Chapter 3). We shall see later that in advanced digital systems a knock sensor is used to detect the onset of undesirable knock. When this occurs the knock sensor sends a signal voltage to the ECU and the engine is retarded until the knock disappears. At present, knock control is not widely used in motorcycle engineering.

## 13 Digital ignition – speed control only

**1** Illustration 13.1 shows a computer controlled digital ignition system as used on Honda's 4-cylinder CBR600/1000F (later models), VFR400R/750/750R, and ST1100 models.

The reluctor has nine projections and a single sensor. The angle between the ninth projection and the first is 120°, the others being 30° apart. This gives a means of finding the crank angle and the starting point for the ignition sequence. Pulses from the sensor first pass through a signal processor where they will be amplified and sharpened up into square-topped pulses.

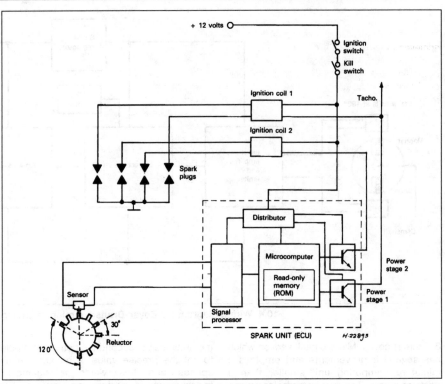

**13.1 Honda's digital ignition system**

**2** As the 120° gap passes the sensor, no pulse voltage will be generated; when the first of the nine teeth passes under the sensor, the firing sequence commences. The 120° gap resets the computer (like pushing the reset button on a tripmeter) and the sequence repeats.

The rate at which teeth pass the sensor is measured by the computer as engine speed. Information stored in the ROM (Read Only Memory) is interrogated and a figure for

ignition timing will be retrieved and passed to one of the two power stages and an ignition coil.

Any engine can be controlled by this system by changing the ROM and position of the sensors.

**3** Ignition timing will be closely that required for optimum engine performance throughout the complete speed range, a typical curve being shown in illustration 13.3.

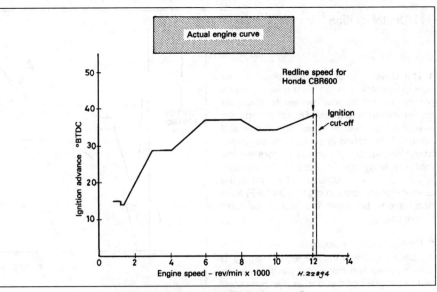

**13.3 Advance curve (Digital control)**

**4** Ignition cut-out provision is built into the memory to prevent engine overspeed. This is achieved in two stages and in the case of the CBR600F the computer cuts off ignition in cylinders 2 and 3 at 11,900 rev/min and cuts off cylinders 1 and 4 at approximately 12,500 rev/min. 'Redline' speed for the CBR600F is 12,000 rev/min.

**5** To prevent the ignition coils overheating if the engine stops and the ignition switch remains on, an inhibitor circuit in the computer will cut power to the coils below a pre-determined speed (90 – 110 rev/min).

## 14 Mapped digital ignition

**1** If a family of ignition advance/speed graphs were plotted separately for each position of throttle opening, there would be a large number of sheets to look up. Imagine them compressed together; the resulting block of graphs is now three dimensional as shown in illustration 14.1. Here, three values are displayed. Ignition advance vertically, load and speed horizontally at right angles. Two spot values of load and speed are shown entered by the arrows. Where they cross on the horizontal grid, erect a vertical line to cut the solid surface. The height gives advance angle. The surface is like a 3 dimensional contour map and for this reason is known as **mapped ignition**. In practice the ignition map may be made up of 1000 – 4000 individual recallable ignition angle advance points.

**2** It is interesting to see the difference between the optimum three dimensional advance curve (map) and the best that might be obtained by a mechanical contact breaker advance system (see illustration 14.2). The electronic ignition map is more complex than that of the mechanical system and is therefore a closer representation of the required ideal.

**3** The condition of overrun is programmed specially for the purpose of fuel shut off above a certain speed when coasting downhill. A switch to signal this condition may be linked to the throttle.

**4** When the engine runs, sensor signals enter the ignition control unit (or Spark Unit, igniter or ECU) and are processed to give digital pulses.

These signal pulse voltages are then interpreted against the pre-programmed Read Only Memory (ROM) which fixes the correct ignition timing. Firing pulses are then sent to the transistor drive stages (usually Darlington Pairs) which operate the ignition coils.

## 15 Computerised ignition processing

**1** We have looked at the speed-only digital control of ignition; now we move a stage further forward to consider computer control of ignition involving extra engine parameters.

**2** Information may be fed into the computer in the form of electrical signals representing some of the following:

*(a) Engine speed and crank position.*
*(b) Engine load.*
*(c) Coolant temperature (on liquid-cooled motorcycles).*
*(d) Battery voltage.*
*(e) Inlet air temperature.*
*(f) Knock detector (may be found on more advanced systems).*
*(g) Road speed is measured and compared with the engine speed to tell the computer which gear is being used (Triumph digital system).*
*(h) Throttle position (Yamaha XJ900S).*

**3** Since computers handle digital pulses only, any electrical signals which are constant or slowly varying (ie analogue signals) will have to be converted to a corresponding train of

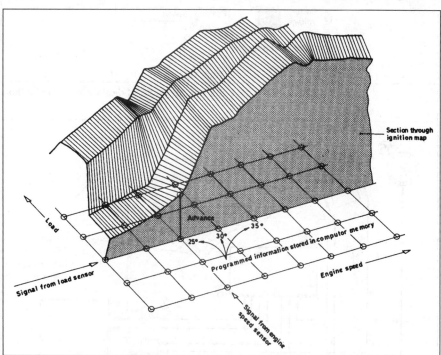

**14.1  Ignition map and stored information concept**

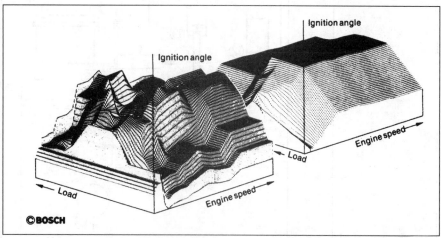

**14.2  Optimised electronic ignition advance map (left) compared with the ignition map of a mechanical spark advance system (right)**

**7**

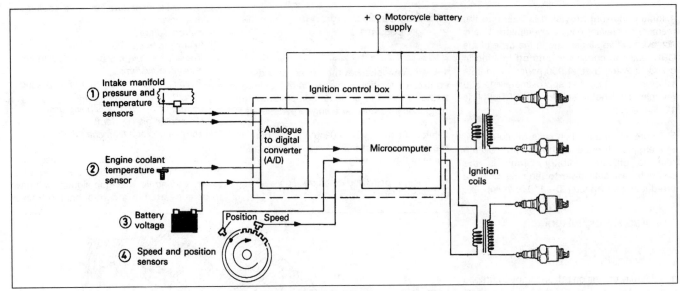

**15.4 Schematic layout of digital electronic ignition system**

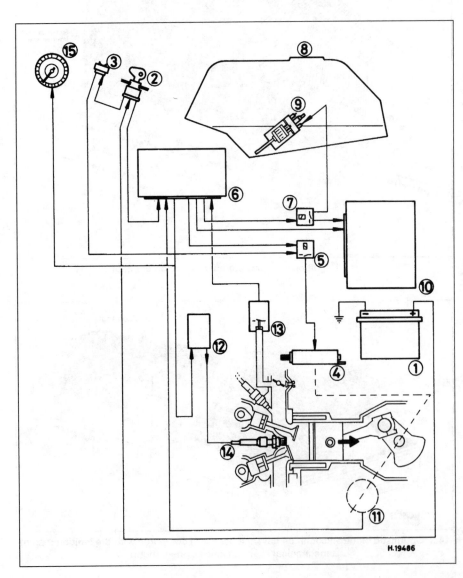

square-topped digital pulses by an AD converter (AD means analogue to digital – see Chapter 2).

**4** Engine speed/position signals are usually in pulse form and require no AD conversion but usually need shaping, while load, temperature and battery voltage are in analogue form and need AD conversion.

Some of the variables listed in paragraph 2 above are now looked at in more detail by reference to illustration 15.4.

### Engine load

**5** Inlet manifold vacuum gives a measure of load and a pressure sensor of the aneroid capsule type can be used. This gives an indirect method of measuring airflow and so is linked to the load condition of the engine. (An aneroid capsule is similar to that in a barometer with a sensor attached to measure the bellows movement with change of air pressure or vacuum.)

**15.6a Ignition system components on the BMW K75 and 100 models**

1 Battery
2 Ignition switch
3 Starter button
4 Starter motor
5 Starter relay
6 Ignition control unit
7 Injector relay
8 Fuel tank
9 Fuel pump
10 Fuel injection control unit
11 Ignition trigger assembly
12 Ignition HT coil
13 Vacuum switch (where fitted)
14 Spark plug
15 Tachometer

H.19486

**15.6b Throttle position sensor (Yamaha XJ900S)**

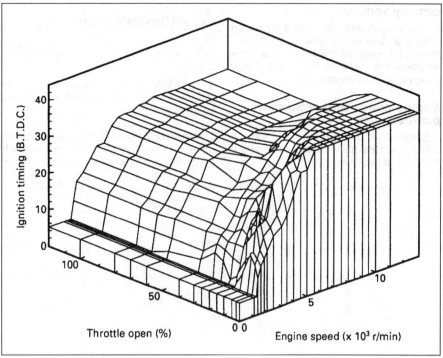

**15.6c Ignition timing map (Yamaha XJ900S)**

Ignition timing (B.T.D.C.) — Throttle open (%) — Engine speed (x 10³ r/min)

**6** If air temperature is measured electrically and this signal also is fed to the computer, an allowance can be made for variation of air density with temperatures. This information is particularly needed for fuel injected engines. It is air *mass* flow that we really want to measure and there are better ways of measurement (see Chapter 8 for details).

Remember:
Air Mass = Air volume x air density

An interesting way of dealing with engine load in the part load condition occurs with pre 1985 BMW K100 models in which a vacuum switch was located in the inlet manifold (see illustration 15.6a). On part load the switch brought in a second advance curve but in practice this had so little effect that it was omitted on later models.

In the case of the Yamaha XJ900S the throttle position is measured by a potentiometer located on the carburettor spindle and the output fed into the spark unit (see illustration 15.6b). The mapping for this machine shows one axis as the percentage throttle opening (see illustration 15.6c).

### Engine temperature

**7** Temperature sensors are usually of the semiconductor type, known as thermistors, which have displaced earlier thermocouple units for situations below 200°C (400°F).

The bead of semiconductor material has a marked negative temperature coefficient of resistance, and a working range of at least -20°C to +130°C. It is suitable for measuring coolant temperature and is mounted in a screw-in capsule (see illustration 15.7) in a coolant channel in the cylinder block if the engine is liquid cooled. The sensitivity is good for accurate temperature measurements to within 0.05°C.

**7**

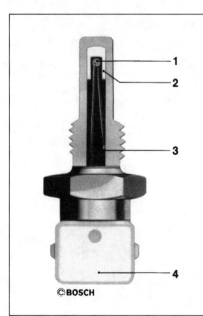

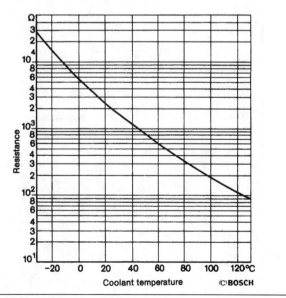

1 Negative temperature coefficient semiconductor resistor (NTC bead)
2 Insulation
3 Sealing compound
4 Electrical connection

*The graph shows the resistance change with temperature of NTC bead (negative temperature coefficient)*

Resistance (Ω) — Coolant temperature (°C) — ©BOSCH

©BOSCH

**15.7 Engine temperature sensor**

### Battery voltage

**8** This is a correcting quantity; if the battery voltage deviates from a set standard, the time allowed for energising the coil (dwell period) is lengthened or shortened so that constant energy conditions are obtained.

### Engine speed and crankshaft position

**9** Sensors of the Hall type or variable reluctance type have already been met in Section 5 of this Chapter.

### 16 Ignition and fuelling

**1** In Chapter 3 we have seen that both ignition and fuelling affect performance and pollution levels.

Along with the developments in ignition has come an increasing use of electronically controlled fuel injection, giving much better use of fuel than is usually achieved with a carburettor.

**2** Fuel injection is explained in the following Chapter and it is interesting to see that initially ignition and fuel injection were controlled as separate units. As both ignition and fuelling systems developed into digital form, it was a logical step to have both controlled by the same computer (ECU).

When the two were so combined, a new term 'Engine Management' came into use and this is developed further in Chapter 9.

# Chapter 8
# Fuel injection

## Contents

8

### 1 Fuel metering

**1** The petrol/gasoline engine requires a supply of fuel in the form of a vapour of air and fuel in a ratio within the range 12:1 to 17:1, the first being a rich mixture and the second a weak or lean mixture.

From the beginning of petrol/gasoline engine technology this has been achieved, not always with precision, by the carburettor. Now anti-pollution regulations require exact metering of fuel, particularly where catalytic converters are used, and have brought about a number of fuel injection system designs for motorcycles.

**2** The early work on fuel injection is credited to the USA Bendix company who produced a working system in the 1950-60 decade. At that stage the equipment involved was too bulky for use on motorcycles but with the parallel developments in electronics eventually there emerged the EFI (electronic fuel injection) units which are now available. The principal advantages of fuel injection are as follows:

(a) *Increased power output per unit of displacement.*
(b) *Higher torque at low engine speeds.*
(c) *Improved cold start, warm-up and acceleration.*
(d) *Lower pollution levels from the exhaust.*
(e) *Lower fuel consumption.*

Disadvantages of the carburettor can be summed up as follows:

(a) *Volumetric efficiency is limited by the venturi constriction and fuel mixture pre-heating requirement:*

Volumetric efficiency =

$$\frac{\text{Volume of mixture actually taken in}}{\text{Swept volume}}$$

*and is about 70% using conventional carburation.*
(b) *It is virtually impossible to distribute the mixture evenly between cylinders. One result is the use of a richer mixture than might otherwise be required so that the cylinder(s) receiving the weakest mixture do not suffer from detonation.*
(c) *In cold conditions, fuel wets the walls of the induction manifold causing running difficulties.*

### 2 Fuel injection

**1** There are several ways in which fuel may be injected; the first consideration is whether injection should be directly into each cylinder (direct injection) or into the airstream before entering the cylinder via the inlet valve (indirect injection) (see illustration 2.1).

**Direct injection** has been ruled out in present designs because of complexity. Fuel would need to be injected at high pressure by

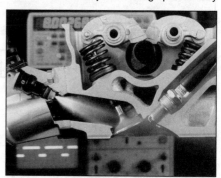

**2.1 Indirect fuel injection**

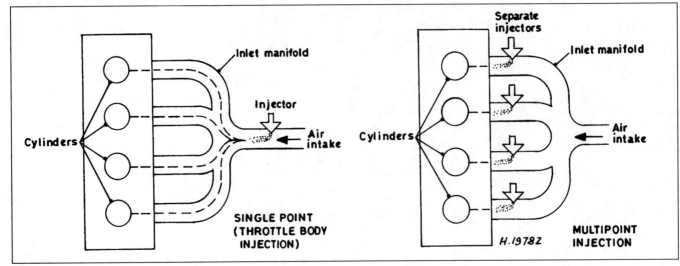

**2.3 Positions for fuel injectors**

an expensive pump; also the injection pulses would need to be synchronised with the engine cycle. However, new direct fuel injection designs have appeared in the car field and as so often happens the motorcycle will quite possibly follow.

**Indirect injection**, in which the fuel is sprayed at one or more points in the air intake system, operates at lower pressures, and the injectors can be triggered simultaneously with no engine-cycle synchronisation.

**2** With indirect injection there are then two ways of supplying the fuel to the injectors:

**Continuous injection** – Fuel is sprayed continuously while the engine is running, the quantity of fuel being governed by changes in the fuel pressure. However, the ratio of idle to full load fuel consumption can be 1:60 with high accuracy at the low end being required.

Pump and system design is complex and is not a favoured option.

**Intermittent injection** – Fuel is sprayed at regular intervals at constant pressure (see later). The quantity of fuel is determined by the length of spraying time. These spraying pulses may take place EITHER without regard to the opening of the inlet valves (simultaneous) OR being correctly phased in relation to the opening of the inlet valves (sequential).

**3** Finally, designers have to choose between the use of only one injector per engine (single-point injection) or one injector per cylinder (multi-point injection) (see illustration 2.3).

**4** Past and present designs favour multi-point injection on motorcycles, but there is no technical reason why single-point injection should not be used in the future.

The single point injector valve is located above the throttle valve and is a relatively low-cost system. Because the injector is so located it is sometimes known as throttle-body injection (TBI). Multi-point injection is in use in the majority of systems, particularly where the extra cost is not an overriding consideration. Whichever method is used, the basic principle is as in illustration 2.4.

The present favoured system therefore is **indirect, intermittent, multipoint fuel injection**.

## 3 Fuel injection control

**1** Bosch have undoubtedly led the way in vehicle fuel injection and in earlier motorcycles the injection system ran separately from the ignition control. As we will see later, when they are combined, the term for the single control is **engine management**. Some of what follows may relate to separate systems and some to the fuel injection part of complete engine management units.

'Jetronic' was the name used by Bosch for earlier units which were separate from the ignition as in the BMW K100 and 75 series.

The latest arrangement is the Motronic MA2.2 version used on the BMW four valve R and K series motorcycles. All Bosch systems which are called Motronic (there are several) have combined fuel and ignition control.

**2** There are now designs from other manufacturers including the Sagem system fitted to Triumph motorcycles, which use multipoint sequential electronic fuel injection on the T595 Daytona and T509 Speed Triple models.

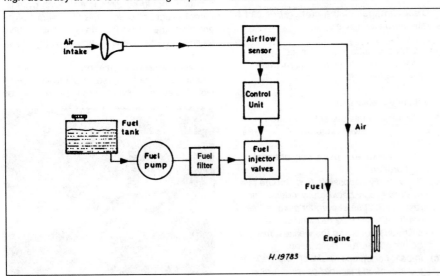

**2.4 Principle of fuel injection**

4.4a Location of Throttle Position Sensor (TPS) – BMW R Series

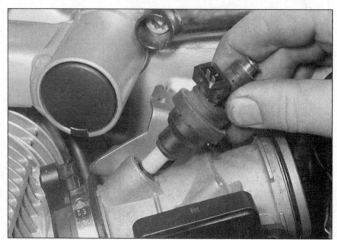

4.4b Location of injector in the throttle body – BMW R Series

4.5a Throttle position switch located on rear end of butterfly assembly

4.5b Air temperature sensor in the mouth of the airflow meter

8

All work on the same fundamental principles and the main differences are in the method of airflow measurement.

In this Chapter we shall concentrate on fuel injection and look at combined systems of fuelling and ignition in Chapter 9.

## 4  Air metering

1 In order that the electronic control system can provide the correct amount of fuel it is necessary to measure the amount of air taken by the engine. This is the key point around which the subsequent operation works.

### *Throttle potentiometers*

2 The simplest method is to measure the angle of throttle opening and this is done by having a potentiometer on the end of the throttle butterfly shaft (see Chapter 2 for

information on potentiometers). While in principle a simple method, it is by itself a crude way of measuring air mass flow since it assumes that air intake will always be proportional to the throttle opening.

3 In the Triumph (Sagem) system the output voltage from the throttle potentiometer is fed into the ECU together with an engine speed sensor signal and two sensors in the air intake box to register air density. Air density is calculated from a barometric pressure sensor and from an air temperature sensor, bearing in mind that air density varies with temperature as well as pressure. Ducati use speed and throttle angle and Yamaha have used speed and air density as metering factors.

4 Bosch Motronic, as used in the four valve BMW motorcycles, uses a throttle potentiometer and some models also use a Lambda sensor in the exhaust when a catalytic converter is fitted. The Lambda

sensor (also called an oxygen sensor) will send a correcting signal to the ECU if the excess air factor is incorrect. This means that any error in the measurement of air intake is automatically corrected by the ECU and so the accuracy of the throttle potentiometer is not important within limits (see Chapter 9).

A BMW throttle position sensor is shown in illustration 4.4a. It is important not to remove the sensor from the body as its position is pre-set and any disturbance will make information sent to the Motronic inaccurate. Illustration 4.4b shows the location of the injector in the throttle body.

5 Other Motronic versions use simply a throttle position switch (see illustration 4.5a) which registers only whether the throttle is closed, fully open or somewhere in between. An air temperature capsule is shown in illustration 4.5b. This is located in the mouth of the airflow meter (BMW K100/75).

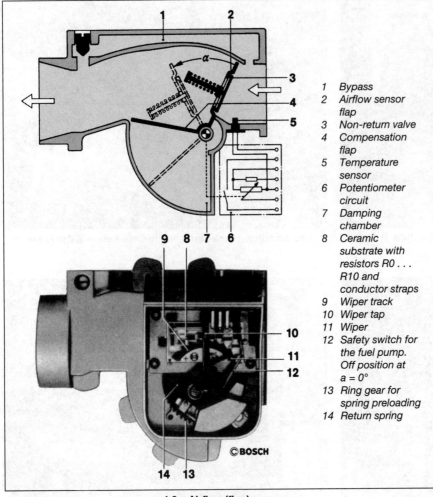

1 Bypass
2 Airflow sensor flap
3 Non-return valve
4 Compensation flap
5 Temperature sensor
6 Potentiometer circuit
7 Damping chamber
8 Ceramic substrate with resistors R0 . . . R10 and conductor straps
9 Wiper track
10 Wiper tap
11 Wiper
12 Safety switch for the fuel pump. Off position at a = 0°
13 Ring gear for spring preloading
14 Return spring

**4.6a  Airflow (flap) sensor**

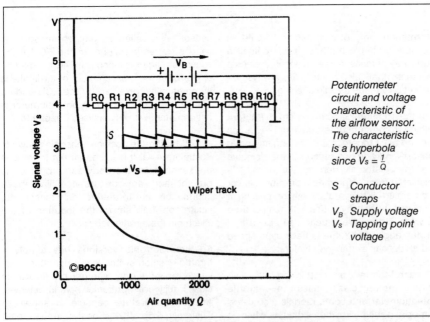

Potentiometer circuit and voltage characteristic of the airflow sensor. The characteristic is a hyperbola since $V_s = \frac{1}{Q}$

S  Conductor straps
$V_B$  Supply voltage
$V_s$  Tapping point voltage

**4.6b  Airflow meter output characteristic**

## Airflap sensors

**6** The airflow (flap) sensor which has been in use for some years is shown in illustration 4.6a. It is located in the air intake and the flap (2) will rotate due to airflow against a spring return. It is balanced by a similar flap in a damping chamber (7) which not only balances the main flap but damps out any tendency to oscillate.

On the flap spindle outside the airflow chamber is an arm with a wiping contact on a resistor potentiometer (see illustration 4.6b). The voltage picked up by this wiping contact corresponds to the angle of the flap and this in turn is a measure of airflow.

The signal voltage is fed into the Electronic Control Unit (ECU) along with signals from other sensors to determine the fuel injection.

The potentiometer is made up of a series of resistors R0 to R10 of ceramic-metal (cermet), connected by narrow conductors to the wiper track which is of high impedance and hard wearing.

Signal voltage is high when the air quantity Q is low and vice versa, resulting in a graph as shown.

**7** The airflap sensor is simple and reliable but suffers from the disadvantage that it measures the *volume* of intake air. Air to fuel ratios are in terms of mass (weight) of air and the flap meter readings will require correction for air density. An air temperature sensor is mounted at the air intake to the flap sensor, the signal being processed by the ECU to obtain a corrected figure for air mass.

**8** The flap is bypassed by a channel for idle air and an adjusting screw partially closes an orifice to regulate the idle mixture (see illustration 4.6a item 1).

## Air mass-flow meters

**9** The disadvantage of the airflap sensor lies in the fact that it measures volume of air intake and not the mass (weight). Errors are introduced according to altitude, since the density of air falls with increasing altitude (Remember: Mass = Volume x Density). In addition, the airflap sensor is subject to slight pulsation errors due to sudden opening or closing of inlet valves. It is costly to make and is not used on current models.

**10** One solution lies in the hot wire air mass meter which will measure the air mass directly, independent of air density (altitude) changes (see illustrations 4.10a and 4.10b). In addition, there is no pulsation error. This type

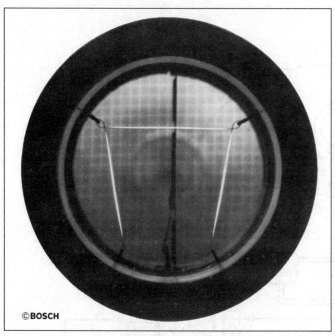

©BOSCH

**4.10a Hot wire air mass flow meter**

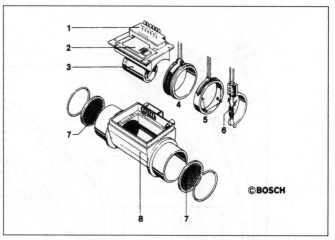

©BOSCH

**4.10b Hot wire air mass flow meter assembly**

1 Printed board
2 Hybrid circuit. In addition to the resistors of the bridge circuit, it also contains the control circuit for maintaining a constant temperature and the self-cleaning circuit
3 Inner tube
4 Precision resistor
5 Hot wire element
6 Temperature compensation resistor
7 Guard
8 Housing

of sensor uses a heated wire of 70 mm diameter mounted in a measuring tube in the incoming airstream before the throttle.

**11** The hot wire air mass meter works on the constant temperature principle. The hot platinum wire is one arm of a Wheatstone Bridge (see Chapter 2) which is kept in balance by changing the heating current so that the temperature (about 100°C, 212°F) of the hot wire is a constant amount above that of the incoming air (see illustration 4.11).

As airflow increases, the wire cools and the resistance falls. This unbalances the bridge, the difference voltage between A and B being fed into an amplifier, the output of which supplies the bridge so heating up the wire and increasing its resistance until balance is restored. The range of heating current is from 500 – 1200mA.

The increase of current will flow through the precision resistor $R_3$ and the voltage drop across it is read as a signal by the ECU as a measure of air mass flow as it then calculates the amount of fuel to be injected.

**12** The hot wire sensor is presently used in automobiles but is included here because it may well appear in motorcycle fuel injection designs of the future. However, it should be noted that the cost of precise metering may mean that airflaps and hot wire methods will not be so important if the use of the Lambda sensor becomes more widespread. This is because the signal feedback from the oxygen sensor can cover up some inaccuracies in the air metering unit. There will be more on this topic in Chapter 9.

## 5 Bosch LE-Jetronic fuel injection

**1** This Bosch system is used on the BMW K-series engines. Illustration 5.1 shows the system fitted to the K75 models and serves here as a good model to explain the principles of intermittent multi-point fuel injection.

### Operation

**2** Fuel and air are admitted as a correct mixture with engine speed and intake air volume as the main controlling factors.

The volume of air supplied to form the combustion mixture is drawn in by the engine and varied by the angle of the throttle butterflies (17). The fuel injection system then supplies the correct amount of fuel in the form

**4.11 Hot wire air mass meter electrical circuit**

$I$    Hot wire current to maintain wire temperature
$V_D$    Signal voltage to electronic control unit (ECU)

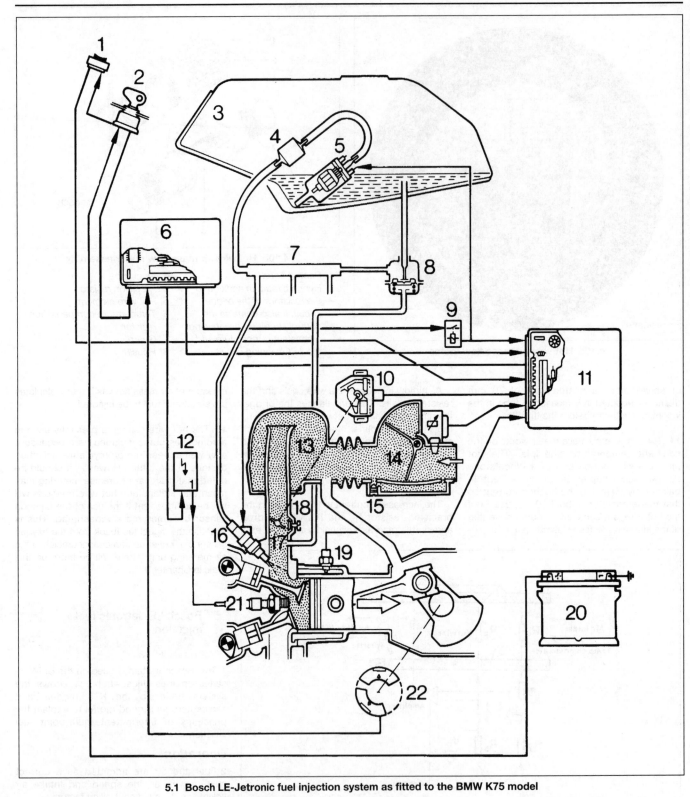

**5.1  Bosch LE-Jetronic fuel injection system as fitted to the BMW K75 model**

1  Starter switch
2  Ignition switch
3  Fuel tank
4  Fuel filter
5  Fuel pump
6  Ignition control unit

7  Fuel supply rail
8  Pressure regulator
9  Injection relay
10  Throttle butterfly switch
11  Electronic Control Unit
    (ECU)

12  HT coil
13  Air collector
14  Airflow meter
15  Bypass air screw
16  Injector
17  Throttle butterfly

18  Idle adjusting screw
19  Coolant temperature sensor
20  Battery
21  Spark plug
22  Hall-effect trigger

of a spray from an injector (16) located in the inlet tract (see illustration 5.2).

**3** The three injectors (one for each cylinder) have nozzles which are opened and closed by solenoids wound in the injector units (see illustration 5.3). All three injectors are electrically connected in parallel and open at the same time once per revolution of the crankshaft.

When open, fuel is sprayed at a pressure of 2.5 bar (36 lbf/in²) until the electric signal current in the solenoids is cut off by the control unit, the 'on' period being between 1.5 and 9 milliseconds (ms). The fuel spray mixes with the incoming air as both move towards the inlet valve, giving a precisely metered combustion mixture. The complete system has three areas as follows:

### Fuel system

**4** Fuel is pumped from the tank by a roller-cell pump (5) through a fuel filter (4) into a fuel rail (7) at the end of which is a fuel pressure regulator (8).

In order to keep the injector pressure differential constant despite variations of inlet manifold depression with load, the fuel pressure regulator senses the difference between pumping pressure and that of the inlet manifold.

Excess fuel is returned to the tank, the continuous flushing keeping the fuel cool and avoiding pockets of fuel vapour.

Filtering of the fuel is important in case dirty fuel gets into the tank; the filter has a 10 μm pore-size paper cartridge requiring eventual replacement. Details of the roller cell pump,

**5.2 Injector showing renewal of O-ring**

pressure regulator and the fuel filter are shown in illustration 5.4.

The petrol (gasoline) has a secondary duty of both lubricating and cooling the roller cell pump, the fuel flowing through the motor, including the brushes and across the armature. It is important never to run the pump without an adequate fuel supply.

### Air intake system

**5** The airflow meter (14) has already been described in this Chapter (airflap type). As the airflow varies so will the angle of the airflap (14). A potentiometer is mounted on the airflap spindle, and a voltage picked off by a sliding contact connected to the spindle will signal the quantity Q of air being taken in by the engine.

The airflow meter has a by-pass screw (15) which may be adjusted externally and is used to set the CO emission of the exhaust gases. One important feature of EFI systems is that they are sensitive to air leaks in the intake tract; the smallest leak will produce serious malfunction of the engine.

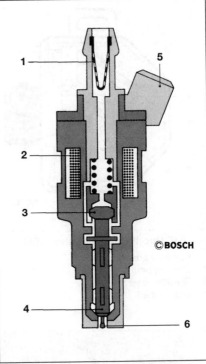

**5.3 Fuel injector cross-section**

*With no current in the solenoid, the needle valve is held against its seating by a spring. When the coil is energised the needle valve is lifted 0.1 mm. The pintle atomises the fuel into a fine spray*

1  *Filter*
2  *Solenoid winding*
3  *Solenoid armature*
4  *Needle valve*
5  *Electrical connection*
6  *Pintle*

**8**

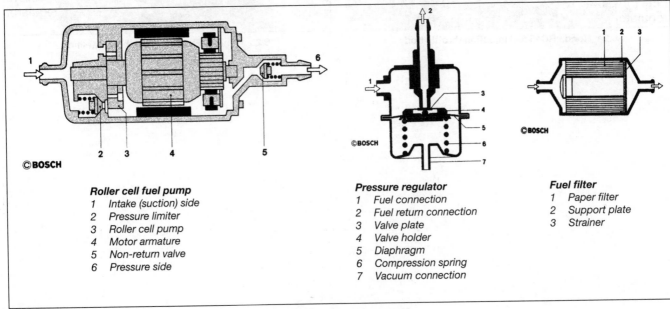

### Roller cell fuel pump
1  *Intake (suction) side*
2  *Pressure limiter*
3  *Roller cell pump*
4  *Motor armature*
5  *Non-return valve*
6  *Pressure side*

### Pressure regulator
1  *Fuel connection*
2  *Fuel return connection*
3  *Valve plate*
4  *Valve holder*
5  *Diaphragm*
6  *Compression spring*
7  *Vacuum connection*

### Fuel filter
1  *Paper filter*
2  *Support plate*
3  *Strainer*

**5.4 Fuel system components**

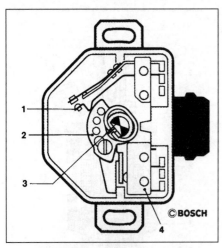

**5.6 Throttle butterfly valve switch**

1 Full-load contact
2 Contact path
3 Throttle valve shaft
4 Idle contact

## Electronic control unit (ECU)

6 The volume of fuel injected per crankshaft revolution into all the intake tracts simultaneously is fixed by the time over which the injectors are open. To control this open period, an Electronic Control Unit (ECU) (11) passes current pulses to the injector solenoid windings (16) which pull open the nozzles. The time length of these pulses depends upon the following five factors:

(a) Engine speed information from the Hall-effect trigger (22) via the ignition control unit (6).
(b) Special cold start and normal start programmes initiated by operating the starter switch (1).
(c) Engine load information from the throttle butterfly switch (10). To achieve maximum power output on full load, the engine must have a richer mixture than when on part load. This switch signals to the ECU (11) that enrichment is required (see illustration 5.6). The idling state is shown when the idle switch closes.

(d) Air volume as indicated by the airflow meter (14).
(e) Engine temperature is measured by the coolant temperature sensor screwed into a coolant channel (19).

## 6 Keihin fuel injection

1 This company, well known for carburettors, also supply injection equipment for Japanese motorcycles. The working principles are the same as in other systems but with interesting variations in detail.

2 The illustrations 6.2a and b show the Honda RC45 throttle body supplying four injectors from a single fuel rail and the VFR800 throttle body using twin fuel rails connected in series. Note the position of the fuel pressure regulators at the entrance to the fuel rails. The throttle angle sensor is shown clearly in 6.2b.

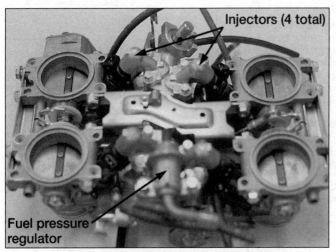

**6.2a Honda RC45 fuel injection throttle body**

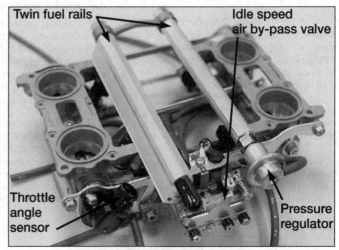

**6.2b Honda VFR800 throttle body (Keihin)**

# Chapter 9
# Engine management

## Contents

**9**

## 1  Combined control of ignition and fuelling

**1** The motorcycle engine has two supplying units for the production of power, one being the supply of atomised fuel in correct quantity and correct air:fuel ratio, the other being the supply of an igniting spark at the correct timing. For most of this century, these two provisions of fuelling and sparks have been dealt with separately. However, Chapter 3 *Ignition and Combustion* shows that the relationships of optimum power, fuel economy and exhaust pollution involve both fuelling and ignition.

**2** Digital ignition circuits use a microcomputer in the ignition control unit and this computer is capable of controlling other tasks. It was logical to use this spare capacity for controlling fuelling also.

Up to this stage of development, fuel injection control units, although fully electronic, did not use digital methods but, instead, analogue multivibrator technology, and these were not compatible with the ignition control boxes.

**3** Bosch then developed a digital electronic control system for fuel injection and combined it with the digital ignition control to form a single controller – this is the Motronic system. It uses one control unit to sense the necessary engine conditions and to produce ignition pulses and fuel injector pulses accordingly. Developed originally for the car world it has now been successfully used on the 16v BMW K1 and K100RS models and the latest version Motronic 2.2 is on the four valve R and K series.

**4** Other manufacturers have followed and as examples Yamaha have used full engine management on the GTS1000 and Honda employ the Keihin design for their RC45FI and VFR800 models. It is interesting that the Honda RC45FI has two ECUs, one for ignition and one for fuel injection, but they use the same sensors so really are together, a full engine management system. The VFR800 has a combined ECU and is an *open loop* design for the UK but in Germany the model has 2 Lambda sensors and is therefore a *closed-loop* system (see Section 3 below for an explanation of open loop and closed-loop). Triumph use the SAGEM system on the Daytona T595 and the Speed Triple T509 models and do not use Lambda sensor feedback, that is, the system is open loop.

## 2  Performance mapping

**1** Three-dimensional mapping has been discussed in Chapter 7 to explain the interlink between engine speed, load and ignition (advance) angle.

**2** With the memory capacity available to the microcomputer, further sets of three-dimensional information can be stored which

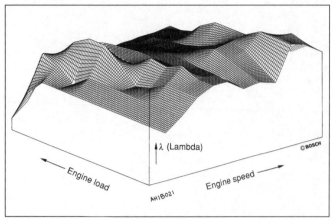

2.2a Lambda map

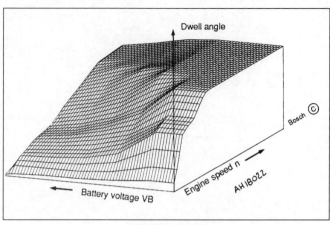

2.2b Dwell map

relate to additional variables. Two examples are shown in illustrations 2.2a and 2.2b. The Lambda map shows how engine speed and load relate to λ, the Lambda factor. (Remember Lambda λ is 1.0 for air:fuel ratio of 14.7:1. Higher than 1.0 is a weaker mixture and lower is a richer mixture.) The value of Lambda λ is critical to keep pollution levels low and assumes special importance where a catalytic converter is fitted.

Another set of information which a control unit may store is the relationship between engine speed, battery voltage and dwell angle (see illustration 2.2b). It is possible in the more complex engine management units to store and use other inter-dependent quantities such as engine speed, load and warm-up enrichment.

The sensors which measure all these variables are often the same type used in both fuel-injection and ignition: it is a matter of natural development that one set of sensors and one control unit should suffice.

### 3 Open- and closed-loop control

**1** When the engine maps are drawn up the results are stored in the permanent memory (ROM) of the micro-processor. The engine will be operated according to the figures in store for any value of speed or load. However, an assumption is made that the engine remains in the same condition as when the performance maps were plotted.

**2** This cannot be so, for as the engine wears there will be wear on the piston, valve guides and throttle spindles so that the air intake, for example, will soon become different from what the micro-processor believes it to be

from the sensor inputs. This situation is one of **open-loop control**, meaning that there is no check on the actual performance of the engine or the actual exhaust emission. Similarly, the ignition performance could go off tune resulting in loss of power (retard) or engine knock if the errors result in advancing ignition too far.

**3** The solution to these possible problems lies in measuring the performance with sensors, the signals from which can be fed back to the Electronic Control Unit (ECU). The ECU can then adjust timing or mixture to standard values.

**4** Engine knock can be detected by a vibration sensor attached to the cylinder block, and incorrect mixture by a Lambda sensor situated in the exhaust gas stream. Feedback by one or both of these sensors gives a **closed-loop** control system, which holds the required values throughout the life of the engine and takes into account engine deterioration with time.

**5** At the time of writing, knock sensors appear to be used in the automobile and not on the motorcycle, but the technology of knock control is firmly established and could well appear in a motorcycle engine management system at any time. Lambda sensors are used for closed-loop control in fuelling and, as stated, find special use in exhaust systems with catalytic converters.

For all the case for Lambda control, open loop systems without it produce excellent efficiency results for engines in good condition.

**6** In the next two Sections we will look at the main features of engine management equipment from examples of popular motorcycles.

### 4 Bosch Motronic – BMW 16-valve models

**1** This digital control was the first engine management system applied to a production motorcycle.

Referring to illustration 4.1, note that the four-cylinder engine has ignition and fuel injection controlled by the single Motronic control unit (12). The system is of the open-loop type, but a closed-loop version is available with a catalytic converter and Lambda exhaust sensor (see Section 8).

**2** The vertical row of boxes on the left side of the Motronic control unit (12) are signal processors. Inputs from sensors are fed into signal processor circuits to ensure that all outputs to the computer are in the form of digital pulses. In the case of the Hall ignition sensors (2), the input will be in pulse form already and only shaping will be required.

Other inputs may be steady or slowly varying voltages; these are said to be in analogue form and will need to be converted into equivalent digital values by an analogue to digital (AD) converter. AD converters constitute those signal processor boxes where inputs are analogue.

The digital outputs of the signal processor boxes are fed to the input/output rail for transporting to the main heart of the computer.

**3** The ROM (Read Only Memory) contains performance maps for optimum engine performance corresponding to any possible set of conditions. Adjacent is the RAM (Random Access Memory) where signal information is stored temporarily and taken out again to aid the CPU (Central Processing Unit) to carry out calculations.

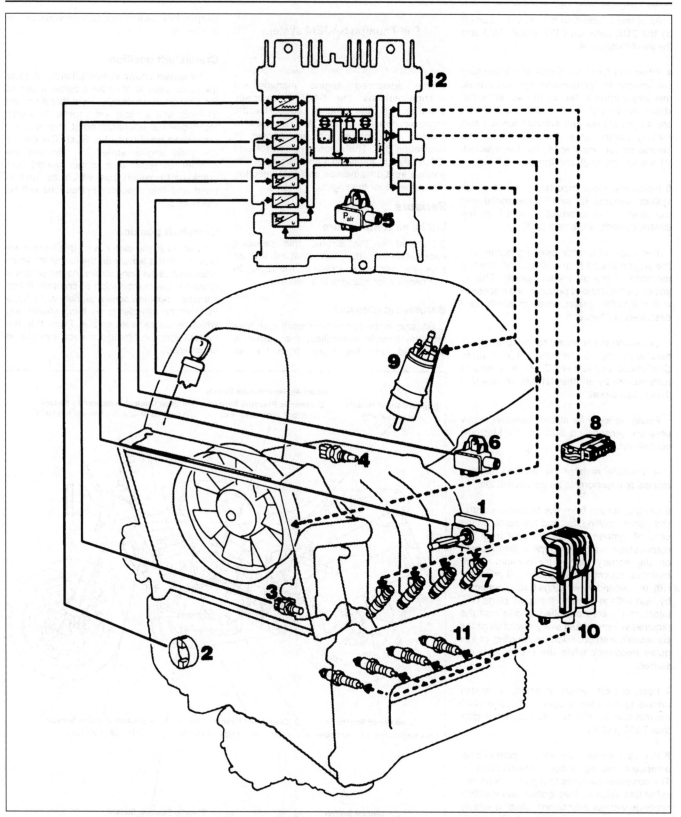

**4.1 Motronic engine management system as fitted to BMW K1 and K100RS 16-valve models**

| | | | | |
|---|---|---|---|---|
| 1 Throttle butterfly angle sensor | 4 Air temperature sensor | 7 Fuel injectors | 10 Ignition coils |
| 2 Hall ignition sensors | 5 Air pressure sensor | 8 Power amplifier | 11 Spark plugs |
| 3 Engine temperature sensor | 6 Variable resistor | 9 Fuel pump | 12 Motronic control unit |

All of this information movement is carried by the BUS between CPU, ROM, RAM and the Input/Output rail.

**4** When the CPU has made the necessary calculations for ignition and injection pulses, this information is fed to the set of boxes shown on the right of the control unit. These are output stages and activate ignition and fuelling components. Outputs are to the ignition power amplifier (8), the fuel injectors (7), the fuel pump (9) and the electric fan.

**5** Inputs are, most importantly, from the Hall ignition sensors (2) which give speed and top-dead centre information, and from the throttle butterfly angle sensor (1).

The angle of throttle opening (alpha) and the engine speed N are, when multiplied, a measure of the air intake volume. This is known as the alpha-N principle and dispenses with the airflow meter, some of which were described in Chapter 8.

Correction is necessary for air temperature measured by a Negative Temperature Coefficient capsule NTC (4) and engine temperature by another NTC (3) mounted in the coolant jacket.

Finally, to allow for altitude variation, an air pressure sensor (5) is built into the Motronic control unit.

A variable resistor (6) enables carbon monoxide emissions to be adjusted at idle.

**6** Output stages from the Motronic control unit control fuelling, fan and fuel pump. In the case of ignition, pulses are sent from the output stage to a power amplifier (8) (mounted on the battery carrier for cooling) which switches current to the ignition coil primaries (10), the secondary windings being connected by high voltage cable to the spark plugs (11). Injectors (7) are controlled to give half the required volume of fuel every revolution of the crankshaft, with provision for doubling of fuel pulse frequency while the engine is being started.

**7** Fuel cut-off when coasting operates providing the engine speed is above 2000 rev/min and the engine temperature is higher than 70°C (158°F).

**8** Fail-safe provision allows for a possibility of an absent input signal due to a fault condition. The computer switches to a pre-programmed substitute value so that ignition and injection continue without interruption. Missing signals from sensors are registered in a fault memory and will be read out at the next service by BMW diagnostic equipment. No substitute signal is available for the engine speed sensor.

## 5  The Triumph SAGEM system

**1** This advanced engine management arrangement by the SAGEM company operates on the engine speed/throttle angle/air density system and sensors to provide this information are shown in illustration 5.1. The electronic control unit (ECU) takes in the signals and calculates the precise ignition advance and fuel injection requirements for the engine.

### Sensors

#### Intake air temperature

**2** Located in the airbox, this sensor's information together with that of the air pressure sensor is used in the ECU to compensate for changes in air density.

#### Barometric pressure

Situated in the airbox between the air filter and the throttle butterflies, the output is combined with the signal from the air temperature sensor to calculate variations in air density.

#### Crankshaft position

The sensor shown in illustration 5.2 detects the rotor teeth as they pass below it due to the change of reluctance. Note that there are 21 teeth and a triple width tooth. This odd tooth gives a reference point showing the crankshaft position to the ECU. The sensor will yield engine speed by counting the number of teeth over a set period and crankshaft position from which the ignition point and fuel injection instructions will be calculated.

#### Camshaft position

Situated in the cam cover, this sensor will pick up from a feature on the camshaft which rotates once per firing stroke. As the engine is cranked, the combination of crankshaft and camshaft position sensor signals will tell the ECU which cylinder is on firing stroke and which is on exhaust stroke. From this the correct ignition timing for each cylinder is determined.

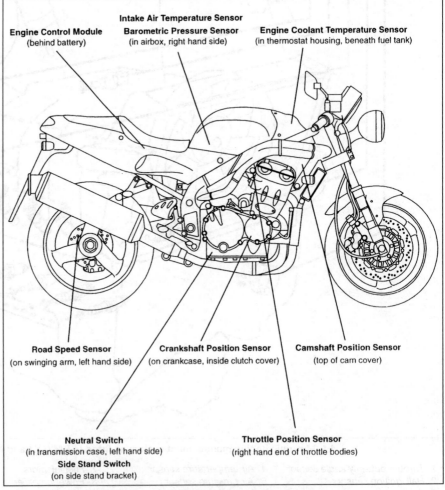

**Engine Control Module**
(behind battery)

**Intake Air Temperature Sensor**
**Barometric Pressure Sensor**
(in airbox, right hand side)

**Engine Coolant Temperature Sensor**
(in thermostat housing, beneath fuel tank)

**Road Speed Sensor**
(on swinging arm, left hand side)

**Crankshaft Position Sensor**
(on crankcase, inside clutch cover)

**Camshaft Position Sensor**
(top of cam cover)

**Neutral Switch**
(in transmission case, left hand side)

**Side Stand Switch**
(on side stand bracket)

**Throttle Position Sensor**
(right hand end of throttle bodies)

**5.1 Triumph SAGEM system: sensors**

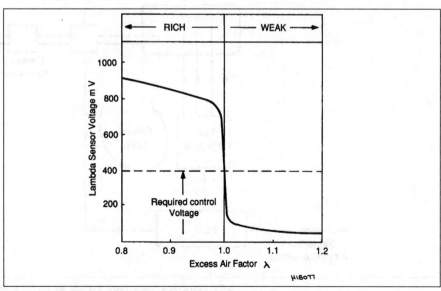

1 Crankshaft position sensor
2 Rotor
3 Air gap of 1.0 ± 0.2 mm

1 Sprocket
2 Air gap of 1.0 mm

**5.2 Crankshaft and road speed sensors**

### Engine coolant temperature

Fuel injection requirements at all engine temperatures are calculated by the ECU from this sensor signal as are the particular settings for cold starting and hot starting.

### Throttle position

Located at the end of the throttle spindle, this sensor gives a base reading at the closed position and a rising value as the throttle is opened. The throttle position calculated from this signal voltage is used by the ECU to generate the correct fuelling.

### Road speed

A sensor probably of the reluctor type counts the movement of the bolts on the rear wheel disc (see illustration 5.2). By comparing the engine speed (as measured by the crankshaft sensor) with the road speed the ECU can work out which gear the motorcycle is in. From this the fuelling, ignition and airflow needs are adjusted according to gear position. The road speed sensor also contributes to a mechanism which engages the adaptive idle speed control system.

### System Actuators

**3** Sensors provide the *inputs* to the electronic control unit (ECU) and when the calculations are complete the ECU then operates actuators by *output* signals to carry out a particular job. The obvious jobs are (a) to send signals to the ignition coils to produce the spark and (b) to send signals to the fuel injectors to give the right amount of fuel at the right moment.

Triumph include also an idle air control system which comprises an air control valve driven by a stepper motor. A stepper motor is a specialised form of electric motor which does not turn continuously but moves in steps forward and backward. The air control valve then corrects for idling, overrun air to give complete combustion with the throttle closed, altitude correction and adjustment for hot or cold starting.

Two further features are:

(a) *The main power relay which provides a stable voltage supply for the ECU and, on switch off, the ECU holds on the power relay so that it may write data to the ECU memory, note the position of the idle valve stepper motor and run the cooling fan until the engine cools down.*
(b) *The use of separate plug top ignition coils which plug straight on to each spark plug. This reduces the length of cable carrying the HT spark current and the accompanying electromagnetic radiation. This is part of the efforts by manufacturers to meet EU requirements that all electrical equipment will have electromagnetic compatibility (EMC). This is to prevent mutual interference by radiation-producing equipment.*

### 6 Lambda exhaust closed-loop control

**1** In Chapter 3, the pollutant products of combustion were discussed and the catalytic converter was shown to be a highly successful solution in reducing toxic outputs to within the limits specified by most countries.

It is an overriding proviso that an engine fitted with a catalytic converter must run on unleaded fuel and have an air:fuel ratio at which combustion will be theoretically complete. This Stoichiometric ratio is 14.7:1 by mass, meaning 14.7 kg of air to 1 kg of fuel. It is convenient to call this figure 1.0 and the international symbol is Lambda ($\lambda$).

A comparison is given in the table between actual numerical ratios and the corresponding Lambda figure. In some literature $\lambda$ is called the Excess Air Factor.

| Air:fuel ratio | 11.76 | 13.23 | 14.7 | 16.17 | 17.64 |
|---|---|---|---|---|---|
| Excess Air Factor | 0.8 | 0.9 | 1.0 | 1.1 | 1.2 |

**2** So far, the fuel injection systems described have no check on the results of injector control as far as exhaust emissions are concerned and are only measured when the engine is serviced. Such a system is said to have open-loop control.

**3** To measure the state of exhaust gases, a Lambda sensor (sometimes called an exhaust gas oxygen (EGO) sensor) is fitted in the exhaust (muffler) pipe. This sensor measures the oxygen left unburned in the exhaust gases (a measure of excess air factor) and generates a signal voltage (see illustration 6.3) which is

**9**

**6.3 Lambda sensor voltage characteristic at 600°C (1112°F)**

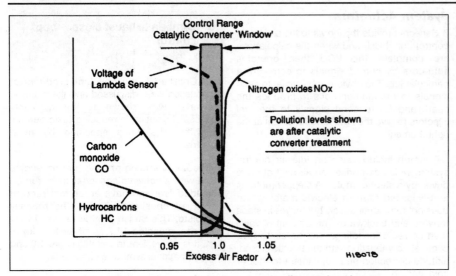

6.4a Lambda sensor voltage curve and pollutants in exhaust

fed back to the Electronic Control Unit (ECU) as an additional unit of information.

**4** In turn the ECU will correct the fuel injection to ensure that the excess air factor is within a narrow range around unity (ie λ = 1); this range is called the catalytic converter window (see illustration 6.4a). Because the output information (ie state of exhaust gas) is fed back to the ECU which in turn controls the output, this is an example of closed-loop control (see illustration 6.4b).

**5** The graphs in illustration 6.4a show that carbon monoxide quantities rise sharply just below λ = 1.0 and nitrogen oxides rise rapidly just above λ = 1.0. From this it will be seen that maintaining the Stoichiometric ratio

at λ = 1.0 is vital to the success of the catalytic converter.

## 7 Operation of the Lambda sensor

**1** The sensor is an exhaust gas oxygen measuring device which works like a small battery. It is about the size of a spark plug, screws into the exhaust (muffler) system and is exposed to the full flow of the exhaust gases. The presence of oxygen in the exhaust gases means that the mixture is weak (λ greater than 1.0), whereas no oxygen indicates a rich mixture (λ less than 1.0).

**2** The Lambda sensor (or exhaust gas oxygen sensor, EGO) uses a ceramic body made of zirconium dioxide ($ZrO_2$) in the shape of a long thimble; the outer surface is exposed to the exhaust gases and the inner surface is in contact with the outside air (see illustration 7.2).

The zirconium dioxide is covered inside and out with two thin layers of porous platinum which act as electrodes from which the output signal voltage is taken. Extra protection is given by coating the surface exposed to the exhaust with a layer of porous alumina through which the exhaust gas can penetrate.

The zirconium dioxide acts as the (solid) electrolyte; the inside surface is exposed to air which has 21% oxygen content and the outer surface is exposed to the exhaust gas.

**3** The sensor develops a voltage between the inner and outer surfaces according to the difference of oxygen concentration and the voltage is collected at the two platinum electrodes (see illustration 7.3).

**4** When the engine is working with a rich mixture the voltage generated will be about 800 to 900 millivolts (mV). This drops abruptly at the Stoichiometric point and levels off to about 50 mV in the weak region.

The change is abrupt so that the sensor acts almost like an on-off switch and the signals it sends to the ECU, together with wave re-shaping and the rapid correction produced by the ECU, mean that the signal is like an on-off square wave maintaining the excess air factor at very close to λ = 1.0 (see illustration 7.4).

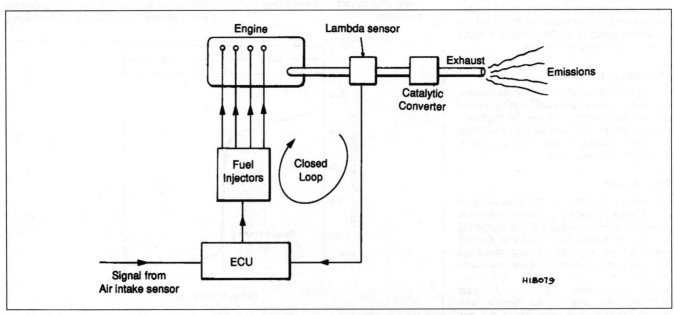

6.4b Lambda closed-loop excess air factor control

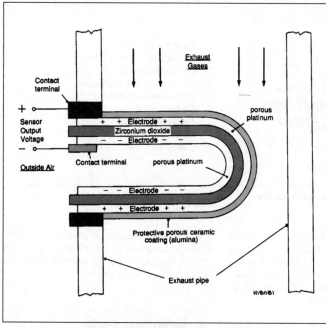

**7.2 Schematic of Lambda sensor**

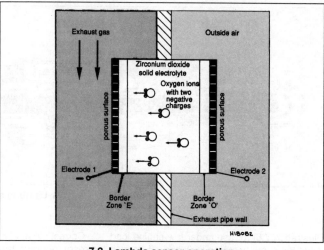

**7.3 Lambda sensor operation**

When in the vicinity of the electrode surface, residual oxygen is bound to hydrogen, carbon monoxide and hydrocarbons. If the mixture goes from weak to rich, border zone E becomes depleted of oxygen. Large numbers of oxygen ions migrate to electrode 1, causing this to go negative relative to electrode 2. This gives the sensor voltage used in the Lambda closed-loop control system

**5** The output voltage is strongly influenced by temperature since the electrolyte $ZrO_2$ does not become conductive below 300°C (572°F); ideally the sensor should work at about 600°C (1112°F). In addition, the response time at 300°C (572°F) is several seconds but at 600°C (1112°F) the sensor reacts in less than 50 ms.

For these reasons the location of the sensor is critical – too far away from the engine and the sensor would not work, too near and on long hot runs the sensor would be destroyed. (Note – maximum temperature should not exceed 850°C, 1562°F.) A Lambda sensor is shown in cross-section in illustration 7.5.

**6** Some units have a built in heater (see

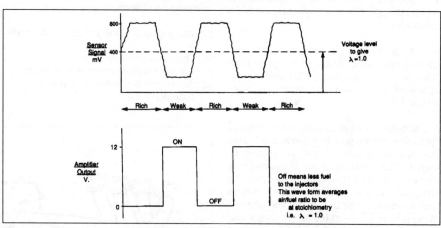

**7.4 Control waveforms in Lambda control system**

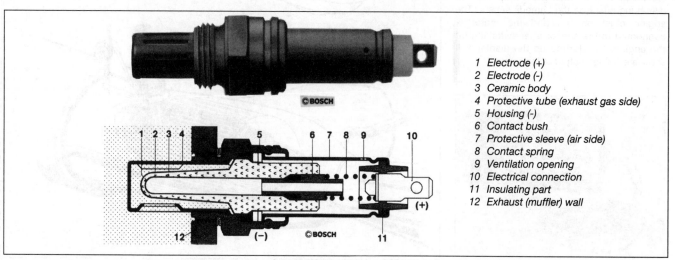

1 Electrode (+)
2 Electrode (-)
3 Ceramic body
4 Protective tube (exhaust gas side)
5 Housing (-)
6 Contact bush
7 Protective sleeve (air side)
8 Contact spring
9 Ventilation opening
10 Electrical connection
11 Insulating part
12 Exhaust (muffler) wall

**7.5 Bosch Lambda sensor**

**9**

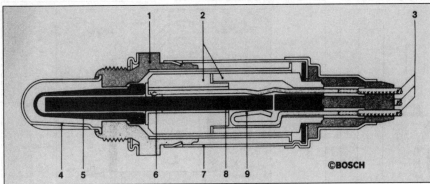

| | |
|---|---|
| 1 | Sensor housing |
| 2 | Protective ceramic tube |
| 3 | Connection cable |
| 4 | Protective tube with slots |
| 5 | Active sensor ceramic |
| 6 | Contact section |
| 7 | Protective sleeve |
| 8 | Heating element |
| 9 | Clamp terminals for heating element |

©BOSCH

**7.6 Lambda sensor with heater**

illustration 7.6) for use under low engine load conditions; the heater is switched off on high loading. The location is still important but the Lambda control is up to temperature and working after 25 seconds.

Properly installed the heated Lambda sensor has an expected life of 62,000 miles (100,000 km). Unleaded fuel must be used to avoid damage to the active outer platinum electrode.

**7** Testing a Lambda sensor is normally carried out with specialised equipment but there is now on the market a low cost test set available from Gunson shown in illustration 7.7.

The output of a Lambda sensor is a voltage, typically in the range 0 to 1.0 volt. It is high at 0.8 volt in an exhaust gas containing no oxygen and low about 0 volt in the presence of even a small percentage of oxygen. The bargraph display of the tester has a measurement range of 0 to 1.0 volt and can show graphically the output of the sensor over the full operating range. With an input resistance of over 500MΩ the meter has no disturbing effect on the Lambda sensor. The engine must be hot and the meter is connected to the sensor after switching off the engine. On starting up the display will show the voltage output of the sensor.

Correct closed-loop operation is shown if a sensor gives a rapidly fluctuating voltage varying between 0.15 volt to 0.8 volt. The rate of fluctuation is around 8 cycles in 10 seconds at idle speed rising to twice this rate at an engine speed of 3000 rev/min.

If a steady bargraph display with only some of the segments illuminated is shown for all operating conditions, this indicates that:

(a) The engine is running in open loop mode, or
(b) There is a circuit fault, or
(c) The Lamba sensor sensor is faulty, or
(d) The engine is running in 'limp home' condition*

*Limp home condition is available in some ECUs when there is a fault which prevents correct fuelling and/or igntion but allows the rider to complete the journey.

## 8  Catalytic converter

### BMW system

**1** This was the first motorcycle catalytic converter with Lambda closed-loop control to be offered.

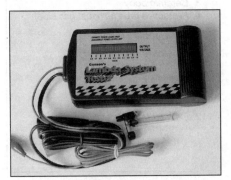

**7.7 Lambda sensor tester**

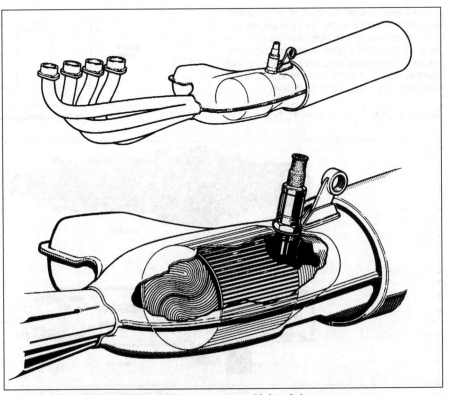

**8.1 BMW catalytic converter with Lambda sensor**

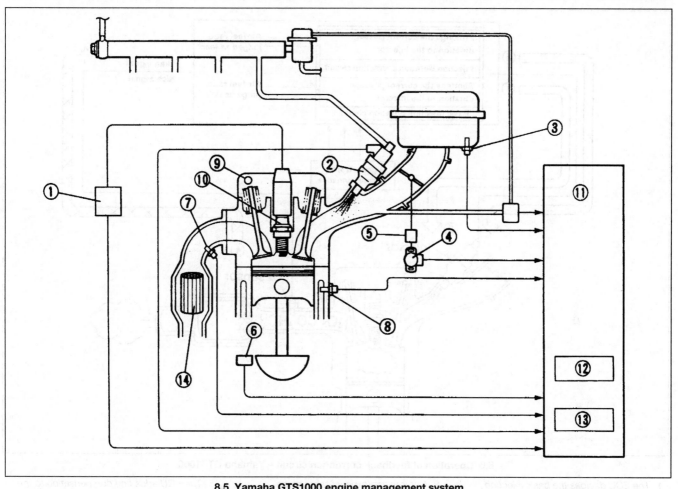

**8.5 Yamaha GTS1000 engine management system**

1 Ignition coil
2 Injector
3 Intake temperature sensor
4 Throttle sensor
5 Intake pressure sensor

6 Crankshaft sensor
7 Oxygen ($O_2$) sensor
8 Water temperature sensor
9 Camshaft sensor
10 Spark plug

11 ECU
12 Igniter
13 Atmospheric pressure sensor
14 Catalytic converter

This catalytic converter (see illustration 8.1) uses a metallic base (or monolith), BMW claiming that this gives a greater exhaust gas through-flow than the ceramic-based type (see Chapter 3) and that the unit reaches operating temperature quicker.

With dimensions of 85 x 74 mm (3.3 x 2.9 in), the cylindrical catalyst holder is located within the exhaust system and insulated from the outer skin of the exhaust.

**2** The catalyser uses precious metals applied to the surface of the monolith in order to stimulate the chemical reactions which oxidise the noxious exhaust gases. Palladium causes oxidisation of hydrocarbons (HC) and carbon monoxide (CO), while the rhodium acts to reduce oxides of nitrogen ($NO_x$). (Palladium is an alternative agent instead of platinum.)

**3** Illustration 8.1 shows the physical layout and the Lambda sensor, which is a heated type. Feedback from this sensor to the Motronic control unit ensures that the engine always runs at Stoichiometric conditions ($\lambda = 1$).

**4** The following advantages over open-loop systems are worth restating:

(a) Efficient exhaust emission control.
(b) Long-term optimum engine settings are maintained.
(c) Fuel consumption rarely alters during the life of the catalytic converter.
(d) Lambda control largely compensates for the effects of engine wear.

### Yamaha system

**5** The Yamaha GTS1000 motorcycle features a closed-loop engine management system. This follows the principles outlined earlier in this Chapter, the arrangement being shown in illustration 8.5. Note the small differences in terminology such as the Lambda sensor which is referred to by its common name of oxygen ($O_2$) sensor, and the electronic ignition unit is here termed the igniter.

**6** A graphic illustration of how precise control of the correct air:fuel ratio is maintained is given in illustration 8.6 (overleaf).

A fuel cut-off device comes into operation when the engine speed is high and the rider has closed the throttle to decelerate. Under these conditions the electronic signal from a sensor attached to the throttle shuts off the injection of fuel. This action prevents generation of carbon monoxide (CO) and hydrocarbons (HC) as only air is then drawn into the combustion chamber.

The additional advantages are prevention of overheating and reduction of fuel consumption.

**9**

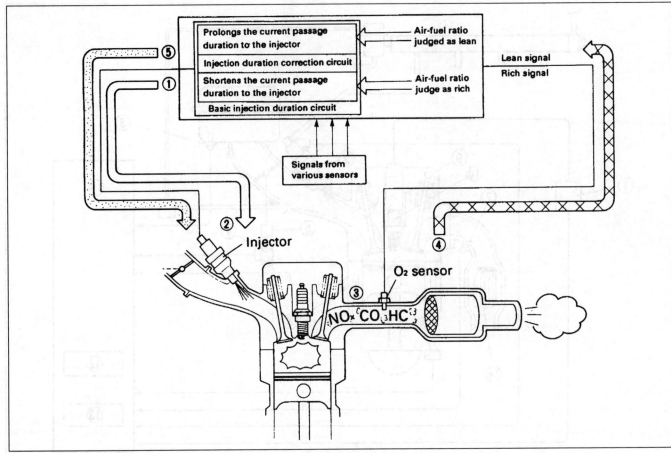

**8.6 Operation of feedback correction circuit – Yamaha GTS1000**

1  The ECU decides the basic injection quantity based on the input signals from various sensors, and gives instructions for current passage duration to the injector

2  Current passes through the injector which injects fuel accordingly

3  Combustion/exhaust takes place

4  The oxygen sensor detects the residual oxygen concentration in the exhaust gas.
It sends the lean signal/rich signal for the fuel:air ratio based on this data

5  The ECU adds fine compensation to the basic injection timing, based on the signals received. It decides the injection quantity for the next stroke and gives instructions to the injector

By repeating the operations described, the theoretical air-fuel ratio is maintained

# Chapter 10
# Spark plugs

# Contents

## 1 The Spark plug

**1** In principle, the spark plug is a simple device for providing a pair of electrodes within the cylinder space. A high voltage provided by the ignition system is applied to the electrodes causing a spark at the correct time and in the correct position to ignite the air/fuel vapour.

It was invented by Jean Lenoir in 1860 and although in principle it remains the same today, in practice it is the result of much research and technological innovation.

**2** A spark plug operates in the combustion chamber of the engine under severe conditions. For example, the combustion chamber temperature can reach 2500°C (4532°F) and pressures of 48.3 bar (700 lbf/in²).

The plug is exposed to sudden changes in temperature and pressure; going abruptly from the temperature of burning fuel to the relatively low temperature of the incoming mixture. It must endure high voltage, mechanical vibration and corrosion attack from the combustion gases and so what seems to be a simple device is in fact an engineering triumph.

## 2 Construction

**1** Plugs are made up of three main components – the shell, electrodes and insulator (see illustration 2.1).

### Shell

**2** Made of steel, the shell has a thread to screw it into the cylinder head while the upper part has a hexagon. The surface is electroplated nickel to deter corrosion, keep the thread free, and to prevent seizure. Prevention of seizure is most important with alloy cylinder heads. The insulator is inserted into the spark plug shell, then swaged and heat-shrunk in position by inductive heating under high pressure.

### Electrodes

**3** The electrode materials are vital to correct plug operation for they must be suitable for easy spark emission, and resistant to high temperature and chemical corrosion.

The centre electrode is held in place in one of several ways. Bosch use a conducting glass seal, and NGK and Champion use a powdered seal which caulks the electrode/insulator and insulator/steel body gaps.

Nickel alloys are suitable for electrodes but in some plugs the nickel alloy has a core of copper to assist in conducting away the heat.

The earth (ground) or side electrode is welded to the steel body and is commonly of rectangular section, but some advantages are claimed by the makers of Champion, Splitfire and Nippon Denso ZU plugs where their earth (ground) electrode structure is special.

**4** The Champion double copper plugs have a copper core for both the centre and earth (ground) electrodes, the latter having a trapezoidal cross-section to give a larger area over which the spark may jump. It is claimed that this plug runs 100°C (212°F) cooler than

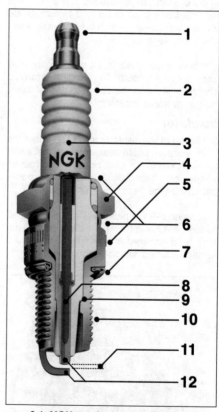

**2.1 NGK spark plug construction**

| | | | |
|---|---|---|---|
| 1 | Terminal | 6 | Caulking (to |
| 2 | Insulator | | ensure gas-tight |
| | ribs | | seal) |
| 3 | Insulator | 7 | Sealing washer |
| | (top portion) | 8 | Copper core |
| 4 | Metal shell | 9 | Inner gasket |
| 5 | Plated finish | 10 | Threaded portion |
| | (to prevent | 11 | Electrode gap |
| | corrosion) | 12 | Electrodes |

**10**

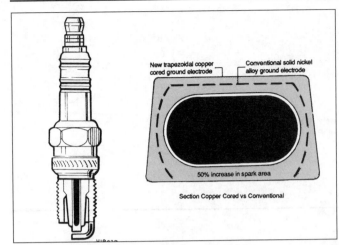

2.4 Champion double copper plug

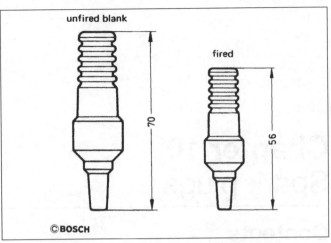

2.5 Spark plug insulator before and after firing

plugs with a solid nickel-alloy earth (ground) electrode (see illustration 2.4) and because the wear rate of the copper-cored earth (ground) electrode is reduced, it is possible to use electrode gaps of up to 0.15 mm (0.006 in) greater than with conventional solid electrode plugs.

It is now accepted that a wider spark plug gap improves both the engine start-up characteristic and the ability to give efficient ignition to leaner fuel/air mixtures.

### Insulator

5 The job of the insulator is to ensure that the high voltage pulse will not leak to earth (ground) within the plug body. It also has an effect on heat dissipation and partly determines the 'heat range' of the plug.

Alumina ($Al_2 O_3$) plus a filling agent is used to form the insulator which starts as a blank and is then fired in a high temperature furnace, during which a shrinkage of 20%

takes place (see illustration 2.5). The exposed surface is glazed to prevent adhesion of dirt, which could provide a leakage path. The effective length is increased by providing five ribs over which leakage current would have to travel.

The insulator houses the centre electrode and the terminal stud. In summary it must possess the following qualities:

(a) Mechanical strength.
(b) High insulation resistance.
(c) Good thermal conductivity.

3.1a Pre-ignition damage to plug

3.1b Piston crown holed by pre-ignition

## 3 Heat range

1 The firing end of a spark plug must operate between the temperature limits of 400 – 800°C (750 – 1470°F) approximately. Below 400°C (750°F) the plug cannot burn off the carbon deposits generated by combustion, and much above 800°C (1470°F) there is increasing oxide fouling and electrode burning. At 950°C (1740°F) the plug tip becomes so incandescent that premature igniting of the fuel vapour occurs (pre-ignition) resulting in damage to the piston and the plug itself (see illustrations 3.1a to 3.1.c).

Between 400 – 800°C (750 – 1470°F) approximately, the plug is self cleaning – the essential condition for good running and long service intervals.

2 Heat flow from the plug has been measured by manufacturers with some accuracy and it is known that about 91% is transmitted via the screw thread and gasket to the engine body, with the remaining 9% lost by radiation

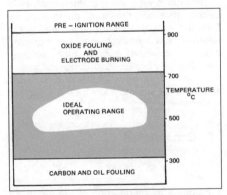

3.1c Plug operating temperatures

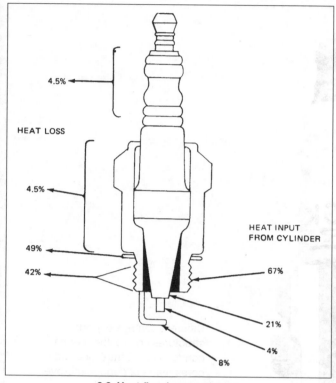

3.2  Heat flow in a spark plug

and convection from the plug shell and the exposed insulator (see illustration 3.2).

**3** The figures do not take into account the cooling effect of the fresh inflowing vapour, but do give an informative picture. It is clear, for instance, that correct fitting and tightening down is vital, since the attached gasket (if fitted) is responsible for nearly half of the heat transmission – failure to maintain good seating contact could result in an overheated plug.

**4** Clearly no one plug can be correct for all operating conditions and some manufacturers distinguish between plug choice for round-town work or for sustained high speed travel. The important dimensions of a spark plug are at the bottom end, and illustration 3.4 shows vital dimensions that MUST be correct.

**5** It is essential for correct plug tip temperatures that the electrodes should JUST project into the cylinder. If the plug reach is too short, the spark is shielded from the fuel vapour; bad misfiring will result and be accompanied by carbon build-up. If the reach is too long, the electrodes will run hot and there is also the chance that the screw threads of cylinder and plug may be damaged by overheating or even by impact with the piston (see illustration 3.5).

**6** Plugs dissipate heat from the centre electrode via the nose of the insulator surrounding it. A short insulator will pass heat to the steel shell more readily than a nose insulator which is relatively long and thin (see illustration 3.6).

**7** A high compression engine generally has hot operating conditions and requires a plug with good heat dissipation. Conversely, a low compression engine has lower combustion chamber temperature and so a hotter grade of plug would be chosen so that the plug tip temperature could be maintained above the oil fouling level (see illustration 3.1c).

Vital dimensions of a spark plug labels: Hexagon, Thread reach, Spark gap, Thread diameter

3.4  Vital dimensions of a spark plug

**10**

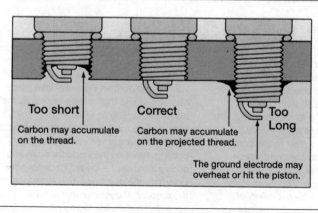

3.5  The importance of correct plug reach

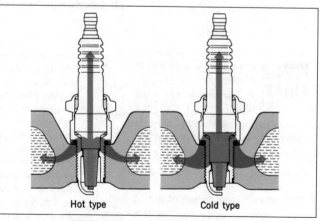

3.6  Heat flow in hot and cold plugs

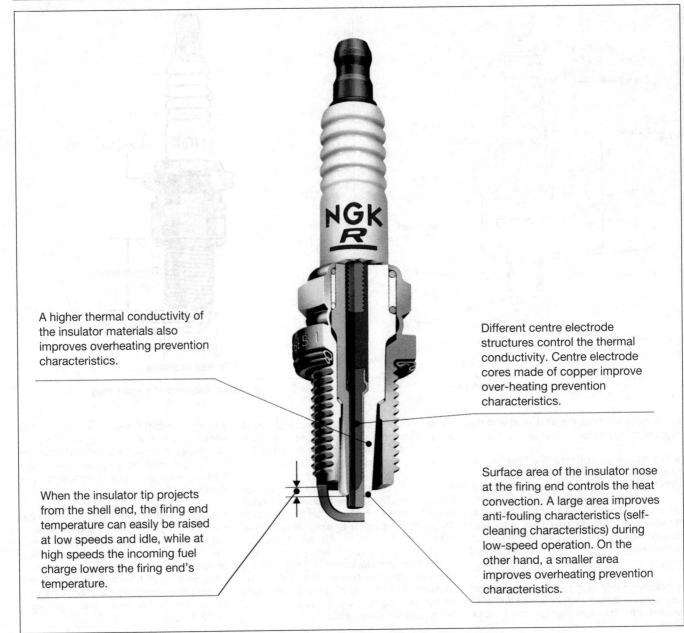

A higher thermal conductivity of the insulator materials also improves overheating prevention characteristics.

Different centre electrode structures control the thermal conductivity. Centre electrode cores made of copper improve over-heating prevention characteristics.

When the insulator tip projects from the shell end, the firing end temperature can easily be raised at low speeds and idle, while at high speeds the incoming fuel charge lowers the firing end's temperature.

Surface area of the insulator nose at the firing end controls the heat convection. A large area improves anti-fouling characteristics (self-cleaning characteristics) during low-speed operation. On the other hand, a smaller area improves overheating prevention characteristics.

**3.8 Influence of design on the heat range of a spark plug**

**HAYNES HiNT**

*A hot engine uses a cold plug*

*A cold engine uses a hot plug*

*Note that sometimes hot plugs are referred to as 'soft' and cold plugs as 'hard'.*

**8** The working temperature of a plug (heat range) depends upon four factors (see illustration 3.8):

(a) *Choice of material used for the insulator and the design of electrodes. Electrodes with materials of high thermal conductivity or copper-cored types will conduct heat well.*

(b) *Insulator nose length will affect tip temperature. This is the length from the tip of the insulator to the point where it can transfer conducted heat to the body.*

(c) *Insulator projection into the combustion chamber is linked to the cooling effect of the incoming fuel vapour. The term 'turbo action' is used to describe the effect of the incoming charge and better resistance to fouling is claimed.*

(d) *Insulator/shell space is important because gas circulates in this 'gas volume'. Exchanges of heat between incoming vapour and outgoing gas will take place here. Enlarging this volume improves the ability of the plug to resist low temperature fouling. Due to the clearance gap there is improvement in charge cooling effect on the insulator nose and allows the use of a longer insulator nose. Enlarging the clearance also increases the amount of deposits that can be accepted before the fouled plug condition occurs.*

**4.1a  Normal condition firing end**

*A brown, tan or grey firing end indicates that the engine is in good condition and that the plug type is correct*

**4.1b  Ash deposits on firing end**

*Light brown deposits encrusted on the electrodes and insulator, leading to misfire and hesitation. Caused by excessive amounts of oil in the combustion chamber or poor quality fuel/oil*

**4.1c  Carbon fouled firing end**

*Dry, black sooty deposits leading to misfire and weak spark. Caused by an over-rich fuel/air mixture, faulty choke operation or blocked air filter*

**4.1d  Oil fouled firing end**

*Wet oily deposits leading to misfire and weak spark. Caused by oil leakage past piston rings or valve guides (4-stroke engine), or excess lubricant (2-stroke engine)*

**4.1e  Overheated firing end**

*A blistered white insulator and glazed electrodes. Caused by ignition fault, incorrect fuel, or cooling system fault*

**4.1f  Lead fouled firing end**

*Yellowish brown deposits on the insulator nose. Caused by lead from petrol (gasoline) adhering to the insulator and will lead to misfiring*

## 4  Plug examination

**1** The state of a spark plug that has been in service will indicate the condition in the engine (see illustrations).

## 5  Ignition timing

**1** Incorrect ignition timing will have a marked effect on plug temperatures.

While advancing ignition beyond manufacturer's figures may show a small power increase, the temperature rise will be disproportionately greater, giving rise to problems on sustained full load (see illustration 5.1).

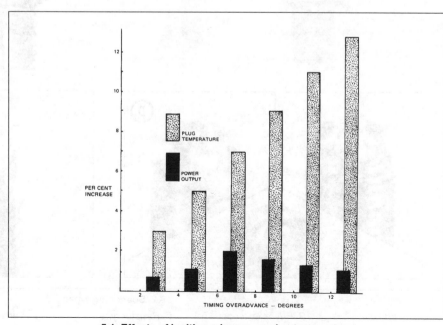

**5.1  Effects of ignition advance on plug temperature**

**10**

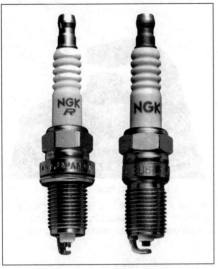

**6.1 Spark plugs with flat (left) and conical (right) seats**

## 6 Types of spark plug

1 Plugs have seats which are either flat or conical (see illustration 6.1).

The **flat** seat uses a gasket washer which is attached permanently to the plug body, and it is important that the plug is screwed properly into the cylinder head. Too loose and the effect can be pre-ignition because there is no proper conductive path for heat: too tight and threads of both plug and cylinder head could be damaged (see Section 8).

**Conical (or taper)** seating plugs do not use gaskets and can be made with a smaller body shell: they are becoming increasingly popular. Special care must be taken when fitting (see Section 8).

2 **The standard plug** has the spark gap just protruding from the bottom of the plug thread (see illustration 6.2, part A). The standard insulator nose plug is suitable for older engine designs.

3 **P-type plugs** (an NGK term) have a projecting insulator nose (illustration 6.2, part B). Better fouling protection and anti-pre-ignition characteristics are claimed for this type of plug, since the nose temperature is raised quickly at idle and low speeds to be within the self cleaning heat band. At high speeds the incoming charge has a cooling effect. This type of plug is suited to modern engine design.

4 **Resistor plugs** have a carbon compound resistor often of about 5 k$\Omega$ resistance in the centre core (illustration 6.2, part C). This gives good radio interference suppression because it is more effective to have a suppression resistor close to the source of radiation – namely the spark.

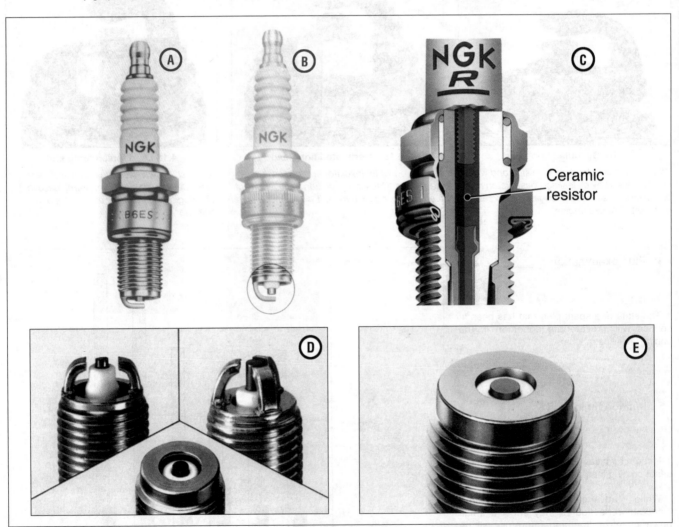

Ceramic resistor

**6.2 Spark plug types**

| A Standard type | B P-type (extended insulator nose) | C Resistor type | D Semi-surface discharge type | E Surface discharge type |

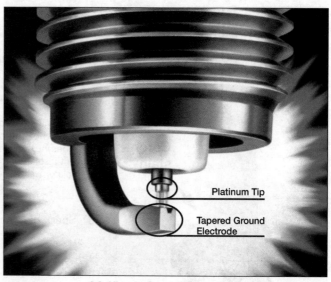

Platinum Tip

Tapered Ground Electrode

6.7 Splitfire spark plug features

6.8 Nippon Denso ZU type plug

**5 Semi-surface discharge plugs** are designed to give a spark along the insulator upper surface to the adjacent earth electrodes or metal shell depending on the plug type (see illustration 6.2, part D). There is greater resistance to plug fouling due to the spark burning off attached carbon.

**6 Surface discharge plugs** are designed for CDI (Capacitor Discharge Ignition) systems and give good sparking even under conditions of fouling (illustration 2.6, part E).

**7 Splitfire plugs** (a trade name). The earth (ground) electrode on these plugs is split in the shape of a 'V' **(see illustration 6.7)**. The twin arcs are said to give better exposure of the flame kernel to the air/fuel mixture not only because of the twin spark but also that part of

the spark flame goes through the fork gap and reaches the air/fuel mixture more efficiently. Also the platinum tipped centre electrode is smaller in diameter giving rise to a more intense electric field at the surface. For added performance the forked earth (ground) electrodes also have platinum spots to aid spark firing and reduce wear. These factors promote easier sparking and lower misfire rate under adverse conditions

**8 Nippon Denso ZU plugs.** Again this design has a small diameter platinum-tipped centre electrode and a specially shaped earth (ground) electrode. The latter is tapered and grooved as shown in illustration 6.8.

Both features will create an intense electric field at the surfaces which will enhance

sparking. The makers claim a lower sparking voltage requirement and superior performance.

## 7 Corona discharge and flashover

**1** If conditions are damp or the plug ribbed insulator is dirty, then in the dark a pale blue light may be seen around the HT cable connector and/or the plug insulator when the engine is running. This is due to ionisation of the air which splits up into free electrons and positively charged ions in the area of high electric stress. It is known as Corona discharge. It can also sometimes be seen on National Grid high voltage cable insulators in wet weather.

The effect on ignition is minimal unless the Corona reaches the terminal stud allowing flashover to the metal shell. This gives an engine misfire (see illustration 7.1). In part A, the plug is on the point of acquiring a corona glow. In part B the glow shows as small and varied streaks of light while at part C there is a full flash when an engine misfire would occur.

**2** Whenever it is suspected that there is unwanted sparking over (often called tracking) run the engine in the dark. Actual flashover is then easy to locate and sometimes corona discharge can be seen, not only on plugs as shown but possibly around HT cables and the tower of an ignition coil.

**3** On examination of a spark plug a discoloration on the insulator surface may be seen which looks as if gas has leaked

**10**

A                    B                    C

7.1 Corona discharge and flashover

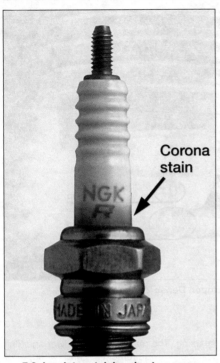

**7.3 Insulator staining due to corona discharge**

between the insulator and the shell, as shown in illustration 7.3. This discoloration is generally called 'Corona stain'.

It is due to oil particles, hanging in the air around the insulator surface, being attracted by the corona discharge; these become charged and adhere to the insulator surface.

The corona stain causes no deterioration in the function of the spark plug. The corona stain does not cause flashover since it has sufficient insulation, but moisture adhering to the insulator will cause flashover.

## 8 Spark plug servicing

1 Plugs should be checked and renewed at the intervals recommended by the machine's manufacturer, for performance to be maintained. Properly serviced plugs have a gradual deterioration and a finite life.

Depending upon riding style, the economical limit of plug life is 6000 – 10,000 miles (10,000 – 16,000 km) for a 4-stroke engine. Due to the oily nature of the 2-stroke engine, plug life is reduced markedly to 4000 – 6000 miles (6500 – 10,000 km). Note that the use of unleaded fuel (where possible) will greatly increase spark plug life.

2 Plug cleaning may be carried out by hand but workshops frequently use an abrasive grit blast machine. It is most important to clean away all traces of grit afterwards with compressed air. Note that some plug manufacturers specifically advise against cleaning due the likelihood of damage to the firing ends. Considering the relative cheapness of spark plugs, renewal is often the best course of action if there is any doubt about their condition.

3 When removing a plug, unscrew it a few turns using a proper spark plug spanner (wrench) and blow or brush away any grit or rust particles lying round the plug well. Do not, under any circumstances, allow foreign matter to drop into the engine through the plug hole. When the plug has been removed put a clean rag into the plug hole to be sure that nothing gets in.

4 Cleaning manually is best carried out with a fine wire brush, going over the external thread, plug tip and earth (ground) electrode CAREFULLY; a harsh abrasive brush may damage the plug. After cleaning, check that no whiskers from the wire brush remain in the plug. Clean the insulator with a rag moistened with solvent to prevent spark-tracking paths developing.

5 Gap resetting should be carried out using a combination tool with an electrode adjuster and wire gauge. Note that flat feeler gauges are not ideal for this job in case of irregular electrode wear and they are unable to check the gap successfully on twin- or triple-earth semi-surface discharge plugs (see illustrations 8.5a to 8.5d).

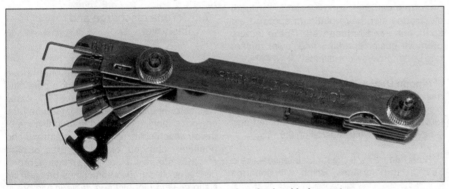

**8.5a Wire type gauges can be obtained in key sets**

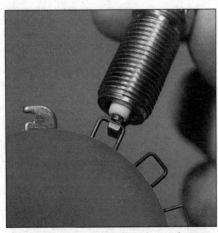

**8.5b Measuring the plug electrode gap using a wire gauge**

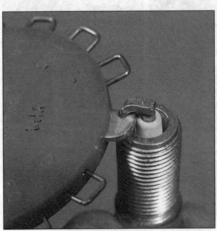

**8.5c Adjusting the plug electrode gap using a special tool**

**8.5d Note the curved faces of multi-electrode plugs**

**6** Refitting needs care, especially with alloy heads. After cleaning the plug thread with a brass wire brush smear a TRACE of graphited or copper-based grease on the thread and start the plug carefully by hand. Withdraw immediately if unusual resistance is felt – this may be due to cross threading. One manufacturer (Bosch) states that their NEW plugs are already lubricated but grease should be applied for all used plugs.

Plugs should ideally be tightened to the torque setting specified by the machine's manufacturer. If a torque setting is not provided by the manufacturer, refer to the recommended torques or tightening angles in illustration 8.6. Note that settings differ for cast iron or aluminium cylinder heads (most motorcycles use aluminium heads), and for flat seat or conical seat plugs.

## 9 Contact numbers

**1** Further information on spark plugs can be obtained from the main plug manufacturers on the following UK telephone numbers:

| | |
|---|---|
| NGK | 0181 202 2151 |
| Bosch | 01895 834466 |
| Nippon Denso | 01622 730939 |
| Champion | 0151 678 7070 |
| Splitfire | 01562 60555 |

## Recommended tightening torques

| Spark plug type (thread diameter) | | Cast iron cylinder head | Aluminum cylinder head |
|---|---|---|---|
| Flat seat type (with gasket) | 18φmm | 35~45N·m 25.3~32.5 lbs·ft | 35~40N·m 25.3~28.9 lbs·ft |
| | 14φmm | 25~35N·m 18.0~25.3 lbs·ft | 25~30N·m 18.0~21.6 lbs·ft |
| | 12φmm | 15~25N·m 10.8~18.0 lbs·ft | 15~20N·m 10.8~14.5 lbs·ft |
| | 10φmm | 10~15N·m 7.2~10.8 lbs·ft | 10~12N·m 7.2~8.7 lbs·ft |
| | 8φmm | ——— | 8~10N·m 5.8~7.2 lbs·ft |
| Conical seat type (without gasket) | 18φmm | 20~30N·m 14.5~21.6 lbs·ft | 20~30N·m 14.5~21.6 lbs·ft |
| | 14φmm | 15~25N·m 10.8~18.0 lbs·ft | 10~20N·m 7.2~14.5 lbs·ft |

## Recommended tightening angle

| Thread size | New gasket plug | Re-used plug |
|---|---|---|
| 18φmm 14φmm 12φmm 10φmm | $\frac{1}{2}$ of a turn (180°) | $\frac{1}{12} \sim \frac{1}{8}$ of a turn (30°~45°) |
| 8φmm | $\frac{1}{3}$ of a turn (120°) | $\frac{1}{12}$ of a turn (30°) |

Note: In the case of a conical seat type, $\frac{1}{16}$ of a turn (22.5°) is recommended.

**8.6 Spark plug tightening recommendations**

**10**

**Notes**

# Chapter 11
# Charging – Direct current (dc) generators

## Contents

## 1 Introduction

**1** The use of a generator to charge a motorcycle battery goes back to the early part of the century, but widespread use of the direct current dynamo began in the 1920's when the Lucas Magdyno first appeared (see illustration 1.3a in Chapter 5).

**2** It is interesting to note that the voltage generated in the dynamo armature is alternating and appears as direct voltage at the output terminals only after passing through a commutator. This is a mechanical means of reversing the negative alternating wave so that the output is a series of uni-directional pulses which are a form of direct current and suitable for battery charging. We shall examine in some detail how the dynamo works, going right back to basics.

## 2 Electromagnetic generation

**1** When a wire is moved through a magnetic field, a voltage is induced proportional to the following (see illustration 2.1).

(a) *The velocity (v) at which magnetic lines of force are cut.*
(b) *The strength of the magnetic field (B).*
(c) *The length of the wire (l) actually in the field.*

*induced emf e = Blv volts.*

This is the basic equation on which all generators, both ac and dc, operate.

**2** The strength of the magnetic field (B) is usually measured in Teslas, the length of wire (l) measured in metres and the wire velocity (v) in metres per second at right-angles to the magnetic field.

**3** This arrangement does not make a practical generator and so the wire was next arranged as a parallel sided loop and the voltage picked off by slip rings with carbon brushes pressing lightly on them. Rotating the coil between the poles of a magnet means that the coil sides are first moving up through the field and then down. Not surprisingly, the voltage generated

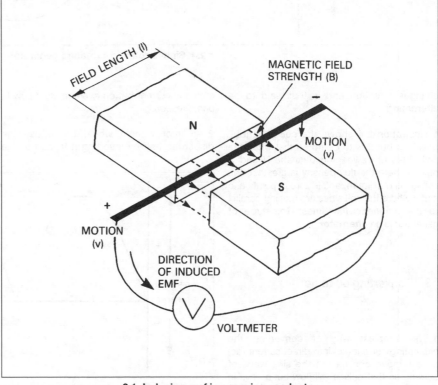

**2.1 Inducing emf in a moving conductor**

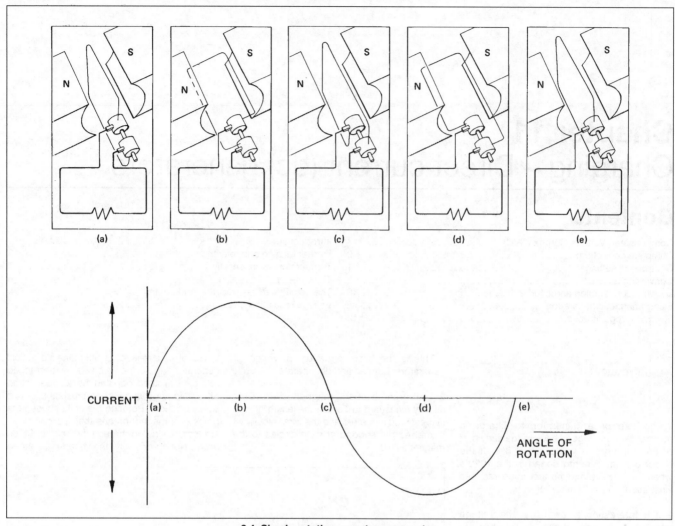

**2.4 Simple rotating-armature generator**

changes direction and is thus said to be **alternating**.

**4** Illustration 2.4 shows the coil in various positions but it is to be noted that when the coil sides are sweeping past the N and S poles (where the flux density is greatest) the voltage is maximum, and is zero at points a, c and e where the coil sides are running parallel to the magnetic flux lines. This type of generator is an **alternator**.

### 3 Converting ac to dc

**1** The simplest way of converting the alternating current (ac) into direct current (dc) is to remove one half of the sine wave of current, so that pulses will flow but always in the same direction. Note that dc need not be

a steady current but on average *must flow in one direction.*

**2** An improvement would be to use the discarded half by inverting it to add to the

current flow (see illustration 3.2a). Today, with the development of electronics, we would use a semiconductor rectifier to do this, but generators on early motorcycles were designed so that alternating current generated

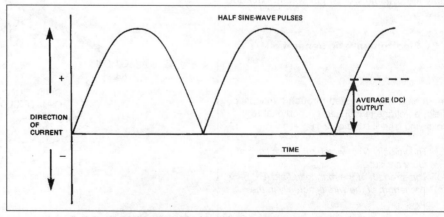

**3.2a Uni-directional (dc) output from single-coil armature**

in the armature coils was rectified by mechanical means for battery charging.

This was achieved by the **commutator** (the word commute meaning 'to change'). Instead of slip rings, a single split ring was used so that the two halves were insulated from one another (see illustration 3.2b).

**3** If you imagine the coil turning slowly through 360° then as the coil sides are exactly halfway between the magnetic poles, the brushes are just passing over the commutator joint. Thus current in the armature coil is reversing in direction but simultaneously the connections to the external circuit are being reversed so that the *current in the load is always in the same direction*: namely, it is direct current, with a waveform as in illustration 3.2a, and may be used to charge a battery.

**4** In practice, a single coil would give insufficient voltage to be of use, so a series of coils is wound round the armature perimeter and the ends are connected to a commutator which has many segments. The result of this arrangement is that at any one time a constant number of coil sides are passing the N and S poles; the voltage and current are both nearly constant but with a ripple which depends on how many conductors and slots are used.

Illustration 3.4 shows a typical armature and it should be noted that the coils are wound in slots of a laminated iron armature. The reason for the iron-cored armature is to create a path for the magnetic lines of force to go through and so the field is stronger and more concentrated.

**5** Referring again to illustration 3.2a the output wave form of the simple single-coil generator is shown. Comparison with illustration 3.5 shows that the multicoil armature gives a higher output which is nearly constant.

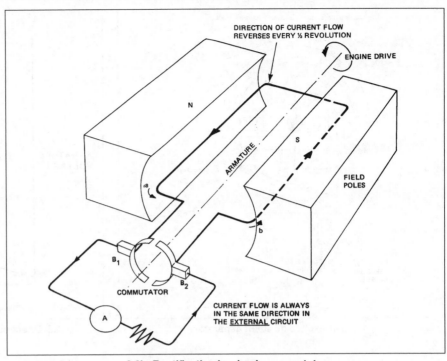

**3.2b  Rectification by simple commutator**

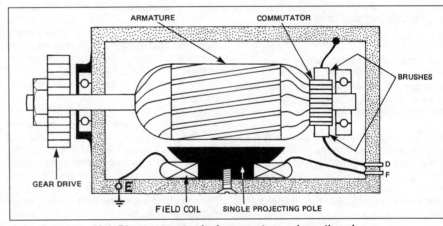

**3.4  Direct current unipole generator – schematic only**

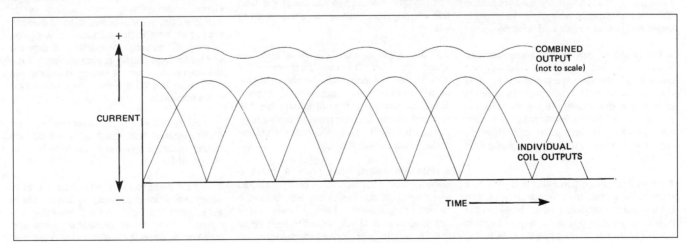

**3.5  Multi-coil armature output**

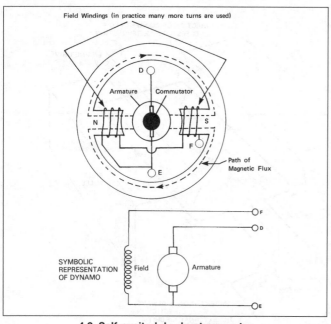

4.2 Self-excited dc shunt generator

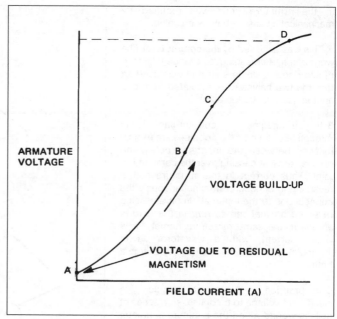

4.5 Direct current dynamo no-load characteristic

## 4 The dc generator – excitation and control

**1** Permanent magnets are not used in motorcycle dc generators because it is possible to obtain stronger fields using electromagnets and, moreover, the magnetic field strength is then controllable.

**2** A field winding wrapped round the poles may be supplied with a small current from the armature and hence this type of generator is said to be a self-excited shunt generator (shunt meaning 'in parallel' as are the armature and field coils). The arrangement is shown in illustration 4.2 together with the conventional diagram for a shunt generator. Two poles are shown in the schematic diagram and the coils wound over them are in series and constitute the **field winding**.

**3** The Lucas E3 type dynamo was standard equipment for many years and used only one projecting pole (see illustration 3.4). It is always necessary to have magnetic poles in pairs but in this model the frame forms the opposite pole. Rather incorrectly, therefore, this dynamo was referred to as a UNIPOLE type. The arrangement allows a smaller overall diameter.

**4** When a dc shunt generator is driven by a motorcycle engine, the armature rotates, and because of the residual magnetism left in the poles, there will be a small voltage induced in the armature which will appear between the armature D and E terminals.

The field coil terminal F is connected externally directly to D (via a pair of contacts in the regulator box) and so the induced armature voltage will drive a small current down the field winding, thus creating more magnetic flux and a rise in armature voltage. In turn, this gives a higher field current, a higher magnetic flux and a higher armature voltage.

You might ask, why does this voltage not continue to rise and rapidly burn out the field winding? The answer is that the iron of the field poles eventually becomes magnetically saturated, providing a natural limit to the armature voltage. Even so, the voltage attained could cause the field winding to fail and dynamos must not be run at high speed without a control box. Another factor in field coil limitation is the resistance of the field coil windings, something we shall return to later.

**5** If the dynamo were run at a constant speed, with F and D terminals connected but with no external load, then the characteristic of armature voltage against field current would be similar to that of illustration 4.5. Points B, C and D correspond to the terminal voltage for decreasing values of resistance added in series with the field.

**6** Note particularly that point A gives a generated voltage dependent on the residual magnetism of the field iron. Sometimes a generator put into service may have insufficient residual magnetism to start up or may generate with reversed polarity. To correct both situations it is usual to *flash* the

field windings by connecting F and E *momentarily* to a battery; if the generator is for negative earth (ground) working then the battery connection would be F+ and E- and vice versa for positive earth (ground) systems. In Section 6, where the cut-out is discussed, it will be seen that this can be done in situ by pressing the cut-out contacts together for a very short time when the ignition is switched off.

## 5 Voltage regulation

**1** The dynamo will be driven by the motorcycle engine over a wide speed-range. Correspondingly the generated voltage will be variable and, without some form of control, the battery and electrical equipment would be destroyed. The voltage required to charge a 6 volt motorcycle battery is approximately 7.8 – 8.0 volts and the device designed to keep the dynamo at this voltage over the speed range is the **regulator**.

Most dynamo-equipped motorcycles used 6 volt systems, but equally a 12 volt battery would require a dynamo charging voltage in excess of 12 volts.

**2** The simplest form of regulation is that in which a resistor is periodically connected in series with the field winding. Inserting the resistor will reduce the generator voltage and conversely, when the resistor is shorted out, cause an increase.

**3** Illustration 5.3 shows a simplified arrangement in which the field resistor (R) is switched in and out of circuit between 40 and 70 times per second, so the generated voltage rises and falls between certain limits, the average of which is that required for charging.

**4** Illustration 5.4 shows a simple regulator circuit, featuring an electromagnet which overcomes the pull of a restraining spring on the iron armature at the voltage setting of 7.8 – 8.0 volts and opens the contacts, thus switching in the additional field resistor (R). As the voltage falls the magnetic pull on the regulator armature decreases and the contacts again close when the spring pull overcomes the magnetic force. Thus the dynamo voltage hunts between two limits, but so long as the average voltage is within the specified limits all is well. The value of R is between 27 – 45 ohms depending upon the model of regulator.

**5** You may ask, what happens if engine speed slows to the point where the dynamo voltage is less than that of the battery? The battery will drive current back into the dynamo and the battery would soon become discharged. There must be some device which breaks the connection between the dynamo and battery when the dynamo speed drops below the charging voltage limit. This device is called the **CUT-OUT** and is discussed in the following Section.

## 6  The Cut-out

**1** Rather similar to the regulator in its mode of working, the cut-out consists of an electromagnet which pulls in its armature at a pre-set dynamo voltage. When this happens, a pair of heavy duty contacts connect the D terminal of the dynamo to the battery. At tickover speeds, the dynamo voltage drops below that of the battery and the cut-out drops out, thus disconnecting the battery from the dynamo.

**2** Illustration 6.2 shows the general idea, although as with the regulator, there are certain practical improvements that can be made to ensure best working, these being dealt with in the following Sections. The regulator and cut-out are usually contained in one control box.

## 7  Compensated Voltage Control (CVC)

**1** There are serious shortcomings of the simple voltage regulator since, as its name implies, it controls the dynamo voltage and

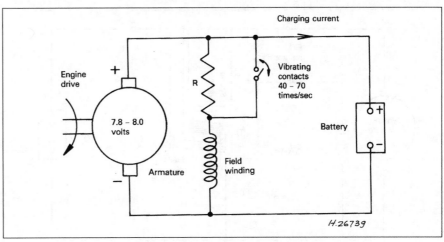

**5.3  Principle of the voltage regulator**

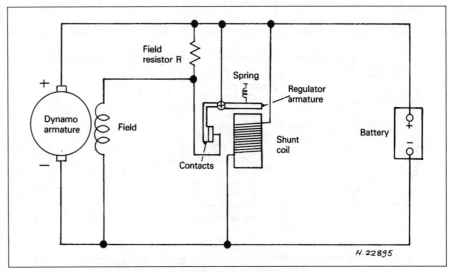

**5.4  Simple voltage regulator**

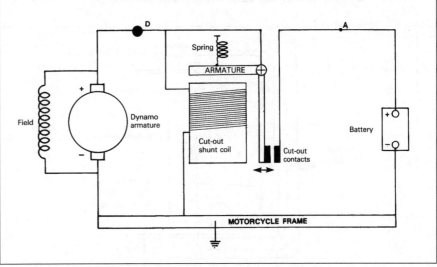

**6.2  Simple cut-out – regulator not shown**

11

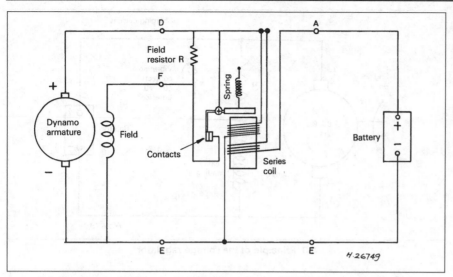

**7.1 Regulator with Compensated Voltage Control (CVC) (cut-out not shown)**

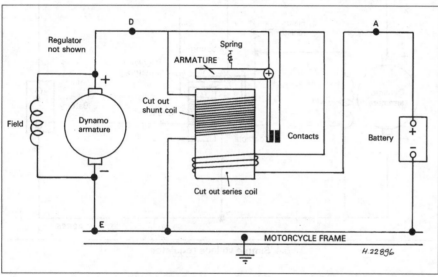

**7.3 Cut-out with series coil (regulator not shown)**

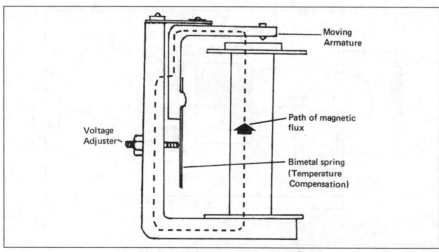

**8.2 Magnetic paths for voltage regulator**

not the current. When a battery is discharged this would result in a very large charging current from the dynamo, which could damage the dynamo, regulator and battery. What is needed is a device which will sense the output current and introduce a fall in the dynamo terminal voltage as the current to the battery increases. This is called Compensated Voltage Control (CVC) and is achieved by winding a few turns of heavy gauge wire over the regulator electromagnet and passing the dynamo charging current through them (see illustration 7.1).

**2** The magnetic effect is to assist the main winding in opening the regulator contacts at a lower voltage. As the battery charges up, the terminal voltage will rise and the charging current will decrease.

**3** The **cut-out** electromagnet also has a series winding of heavy gauge wire wound over the main shunt winding. Charging current passes through this series winding. The main shunt winding senses the dynamo voltage and pulls in the contacts at about 6.5 volts so that the dynamo connects to the battery and charging occurs (see illustration 7.3).

Charging current passing out to the battery creates a magnetic field in the series winding which assists that of the main shunt winding. The effect is to *reinforce* the pull on the armature, so keeping the contacts more firmly together.

**4** However, when the dynamo speed drops to tickover, the generated voltage drops below that of the battery and current reverses, flowing back into the dynamo. This reverse current, flowing through the series winding creates a magnetic field which *opposes* that of the main shunt winding and throws open the cut-out contacts. The contact-opening voltage is between 4.8 – 5.5 volts according to the control box model and the temperature. This is also called the *drop-out voltage*.

## 8 Temperature compensation

**1** The effect of a temperature rise is to increase the resistance of the main shunt coils of both the regulator and the cut-out. Higher coil resistance means that the dynamo voltage must rise to push through the current necessary to open the contacts (regulator) or close the contacts (cut-out).

**2** In practice, the armature return springs are flat strips made in bimetal form which bend with temperature change and accordingly change the spring pressure. Illustration 8.2 shows the arrangement of bimetal spring temperature compensation and the complete magnetic circuit.

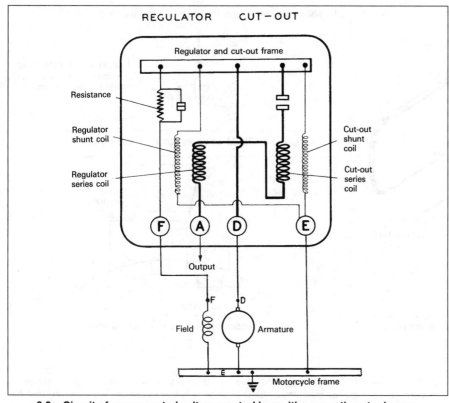

REGULATOR     CUT – OUT

Regulator and cut-out frame

Resistance

Regulator shunt coil

Regulator series coil

Cut-out shunt coil

Cut-out series coil

F   A   D   E

Output

F   D

Field   Armature

E

Motorcycle frame

**9.2a  Circuit of compensated voltage control box with connections to dynamo**

**9.2b  Lucas RB107 control box**

## 9  Complete control box

**1** Control boxes containing a regulator and cut-out for use with a two brush dynamo were produced by Lucas from 1936. The popular MCR1 used a wire wound resistor of about 30 ohms and continued in use until the 1950's, when the similar MCR2 replaced it. One difference was the resistor which now became a round carbon disc fixed to the frame. Its ohmic value was slightly higher at about 40 ohms.

In 1954 the RB107 was introduced and used in great numbers; the last of the range was the RB108 of 1960 which was finally superseded by alternator systems.

**2** Illustration 9.2a shows the circuit diagram for a complete control box with connections to the dynamo, and illustration 9.2b is the RB107 in cutaway form.

## 10  Dynamo construction and overhaul

**1** The two brush dynamo came into service in 1936 to replace the earlier three brush dynamo. This became the standard charging set (with certain variations) up to the time when it was superseded by the alternator. Space does not allow us to go into detail about the early 3 brush dynamo but please see 'Restoring Motorcycles; Electrics' by Roy Bacon and 'The Vintage Motorcyclists' Workshop' by Radco listed in Section 13.

### Construction

**2** Illustration 10.2 shows the construction of the E3 series also used as part of a Magdyno. Early models E3 and E3HM were of 35 watt output and negative earth (ground) up to 1951, when positive earth (ground) systems were introduced; up to 1949 the commutator end bearing was of the plain type but this was

**11**

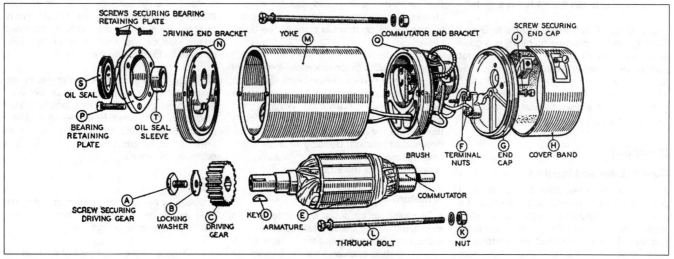

**10.2  Lucas dynamo (E3 series)**

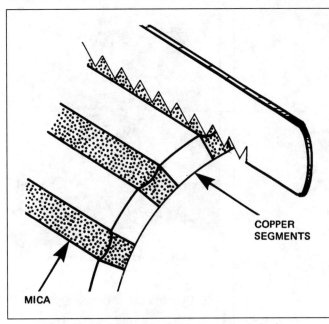

MICA

COPPER
SEGMENTS

**10.5a Undercutting mica between commutator bars**

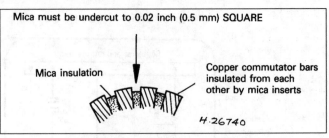

Mica must be undercut to 0.02 inch (0.5 mm) SQUARE

Mica insulation

Copper commutator bars
insulated from each
other by mica inserts

H.26740

**10.5b Mica undercutting measurement**

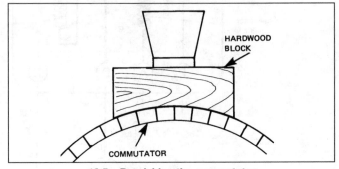

HARDWOOD
BLOCK

COMMUTATOR

**10.5c Burnishing the commutator**

changed to a ball bearing for the 1950 range onward. At the same time, the dynamo was lengthened and the output uprated to 60 watts (E3L and E3LM).

Larger 3.5 inch diameter dynamos with 75 watt output were also introduced for motorcycles with coil ignition (C35S series).

**3** Servicing is mainly concerned with cleaning away brush dust, checking bearings for wear, brushes for free movement and remaining length, electrical testing of field and armature. See the appropriate sub-Section for details.

### Testing

**4** A preliminary check on the electrical health of a dynamo is to see if it will run as a motor.

Join D and F and apply 6 volts to D and earth (ground); if the dynamo runs it is a good indication that all is well. This test is not conclusive, however, because a dynamo may run as a motor even if there is an armature winding fault which would prevent it generating, but it does at least indicate that the field connections are correct.

### Overhaul

#### Commutator and brushes

**5** Commutators wear after a long period of use and may be cleaned up by the use of a thin strip of glasspaper wrapped completely round the commutator bars. Thorough cleaning-off with methylated spirits (stoddard solvent) is essential to remove abrasive particles.

If the bars are too badly scored for this treatment then the commutators must be dry skimmed (ie no lubricant) on a lathe. The insulation (mica) must then be undercut to a depth of about 0.02 inch (0.5 mm) using a hacksaw blade with the blade teeth ground to the correct width (see illustrations 10.5a and 10.5b).

After undercutting the commutator bar mica insulation, all burrs must be removed with a Swiss file and the commutator polished with very fine glasspaper, or burnished with a small block of hardwood (see illustration 10.5c).

**6** Brushes should always be renewed when the dynamo is overhauled, but for routine checks only renew if the hairspring holding the brush down is close to the brush carrier.

Genuine Lucas brushes are pre-formed but it is safest to bed-in all new brushes. This is done by wrapping a strip of fine glass paper (abrasive side outwards) round the commutator and pressing the brush lightly down while the commutator is rocked in the direction of rotation. Bedding-in is complete when full contact over the brush working face is evident. *Do not use emery paper.*

#### Armature

**7** To check an armature it is necessary to strip it out of the casing, taking care when withdrawing it to safeguard the brushes which should be lifted back and held in position (or taken out of their carriers).

With a test meter on high ohms range (or use a battery in series with a bulb) test the insulation between the commutator and the iron armature laminations. The insulation resistance should be very high and if low (or the bulb lights) there is a short between the windings and frame.

If all is in order, use the test meter on low ohms range to check the resistance between adjacent commutator bars all round. Each reading should be the same; if one is higher then that armature coil is open-circuit. Checking for shorted turns ideally needs a growler in which the armature is slowly rotated by hand between a V-block laminated core which has a mains ac primary winding on it. When shorted turns on the armature span the growler laminations, the buzzing note changes because the shorted turns are like a heavy load on the growler secondary (see Chapter 15 for more on the Growler).

Finally check for solder splashes in the frame. It may be that a connection between the commutator bars and windings has been electrically overloaded. Re-soldering might be possible but if any faults are found in an armature it is advisable to send it to a professional repairer.

#### Field coil

**8** Check by using a high range ohmmeter that the insulation resistance between the windings and frame is high.

Next measure the resistance of the field coil which for early E3 models is 3.2 ohms, and

2.8 ohms from 1950 on. A single shorted turn, enough to stop the dynamo working, would not show up conclusively on this test but an open circuit would.

If a field coil rewind is necessary, the awkward part is removal and refitting the field pole shoe. It is put on very tight in manufacture and the fixing screw then caulked by pin-pinching the case metal into the head slot.

To refit, an expander of some sort must be used (see illustration 10.8) to force the pole shoe hard up against the case – so unless the workshop equipment is available it is again best to send it to a professional.

### Bearings

**9** Examine the armature and field poles to see if rubbing has occurred. If bright patches are evident, the bearings have probably worn. Early models used a bush at one end and a ball bearing at the other. Later units had ball bearings at both ends.

The sintered bronze bush requires soaking in thin oil overnight before installation, whereas the ball bearing(s) should be lightly packed with high melting-point grease (HMP).

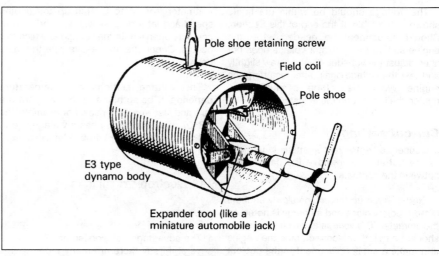

**10.8 Refitting a pole shoe**

## 11 Control box settings

**1** The most frequently found types of control boxes containing both cut-out and regulator are the Lucas MCR1, MCR2 and the RB107

(see illustrations 11.1a, 11.1b and 9.2b). The settings to be checked are as follows:

*(a) Voltage of the regulator.*
*(b) Cut-in voltage of the cut-out.*
*(c) Drop-out voltage of the cut-out.*

For full servicing, the gap settings of points and armatures should also be checked; readers are referred to Roy Bacon's and Radco's books listed in Section 13.

### Voltage regulator setting

**2** Voltage regulator setting is checked by slipping a piece of paper between the cut-out contacts so that no charging can occur. Connect a voltmeter between D and E and then start the engine, running up speed slowly until the voltmeter needle flicks showing that the regulator is working.

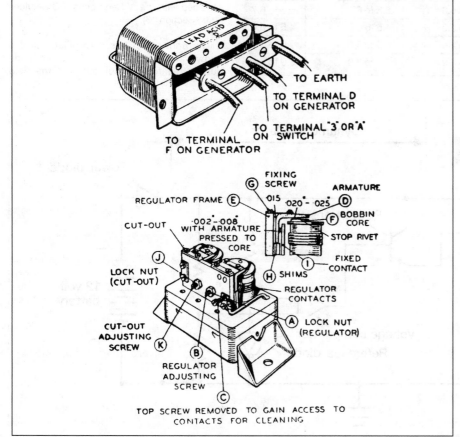

**11.1a  Lucas MCR1 control box**

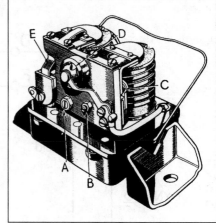

**11.1b  Lucas MCR2 control box**

A  *Cut-out adjuster*
B  *Regulator adjuster*
C  *Regulator contacts*
D  *Field resistor*
E  *Cut-out contact blade*

**11**

The voltage should be within the limits shown in the table at the end of this Section. Should adjustment be needed, stop the engine so that the regulator voltage does not alter, adjust the voltage adjuster screw slightly and test the voltage again after restarting the engine. When the setting is satisfactory, tighten the locknut on the adjuster screw.

### Cut-out settings

**3** Connect a centre-zero ammeter in the lead to the battery and remove the paper from between the contacts.

Start and run up the engine slowly until the cut-out points close and a charge is noted on the ammeter. The voltage at which this occurs should be noted. If incorrect, stop the engine and make a small adjustment to the cut-out screw (in for high voltage). Repeat the check until the correct cut in voltage is obtained.

When the revs are allowed to drop slowly, there will be a reverse current before the cut-out contacts open. This should not exceed 5 amperes (MCR2 and RB107). Take off the lead from the A terminal and connect a voltmeter from A to E. Run up the engine speed and let it drop slowly until the cut-out contacts open – note the voltage at which this occurs. Check the test results with the table below.

The voltage settings are temperature dependent, being higher if the temperature falls and vice versa if it rises. For example, the RB107 regulator setting has a voltage rise of 0.2 volt per 10°C (50°F) drop in temperature.

## 12 Electronic regulators

**1** The advantages of working at 12 volts are several. Firstly there are many more spares available including bulbs and other components but the major gain is that, for a given power output, the current is half that of a 6 volt system.

The resistive power losses in a dynamo will be reduced dramatically by a factor of four times remembering that power loss is proportional to the *square* of the current (see Chapter 2). The volt drops which inevitably occur will be a lower proportion of 12 volts for a 6 volt system. The overall output is therefore higher after conversion to 12 volts and as an example a nominal 60 watt Lucas E3 dynamo can be made to produce 90 watts.

**2** Electronic regulators have been developed for both 6 volt and 12 volt working and for both positive and negative earth (ground). Given a choice, it would seem better to aim for a 12 volt system for the reasons above.

**3** Fortunately the 6 volt dynamo will usually run up to 16/18 volts and this will allow it to be regulated for 12 volt operation without problem but there has to be a system of controlling the field current.

This is achieved with an electronic regulator of which there are several designs. Some Lucas E3 6 volt dynamos will not *always* run with 12 volt regulators according to some reports (but better results are usual with Miller dynamos). In this case it is due to the need for a rewind anyway and owners would be well advised to have the machine rewound for 12 volt working by a professional rewind company. When this has been done the application of an electronic regulator will present no problem. Good results have been obtained with the 'V Reg.' units (AO Services – see Section 13).

**4** The principle of this dc regulator unit is shown in illustration 12.4. A power diode substitutes for the cut out and the field

### Voltage settings for Lucas control boxes

| Check | MCR1 | MCR2 | RB107 |
|---|---|---|---|
| Cut in voltage | 6.2 to 6.6 | 6.3 to 6.7 | 6.3 to 6.7 |
| Drop out voltage | 3.5 to 5.3 | 4.5 to 5.0 | 4.5 to 5.0 |
| Reverse current (amperes) | 0.7 to 2.5 | 3.0 to 5.0 | 3.0 to 5.0 |
| Regulator voltage @ 20°C (68°F) | 7.8 to 8.2 | 7.6 to 8.0 | 8.0 to 8.4 |

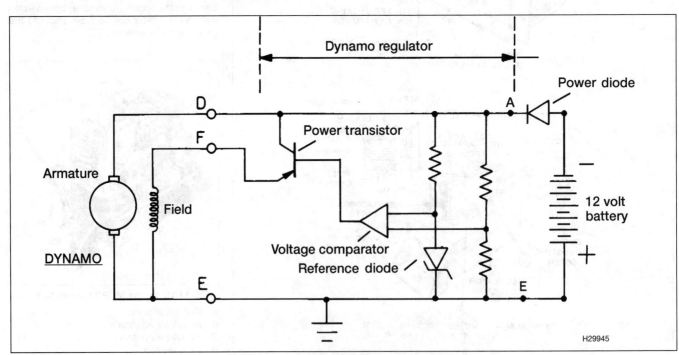

**12.4  dc dynamo electronic regulator (schematic only)**

**12.5  6-volt JG6 dynamo electronic regulator**

winding is fed from a power transistor. A comparator will switch on field current when the dynamo voltage drops below a set level.

**5** Illustration 12.5 shows another popular electronic unit, the JG6 which may be obtained in 6 volt or 12 volt versions and also for positive or negative earth (ground) (Dave Lindsley – see Section 13).

For further details of suppliers see *'Old Bike Mart'* in the references below.

## 13  Further reading and references

**1** For further reading refer to *'Restoring Motorcycles; Electrics'* by Roy Bacon (Out of print but try the public library), and *'The Vintage Motorcyclists' Workshop'* by Radco (Haynes).

**2** More information on dynamo regulators can be found on www.teb-tec.demon.co.UK.

**3** The following are good sources for spares and repairs in the UK:

*Old Bike Mart* (Monthly journal: a good source for specialist repairers), telephone 01507 524004.

*AO Services* (Dynamo regulators and other British bike equipment), telephone 01953 884681.

*Dave Lindsley* (Regulators, magneto rewinds, starter reconditioning), telephone 01706 365838.

**11**

**Notes**

# Chapter 12
# Charging – Alternators

## Contents

## 1 Introduction

**1** The dc generator (dynamo) was standard in all but small motorcycles until 1953, when Lucas fitted the Triumph Speed Twin with an alternator. From then on, the alternator reigned supreme and underwent several stages of development so that today it is a high efficiency assembly of first class design.

**2** It is worth looking at the shortcomings of the dc generator. First, the current from the armature had to be collected from the commutator by brushes. This was a considerable technical achievement but, nevertheless, meant that maintenance for wear on brushes and commutator was necessary. A characteristic feature of the alternator is that the armature in which the output current is generated is always stationary and hence an improvement in efficiency is possible (see illustration 1.2).

**3** The alternator can be run faster than the dynamo because there is no problem of the commutator. This means that charging can begin at lower engine speeds than is the case with the dynamo (see illustration 1.3).

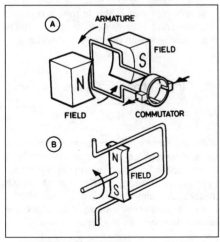

**1.2 Essentials of the dynamo (dc) and alternator (ac)**

A   Dynamo (stationary field)
B   Alternator (rotating field)

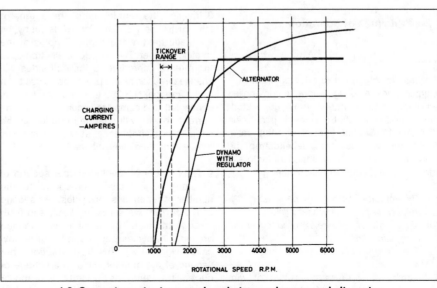

**1.3 Generator output comparison between dynamo and alternator**

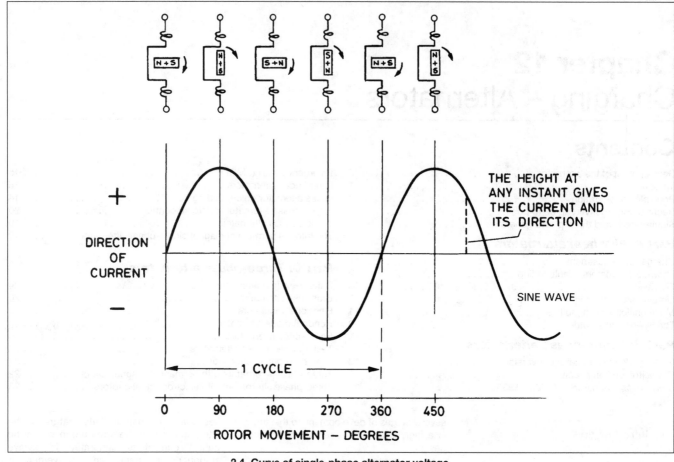

**2.4 Curve of single-phase alternator voltage**

**4** The rectifier used to convert alternating output to direct current will not allow battery current to flow back into the alternator so there is no need for a cut-out.

## 2 Principles of operation

**1** When an electrical conductor crosses a magnetic field a voltage (more properly called an electromotive force – emf) is generated. The same formula that governs dc generation (Chapter 11, Section 2) applies in this case. Generated voltage (emf) depends on the following, all of which are important factors in the design and control of alternators.

(a) The **velocity** of the wire(s) passing at right-angles to the magnetic field.
(b) The **length** of the wire exposed to the magnetic field.
(c) The **strength** of the magnetic field.

**2** In order to increase the length of wire exposed to the magnetic field, coils are used; one or more coils is known as a winding. The magnetic field density (flux density) is always enhanced by using laminated iron frames on which the field coils and armature windings are wound.

**3** Imagine the simple coil of the alternator (see illustration 1.2, item B) which is cut by the magnetic field of the N and S poles of the rotating magnet. The voltage or electromotive force (emf) generated in the coil sides will change direction as the poles pass close by in cyclic rotation, N S N S etc. Thus if the coil is connected to a complete circuit externally current flowing will change direction at the same rate, or frequency, at which the poles rotate, hence the name *alternating current*.

**4** The number of revolutions per second of the magnet will also correspond to the number of repetitions, or cycles, per second of the current wave flowing back and forth through the coil. This number was defined originally in cycles per second, but is now called Hertz (Hz); thus 50 revolutions per second of the magnet will give a voltage or current frequency of 50 Hertz. A graph or waveform of the way in which the electric waves change with time is shown in illustration 2.4.

The sine wave occurs throughout nature – twanging a spring will cause it to oscillate with an amplitude in the form of a sine wave, which gradually dies away. This is then a *damped* sine wave and is the same form as oscillations in a motorcycle with poor shock absorbers!

## 3 Single-phase and three-phase generation

**1** An alternator which produces a single sine wave of current is a single-phase generator; it is the type of output from cycle dynamos, flywheel alternators, the range of British motorcycle alternators from the 1950's onwards, and other motorcycles where current demand was moderate.

**2** A better way of utilising the winding space round the stator (the stationary part of the alternator on which the output coils are wound) would be to use three pairs of coils,

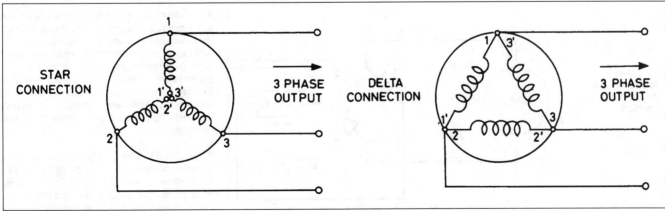

**3.3 Three-phase alternator and its waveform**

but there has to be a special way of connecting them to bring out the power: this is a three-phase alternator.

**3** If a rotating magnet sweeps past the three sets of coils, then each will produce a sine wave of induced voltage, but in sequence. Since a complete revolution of the magnet corresponds to 360° rotation, then each sine wave of voltage will be 120° apart from the other two (see illustration 3.3). Each coil will have the same voltage generated within it by the rotating magnetic field, but there is a time difference corresponding to the time it takes the magnet to travel from one coil to the next, from 1 to 2, 2 to 3, 3 to 1, etc. The voltages generated are said to have a 120° *phase difference* from each other.

**4** It is possible to avoid using six output wires by connecting the coils together in either a 'star' or a 'delta' configuration. Illustration 3.4 shows these connections, both of which are possible for motorcycle alternators.

**5** The 'star' connection will result in a higher voltage between any pair of output terminals than is generated by one coil alone, but will not be twice one coil voltage because of the time phase difference between any pair. In fact, the voltage between lines (as the output leads are called) is 1.732 x coil voltage.

In the 'delta' connection, the output voltage will be that of any one coil in value, but the currents generated in each coil will add to give a line current of 1.732 x one coil current. For this reason, where heavy output current is required, the stator windings are preferably connected in delta.

**6** Looking again at the waveforms of the three phases (see illustration 3.3); if a vertical line is drawn at any point on the time axis, the nett sum of the waveforms is always zero. This means that there is no need for a return wire from the centre point of the star winding, and additionally that current flowing outwards on any one line is balanced by the inward flow in

the other two lines for both star and delta. Under these conditions, the three-phase circuit is said to be balanced. There are circumstances, in mains power systems, where the star point is earthed but is not usual in motorcycle or car three phase equipment. There is one exception in a Honda case and is considered later in this Chapter.

### 4  Rectification – converting ac to dc

**1** The motorcycle battery acts as a storage unit for electrical energy and is a direct current device. Current flowing out from it is direct current as is the current flowing into it when being charged.

**2** It is necessary to convert the alternating current from the alternator into a form of direct current before it is useful in a

**12**

**3.4 Star and delta connections**

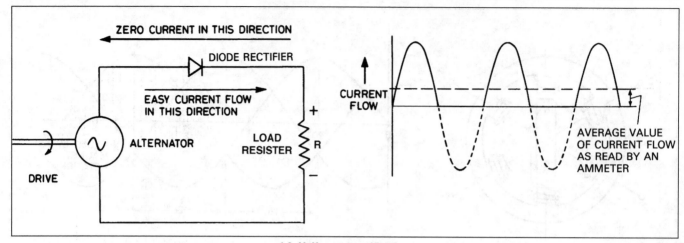

**4.3 Half-wave rectification**

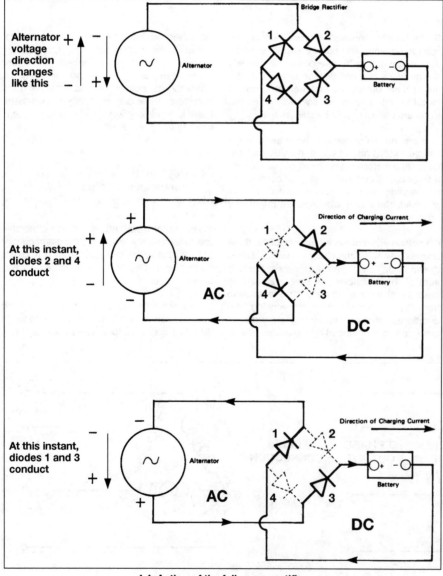

**4.4 Action of the full-wave rectifier**

motorcycle electrical system. Referring to illustration 2.4, note that the sine wave shows that alternating current flows first one way round a circuit and then in the opposite direction. If the lower half of the sine wave could be eliminated then current would flow in pulses, but always in the same direction. For battery charging this pulsation of current does not matter, and an ammeter would register the *average* value of current.

## Rectifier operation

**3** A device which will prevent current flowing in one direction, but allow it to flow in the opposite direction, is called a rectifier. Modern rectifiers are usually made of semiconductor materials and are highly efficient. Illustration 4.3 shows a simple circuit consisting of an alternator connected to a resistive load, via a rectifier. The lower half of the current wave is stopped by the rectifier, allowing pulses to flow through the resistor, but always in the same direction – that is, direct current. For obvious reasons this is known as half-wave rectification: it is inefficient because the lower half of the current wave is wasted. Note the polarity of the voltage across the load resistor R.

**4** A better method of conversion is to use full-wave rectification. As the name implies, the whole of the alternating sine wave is used, and to accomplish this, four rectifiers are used (see illustration 4.4). The alternator will produce an output voltage which changes polarity so that it is, in effect, like a battery which rapidly reverses its leads – and we may give *instantaneous* + and – signs to the output terminals.

**5** Current will flow through a rectifier in the direction of the arrow, but not against it, so if the positive (+) wire at the alternator is traced through, current will flow through the battery and two rectifiers. When the polarity reverses, current flows through the opposite pair of

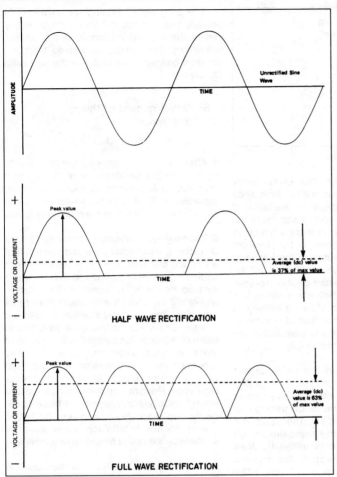

**4.5a Alternating current and rectified waveforms**

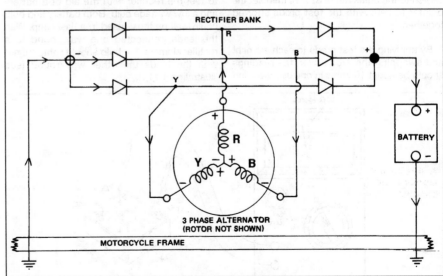

**4.5b Layout of full-wave (bridge) rectifier**

rectifiers, but always in the same direction through the battery. *Thus the whole of the ac wave has been routed to the battery.*

Illustration 4.5a shows the waveforms from half-wave and full-wave rectifiers. The physical layout of one type of full-wave rectifier (a bridge rectifier) is shown in illustration 4.5b. The individual rectifier elements are often known as diodes, or sometimes as diode rectifiers.

**6** Note that the diodes 1, 2, 3 and 4, although mounted on a single spindle, can be drawn in a square for easier visualisation. The second sketch shows the electrical arrangement and this can then be rearranged to give the bottom sketch which is the usual way to portray a full-wave rectifier. The two negative sides of diodes 1 and 4 are connected together. To remember how to draw a full-wave bridge rectifier make the left terminal negative (-), the ac being fed in at top and bottom terminals. Then the right-hand terminal is positive. Draw in the diode symbols (arrow heads) going from the negative terminal to the positive terminal.

**7** Three-phase rectification is along the same lines as the single-phase full-wave rectifier

and is shown in illustration 4.7. This shows a three-phase alternator connected to a three-phase full-wave rectifier. As in the case of the single-phase rectifier, the negative

halves of each phase wave are reversed giving a direct current or voltage wave which has a high average value with a superimposed ripple.

**RECTIFIER BANK**

**BATTERY**

**3 PHASE ALTERNATOR (ROTOR NOT SHOWN)**

**MOTORCYCLE FRAME**

**4.7 Three-phase rectification**

*Current flow is shown at instant when R phase is at maximum voltage*

**12**

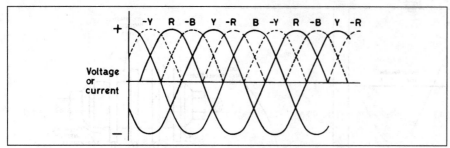

**4.8 Waveforms of the full-wave three-phase rectifier**

**8** The effect of reversing each negative half cycle is to give an output voltage or current which has a high average value and a much lower ripple than in the single-phase case. In fact there will be six 'half-waves' per 360° (see illustration 4.8) and the average value of direct current or voltage is higher than for a single-phase full-wave rectifier.

The current arrowheads in illustration 4.7 show the path of currents in the three lines at the instant when the top 'R' coil of the alternator is a positive (+) max and the other two will be negative (-) at half max value. Note that this is not a diagram of a complete charging circuit since some form of regulating the alternator output is needed.

### Rectifier testing

**9** If the battery is found to be discharged even after a prolonged run, or after the machine has been standing for only a short while, then the rectifier may be at fault.

Each element of the bridge rectifier should pass current in one direction but not in the other. (In practice a small 'back leakage' can be tolerated.) To test the rectifier an analogue multimeter (ie, one with a pointer on a scale) on the ohms range may be used. Switch to the ohms range ($\Omega$ x 1), then set the pointer to zero with the test prods shorted together.

By applying the test prods to each element and swapping the prods over, the readings should be about 10 ohms in one direction and very high (full scale) in the other. Do not worry if the forward resistance is not 10 ohms since the exact value will depend on the make of rectifier and also on the internal voltage of the meter – what is important is that each rectifier element reads the same. If the forward resistances are not the same, or there is a low reverse resistance, the rectifier must be renewed. When measuring the reverse resistance, switch to a high ohms range. It is this reverse path which allows a battery to discharge so it is vital that the reverse resistance of all the separate elements of the rectifier is high (see illustration 4.9).

**10** Digital meters usually have a diode test facility. In the case of one typical meter (the Gunson Digimeter) the meter applies a voltage of about 2.8 volts to the diode through an internal resistance of 1.0 k$\Omega$. The display on the meter then shows the approximate volt drop across the diode in millivolts. Now diodes exhibit a volt drop in the forward direction between 0.3 and 0.8 volts. The reading when connected to a good diode in the forward direction will be 300 to 800 mV and in the reverse direction the meter will read simply 1.

**11** If no ohmmeter is available, it is possible to test the rectifier with the aid of a battery and a low wattage bulb. Both battery and bulb could well be those used in a flashlamp. With the leads connected one way round to a rectifier element, the bulb should light, but not with the leads the other way round (see illustration 4.11).

The principle of testing the elements is clearly that current will flow through easily when the applied voltage is in the correct direction; this voltage is derived from the internal battery of the tester or the flashlamp battery.

## 5 Development of the alternator

**1** Alternators really entered the motorcycle scene with the development of the flywheel magneto. This found application with smaller machines only, due to the limitation on coil sizes in order to fit inside the rotating flywheel.

**2** The early Lucas alternators generated 6 volts dc (approx) after rectification and consisted of a rotating permanent magnet system with a stationary armature (called a stator) on which was wound six coils. There are difficulties in regulating the charge with machines of this type since the magnetic strength is fixed but coarse control was achieved by switching in some of the coils for daylight riding and all of them at night. Later this alternator was produced for 12 volt working and was fitted with a Zener diode to achieve charge regulation. Present day designs now include wound fields (electromagnets) in place of the permanent magnets, thus giving far better charge control. In addition, more power is available by the use of three-phase windings.

**3** The categories of alternator discussed in this chapter are as follows:

*Part A:  Flywheel alternators.*
*Part B:  Permanent magnet single-phase inductor alternators.*
*Part C:  Permanent magnet or electromagnetic three-phase alternators.*

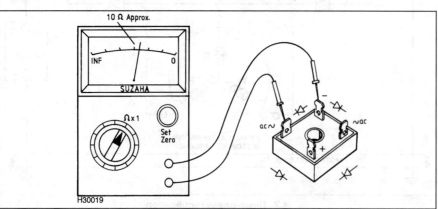

**4.9  How to test a rectifier with a multimeter**

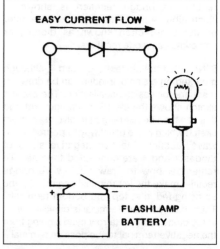

**4.11  Use this method if a tester is not available**

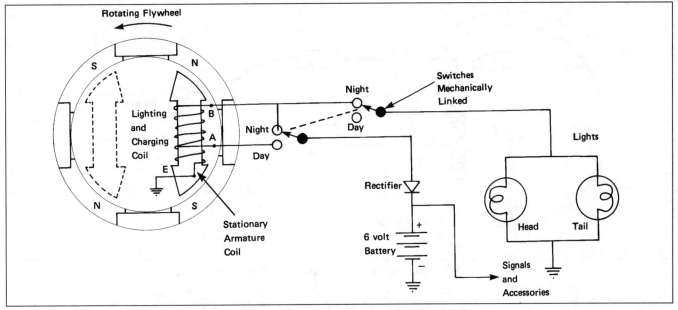

**7.2 Lighting and charging by flywheel alternator**

# Part A: Flywheel alternators

## 6 The flywheel alternator

**1** Generally trouble-free, this set has been touched upon in Chapter 5 where illustrations 5.4a and 5.4b show the details of construction. The flywheel has magnets cast into the rim and these pass over laminated pole shoes on which the lighting and ignition feed coils are wound. As the magnets pass in sequence N→S→N→S, the direction of the magnetic flux changes through the coils and so an alternating voltage is generated in them. If connected to a load such as a bulb an alternating current will flow in the bulb.

## 7 Lighting and charging

**1** The lighting/charging coil of the flywheel assembly has a generated voltage of approximately 6 volts ac.

**2** One end of the coil is earthed (grounded) to the motorcycle frame at point E (see illustration 7.2) and the electrical output comes from either terminal A or B. The higher output comes when the whole of the coil is used (terminal B) and this is switched in when the lights are on. For daytime use without lights, it is sufficient to pick off only part of the output at tap A.

**3** The voltage coming from taps A and B is practically the same when on their respective loads; it is to be expected that the total **generated voltage** at tap B is greater than that at point A, but so also is the load current, since the lights must be supplied. The effect of the heavier current flowing through the whole coil from E to B is to produce a voltage loss so that in fact the voltage that is left is still 6 volts approximately.

**4** It is interesting to see what happens when the engine speed rises. Since the flywheel magnets are passing over the armature coil at a faster rate (or higher frequency) one might expect the generated voltage to rise. There are, however, losses in the coil which increase in proportion to the frequency of the current and the rise in voltage is offset by these losses, so that what finally emerges (known as the terminal voltage) is nearly constant after the first 2000 rpm.

Reference to the graph (see illustration 7.4) shows this, and also shows that if a higher wattage bulb is used in an attempt to raise the illumination level, this simply results in a further lowering of the terminal voltage, and so a probable lowering of the illumination.

 **HAYNES HiNT** *Note that using of a bulb of too low a wattage gives too high a terminal voltage and the bulb then runs at such a high temperature that its life is very short. It is important, therefore, that the correct wattage bulb is always used.*

**12**

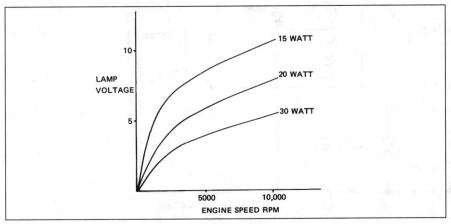

**7.4 Lighting curves**

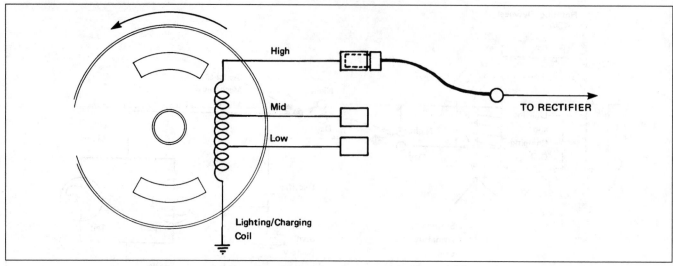

**8.1 Tap changing to alter charge rate (early models)**

## 8 Charge rate adjustment

**1** Some flywheel assemblies make provision for different rates of charge depending on the use to which the machine is put. Up to 3 tappings are made on the lighting/charging coil in illustration 8.1.

**2** The simple lighting/charging assembly has been used for many years, but modern versions now have electronic regulation. One version is shown in illustration 8.2a. The charging output of the alternator is connected to a regulator/rectifier unit in which diode D1 rectifies the current to the battery.

As the engine speed increases, the alternator voltage rises. Diode D2 conducts on the positive half cycles and at a certain voltage, the Zener diode ZD abruptly conducts, feeding current to the gate of the Silicon Controlled Rectifier SCR (or thyristor). The SCR turns on, short circuiting the output of the alternator to earth (ground). This happens on each positive half cycle of the alternator output and so regulates the voltage to the battery (see illustration 8.2b).

**3** If the alternator has a combined lighting and charging coil, the charging will be affected by whether the headlamp is on or off.

Referring again to illustration 8.2a, the headlamp switch connects the load resistor (R) to the alternator lighting tap (L) when the headlamp is off, creating a load equivalent to that of the headlamp bulb. This stabilises the output voltage to the battery. This type of regulator is also used on three-phase alternators.

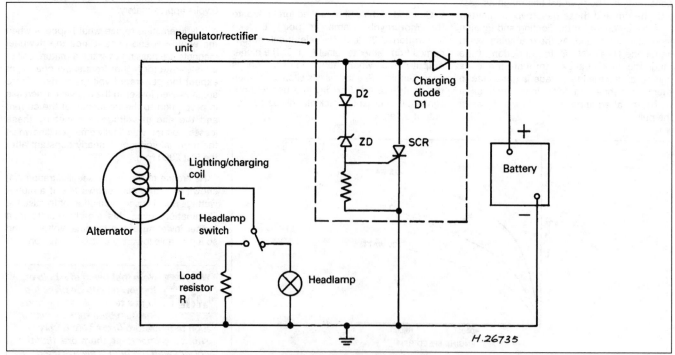

**8.2a Voltage regulator for low power alternator**

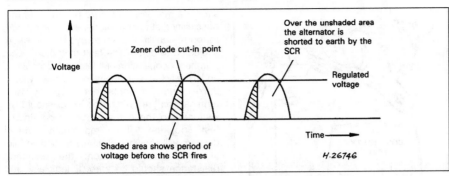

**8.2b  Regulator circuit output waveform**

with no electrical conduction (very high resistance). Lighting/charging coils should show a very low resistance of a few ohms only. Some meters have no scale for continuity checks, but instead a built-in buzzer sounds when there is continuity.

## 10  Flywheel removal

**1** In order to inspect the coils it will be necessary to remove the flywheel with its built-in magnets. To do this correctly, the flywheel must be prevented from rotating, preferably using a special holding tool, whilst its central mounting nut or bolt is removed (see illustration 10.1 overleaf). Note that the flywheel is mounted on a taper, which usually houses a Woodruff key.

**2** A typical flywheel puller is shown, the outer thread of which screws into the flywheel boss once the retaining nut/bolt has been slackened and removed. The puller centre bolt is tightened down on the crankshaft end to dislodge the flywheel from its taper. Note the following precautions:

(a)  *Never hammer the flywheel on or off, otherwise the magnets may be damaged.*

(b)  *Avoid the use of a legged-puller to withdraw the flywheel; this may cause distortion.*

(c)  *Check for wear of the Woodruff key in its crankshaft slot and corresponding flywheel slot.*

(d)  *Check that no foreign objects adhere to the flywheel magnets on reassembly, eg nails, washers, swarf, etc. The poles must be thoroughly clean before refitting.*

(e)  *Tighten the flywheel nut/bolt to the torque setting specified by the machine manufacturer on refitting.*

## 9  Flywheel alternators – fault finding

**1** The majority of faults occurring in motorcycle electrical systems are simple, but finding them may not be so easy. However, a systematic approach will pay dividends, there being no need for the replacement of every item until 'it works'.

### Charging output check

**2** An examination of the basic circuit of the flywheel assembly charging system shown in illustration 9.2 will provide a good example of how to conduct a test routine.

If the battery runs down even though the motorcycle is used regularly, the first thing to check is the charging rate. To do this the circuit between the rectifier and the battery must be broken and an ammeter connected in. *Remember the ammeter is connected always in series with the circuit components as shown.* Note also that if the charging system is working correctly, current will flow through the rectifier in the direction of the arrowhead and down through the battery when the engine is run; thus the ammeter terminals should be connected with polarity as shown in illustration 9.2.

**3** The ammeter should read zero when the engine is not running; if the needle shows a small reverse current, this indicates a leaking rectifier since it should only pass current from left to right in the diagram. If engine speed is briefly run up to 5000 rev/min the charge rate should be about 1 ampere.

If there is no charging current, the next thing is to check the circuit and its components for continuity, that is, to see whether there is an electrical path.

### Continuity check

**4** Use an ohmmeter or a pocket multimeter for this check. If using a multimeter, the 'ohms' or resistance range is required. It is important not to use an ohmmeter on a live circuit. This means disconnecting the battery before the ohmmeter is used.

The two leads from the tester should be applied to the part under test. The meter scale should, of course, read zero for a continuous path and full scale (or infinity) for a component

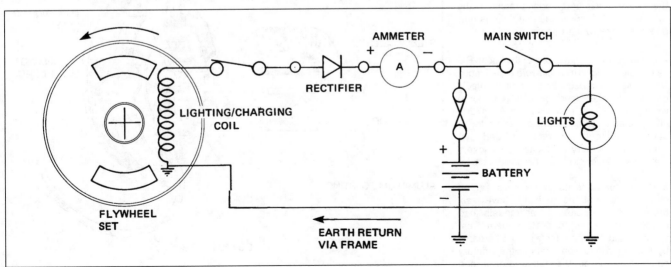

**9.2  Measurement of charge current**

12

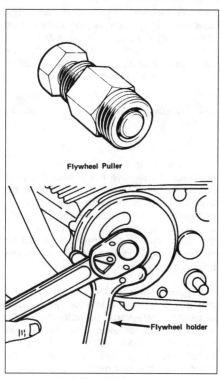

**Flywheel Puller**

**Flywheel holder**

**10.1 Flywheel removal**

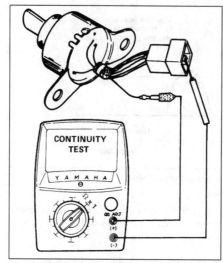

CONTINUITY
TEST

YAMAHA

**11.2 Testing a main/ignition switch for continuity**

## 11 Main/ignition switch faults

1 Switches are made down to a price and are by no means trouble-free. Sometimes there is simply a mechanical failure but there is the possibility that poor contacts will develop due to corrosion if the motorcycle has been subjected to damp. The fault may then result in imperfect operation of lights or accessories, and usually the only cure is to fit a new switch.

2 To check contacts between any two terminals on the switch, the tester should be switched to the ohms range or continuity test position. The machine's wiring diagram will show which contacts should join at each switch position; the resultant resistance should be zero. Check also for intermittent contact by 'wiggling' the key or knob to the switch (see illustration 11.2).

3 Note that bullet or prong connectors can sometimes come apart underneath their plastic weatherproof covers, without it being apparent; check each one by direct inspection.

Wires can occasionally break internally, even though the outer insulation looks sound, especially where the wire passes close to frame components. Breaks can usually be located by lightly stretching the wire until the insulation 'gives' at the fault point.

4 For more on switches see Chapter 16 and for fault tracing see Chapter 18.

# Part B: Single-phase alternators

## 12 The internal permanent magnet single-phase alternator

1 Alternators of this type are usually mounted on the end of the crankshaft, with the rotor running inside a set of stator coils. The principle of operation is thus the same as for the flywheel alternator. One difference, due to the smaller mass and working radius of the rotor magnets, however, is that there is now no significant flywheel effect.

2 Illustration 12.2 shows one of the Lucas RM series alternators. Troubles were experienced with earlier types because of vibration effects on the coils, often causing the entire stator to work loose. The much improved 47204 encapsulated stator shown cured the loose coil trouble, but it is recommended that whenever a primary chaincase is removed, the stator bolts or studs are fixed with Loctite.

3 The stator consists of six coils set on circular laminations which have six projections or poles. Later models had encapsulated coils to protect them from vibration and also from metallic swarf created by the chain and sprockets in the primary chaincase. It is good practice to drain and change the chaincase oil regularly to prevent swarf attaching itself to the magnetised rotor and to protect stator coils if they are of the older unencapsulated type.

4 Two types of stator are likely to be found, those with 3 wires (early types 1953 to 66) and those with 2 wires (later 12 volt version).

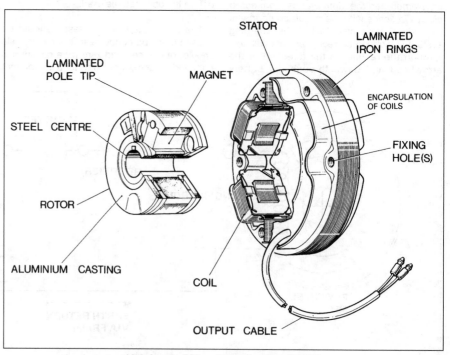

LAMINATED POLE TIP

STEEL CENTRE

ROTOR

ALUMINIUM CASTING

MAGNET

STATOR

LAMINATED IRON RINGS

ENCAPSULATION OF COILS

FIXING HOLE(S)

COIL

OUTPUT CABLE

**12.2 Lucas RM series alternator (RM21)**

The 2-wire version is electrically similar to the early type but the coils are internally connected, and hence give maximum output at all times when running. Early Lucas alternators were designed for 6 volt systems but 12 volt assemblies were supplied for the Triumph Thunderbird in 1965.

**5** The rotor has a steel centre which is hexagon shaped like the head of a bolt. A powerful permanent magnet is mounted on each hexagon, the outer face of which is keyed to a laminated pole tip. The whole is then cast into aluminium (which will not affect the magnetism) and lathe-turned to give a smooth external finish. Thus there are six magnetic poles which pass simultaneously under the six stator windings, and the current from the stator will alternate at a frequency dependent on the crankshaft speed. It is important to maintain a gap between rotor and stator of 0.2 mm (0.008 inch). Note also that early rotors suffered from the centre of the rotor separating from the rest of the casting with disastrous results.

## 13  Early Lucas alternators – 1953 to 1966

**1** The main switch has 3 positions, OFF, PILOT and HEAD, and the six coils are switched so as to give 3 levels of output as shown in illustration 13.1. This shows the lighting switch at HEAD (Headlight) position and all three pairs of coils are in parallel to give maximum output.

**2** In illustration 13.2 with the lighting switch at PILOT position, the output control coils are inoperative and the rectifier receives the current from the battery charging coils only. This is enough to power the pilot and rear lights.

**3** When the main switch is OFF (see illustration 13.3) only a trickle charge is required by the battery. Now the output control coils are working into a short circuit and as a result a heavy current will flow through them. This current will create a magnetic field which tends to offset the magnetic field of the permanent magnet rotor so that the net field strength linking with the battery charging coils is reduced and the electrical output is low.

**4** Lucas made variations so that in some models two sets of coils are connected permanently for battery charging and only one set for output control. The principle of operation, however, remains the same for all cases.

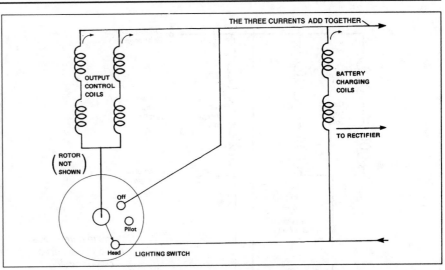

**13.1  HEAD switch position – early Lucas alternator**

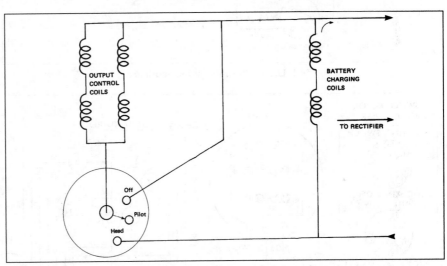

**13.2  PILOT switch position – early Lucas alternator**

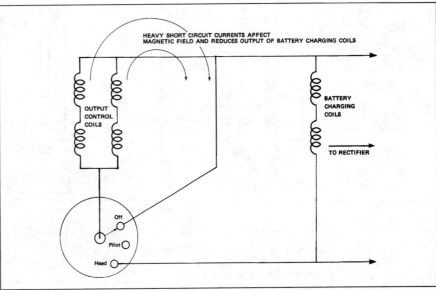

**13.3  OFF switch position – early Lucas alternator**

**12**

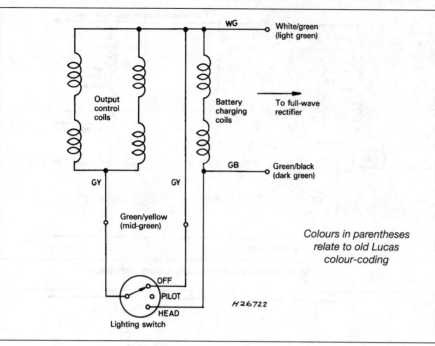

**14.1 Lucas alternator colour-coding**

## 14 Lucas alternator colour-coding

**1** Wiring codes for the three-wire alternators started out using three shades of green but with ageing they became difficult to identify.

A change was made to dark green, green/yellow, and light green, but eventually the colours of green/black, green/yellow, and white/green were chosen for easy identification (see illustration 14.1). For a table of Lucas cable colour codes see illustration 15.2.

## 15 Emergency start (EMG)

**1** One of the many possible wiring options is the Lucas emergency start connection, for use when a battery is flat. With the switch in the EMG position, the output of four coils is taken to the ignition coil via the two coil wire connected to the lighting switch.

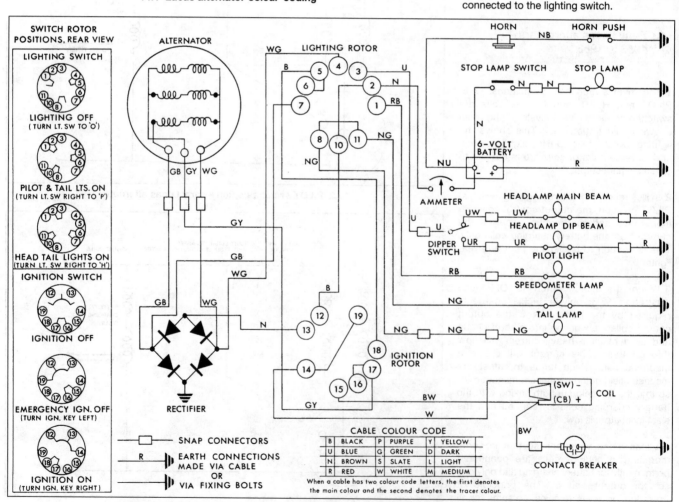

**15.2 6-volt single cylinder motorcycle wiring diagram with emergency start (EMG) facility**

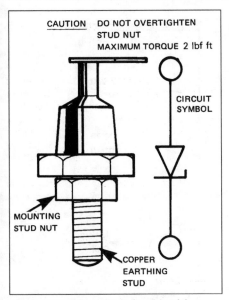

**16.1  Zener diode (positive (+) earth/ground)**

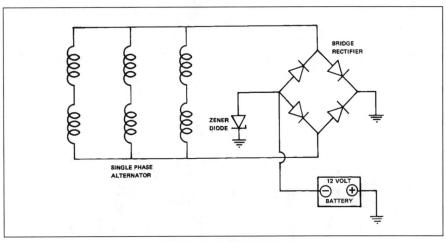

**16.2  Zener stabilised circuit**

**2** The engine may be started and run temporarily in the EMG mode provided the ignition has been accurately timed. Misfiring may soon occur, however, and the switch should be returned to the ignition IGN position. In the EMG connection, the ignition system is converted to Energy Transfer (ET) (see Chapter 5). A connection is still made to the battery, however, and, as its voltage rises, will cause misfiring (see illustration 15.2). This diagram requires some patience to follow but use the switch rotor position as shown in the table on the left of the diagram to see the connections for each mode.

## 16  Later Lucas alternators

**1** Some degree of battery charging control was achieved by switching coils in early circuits but the method was by no means perfect. Motorcycle electrical designers had long wished to use 12 volt circuits and the opportunity came in 1963 with the arrival of the power Zener diode (see illustration 16.1).

Using the standard Lucas RM alternator, which has the ability to run a 12 volt circuit, the solution was a vast improvement over earlier arrangements and was quickly adopted in new motorcycles and by owners who wanted to convert their machines from 6 volt to 12 volt.

**2** Basically, the Zener diode behaves like a pressure relief valve. Until the pressure on it reaches about 14 volts it will not pass current, but at this voltage it becomes partially conductive and drains off to earth (ground)

some of the charging current. As the voltage rises to 15V the Zener passes a large current and virtually none reaches the battery.

If an electrical load, such as the head and tail bulbs is now switched on, this will lower the system voltage and the Zener diode becomes less conductive and more rectified current flows to the battery. It is thus a highly efficient regulator which has no moving parts and requires no maintenance. Connections for later Zener diode 12 volt systems are shown in illustration 16.2 and for this arrangement it is necessary to use a heat sink (a cooling fin or fins on which the Zener diode is bolted) of at least 36 in² and mounted in a good airstream for cooling. Note that all six coils are connected to give maximum power output and the connections are for positive earthing (grounding).

**3** The change to full power output with six coils permanently connected did not occur straightaway with the introduction of the Zener diode and some machines may be found with switched coils. In these cases four coils are used for charging in coil ignition machines, the remaining two being switched in for headlamp loads. Magneto ignition machines used two coils for charging and switched in the remaining four coils for headlamp work. Smaller heat sinks are also used for the Zener diode.

**4** Lucas improved the power rating of alternators and the RM15 and RM18

machines of only 80 watt output were superseded by the RM19 110 watt and the RM21 (2-wire 110 watt) alternators. Inevitably the advantages of using three-phase led to the availability of the RM24 alternator (180 watt). A table of alternators presently available from one source is given below.

The increase of power, even at kickstart speeds, means that with a flat battery, starting is possible at the third or fourth kick if the ignition system is in good order. Emergency start (EMG) was rendered obsolete by these later designs.

## 17  Capacitor ignition circuit

**1** A capacitor will store electrical charge and allow it to discharge again when a suitable circuit is connected to it. If a large capacitor is connected on the dc side of the rectifier then each alternator pulse will charge up the capacitor; it is then possible to use this stored charge to supply an ignition coil when the battery is disconnected.

Sufficient energy is stored to ensure adequate plug sparking for starting and running at all speeds throughout the engine speed range. The main use of this ignition capacitor is for competition work where the battery is removed, or in cases of a flat battery. It is wise to check that the capacitor

**12**

| Model | Power | Phases | Comment |
|-------|-------|--------|---------|
| RM19 | 110 watt | Single-phase | 6 volt 3-wire (can be converted to 12 volt 2-wire) |
| RM21 | 110 watt | Single-phase | 12 volt 2-wire |
| RM23 | 180 watt | Single-phase | Needs extra Zener |
| RM24 | 180 watt | Three-phase | Zener control |

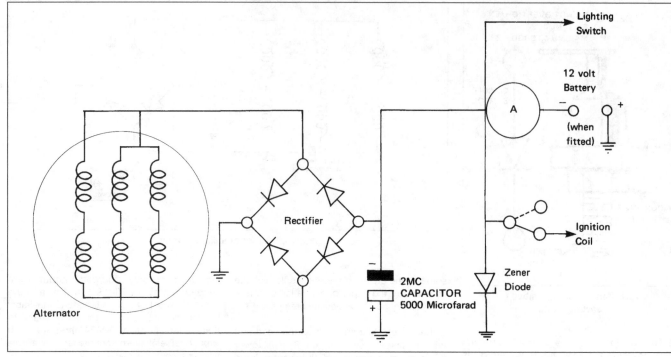

**17.2a Capacitor ignition circuit**

is working correctly from time to time by disconnecting the battery and starting the engine.

**2** The Lucas 2MC capacitor of 5000 μF capacity is of the electrolytic type, meaning that it *must be connected with the correct polarity* or it will be quickly destroyed. Illustration 17.2a shows the basic circuit employing both a 2MC capacitor and a Zener diode; the physical mounting of the capacitor is important for the terminals must point downwards. The aluminium case housing the capacitor is pushed into the coiled spring until

it locates on the groove and the spring is then bolted securely to the frame (see illustration 17.2b).

Check the connections carefully, noting that the positive (+) terminal (the small Lucar connector) is taken to earth (ground). The capacitor negative (-) terminal and the Zener diode must both be connected to the negative output terminal of the rectifier or any other convenient point on that line.

Note that the 2MC capacitor is for positive (+) earth (ground) wiring only. Do not run the

engine without the Zener diode or the rise in voltage will destroy the capacitor. Also ensure that the negative (-) lead from the battery is insulated from the frame by taping up the terminal.

**3** Although there are many 2MC capacitors still in service they are no longer available new. Several suppliers offer a substitute of an electrolytic capacitor of 4700 microfarads (AO Services or Boyer Bransden). If a capacitor from an electronics store is used be sure it is for at least 25 volt working and that it is connected in circuit with the correct polarity.

## 18 6 volt to 12 volt alternator conversion

**1** Alternators designed for a 6 volt system can easily run up to 12 volts and beyond without modification if they are in good electrical condition.

In the case of Lucas RM series alternators the full six coil output may be obtained by joining the green/yellow to the green/black lead. This effectively converts the three-wire alternator to a two-wire type RM21.

**2** Illustrations 18.2a and 18.2b show the conversion, which involves fitting a Zener diode, new 12 volt bulbs, a 12 volt battery, a 12 volt ignition coil and, to be safe, a new capacitor across the ignition points. It is strongly recommended to fit a fuse in the

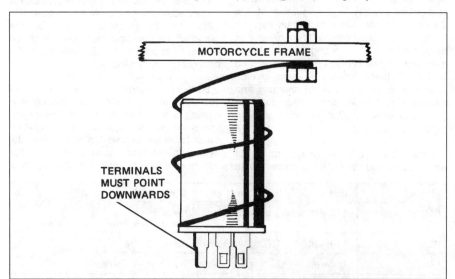

**17.2b Lucas 2MC electrolytic capacitor mounting arrangement**

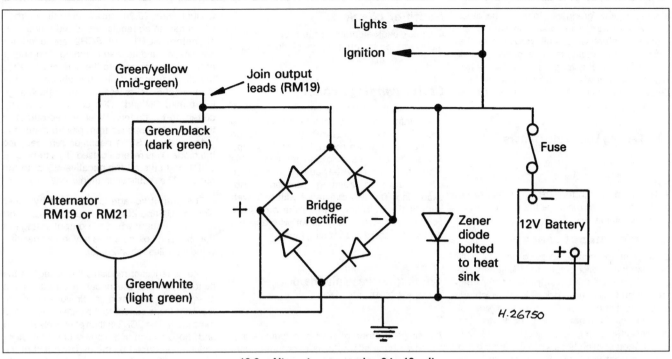

**18.2a  Alternator conversion 6 to 12 volt**

battery output cable (it can be an in-line type) because of the higher system power. The horn may be left in place but it may need adjusting if it gives a peculiar note on its new 12 volt supply!

**3** Before undertaking this conversion it is worth thinking about the condition of the alternator. If of the older type, RM15 or RM18 (which give low output), it might be better to fit an RM21 alternator. One other reason is that the rotor may have lost some of its magnetic strength; it is not cost-effective to have it

re-magnetised, although it can be done. Similarly, if the rectifier is of the old selenium type it should without doubt be replaced with a modern silicon rectifier. Semiconductor developments have resulted in high performance, compact size and low cost, making the retention of a suspect rectifier pointless.

**4** An alternative to the Zener diode method is to use the Boyer-Bransden Power Box shown in illustration 18.4. This unit contains a back-to-back SCR (thyristor) circuit which limits the

amplitude of the incoming alternating voltage wave from the alternator. The clipped wave is then passed through a bridge rectifier and is terminated with a 10,000 µF capacitor so that the motorcycle can be run without a battery, if required, for off-road or competition use.

The maximum power handling capacity is 180 watts with positive or negative earth (ground) and if fed with a three-wire Lucas alternator, the green/yellow and green/black wires must be joined and connected to one of the yellow input wires to the box. The

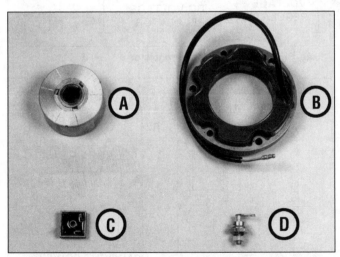

**18.2b  Components necessary for conversion from 6 to 12 volt**
A Rotor    B Stator    C Rectifier    D Zener diode
Components shown were supplied by AO Services

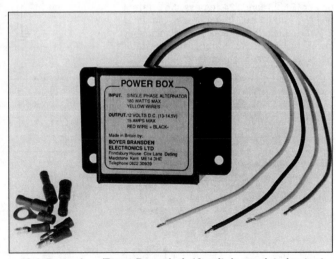

**18.4  Power box (Boyer Bransden), 12-volt dc regulated output**

**12**

alternator white/green wire goes to the other yellow input wire. The version shown has an optional feature which delays power to the lights until the engine is running, allowing all the available energy to go to the ignition while kick-starting. However, if a battery is used the delay is inoperative. A three-phase version is also available.

## 19 Testing Lucas alternators

1 The most straightforward way of checking an alternator is to measure the direct current output when loaded.

### Charging output check

2 Connect an ammeter in the charging circuit between the rectifier output and the battery. To do this, take off the dc output lead from the rectifier and make up a pair of leads which will take current from the rectifier dc output terminal through an ammeter and back to the disconnected output lead. Use wire to and from the ammeter which is capable of carrying the output current (say 14/0.3) There should be no discernible reverse current from the battery to the rectifier as measured on a low ampere range of the ammeter when the engine is off. If you have a multimeter which is capable of measuring the expected output current use that with the test leads provided. Note also that there is now a clip-on ammeter available which does not require the disconnection of the alternator output leads (see Chapter 18). This meter is excellent for high current measurement but will not detect small leakage currents.

3 Switch to a high range (at least 10A), start the engine and switch on all the lights. RM19 or RM21 alternators should read about 9 amperes at 3000 rev/min. For the higher power RM23 and 24 types, the current delivery should be 10 amperes or higher at 2,300 rev/min. If the results are significantly lower, this points to trouble with the stator windings or a weak rotor magnet.

### Rectifier check

4 Check each element of the rectifier with a multimeter on the ohms range as described in Section 4 of this Chapter.

### Stator windings check

5 Measure the resistance between any pair of the 3 stator wires – the ohmmeter should read virtually zero. Measure the insulation resistance between the stator windings and the laminations. It should be very high on the high ohms range. Alternatively, use an ac supply from an isolating transformer not exceeding 40 volts ac in series with a 25 watt bulb. If the bulb lights when the prods are connected between any stator wire and the laminations there is a winding fault.

## 20 Single-phase alternator electronic control

1 A simple method of electronic regulation of a single-phase alternator is in common use. The principle is that of bypassing to earth (ground) excess generated current on the ac side of the rectifier. This is sometimes called 'load dumping'.

2 Illustration 20.2a shows an outline circuit which has an ac regulator and a dc regulator. Thyristors SCR1 and SCR2 are used for rectification and ac load dumping. The output of the alternator goes to the gate of SCR1 via the dc regulator. When the voltage at the cathode of SCR1 is less than the gate voltage it is turned ON and SCR1 conducts charging current to the battery. When the ac output of the alternator changes from plus to minus the gate voltage of SCR1 becomes zero because the diode D1 is reverse biased. This turns OFF SCR1 and cuts off the negative signal to the battery. The rectification then is half-wave.

The output voltage is regulated by zener diodes ZD1 and ZD2 which turn on and short to earth (ground) when the output voltage of the charging coil increases beyond a specified value (see illustration 20.2b).

3 The ac regulator regulates the voltage to the headlight. When the negative output of the charging coil reaches a certain voltage, the ac regulator feeds current to the gate of SCR2 and turns it ON. The SCR2 is then effectively shorted and chops off part of the power to the headlight which is produced by the negative half of the waveform (see illustration 20.3). Since the negative output voltage of the charging coil is not used for battery charging the ac regulator has no effect on charging the battery.

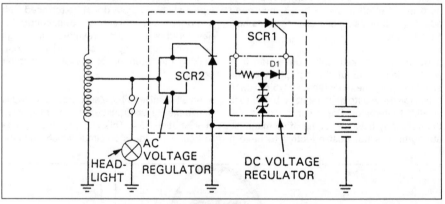

**20.2a Single-phase alternator regulator**

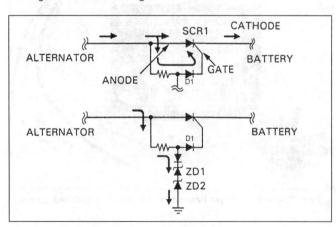

**20.2b dc output voltage regulation (operation)**

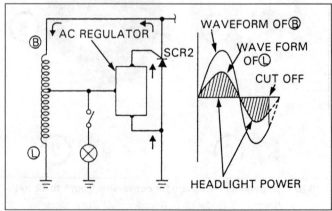

**20.3 ac regulation for lights (operation)**

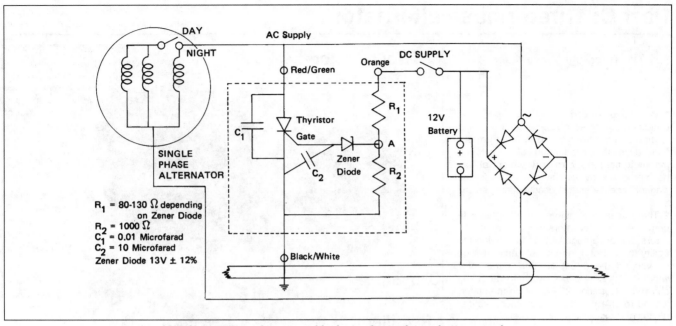

**20.4 Single-phase alternator with electronic regulator – battery-sensing**

R₁ = 80-130 Ω depending on Zener Diode
R₂ = 1000 Ω
C₁ = 0.01 Microfarad
C₂ = 10 Microfarad
Zener Diode 13V ± 12%

**4** The circuit in illustration 20.4 has the advantage that the operation of the regulator depends on the state of charge of the motorcycle battery. As the battery voltage eventually rises with charge, the voltage at point A will eventually reach a value at which the Zener diode begins to conduct. Current through the Zener diode will flow into the thyristor gate, thus turning the thyristor ON.

This has the effect of shorting out a portion of one half cycle from the alternator but will not affect the following negative half cycle since the thyristor can only conduct in one direction. Remember that negative half cycles will pass through the full-wave bridge rectifier and emerge as charging current into the battery as well as positive half waves. By effectively throwing away part of the positive half cycles of energy from the alternator, the regulator has achieved battery-voltage-dependent control. Note that the capacitors serve only to protect the thyristor against transient voltages.

**5** Resistance checks can be made from the orange to black/white leads when, from the diagram it will be seen that the resistance should be about 1.1 kΩ. Measure the resistance in both directions with the ohmmeter between the red/green and the black/white wires. No continuity indicates that the thyristor is likely to be in good condition.

It is important not to alter connections with the ignition switch on or with the engine running since this may give rise to transient voltages which can destroy the thyristor or the Zener diode. Little can be done with a faulty

unit since the components are encapsulated in epoxy resin – renewal is essential.

**6** Another type of single-phase alternator regulator used in smaller motorcycles is shown in illustration 20.6. The bridge rectifier incorporates

two thyristors (SCR) in place of normal diodes. An integrated circuit (IC) measures the alternating voltage and when the required voltage is reached the IC cuts off the gate signals, so blocking both halves of the ac cycle. The rectifier comes complete with the IC and cannot be repaired.

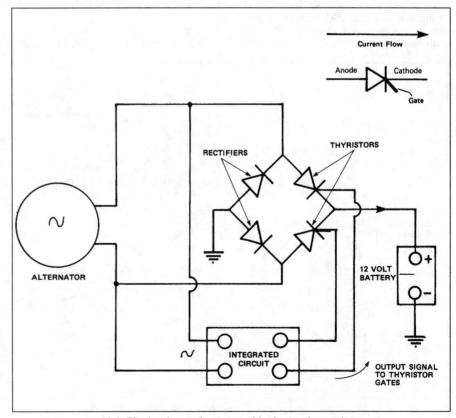

**20.6 Single-phase alternator with electronic regulator**

**12**

# Part C: Three-phase alternators

## 21 The Three-phase alternator

1 We have already touched upon the principles of three-phase alternators and rectifiers in Sections 3 and 4. An important feature is the production of a rotating magnetic field in the rotor which so far has been produced by permanent magnets for the single-phase generators described earlier.

2 Three-phase alternators may be fitted with permanent magnet rotors or electromagnetic rotors, the advantage of the latter being the ability to control three-phase output voltage by varying the direct current in the rotor winding. An example of present practice is shown in illustration 21.2 in which the stator, wound rotor, rotor slip ring brushes, rectifier diodes and regulator are displayed.

## 22 Three-phase alternators with permanent magnet rotors

1 A simple two-pole permanent magnet has been shown so far to illustrate the principle of the three-phase alternator. In practice more pairs of poles are used, as shown in the example in illustration 22.1. Here an outboard set of magnets are cast into the rotor (outboard meaning that the rotor spins outside the stator windings). Inboard rotors are also to be found, but the essential requirement is that a magnetic field should pass through the stator windings in sequence.

2 Control of a three-phase alternator with a permanent magnet rotor always comes

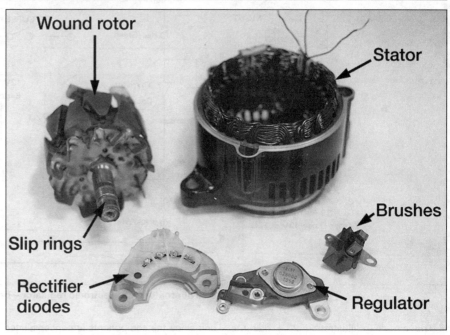

**21.2 Three-phase wound rotor alternator with electronic regulator**

down to load 'dumping' when the correct voltage for battery charging has been reached. The Honda circuit shown in illustration 22.2 shows the principle: 6 rectifiers form a three-phase full-wave bridge and connected to the centre point of each pair is a thyristor (SCR).

When the dc voltage at the battery reaches the required level the voltage sensor's integrated circuit (IC) sends a gate signal to all three thyristor gates. The thyristors conduct and effectively short-circuit the stator output until the dc voltage drops to an accepted level. Note that the stator windings are connected in delta form, the current output being greater than when connected in star form.

3 A similar load dump circuit has been used by Kawasaki; the circuit diagram is shown in illustration 22.3.

One side of the Zener diode ZD is connected to the positive (+) side of the battery via a resistor, to keep a check on charging voltage. The other side goes to the gate terminal of thyristor No 1 (Th$_1$); it will be seen that each phase has a thyristor and that they are all interconnected.

When the battery terminal voltage is low, say at low engine speed or when heavily loaded, the voltage across the Zener is too low for it to pass current and so all the charge goes from the three-phase rectifier straight to the battery.

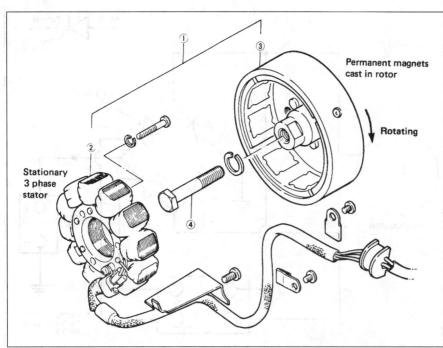

**22.1 Permanent-magnet three-phase alternator – Suzuki**

*1 Alternator assembly    2 Stator    3 Rotor    4 Centre bolt*

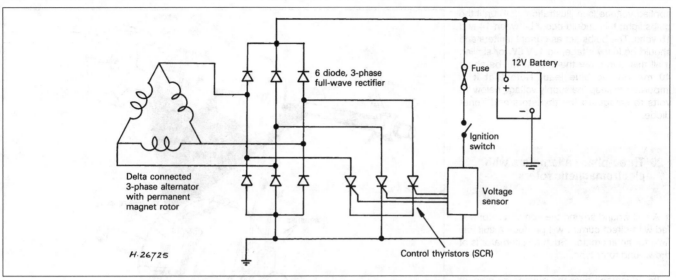

**22.2 Permanent-magnet three-phase alternator with load dumping regulation**

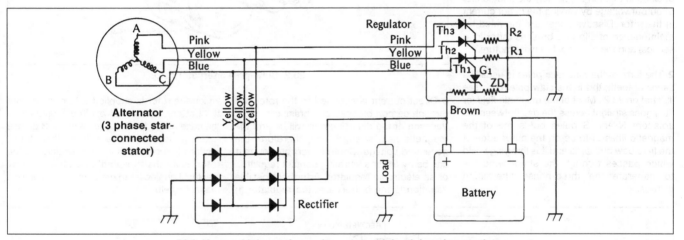

**22.3 Kawasaki three-phase alternator with load dumping regulator**

When the voltage reaches a predetermined value, somewhere between 14 and 15 volts, the Zener diode conducts and switches on thyristor No 1 ($Th_1$). The flow of current through $R_1$ creates a voltage difference between the gate and cathode of thyristor $Th_2$ which promptly switches on and this acts in the same way to trigger thyristor $Th_3$. All thyristors bleed off current from the alternator until the battery voltage falls to the required level.

**4** The regulator cannot be repaired and, if faulty, renewal is essential. To test the regulator, check the resistance between the brown wire and earth/ground (black); the reading will be about 300 ohms with the meter positive (+) prod connected to the brown lead and the meter negative (-) prod connected to the black lead. Reversing the meter prods will give a reading of about 1050 ohms.

Beyond this it is possible to test the thyristors by gradually increasing the dc

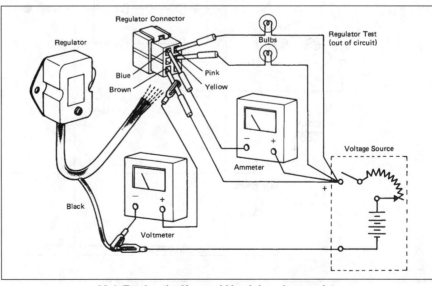

**22.4 Testing the Kawasaki load dumping regulator**

applied voltage (see illustration 22.4) until the bulbs light; this should occur between 14 and 15 volts. The bulbs act as current limiters and should be low wattage, eg 12V 5W or similar. If all this is in order the current will be about 40 mA on the blue lead. Note that it is important to keep the supply voltage below 18 volts to safeguard the thyristors and Zener diode.

## 23 Three-phase alternators with electromagnetic rotors

**1** A coil wound around the iron of a rotor and fed with direct current will produce a suitable field for an alternator. Such an alternator is of the wound rotor type.

Its advantage over the permanent magnet three-phase alternator has already been outlined in Section 21, namely the fine control of output voltage by varying the direct current in the rotor. Disadvantages are the need for maintenance of slip ring brushes (after long service) and the extra cost of manufacture.

**2** The form of the magnetic poles is usually a series of teeth; this is the claw pole rotor (see illustration 23.2). Most of the magnetic field (or flux) goes straight across the gap between the adjacent N and S poles but some of the magnetic lines of force on the outer edge of the field bow outwards and it is this fringe field which passes through the stator windings to generate the three-phase alternating voltage.

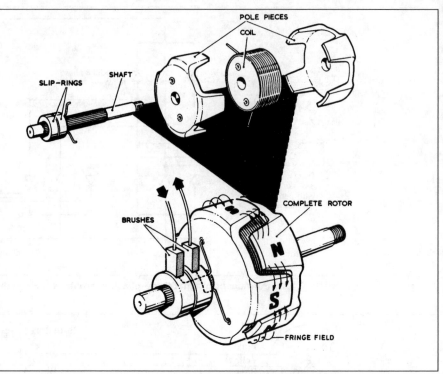

**23.2 Claw-pole alternator rotor**

**3** Direct current is supplied to the rotor coil through carbon brushes and brass slip rings. Variation of the direct current will control the magnetic field strength and, therefore, the generated voltage. Control over rotor current can be by either a vibrating contact regulator, or an electronic regulator. A further possible variation is the battery-excited regulator in which the rotor is supplied with current from the battery, or the self-excited regulator. In the case of the latter, an extra set of 3 diodes takes generated current from the stator, rectifies it and passes it via a regulator to the rotor. Note that 'excited' is a term used by electrical engineers to mean the provision of a magnetic field.

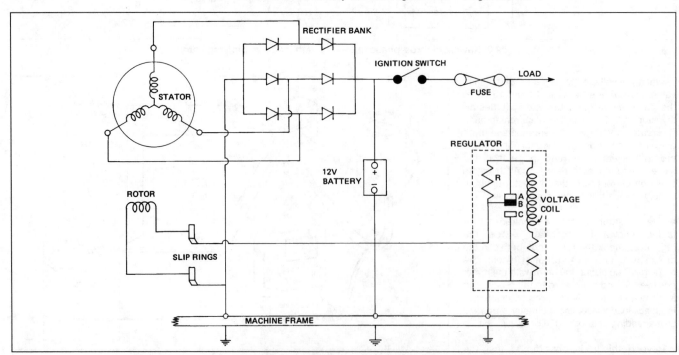

**24.1 Battery-excited alternator and electromechanical regulator – now old technology**

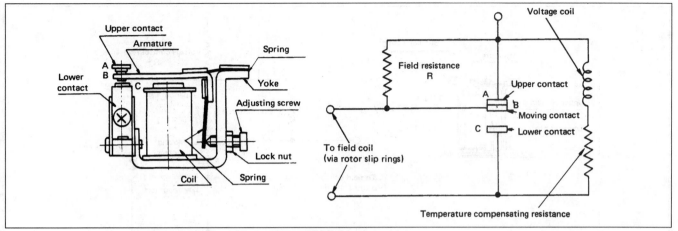

**24.2 Regulator construction**

## 24 Battery-excited alternators

**1** The diagram in illustration 24.1 shows a rectifier unit supplied from the stator windings. Note that the battery is connected straight to the rectifier; there is no need for a cut-out as with dc generators because the rectifier will not permit battery current to flow back into the stator windings. Here we have an electromechanical regulator which is definitely old technology but there are many

still about and technicians should know about them.

**2** When the ignition switch is closed and the motorcycle is started, battery current will flow through the coil of the regulator which exerts a magnetic pull on the regulator armature (see illustration 24.2). Until the voltage generated on the dc side of the rectifier reaches 15.5 – 16.5 volts (for the exact figure see the motorcycle workshop manual), the current flow to the rotor passes straight through contacts A and B which are normally CLOSED.

**3** As the rotor becomes magnetically excited, the alternating voltage generated in the stator winding increases. This means that more current flows into the voltage regulator coil and the armature is attracted so that the contacts A and B separate. Now the current to the rotor must pass through the field resistor R and this has the effect of reducing the rotor current and hence regulating the direct voltage emerging from the rectifiers.

**4** If the alternator speeds up, the armature is pulled down further, to close contacts B and C, thus the rotor is short circuited, the

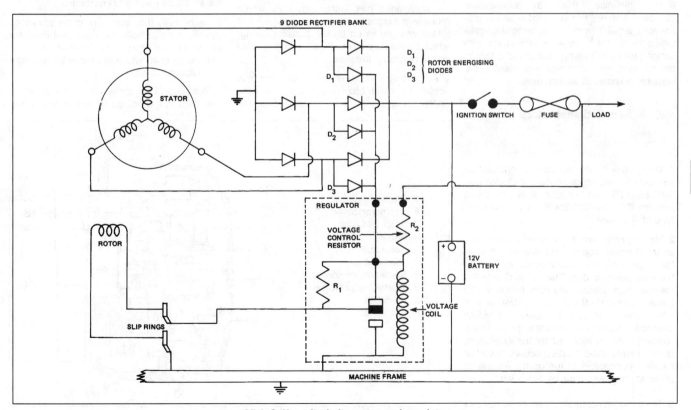

**25.1 Self-excited alternator and regulator**

12

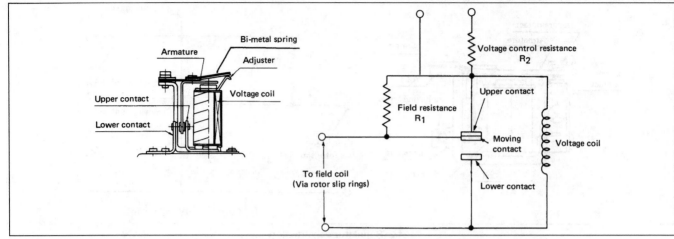

**25.5 Regulator with bimetal spring temperature compensation**

alternator voltage falls rapidly and the contacts separate.

**5** The result is that the movable contact B vibrates between A and C, depending on the alternator speed and the load on the battery. Remembering that copper wire increases in resistance with temperature, it will be seen that the current flowing through the voltage coil will decrease as the coil heats up in use. This would affect the output voltage of the alternator since the magnetic field strength would also decrease.

**6** To minimise this, a temperature compensating resistor is added in series with the voltage coil. This resistor is made of material which does not change in resistance with temperature and swamps out any changes in the coil itself. For this reason such resistors are sometimes known as swamp resistors.

## 25 Self-excited alternators

**1** These may be immediately recognised by the rectifier unit, which contains 9 diodes (see illustration 25.1 on previous page) compared with the 6 diode pack for the battery-excited type of alternator.

**2** The regulator works in much the same way as the 6 diode type but the magnetic field of the rotor is derived from current rectified by the energising diodes. Start up is due to the residual magnetism in the rotor iron aided by battery current via the voltage control resistor; when the alternator is driven, a small alternating voltage is generated in the stator winding. This is rectified by the energising diodes and so rapid build-up occurs. In certain cases it is possible to fire up the engine by bump starting even if the battery is flat.

**3** The battery is not totally independent however for it is linked to the regulator coil by a resistor $R_2$

so that the operation is to some extent determined by the state of battery charge.

**4** Additionally, the flow of current through $R_2$ from the battery when ignition is switched on helps to strengthen the residual magnetism in the rotor and ensures a rapid build-up of alternator voltage.

**5** In the regulator shown in illustration 25.5 the spring is a bimetal strip to take temperature variation into account. If the temperature rises, then the copper voltage regulator coil would take less current because the resistance has increased. This would mean less magnetic pull on the armature but this is compensated by the bimetal spring, which bends so as to reduce the spring force on the regulator armature.

**6** All motorcycles now have an electronic control box which has superseded the moving contact regulator. The principles remain the

same in that the rotor current is switched on and off to maintain the required charging voltage.

## 26 Brushless alternator

**1** This type is the most powerful of the three-phase alternators and is sometimes mounted externally to the engine, not unlike the mounting of a car alternator. It is used for high capacity motorcycles and is run at a speed higher than the engine by gearing or chain drive.

**2** Technically this alternator is an advanced design because both the stator and the rotor windings are stationary. The absence of moving parts should lead to long life and little or no maintenance.

Illustration 26.2 shows that both stator (1) and the rotor windings (3) are bolted to the

1 Stator windings
2 Alternator cover
3 Rotor windings
4 Rotor
5 Rotor bolt
6 Allen bolt
7 Starter motor sprocket
8 Starter motor clutch
9 Allen bolt
10 Crankshaft

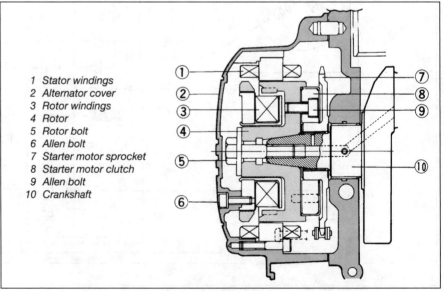

**26.2 Kawasaki brushless alternator in cross-section**

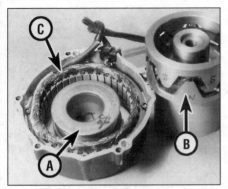

**26.3 Yamaha brushless alternator**

*See text for details*

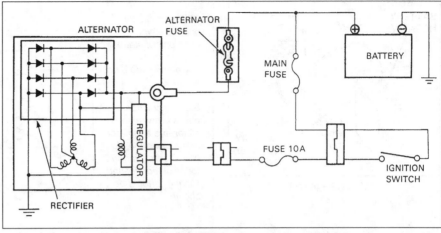

**27.2 Honda 8-diode rectifier arrangement (ST1100)**

cover; the magnetic field created by the rotor windings is picked up by the iron of the rotor (4) to reach the stator windings (1). The magnetic flux must jump airgaps to complete its path but nevertheless can be made sufficiently strong to generate the voltage required in the stator windings (1).

**3** A Yamaha alternator of similar design is shown in illustration 26.3. The inner coil (A) is the provider of magnetic flux which magnetises the inner part of the rotor. Flux then passes round to the claw poles (B) which have been marked N S for the purpose of identification. The fringe field cuts the stator windings (C) to generate three-phase in them when the rotor iron is running.

## 27 Honda 8 diode alternator

**1** The three-phase alternator stators seen so far in this Chapter have been star connected or more rarely, delta connected. In the star connection, the return path normally has to be through the two phases that are not positive when the third is positive and there will be a small resistive loss in the windings.

**2** Honda have used on the ST1100 a variation on this star arrangement by connecting the star point to two diodes which feed the return current. This results in an 8 diode rectifier pack as shown in illustration 27.2 and will avoid return currents having to flow through the phase windings.

## 28 Electronic regulators

**1** The electronic control unit switches rotor current on or off to maintain the alternator dc output voltage at the required level.

**2** Referring to illustration 28.2: at low speed the Zener diode ZD does not conduct and so transistor $Tr_2$ is cut off. Absence of collector current means that the volt drop in resistor R will be low, thus the base/emitter voltage difference of transistor $Tr_1$ will be sufficient to switch on and the current flows down through the field coil into the collector of $Tr_1$. Current flow in the alternator field coil will allow the voltage output to rise.

**3** As the speed rises and alternator voltage rises to the preset value, the zener diode conducts and the transistor $Tr_2$ switches on. Collector current flows in resistor R and the volt drop in it causes transistor $Tr_1$ to cut off the current flow in the field coil. This cycle of switching repeats rapidly and holds the output voltage of the alternator steady. The diode D is to absorb shock transients such as occur when voltages are suddenly changed. The circuit shown is simplified to show the principle of voltage regulation.

**12**

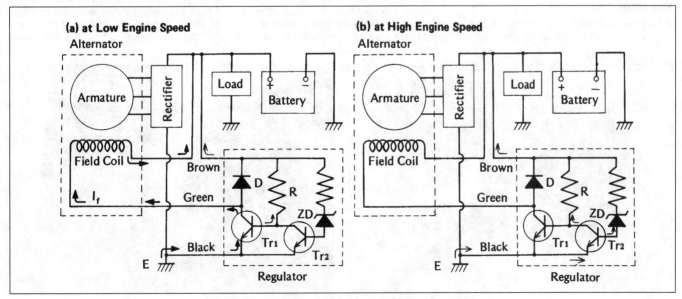

**28.2 Electronic regulation of wound rotor alternator**

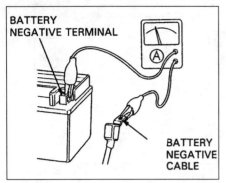

**29.3 Leakage test**

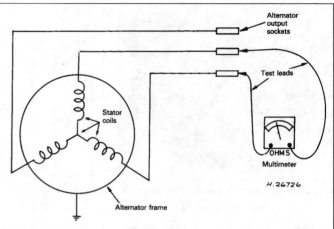

Stator continuity: check between each pair of stator coils as shown – low ohms should be shown

Stator insulation: check between any stator and alternator frame using the high (x 100 ohms) range for insulation testing – infinity should be shown

**29.4a Alternator stator testing**

## 29 Testing three-phase alternators

1 If the battery goes flat without any obvious reason then it could be a faulty battery, alternator or regulator. For information on batteries see Chapter 13.

2 Switch on the lights, then start the engine, if possible. Increase engine speed to about 3000 rev/min and note if the lights brighten up. If they do, the alternator is charging. A voltage check at the battery while charging with the engine running at mid speed should be within the range 13.5 – 15.5 volts. Any serious variation from these figures points to a faulty regulator. There is no way of repairing modern electronic regulators and replacement is necessary. However it is possible that current is leaking away out of the battery due to a faulty rectifier. The usual cause is a rectifier with low reverse resistance on one or more of the diodes.

### Rectifier

3 To check if leakage is occurring, stop the engine and switch off all loads. Use a multimeter on the amperes range to measure current from the battery to the rectifier. A simple way to do this is to disconnect the battery negative terminal and connect the ammeter as shown in illustration 29.3.

Always start on the highest range of the ammeter and switch down ranges until the leakage current (if any) can be measured. It should be less than 0.1 ampere according to one manufacturer but a personal view is that even this is too high to be acceptable. A new rectifier is required if leakage is shown. If the motorcycle is used infrequently the rider can defer the replacement by disconnecting the earth (ground) lead after use: but do not delay too long!

To check individual diodes (which make up the rectifier), test each one separately as explained in Section 4, of this Chapter.

### Stator

4 The 3 stator wires can usually be reached at a block connector joint. Separate the connector and make the test on the alternator side. Testing between any pair should show

the same resistance (see illustration 29.4a). A stripped down stator being checked for line to line resistance is shown in illustration 29.4b.

For a typical three-phase 180 watt permanent magnet alternator the resistance between any pair should be in the range 0.1 – 1.0 ohm. For a three-phase 350 watt wound rotor alternator this figure might typically be 0.4 – 0.6 ohm. Whatever the value of resistance the important thing is that all three results should be the same. If there is a significant difference it points to a stator winding fault.

Next check the insulation between any stator wire and the alternator frame. It should be infinite or very high, at the top of the x 100 ohms range of a multimeter.

### Rotor

5 If the alternator is of the wound rotor type it will have a pair of slip rings with brushes. Check the resistance between the slip rings as shown in illustration 29.5a. If the alternator has not been removed from the motorcycle,

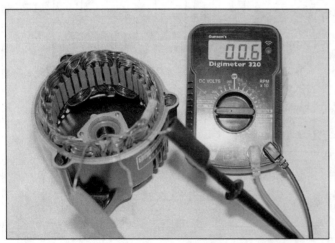

**29.4b 3-phase alternator stator winding test**

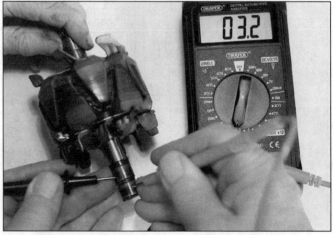

**29.5a Check rotor resistance between the slip rings**

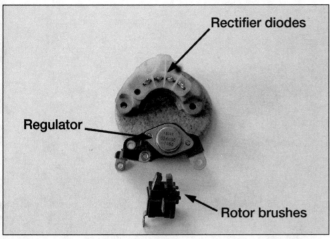

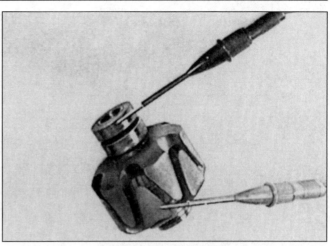

**29.5b  3-phase alternator regulator, brushes and rectifier diodes**

**29.6  Slip ring insulation test**

make the test connections to the appropriate terminals of the block connector socket. A low ohms figure should be read, the Yamaha rotor shown being within the tolerance given in the handbook of 2.8 to 3.5 ohms.

Next examine the carbon brushes to see if they are not worn down and are free to slide in their holder. Sometimes brushes can stick in

the brusholder and the result is eventual loss of charging current. The separated brushgear, regulator and rectifier diodes are shown in illustration 29.5b.

**6** Finally, check the insulation resistance from the slip rings to earth (ground) as shown in illustration 29.6. This can be done with the multimeter on the high ohms range or a

40 volt ac test with a 25 watt mains lamp in series. This ac voltage should be derived from an isolating transformer and not directly from the mains. The multimeter should show infinite (very high) resistance between the rotor slip rings and the iron laminations. If using the lamp method there should be no glow from the lamp. Any fault in either the stator or the rotor means replacement.

**12**

**Notes**

# Chapter 13
# Batteries

## Contents

 **Warning: Lead acid batteries give off explosive gases. Keep sparks, flames and cigarettes away. Batteries contain sulphuric acid as the electrolyte. Contact with the skin or eyes will cause severe burns. Use eye protection. Wash skin thoroughly if acid gets on it. If acid gets in your eyes, flush with water and get first aid. Acid is corrosive to clothes, metal and paintwork.**

## 1 The lead-acid battery

**1** Motorcycles invariably use the lead-acid battery for the storage of electrical energy.

A battery is made up of several cells connected in series packed together in one container. Each cell contributes a nominal 2 volts; a 12 volt battery has six 2 volt cells (see illustration 1.1). The principal features of the lead-acid cell are as follows:

(a) *It may be recharged after giving up its stored electrical energy.*
(b) *The internal resistance is low, so that heavy currents may be drawn without great loss of terminal voltage.*

**2** Until 1983, motorcycles always used batteries with free liquid acid and a filler plug/gas vent for each cell. Periodically the acid must be topped up with *distilled water*

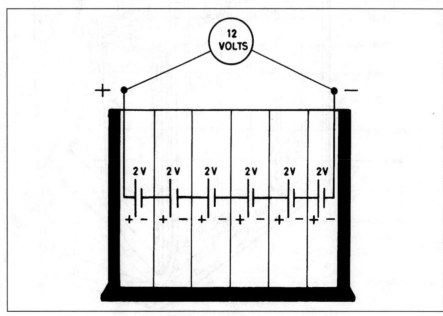

**1.1 A 12 volt battery of six 2 volt cells**

13

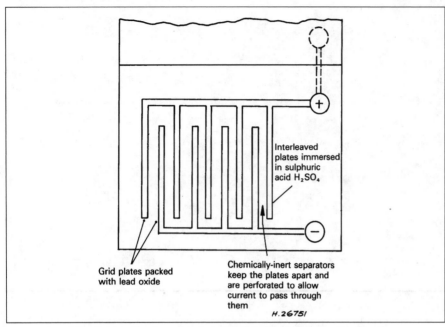

**2.2a  Schematic view showing plate interleaving in one 2 volt cell**

Interleaved plates immersed in sulphuric acid H₂SO₄

Grid plates packed with lead oxide

Chemically-inert separators keep the plates apart and are perforated to allow current to pass through them

H.26751

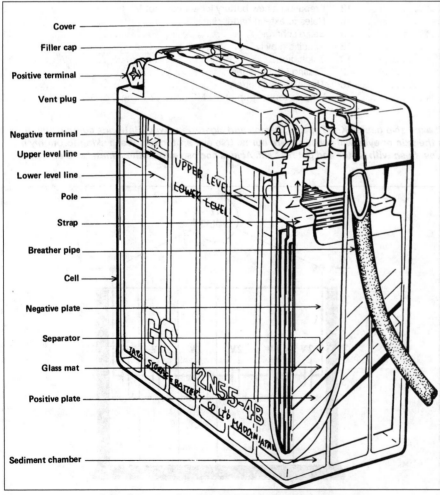

**2.2b  Cutaway view of a 12 volt motorcycle battery**

Cover
Filler cap
Positive terminal
Vent plug
Negative terminal
Upper level line
Lower level line
Pole
Strap
Breather pipe
Cell
Negative plate
Separator
Glass mat
Positive plate
Sediment chamber

(not tap water) due to evaporation. These batteries are still in widespread use, but in that year Yuasa introduced the maintenance-free (MF) battery for motorcycles.

The maintenance-free battery is still of the lead-acid type but with some important differences in construction. For these reasons we will consider the **conventional** and **maintenance-free (MF)** types separately.

## 2  Conventional lead-acid batteries

**1** The battery used for energy storage in motorcycles is a secondary type, that is, it may be recharged when exhausted. This is in contrast to primary cells or batteries such as those in hand-held flashlights, which are expendable and cannot be recharged.

**2** For storing electrical energy it is necessary to have two suitable dissimilar conducting materials immersed in close proximity in a conducting liquid (or compound) called the electrolyte.

The lead-acid battery uses lead-antimony grid plates (several per cell) and the grid holes are filled with lead oxide pastes. These grid plates are interleaved, one set being connected to one battery terminal and the other set to the other battery terminal (see illustration 2.2a). Glass matting helps to retain the grid paste in place and the plates are kept apart by separators. Illustrations 2.2b and 2.2c show the components and construction.

**3** When current is passed through the battery, chemical reactions take place which convert the pastes into the required dissimilar conducting materials.

## 3  Charging, overcharging and discharging

### Charging

**1** When a battery is charged, current is forced through it in the opposite direction to normal, in much the same way as filling a tank via its outlet tap (see illustration 3.1). The battery gives a direct current (dc) and so it follows that a direct current is required to recharge it. Clearly, if the battery has a terminal voltage of, say, 12 volts, then in order to force current into it, it will require a battery charging voltage somewhat in excess of this, say, 14 to 16 volts depending upon the charge rate required and the internal resistance of the battery.

**2** Looking now inside the battery (see illustration 3.2), while under charge conditions

**2.2c Construction of a 12 volt motorcycle battery with two cells sectioned**

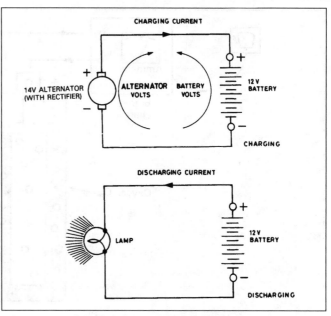

**3.1 Charging and discharging action**

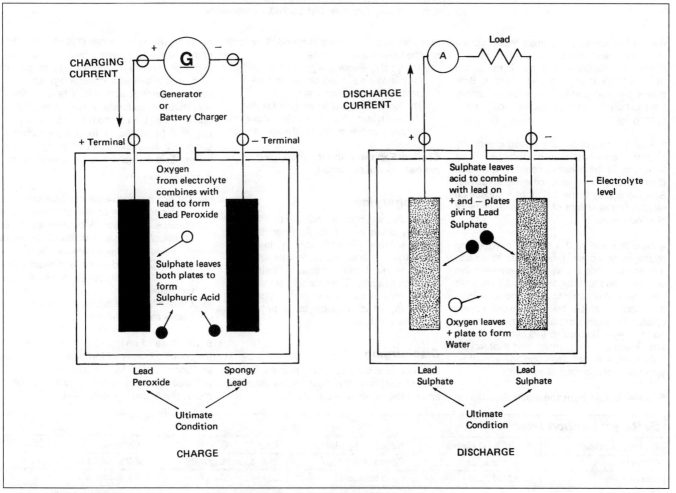

**3.2 Charging and discharging a lead-acid battery**

13

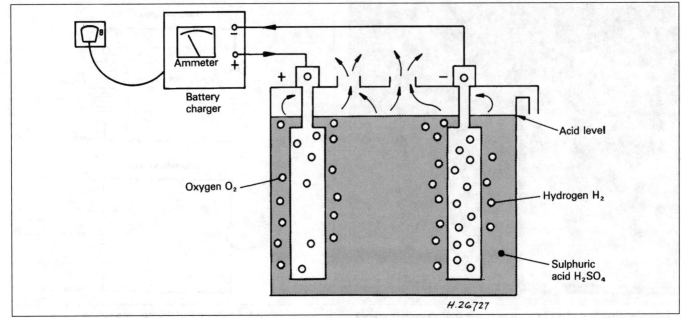

**3.4 Gas emissions from a battery on charge**

*Gases are given off a battery when being charged, but mostly at the end of charge period. Unscrew the battery filler caps when bench charging and do not allow sparks, cigarettes or flames near.*

**Hydrogen with Oxygen is an EXPLOSIVE combination**

we see that the flow of current breaks up the electrolyte and that the electrolyte oxygen moves to combine with the lead of the positive (+) plate to form lead peroxide. Both plates give sulphate to form sulphuric acid in the electrolyte, and the negative plate turns to spongy lead.

3 Thus the two plates are altered chemically and the concentration of sulphuric acid increases, ie the density or specific gravity of the electrolyte goes up as charging continues. Specific gravity is the weight of a substance relative to the weight of the same volume of distilled water.

4 Near the end of the charge, oxygen and hydrogen gases are given off (see illustration 3.4) and the cells are said to be gassing; this occurs when the voltage reaches 2.4 volts per cell. The combination is an explosive mixture and care must be taken to avoid having sparks, cigarettes or naked flames near the battery vents. Remember that battery acid will attack eyes, skin, clothing and motorcycle paintwork. Affected parts should be washed with cold water in case of accidents.

5 Water is lost from the electrolyte during charging especially near the end. This loss has the following two effects:
(a) *The level of electrolyte goes down and, if the plates are partially uncovered, the battery capacity decreases.*
(b) *The lost water must be replaced with distilled water. This process is 'topping up' and must be to the level mark and no more.*
**Caution: Tap water must not be used or the battery will be ruined.**

## Overcharging

6 Overcharging occurs when the positive and negative plates have been fully converted to lead peroxide (+) and spongy lead (-) respectively. It is at this stage when gassing increases, and if left on charge, the battery will lose water rapidly. The charging current now serves only to split water into oxygen and hydrogen, which escape as a potentially explosive combination.

## Discharging

7 When discharging, the battery sends current out from the positive (+) terminal, around the external circuit and back in again at the negative (-) terminal. (It is useful to think of the battery as a pump which sets electricity in motion round a circuit, like a pump pushes fluid round a liquid cooling system.) The reverse chemical action now takes place in the battery; sulphate leaves the acid to combine with lead on both the positive (+) and negative (-) plates to form lead sulphate. Oxygen leaves the positive plate to form water. Two things have happened at this stage.

(a) *The positive and negative plates are converted to both be lead sulphate. Because they gradually become identical chemically, there is no difference between them and the voltage between them drops, but should never be allowed to fall below 1.8 volts per cell (10.8 volts for a 12 volt battery).*
(b) *Water dilutes the sulphuric acid and lowers the specific gravity.*

8 The state of charge can be measured by the specific gravity of the battery acid using an hydrometer or by the terminal voltage. In practice, specific gravity measurement is more reliable and is widely used.

| Battery condition table | | | | |
|---|---|---|---|---|
| **Battery condition** | **Positive (+) plates** | **Negative (-) plates** | **Acid** | **Voltage** |
| Charged | Lead peroxide | Spongy lead | High specific gravity | 2.2 volts (approx) per cell* |
| Discharged | Lead sulphate | Lead sulphate | Lower specific gravity | 1.8 volts per cell |
| | | | | * After a rest period |

## 4 Battery capacity

**1** This is a measure of the total quantity of electricity which a fully charged battery can pump round a circuit. It is measured in ampere-hours (Ah).

**2** The rated current is the steady load current which would completely discharge the battery in 10 hours; it is known as the 10-hour-rate current. If the actual discharge rate is higher, then the output capacity is reduced. For example, the 10-hour-rate of a 15 Ah battery is 1.5 amperes. If the battery were actually loaded at 3 amperes it is unlikely that the battery would last as long as 5 hours (3A x 5h = 15 Ah) but would probably be exhausted in, say, 4.5 hours.

**3** As a rough guide, the charging Ah should be about 1.3 x the rated ampere-hour figure; for example, if the above 15 Ah battery were in a state of complete discharge it could safely be given about 15 x 1.3 = 19.5, say, 20 Ah of charge.

## 5 Charging rate

**1** The battery manufacturer sometimes displays the charge rate on the case, but if no figure is available, use between $\frac{1}{10}$ and $\frac{3}{10}$ of the battery capacity. Using the Kawasaki GPZ900R as an example, which has a 14 Ah battery, the charge at the $\frac{1}{10}$ rate is determined as follows:

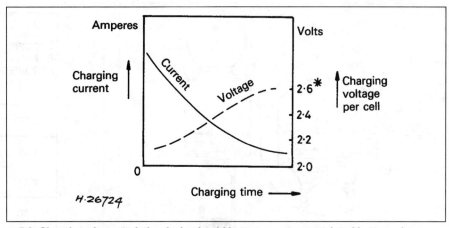

$$\text{Charging current} = \frac{1}{10} \times 14$$

$$= 1.4 \text{ amperes}$$

$$\text{Charging time} = \frac{18}{1.4}$$

$$= 12 \text{ hours } 50 \text{ minutes}$$

**2** Quick-charging is sudden death to motorcycle batteries and should be strictly avoided. The main trouble is overheating, causing the plate paste to swell and severe distortion of the grid structure to occur. Paste drops to the bottom of the battery, reducing the Ah capacity and eventually shorts out the plates.

**3** In practice, the charge rate is not constant (but see MF batteries) since the battery charger is often a constant voltage supply.

**5.3 Charging characteristic of a lead-acid battery on an unregulated battery charger**
*\*Cell voltage falls after disconnection from charger*

With an unregulated battery charger of this type the battery voltage will rise over the charging period and the charging current will fall. This is because the difference in voltage between the charger and battery becomes less (see illustration 5.3).

## 6 Specific gravity

**1** Battery acid varies in specific gravity throughout the charging period (see illustration 6.1) and the state of charge may be accurately assessed by using an hydrometer. Since the graduations are often closely spaced, read off as indicated at the bottom of the curved surface of the liquid (the meniscus).

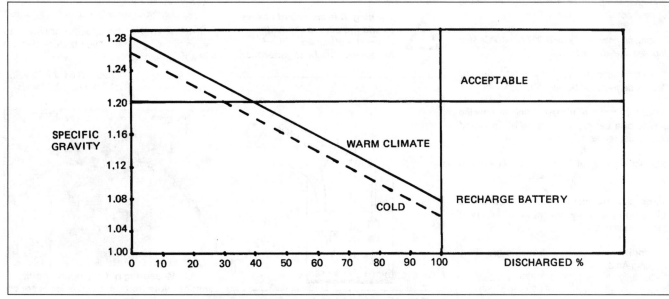

**6.1 Specific gravity of battery acid during charge/discharge**

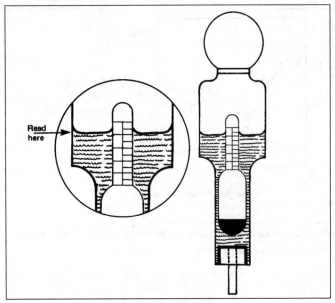

**6.2 Reading the hydrometer**

| SPECIFIC GRAVITY REQUIRED | PARTS OF DISTILLED WATER TO 1 OF CONC. SULPHURIC ACID |
|---|---|
| 1.25 | 3.4 |
| 1.26 | 3.2 |
| 1.27 | 3.0 |
| 1.28 | 2.8 |
| 1.29 | 2.7 |
| 1.30 | 2.6 |

**7.2a Distilled water/concentrated sulphuric acid ratio by volume**

**2** Illustration 6.2 shows an hydrometer which consists of a float inside a suction vessel. The nozzle is inserted into a battery cell and enough acid is withdrawn to read the float. The reading gives a good indication as to the battery charge state, assuming that the correct specific gravity of acid was used for the initial filling.

**3** Electrolyte specific gravity temperature correction is necessary because the volume varies with temperature. The volume rises with temperature so the weight per unit volume will decrease, ie the specific gravity will decrease. The standard temperature at which makers' figures are quoted is 15°C (60°F), so if an hydrometer reading is taken at any other temperature it should be corrected for best accuracy. A rule of thumb is:

*Specific gravity falls by 0.007 per 10 Celsius degrees rise above 15°C*

*Specific gravity rises by 0.007 per 10 Celsius degrees fall below 15°C*

So, for example, if the reading of specific gravity of a battery were taken at 25°C and was measured as 1.22 then:

Specific gravity at 15°C = 1.22 + (1 x 0.007)
= 1.227

**4** For climates normally below 25°C the following figures are typical for a battery in good condition:

| Condition/use | Specific gravity |
|---|---|
| Filling Acid | 1.260 |
| Cell fully charged | 1.270 to 1.290 |
| Cell 70% charged | 1.230 to 1.250 |
| Cell nearly discharged | 1.110 to 1.130 |

## 7 Battery filling

**1** If battery acid is to be prepared from the concentrate, great care should be taken and the wearing of goggles gives essential protection for the eyes.

**2** To mix electrolyte first work out roughly how much distilled water and concentrated acid is required. The table (see illustration 7.2a) gives the proportions (by volume) of distilled water required to 1 part of concentrated sulphuric acid (specific gravity 1.835). Add slowly and stir until the required specific gravity is obtained (see illustration 7.2b).

 *Warning: It is important always to add the acid to the water never the other way round because of the heat generation.*

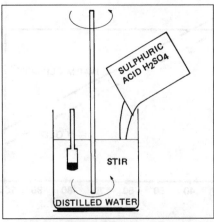

**7.2b Mixing acid and distilled water**

## 8 Open-circuit voltage

**1** Battery terminal voltage on no-load is the open circuit voltage and it is related to the state of charge (specific gravity).

**2** If the battery has recently been on charge, a false reading (high) will be obtained. It is necessary to let the battery rest for an hour before connecting the voltmeter which should be a large scale accurate instrument (see illustration). The approximate relationship between open circuit voltage and specific gravity is as follows.

*Open circuit voltage = Specific gravity + 0.84 volts per cell*

If, for example, the specific gravity was known to be 1.25 in a 12 volt battery then the following would apply.

*Cell voltage . . . . . .1.25 + 0.84 = 2.09 volts*
*Battery voltage . . .6 x 2.09 = 12.54 volts*

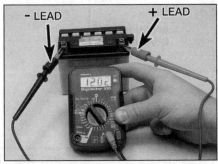

**8.2 Measuring battery open-circuit voltage. Note that the multimeter is set on the 0 – 20 dc volts range**

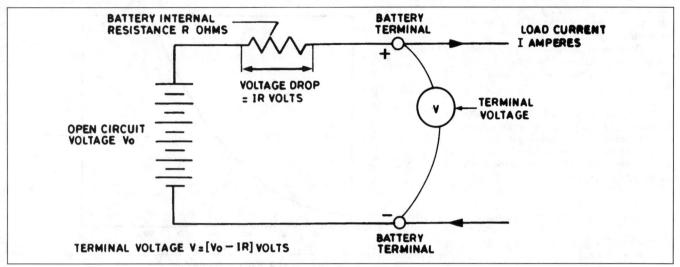

**9.2 Internal resistance of a battery**

## 9 Internal resistance

**1** All batteries have an internal resistance, but this is very low in the case of a lead-acid battery in good condition. In fact, it is because of its inherent low internal resistance, that this type of battery is favoured for vehicle work where starting current demand can be very high.

**2** Illustration 9.2 shows a battery with its equivalent internal resistance. Calculation will show that if, for example, the internal resistance were 0.05 ohms and the open circuit voltage 12.0 volts, then, with a lighting load of 10 amperes the terminal voltage would be as follows.

> *Battery terminal*
> *voltage*        = 12 – internal volt drop
>         = 12 – (10 x 0.05)
>         = 11.5 volts

The table below shows terminal voltages for this battery under various loads. It does not represent a good battery or any particular size, but serves to show the importance of even a small internal resistance.

| Open circuit voltage | Load current (A) | Internal drop | Terminal voltage |
|---|---|---|---|
| 12 volts | 10 amperes | 0.5 volt | 11.5 volts |
| 12 volts | 20 amperes | 1.0 volt | 11.0 volts |
| 12 volts | 50 amperes | 2.5 volts | 9.5 volts |
| 12 volts | 100 amperes | 5.0 volts | 7.0 volts |

**3** The internal resistance is made up of various individual resistances, namely between electrodes and the electrolyte, the plate resistances, internal connectors and resistance of the electrolyte to ion flow (ions are particles moving through the electrolyte and carrying a positive (+) or negative (-) charge).

Additionally, the internal resistance depends upon the state of discharge and cell temperature, the value being higher as the battery is discharged. The designer controls one factor of the internal resistance by the surface area of the plates. Batteries with a larger number of plates (and therefore larger ampere-hour capacity) will have a lower internal resistance.

**4** As batteries age, one of the effects is a rise in the internal resistance. Clearly there will come a point where there will be insufficient terminal voltage left to turn the starter motor fast enough for the engine to fire. For a cold morning start, extra torque will be required to free the crankshaft and the minimum engine turnover speed for firing will be about 100 rev/min. It is under these conditions that the end of the battery life is determined.

## 10 Cold cranking

**1** All motorcyclists know that the battery has a tough time in cranking the engine on a cold morning. Where a battery is intended for starter motor work (not all are), the manufacturer gives a figure for cold cranking. Yuasa give the following specification which complies with that stated by the Society of Automotive Engineers (SAE) standard and Japanese JASO Automotive Battery Standard.

*Cold cranking = Current in amperes at which the voltage is 7.2 volts at -18°C after 30 seconds*

There are other standards in use by European battery manufacturers and more details are given in the author's *'Automobile Electrical and Electronic Systems Manual"* (Haynes).

## 11 Self discharge

**1** Over a period of time a battery which is not used will gradually lose its charge due to several factors:

(a) *Internal chemical processes.*
(b) *Leakage currents.*
(c) *Self discharge.*

### Internal chemical processes

**2** Batteries which have been in service for some time suffer from the effect of antimony deposits on the negative plates. These set up miniature batteries, in effect, which are short circuited upon themselves and use up the charge of the negative plate. In addition, impurities in added water, particularly traces of iron, will result in the self discharge of both positive and negative plates.

### Leakage currents

**3** Dirt and the effects of acid fumes on the top surface of the battery can result in conducting film paths between the positive (+) and negative (-) battery terminals. This trouble can be minimised by periodic cleaning of the battery top (throw the rag away afterwards).

Sediment paths at the bottom of the battery case can also lead to leakage paths.

### Self discharge

**4** Self discharge takes place at the rate of 0.2% to 1% of the battery ampere-hour

**13**

capacity per day, depending on the age of the battery. The rate of discharge goes up with temperature and also with the specific gravity value. Batteries of quality use lead of highest purity in the active plate area with the antimony proportion kept small (see illustration 11.4).

The remedy for self discharge is to charge the battery periodically or to maintain a trickle charge approximately equal to the self discharge rate, this being found by trial and error; a rule of thumb to calculate the trickle charge rate is as follows:

Trickle charge rate = $\frac{1}{1000}$ x ampere-hour rating

From this a 14 Ah battery would be trickle charged at 14 mA.

**5** If a simple battery charger with no rate control is used for this purpose, a good way of reducing the charge rate is to run the battery on charge with a bulb in series. Again the bulb is chosen by trial and error with an ammeter in circuit to check the charge rate.

**6** Note: Although here we are looking at the *natural* self discharge of the battery, often a flat battery is due to other factors such as a faulty rectifier which allows a small leakage current back to the generator when stationary. If the motorcycle is not to be used for a long period it is wise to disconnect the negative earth (ground) lead to prevent this.

## 12 Sulphation

**1** Under normal discharging, fine crystals of lead sulphate are formed on the plates and, by recharging, these are convertible. If the battery is left discharged for a long period, however, these crystals turn into coarse lead sulphate crystals which are not easily converted back to the fine state and may ruin the battery.

**2** Sulphation will reduce the battery Ah capacity and impede the charging process, causing the battery to become very hot. In minor sulphation cases, extended periods of charging at low currents will improve the situation, but in serious cases the battery becomes unusable because of the internal short circuits which result.

**3** When a sulphated battery is first put on charge the terminal voltage rises rapidly, whereas that of a healthy battery rises slowly. As the sulphation breaks down, the battery voltage falls and slowly rises again as normal chemical changes associated with charging take place.

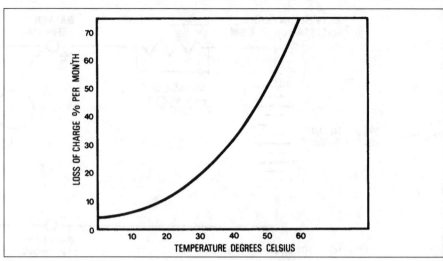

**11.4 Self discharge curve**

## 13 Battery maintenance and fault finding

**1** If a battery is suspected of being defective this can usually be determined by its performance on the motorcycle. A dramatic change in headlight illumination between tickover and high revs, or poor starter motor turnover, are both indications of a battery with high internal resistance. Before condemning the battery, however, check that good connections are being made to earth (ground) and that the battery terminals are not corroded (if so, clean off with a solution of baking soda and water).

**2** Measure charging current with an ammeter, remembering **not** to use a starter motor with an ammeter in circuit! If all appears to be in order, remove the battery for inspection and refer to the following table to assess its condition.

**3** Test charging often reveals troubles; firstly charge at the ordinary rate and if the voltage and specific gravity come up to normal the battery may be returned to service.

**4** Check the voltage of the battery by switching off the charge shortly after starting. A good battery will rise to 12 volts and then gradually rise to 12.5 – 13 volts within an hour after charging has started; fully charged it could reach even higher for a short period.

**5** A battery which exhibits a rise to 13 volts plus, just after the start of charging probably has a high resistance due to sulphation of the plates. Look for even bubbling of all the cells as the battery charge rises – no gassing in one cell indicates an internal short, especially if the cell specific gravity is low.

### Battery fault guide

| Component | Good battery | Suspect battery | Action if suspect |
|---|---|---|---|
| Plates | + chocolate brown colour, – grey colour | White sulphation on plates, plates buckled | Scrap |
| Sediment | Little or none | Deep sediment up to plate level | Scrap |
| Voltage | Above 12 volts | Below 12 volts | Test charge |
| Electrolyte | Normal level | Low, especially if one cell is low | Fill and test charge |
| Specific gravity | Above 1.200 in all cells, with no more than 0.020 difference | Below 1.100 or wide difference between cells | Test charge |
| Case | Sound and leak proof | Leaking case | Scrap. Wash down affected bike parts in baking soda solution |

## 14 Rules to extend battery life

1 Use only distilled water – do not believe stories that the tap water in your district is safe for batteries.

2 Never leave a discharged battery to stand a long time.

3 Recharge a stored battery every 30 days. If it is on the bike then disconnect the negative earth lead. If you recharge it in situ then it is *safer to disconnect it from the bike circuits altogether*.

4 Never add sulphuric acid to battery electrolyte – only distilled water.

5 Never quick-charge a battery.

6 In cold weather keep the battery charged. Discharged batteries freeze more easily.

7 Check that the battery vent pipe is in order; it can get blocked by bending, pinched between frame components or even melted shut if in contact with a hot surface.

8 Never get the battery leads reversed. This is an expensive accident that need not happen.

## 15 Preparing a new battery for service (not MF types)

1 New batteries are usually supplied with servicing instructions but if not then a few simple rules will ensure a long life for a new battery.

2 Remove the six cell caps of a 12 volt battery. Fill to the upper level with battery acid of the correct specific gravity (see Section 7).

3 Leave the battery to 'soak in' the acid electrolyte for 30 minutes before charging.

4 Charge the battery at the rate recommended by the manufacturer, usually for half to one hour. Recheck the acid level and top up if necessary. All future topping up must be with distilled water only.

5 Put in the six cell caps and ensure that they are tight but not overtight. Wipe the battery case clean of any acid film.

6 Install the battery into the frame on the motorcycle and route the plastic breather tube correctly. A kinked or twisted breather tube can cause pressure build up in the battery with the risk of a cracked case or explosion.

7 Connect the positive lead first, then the negative lead.

8 Special treatment must be given to maintenance-free batteries which are discussed in the next Section of this Chapter.

> **HAYNES HiNT** *Battery terminal corrosion can be kept to a minimum by applying a smear of petroleum jelly to the terminals after they have been connected.*

## 16 Maintenance-free (MF) batteries

1 In 1983 Yuasa introduced the maintenance-free (MF) battery for motorcycles (see illustration 16.1). With proper use the MF battery will last for some years, but does require somewhat different care from the conventional battery. Its main properties are as follows.

2 The battery is sealed after the initial filling of sulphuric acid; it is neither possible nor necessary to top up the acid during its lifetime. There can be no spillage, even if the motorcycle falls over because the battery is sealed and there is no free liquid acid. When filled, the glass fibre mat separators absorb all the acid.

3 Under charging, the 'Oxygen Cycle' will recombine gases generated at the plates to return as water to the electrolyte (see illustration 17.3). It is not necessary to top up with distilled water because under normal conditions there is no water loss.

4 In the event of severe overcharging, gas pressure may build up inside the sealed case. The MF battery has safety valves which release the pressure but close again when the internal pressure reduces. No breather tubes are fitted as with conventional batteries and because also there is no need for gas space above the plates, the MF battery is more compact and has no breather protrusions.

5 The plates are constructed of a lead-calcium alloy which gives much less self discharge than lead-antimony. Because the expanded-foam separators fill the space between the plates completely, the MF battery can stand vibration better than the conventional type. In addition, if accidental electrical overload occurs, the active pastes in the plates are held firmly in place by the separators.

6 On the debit side, the MF battery becomes heavily sulphated when it is completely flat. It is sometimes thought that the battery is scrap because it will not accept a charge with an unregulated constant voltage battery charger. What is required is recharging from a constant-current battery charger which may initially produce up to 24 volts to break down the sulphate. The charger should also monitor the *battery* voltage so that charging is discontinued at 16.9 volts. A conventional home charger will not be satisfactory for MF batteries and there are more sophisticated chargers available which have built-in sensing (see Section 19).

## 17 Why no topping up of the MF battery? – The OXYGEN CYCLE

1 When the conventional battery is fully charged the negative plate is converted to spongy lead. The MF battery has a larger negative plate (pole) design, such that it is

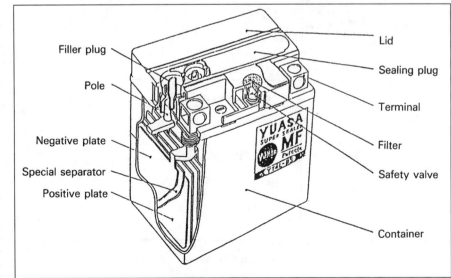

**16.1 Maintenance-free (MF) battery**

Filler plug
Pole
Negative plate
Special separator
Positive plate
Lid
Sealing plug
Terminal
Filter
Safety valve
Container

**13**

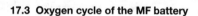

### THE MAINTENANCE FREE BATTERY OXYGEN CYCLE

Two reactions occur simultaneously when the battery is overcharging:-

(1)  $O_2 + 2Pb \Rightarrow 2PbO$
Oxygen ($O_2$) reacts with lead (2Pb) on the negative plate to produce a layer of lead oxide (2PbO)

(2)  $PbO + H_2SO_4 \Rightarrow PbSO_4 + H_2O$
Lead oxide (PbO) reacts with the sulphuric acid ($H_2SO_4$) to give lead sulphate ($PbSO_4$) and WATER ($H_2O$)

This means no loss of water under normal conditions, therefore the battery may be sealed

**17.3 Oxygen cycle of the MF battery**

**18.3 Maintenance-free (MF) battery, ready, filled and charged**

never fully converted to lead by the time the positive plate has been changed to lead peroxide.

**2** When the overcharging point is reached, oxygen is given off from the positive plate but since the negative plate never reaches the overcharge condition, **no hydrogen is given up from it**.

**3** Oxygen migrates through the separators from the positive to negative plate and reacts with the lead of the negative plate to give a layer of lead oxide on it. The lead oxide reacts with the sulphuric acid to give water. This is the **Oxygen cycle**. The battery suffers no water loss because of this process and may therefore be sealed for life.

A summary of the chemical reactions is shown in illustration 17.3. The process is explained but for those familiar with chemistry the reaction equations are also given.

### 18 Filling MF batteries

**1** New Yuasa-type MF motorcycle batteries come supplied with a special acid container. This is pushed into the filler apertures in one movement to provide the correct amount and specific gravity of acid, and the battery is then sealed.

**2** Because of the need to absorb all the acid in the separators, a highly concentrated filler acid of specific gravity 1.310 kg/litre is used instead of 1.280 as in conventional batteries. Additionally, to prevent sulphation, a quantity of sodium sulphate ($Na_2SO_4$) is added to the battery acid. *Standard battery acid must not be used.*

**3** More recently a new form of MF battery has been developed which comes ready filled and charged (see illustration 18.3). A pressure relief valve will vent excess gas pressure if the battery suffers gross overcharging or other catastrophe.

**4** The characteristics of this type are somewhat different from the normal Yuasa type MF battery and when charging, current should be stopped at a battery voltage of 14.5 to 15 volts (not 16.9 volts as with the Yuasa type).

### 19 Charging MF batteries

#### Constant-voltage charging

**1** On the motorcycle the alternator electronic regulator will hold the charging voltage steady at between 14 – 16 volts (or less according to the motorcycle specification). This is the constant-voltage charge characteristic (see illustration 19.1).

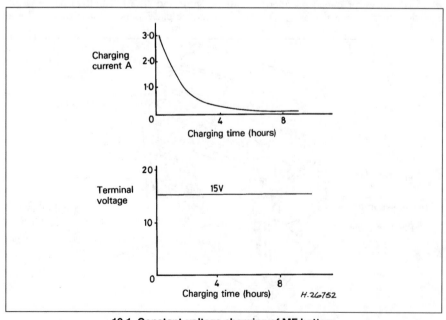

**19.1 Constant-voltage charging of MF battery**

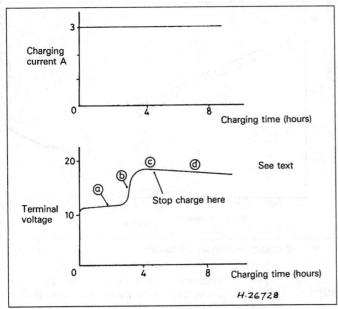

**19.3 Constant-current charging – 1**

*Battery not dead flat*

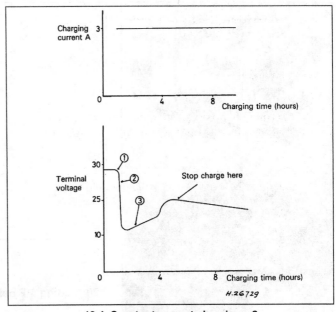

**19.4 Constant-current charging – 2**

*Battery completely flat*

Assuming the battery is not completely flat then:

(a) *A high initial current flows, decreasing rapidly as the battery voltage rises.*
(b) *A small current (say about 0.1A) will continue to flow after the battery reaches full charge.*

If the battery starts off completely flat, it takes a long time to break through the lead sulphate crystals and may not be possible at all with this type of charging. This is why many batteries are thought to be scrap after being deeply discharged.

### Constant-current charging

**2** With this type of charger, the charge current is set according to the battery label information.

**3** For conditions where the battery is not completely flat, refer to illustration 19.3 in conjunction with the following:

(a) *The battery voltage rises steadily up to about 15 volts.*
(b) *The oxygen cycle starts and the voltage rises – bubbling may be heard.*
(c) *This is the fully-charged condition. Stop charge at 16.9 volts in the case of a healthy non-sulphated battery.*
(d) *The negative plate acquires lead sulphate as part of the oxygen cycle and this causes the voltage to fall again.*

**4** Where the battery is completely flat, refer to illustration 19.4 in conjunction with the following:

(1) *Sulphation on the plates needs to be broken down and setting the current (according to battery spec) will raise the charger voltage to the maximum level.*
(2) *The lead sulphate layer is broken through. The voltage decreases and the current rises to the pre-set level.*
(3) *From this point onwards the charging is the same as for the case above.*

### Summary

**5 Constant-voltage chargers** are acceptable to keep the battery in charged condition. The motorcycle alternator is a constant voltage charger and constant voltage bench chargers are available.

**6 Constant-current chargers** are ideal for bench charging. They will 'recover' sulphated batteries quickly but must be used with a timer or voltage sensor to avoid overcharging. Modern sophisticated bench chargers will have all the required sensing built in to them (see below). The battery must not be charged in situ on the bike or damage to the electrical system will occur using a constant-current charger, with the possible exception of a low current charger like the Optimate (see para 8 below).

**7 Unregulated chargers** should not be used with MF batteries, for they will destroy them by overcharging.

**8** It is not surprising that, with the special requirements for charging maintenance-free batteries, new charger designs have emerged. The Tecmate range of battery chargers will service charge all motorcycle lead acid

batteries including MF and Gel types from 2.5 Ah to 25 Ah. This covers most motorcycle batteries and the special features of these chargers are that they are not only fully automatic but will monitor the battery condition by voltage sampling at regular intervals.

For private owners the Optimate model is suitable for 2.5 Ah to 25 Ah batteries (see illustration 19.8a) and will charge at constant current until the battery voltage reaches 14.3 volts and then switches to a constant voltage mode. This change over voltage means it is suitable for any lead acid battery including MF and Gel types.

For professional use the Batterymate covers 2.5 Ah to 45 Ah batteries (see

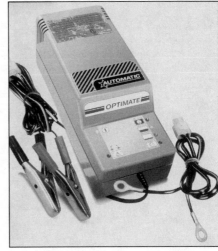

**19.8a 'Optimate' battery charger**

**13**

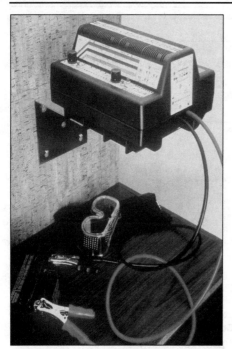

**19.8b 'Batterymate' workshop battery charger**

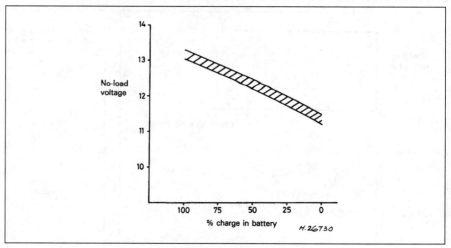

**20.1 Capacity testing an MF battery**

illustration 19.8b) and the voltage at which it switches from constant current to constant voltage mode is selectable at either 16.9 or 14.5 volts.

## 20 Testing MF batteries

**1** As hydrometer testing is not possible, the simplest test is to measure the open-circuit voltage (ie with no electrical load) (see illustration 8.2). The method is, however, not very accurate since variations occur between batteries and the result will not indicate starting performance.

The open circuit voltage should be measured with a good quality voltmeter allowing first a rest period of 30 minutes after charging. Illustration 20.1 shows the approximate relationship between terminal voltage and remaining charge.

**2** If the battery will turn the starter motor then this is the definitive test. An alternative is to test the battery using a high current discharge tester. This should be arranged to take a current equal to starter current load and consists of a resistance load clipped across the battery terminals with a voltmeter in parallel.

# Chapter 14
# Lighting and signalling

# Contents

## 1 Introduction

**1** The lights fitted to a motorcycle are all in parallel (see Chapter 2), which means that each is connected across the battery supply and that the total current is the sum of the separate bulb currents.

**2** Simple lighting circuits are shown in illustrations 1.2a and 1.2b. Many large capacity motorcycles may have more facilities, but still work on the same principle that each lamp is switched in circuit and all are in parallel with the battery and alternator or dynamo. Lighting circuits are generally uncomplicated, but when shown as part of the whole electrical wiring diagram can look more involved than they really are.

**3** In the examples shown, protection is by a 20A fuse and all lights can be operated only after the ignition switch is on.

In the ON position, the headlight switch will illuminate all lights, the dip (or dimmer) switch controlling the high and low beam of the headlight. The lighting switch also has a mid position which only illuminates the position light, tail and instrument lights. For main beam

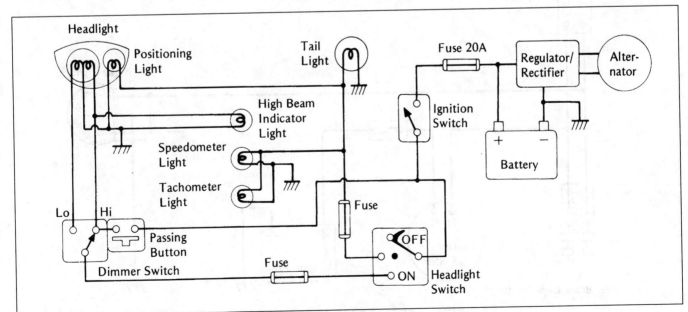

**1.2a Typical lighting circuit for European models**

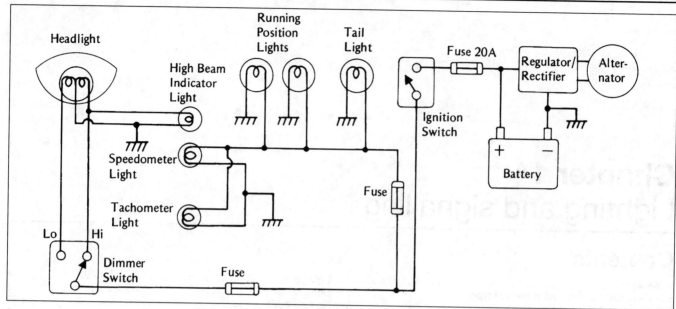

**1.2b  Typical lighting circuit for US and Canadian models**

flashing a wire is taken from the main supply before the headlight switch, and then to the passing button.

**4** The lighting circuits on US and Canadian models have no lighting switch, all lights come on when the ignition is on. The front turn signals often double as running lights and also come on with the ignition; twin filament bulbs are used for this purpose. Sealed beam headlight units may be encountered on certain older models; which means that the complete unit must be renewed if bulb failure occurs.

## 2  Brake lights

**1** Brake light switches are fitted to both front and rear brakes. Older British motorcycles generally have only a rear brake light switch. The switches are usually operated mechanically being of the plunger type, but may be operated hydraulically on some hydraulic disc brake systems.

**2** When the brake lever or pedal is operated, the switch contacts are brought in contact, completing the electrical circuit. Such switches are normally very reliable, corrosion due to road dirt and water normally being the only problem; water dispersant aerosol works well here. Illustration 2.2 shows how either or both front and rear brake switches will operate the brake light.

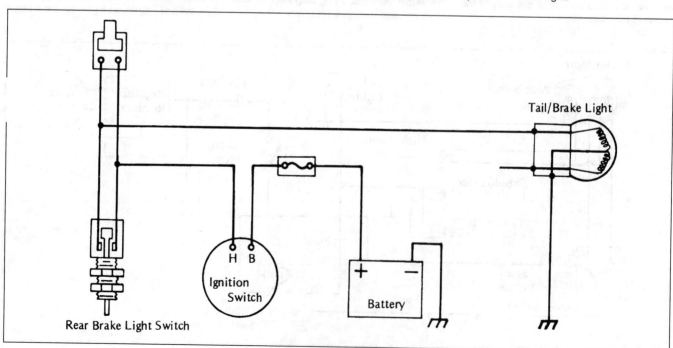

**2.2  Brake light circuit**

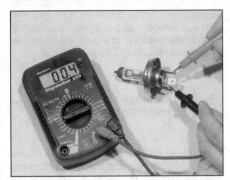

**3.1 Bulb test on the ohms range of a multimeter**

## 3 Lighting faults

**1** Vibration failure used to be the most common fault for motorcycle bulbs although improved engine mountings and lamp design make this less of a problem nowadays. In any event, if a lamp does not light check that the filament has not burned out. Usually a burned out filament is obvious by inspection; there is frequently staining of the glass and tungsten debris in the envelope. If in doubt, check using an ohmmeter between the bulb pins and the metal case (see illustration 3.1). If the bulb filament is good it will read low on the ohmmeter scale and if it is blown, the reading will be very high (infinite).

**2** Blown bulbs frequently take a circuit fuse with them, so after checking and possibly renewing the bulb, look next at the fuse if there is still no light. Again, if uncertain test the fuse with the ohmmeter or a continuity tester.

If all is well here and supply voltage is getting to the bulb pins, then earthing (grounding) should be checked. Corrosion sets in all too easily at the frame or lamp shell connection points on road vehicles, so make sure that the earth (ground) leads are really making good contact. If necessary, unscrew the tag and scrape both tag and frame point clean before screwing/bolting up tight again. A light spray of water dispersant fluid in the bulbholder and on the bulb metal body will be good protection.

**3** Switches may be checked with an ohmmeter in conjunction with the machine's wiring diagram. The switch leads usually terminate in a multi-pin connector, making checking possible without dismantling. Most switch faults are due to internal corrosion of contacts or water contamination, and these can usually be cured by cleaning and the application of a water dispersant fluid. Switches which are particularly susceptible to water contamination should be packed with silicone-based grease.

**4** Certain US motorcycles use a reserve lighting system which automatically switches in the remaining bulb filament in the event of a headlamp beam failure. If the dip beam fails, then the main beam is switched on as a get-you-home facility, although the light intensity may be reduced (vice versa if the main beam fails).

This is achieved by a detector which senses a lack of current in the alternative filament and operates a blown filament warning light in the instrument cluster. To test, switch to the dip beam and then pull off the dip beam connector to the bulb in the headlamp. The main beam and the warning light should come on. Check for broken wires and if necessary replace the reserve lighting unit.

## 4 Light units

**1** A headlight needs a concentrated source of white light at the focal point of a reflector to project the light forward. This source can be a bulb, which is plugged in place in a reflector or, alternatively, an integral system called a sealed beam unit in which the light-emitting filaments are built into a lens and reflector assembly which is sealed against ingress of air and, of course, dust.

## 5 Bulbs – conventional tungsten filament types

**1** Pre-focus bulbs are made with accurately located tungsten filaments and have a metal flange with some form of location tab to give precise positioning of the bulb inside the reflector (see illustration 5.1a). Note the bulb electrical contacts shown here are more usually prongs but solder-type contacts are still used on many bulbs.

The main beam filament is located at the focal point of the reflector and the dipped beam filament situated above and to one side of the main beam filament so that its light is projected downwards and to one side of the road (see illustration 5.1b).

Sometimes a small metal shield welded to the filament supports is used to give a good dipped beam since light is allowed to the upper half of the reflector only (see illustration

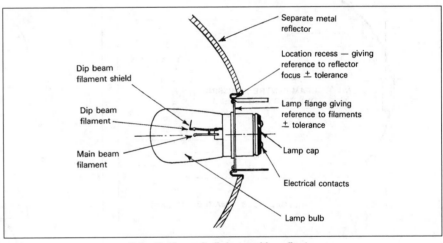

**5.1a Prefocus bulb located in reflector**

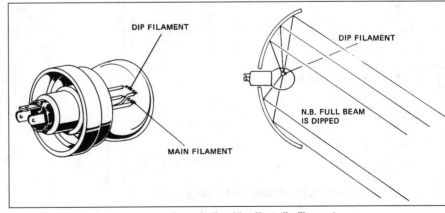

**5.1b Headlamp bulb with offset dip filament**

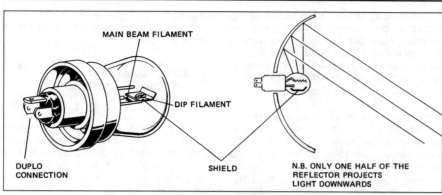

**5.1c  Headlamp bulb with shield dip filament**

5.1c). Ideally the filaments should be a white light spot of infinitely small size, but practically, this cannot be.

**2** The coil of the filament is wound horizontally so that any stray light will illuminate the road edges and not the sky. This is important since upward rays will be reflected by fog back to the rider and may cause dazzle.

One final point on the pros and cons of shield dip and offset filament dip bulbs – the shield does have an effect on the main beam in that the 'centre' of the parallel rays is missing and also on dip only the top half of the reflector is projecting light downwards (see illustration 5.2).

**3** Bulb ratings are usually given in **watts** as shown in Section 12 but in the US, smaller power bulbs are often marked in candle power (cp). Candle power is a measure of luminous intensity and has been superseded by the international standard candela, but nevertheless the older item is still found.

## 6  Disadvantages of separate bulb and reflector

**1** The makeup of the main and dipped beams is primarily dependent upon the filament position relative to the focal point of the reflector, and for many years road vehicles used the prefocus bulb in which the filaments were welded in place with precision.

**2** Even the close tolerances to which this design could be made were too wide for proper beam control. To them should be added the tolerances between the lamp seating in the reflector and the focal point (see illustration 6.2a). Additionally, about 20% of light from the filament is lost due to obscuration by the bulb and cap; also in service the evaporated tungsten from the

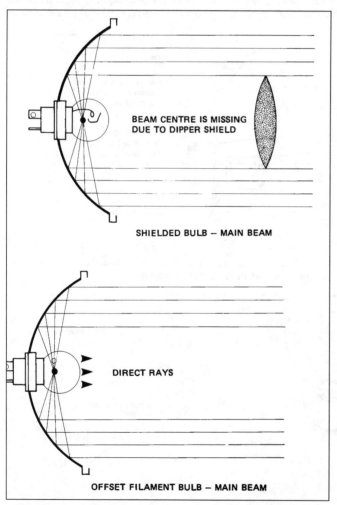

**5.2  Main beam patterns for shielded and offset filament bulbs**

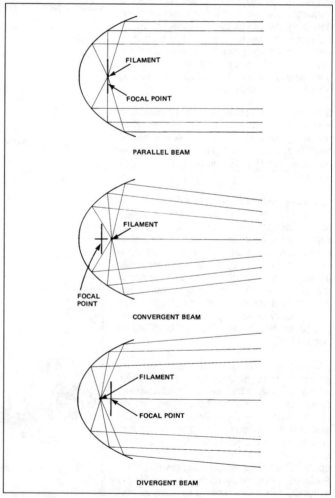

**6.2a  Filament location should be at focal point of reflector**

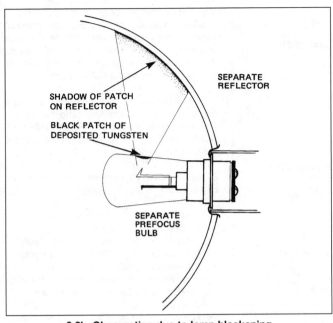

**6.2b  Obscuration due to lamp blackening**

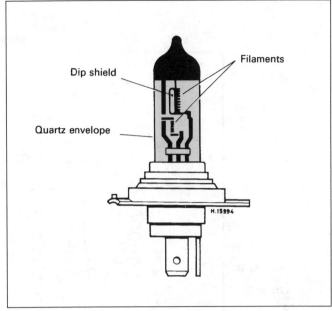

**8.1a  H4 quartz-halogen bulb construction**

filament settles on the upper surface of the bulb, and although the total light from the lamp is reduced by 10% – 15% only at half life (about two years say) the obscuration presented to a large section of the reflector is of serious consequence and the beam is disturbed (see illustration 6.2b).

3 Finally, due to oxidation and the effects of dust and dirt, the reflector loses efficiency so that after four years' service the beam intensity may be reduced to about 60% of the original value. Most of the troubles mentioned occur because in the design, reflector and bulb were considered as separate entities. When combined into a single sealed-beam unit a considerable improvement is obtained.

4 Despite the possible troubles of a separate bulb and reflector, most motorcycles still use a semi-sealed system in which the front glass and reflector are in one piece with the bulb clipped accurately in place. With the arrival of the tungsten halogen bulb the combination is proving successful. Sealed beam headlamps have been used in the past (see Section 9).

## 7  Bulbs – service life (tungsten types)

1 Bosch give figures for the life and light intensity of vehicle bulbs against applied

voltage, but although the information relates to automobiles the same general pattern should apply to the motorcycle.

2 Assuming that the standard life of a bulb in hours of working is attained at 6.75 volts for a 6 volt system and 13.5 volts for a 12 volt system, then the relationship between applied voltage, light intensity and life is as shown in the table below.

It will be seen that the light and life of a vehicle bulb depend upon a correct working voltage; it is therefore important that the voltage regulator is working correctly.

## 8  Bulbs – quartz halogen types

1 The quartz-halogen bulb is in now in common use on all but the smallest motorcycles. It is known by various other names: quartz-iodine, tungsten-halogen or tungsten-iodine, but all are really the same thing, namely a bulb giving a much higher illumination and longer life than a conventional type. Several considerations determine the high efficiency, shape and life of quartz-halogen bulbs (see illustrations 8.1a and b).

2 The normal wearing-out of a conventional filament bulb is due to the evaporation of tungsten from the filament surface (for a mental picture of evaporation think of steam coming from the surface of water). As the filament temperature is raised then evaporation increases rapidly and not only does the filament become thinner but the tungsten vapour blackens the inside of the bulb and illumination decreases.

3 It is found that if one of a group of chemical elements known as halogens (elements that compound themselves to form salts) is added in precise quantity to the normal inert gas filling of a bulb, great improvements are possible in terms of life and illumination.

4 When tungsten vapour leaves the filament surface it works its way towards the glass envelope. Between the filament and the glass there exists a temperature gradient; when the tungsten atoms reach the zone of about 1450°C (2640°F) the halogen combines with

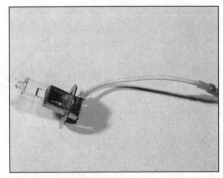

**8.1b  55 watt H3 quartz-halogen headlamp main beam bulb**

**14**

| Applied voltage | 85% | 90% | 95% | 100% | 105% | 110% | 120% |
|---|---|---|---|---|---|---|---|
| Light intensity | 53% | 67% | 83% | 100% | 120% | 145% | 200% |
| Life | 1000% | 440% | 210% | 100% | 50% | 28% | 6% |

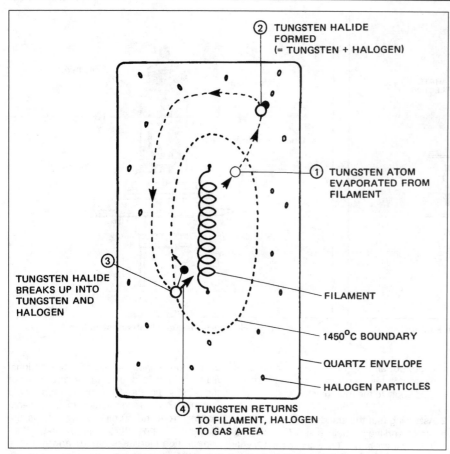

② TUNGSTEN HALIDE
FORMED
(= TUNGSTEN + HALOGEN)

① TUNGSTEN ATOM
EVAPORATED FROM
FILAMENT

③ TUNGSTEN HALIDE
BREAKS UP INTO
TUNGSTEN AND
HALOGEN

FILAMENT

1450°C BOUNDARY

QUARTZ ENVELOPE

HALOGEN PARTICLES

④ TUNGSTEN RETURNS
TO FILAMENT, HALOGEN
TO GAS AREA

**8.4 Regenerative cycle in quartz-halogen bulb**

tungsten to form tungsten halides (see illustration 8.4) and these diffuse back to the region of the filament without the glass-blackening effect taking place.

**5** As the filament is approached the temperature rises again towards 2000°C/3630°F (the surface temperature) and the tungsten halides break up again into tungsten and halogen at the 1450°C/2640°F boundary. The halogen goes back to the gaseous area whilst the tungsten atoms return to the filament, although some surround the filament and tend

to reduce evaporation. Because evaporation is thus reduced it is possible to have a hotter filament and so there is a corresponding increase in illumination. Also because the filament is being constantly replenished with tungsten atoms it has a very long life and, because the tungsten atoms do not reach the glass there is no blackening of the inner surface.

**6** Note that the usual halogen is presently iodine and the tungsten-halogen formed with it is gaseous only above 250°C (480°F). For this reason the bulb must be small so as to

stay hot and so not only are the bulbs much smaller in volume but also they are made of quartz to withstand the temperature. Because quartz is stronger than normal bulb glass, designers increase the gas pressure which in turn reduces the amount of evaporation.

**7** The increase in gas pressure and the halogen cycle of returning tungsten to the filament produces a lamp of high luminous power which is almost constant throughout the life of the lamp.

**8** There are two vital factors relating to the life of the bulb:

*(a) The bulb should not be handled with the fingers because the salt from body perspiration will stain the quartz: should the bulb be accidentally touched it may be wiped carefully, whilst cold, with methylated spirit (stoddard solvent) and allowed to dry before use again (see illustration 8.8).*
*(b) Life is reduced rapidly if the quartz bulb and the gas filling are not maintained at the correct working temperature. A low supply voltage results in not only a drop in luminous power but a serious fall in service life.*

## 9  Sealed beam unit

**1** Lighting engineers, conscious that separate bulb and reflector headlights had serious disadvantages, eventually combined these two elements, the result being the sealed beam unit. This consists of an all-glass sealed unit containing two filaments but without a bulb; the back of the unit is 'silvered' to form a reflector and the front glass is moulded in the shape of a lens (see illustration 9.1).

In effect the unit is a large bulb which is sealed for life against the entry of dirt or damp; they have not been in use for some years.

## 10 Lens design aspects

**1** Lenses are cast into the front glass of headlamps to produce correct lighting patterns on the road for both main and meeting (dip) beams. The complex block lens shown in illustration 10.1 is an excellent example of applied optical principles.

**2** For a single, central, filament the beam emerging from the parabolic reflector is approximately circular. However, this gives no side spread to kerb and road centre line and the upper part of the beam is largely wasted in

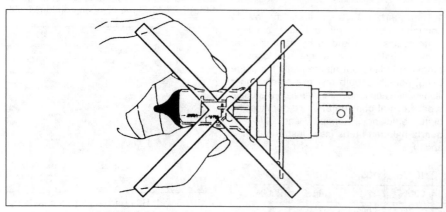

**8.8 Do not touch the glass of a quartz-halogen bulb!**

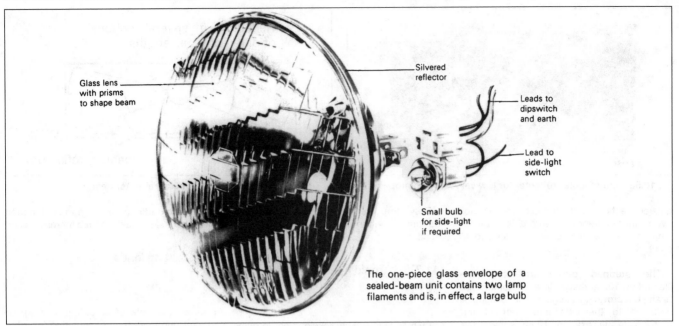

**9.1 Sealed beam unit**

*(From the 'AA Book of the Car', reproduced by kind permission of the Publishers, Drive Publications Limited, London)*

illuminating objects above the rider's eye level.

The refracting (light bending) prisms (see illustration 10.1) can give any desired configuration of the light beam and because the borosilicate glass is so thick (3 – 5 mm) it is ideally suited to moulding into prisms during manufacture. Reflector surfaces are evaporated aluminium.

**3** Quartz-halogen lamp designs were soon incorporated into motorcycle headlamps. They are now standard original equipment on many motorcycles and may have twin filaments for dipped lights. However headlight dipping (dimming-US) is also carried by using two separate headlamps, one used as a main beam and the other switched in as a dipped (dimmed) beam. This allows the main beam lens to be specifically designed for its purpose

with minimal glass lenses and the dipped beam headlight also purpose designed just for dipped beaming.

**4** A comparison of conventional and tungsten halogen bulb illumination patterns is seen in illustration 10.4.

**5** Homofocular headlamps have an advanced design of reflector which is divided into

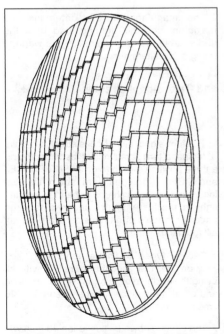

**10.1 Complex block lens for twin filament headlamp**

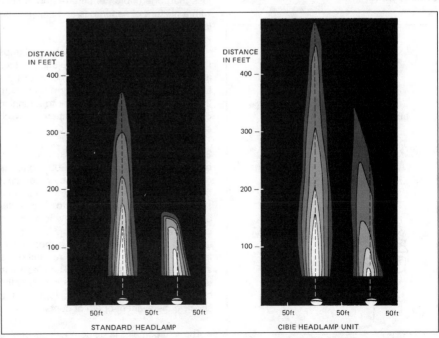

**10.4 Comparison of standard tungsten and quartz-halogen headlamp units**

**14**

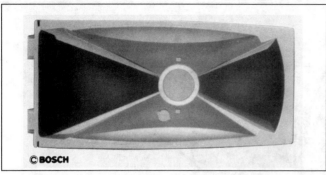

**10.5a Homofocular reflector for low vertical headlamp light**

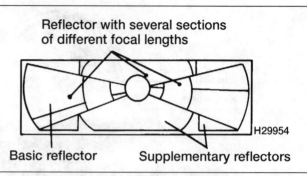

**10.5b Homofocular reflector design**

different sections. In the homofocular reflector two or more paraboloids with different focal lengths are arranged round the same focal point.

The stepped plastic reflector (see illustration 10.5a) results in a low long range beam, but providing a large amount of light for diffusion to the side and front of the motorcycle. Illustration 10.5b shows the separate lenses as a group.

**6** Modern headlamp designs have moved toward single plastic outer shells with two quartz bulbs and reflectors side by side. In the UK the bulbs are rated at 55 watts (dip) and 60 watts (main beam) with both on dip or both on main at the same time. This gives a huge light output of 120 watts and it is not surprising that relays are used in order to shorten the length of cables carrying the current required. Note that in certain European countries the bulb ratings are lower at 45/45 watts.

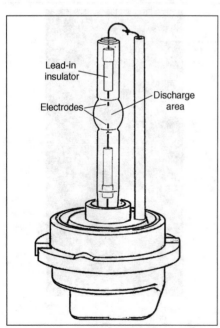

**11.2 Litronic headlamp gas discharge bulb**

'Grey' imports are wired so that one headlamp is on for dip and the other for main beam.

## 11 The Litronic headlamp

**1** A remarkable Bosch development in bulbs has resulted in the Litronic headlamp system. It features a xenon gas-discharge bulb as the central element and although it is not used in motorcycles at the time of writing it must surely only be a matter of time before it appears in a new model. Like most equipment with an electronic element, price and size will both reduce to the point where it will be cost effective for use in the motorcycle.

**2** The 35 watt D2S bulb produces a light flux twice as intense as some 55 watt quartz-halogen bulbs. The light combustion area is less than one cubic centimetre and is filled with a mixture of xenon gas and halogenides (see illustration 11.2).

Normally, industrial gas-discharge lamps take several minutes to warm up and produce maximum light output. To overcome this the Litronic has an initial boost current of up to 2.6 amperes and the drops back to a running current of approximately 0.4 ampere at which point the bulb is running at 900°C.

**3** To ignite the discharge an initial voltage of between 10 and 20kV (20,000 volts) is required, and this is achieved by a compact control unit which resides in the headlamp shell. The 12 volt input goes into a converter and an ignition unit, the whole being controlled by a microprocessor. Should the lamp go out, say because of a momentary lapse in the supply voltage, re-ignition is spontaneous and automatic. The electronic unit will also interrupt the power supply in the case of a damaged bulb to avoid electric shock in the event of operator contact.

**4** The light contains large components of blue and green light and is similar to sunlight. The present application is to use the Litronic lamp

for a dipped (dimmed) beam in conjunction with a normal H4 halogen bulb for main beam.

## 12 Lighting loads

**1** As an example of electrical loading for lighting purposes the specification for a UK specification Kawasaki GPZ500S is given below.

| | |
|---|---|
| Headlight | 12V 60/55W |
| Parking light | 12V 5W |
| Stop/taillight | 12V 21/5W x 2 |
| Licence plate light | 12V 5W |
| Turn signal light (front/rear) | 12V 21W x 4 |
| Instrument light | 12V 1.7W x 3 |
| Neutral light | 12V 3W |
| High beam indicator light | 12V 3W |
| Oil pressure warning light | 12V 3W |
| Left turn signal indicator light | 12V 3W |
| Right turn signal indicator light | 12V 3W |

**2** The manufacturer will determine the maximum possible lighting load from the above table in order to specify the wattage rating of the alternator.

## 13 Turn signal circuits

**1** The turn signal circuit consists of two pairs of lamps, a turn signal relay (flasher unit), and a three position switch to give LEFT, CANCEL and RIGHT. Additionally, most circuits also incorporate either a shared or handed warning light in the instruments, and mid to large capacity models often have a hazard facility (all four lamps light).

Several types of flasher units exist (see Section 14), the essential principle with all being the ability to switch turn signal lamps on and off at a repetition rate between 60 – 120 times per minute.

**2** The circuit shown in illustration 13.2 shows a turn signal circuit, complete with indicator lamps mounted in the instrument cluster. A separate heavy duty hazard relay connects to all four lamps by the hazard switch.

**3** Local regulations govern the bulb wattage requirements; in the UK this is 21 watts, and 23 watts in the US. On certain US models the front turn signal bulbs are dual filament 23/8W and operate as running lights.

**4** Some motorcycles do not have a facility for switching on all four turn indicator lamps for signalling 'hazard'.

It is simple to make an adaptation as shown in illustration 13.4 to achieve this. From the lamp side of the flasher relay, connect a switch to two diodes of 30 volt 5 ampere rating (minimum) to the two output terminals of the flasher switch. Diodes may be obtained from any electronics component shop.

When the new hazard switch is ON, all four lamps will flash. If required, an optional warning lamp can be incorporated in the instrument panel. Most flasher relays will operate four bulbs successfully.

## 14 Turn signal relays (flasher units)

**1** There are several types of flasher units. All have the same purpose of making and breaking the circuit to the turn signal lamps at

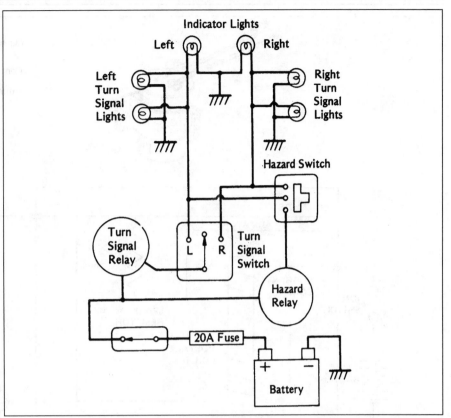

**13.2 Turn signal circuit**

*In this example a second relay is used to operate the hazard function*

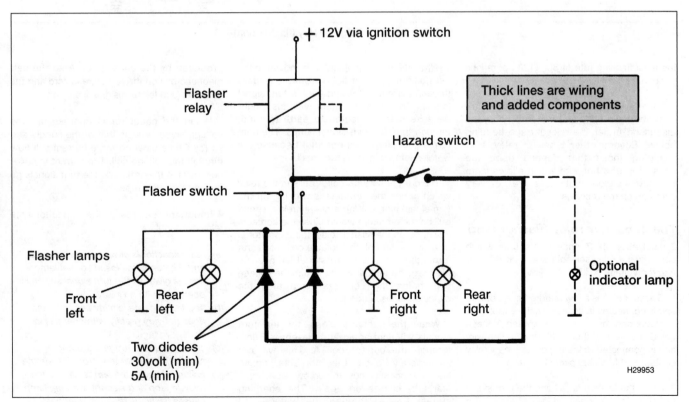

**13.4 How to add hazard flash facility**

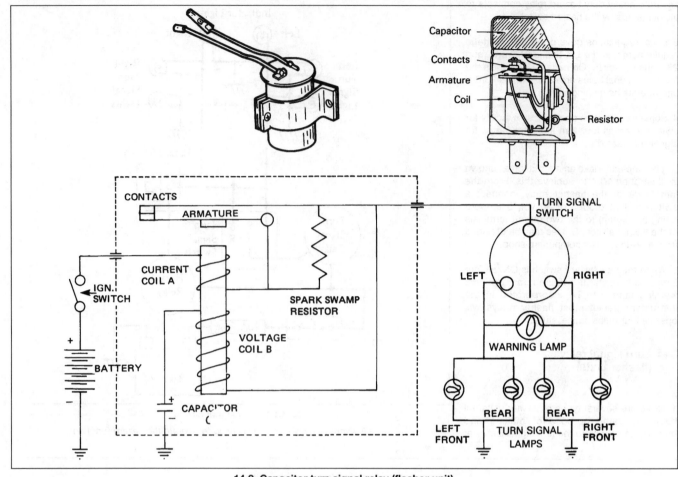

**14.2 Capacitor turn signal relay (flasher unit)**

the legal flashing rate of 60 – 120 operations per minute.

There are three main types, the capacitor relay, bi-metal relay and transistor; they are discussed under the relevant sub-heading below. Several other types of relay exist including those that depend upon the expansion of a hot wire which allows lamp contacts to close but these are not very common on motorcycles.

### The capacitor relay (flasher unit)

**2** Illustration 14.2 shows this unit which comprises a relay solenoid with a current coil A and a voltage coil B.

Current coil A is a few hundred turns of wire and is connected in series with the supply, the contacts and then the flasher switch. Voltage coil B has several thousand turns of fine wire and is connected to the upper stationary relay contact and to a capacitor C.

**3** When the ignition is ON and the turn signal switch is OFF, capacitor C will charge up to the battery voltage with the polarity shown.

When the turn signal switch is moved to the left position, current flows from the battery through current coil A and the left turn signal lamps. The warning lamp will also light because it is connected to earth (ground) through the right turn signal lamps. The right turn signal lamps will not light because the warning lamp current is too small.

The current through coil A pulls in the relay which opens the contacts, switching off the turn signal lamps. With a simple relay, spring pull on the armature would close the contacts again, but in the flasher relay, the capacitor C discharges through the voltage coil B to earth (ground) via the left turn signal lamps. The discharge current, flowing through the voltage coil, holds the contacts open until the capacitor is discharged.

When the contacts close, the left turn signals will light again and current will flow through the current coil A. This will not immediately open the contacts again, however, because now the empty capacitor C starts to charge up again. The charging current flowing through the voltage coil produces a magnetic flux **opposite** to that

produced by the current coil A so the nett magnetic pull on the armature is zero and the contacts (and left turn signals) stay on.

When the capacitor C charges up, the voltage across equals that of the supply and so (by Ohms Law) no more current will flow through the voltage coil. The current in coil A now pulls in the armature, the turn signals go out and the cycle repeats.

**4** Important features of the capacitor-type relay are as follows:

*(a) The capacitor is always ready charged and the contacts closed so that lamp flash is given as the turn signal switch is operated, with no delay.*

*(b) The flashing rate is fairly accurate and does not vary greatly with changes in battery voltage.*

*(c) The relay unit is rugged and not susceptible to vibration from the engine.*

*(d) Failure of any of the lamps causes the relay to stop and also the warning lamp ceases flashing. Thus the rider has definite warning of failure.*

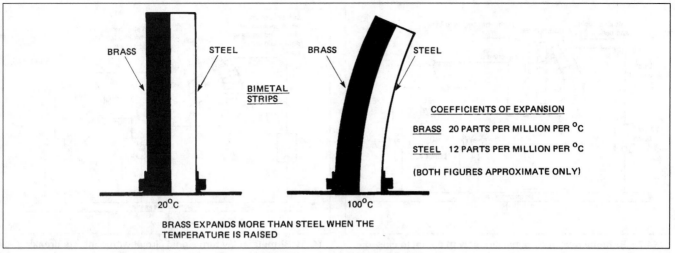

**14.5 Principle of the bi-metal strip**

## The bi-metal relay (flasher unit)

**5** The principle of the bi-metal strip is based on the fact that metals expand at different rates when heated. If two such dissimilar metal strips are riveted or spot welded together then a rise in temperature will cause the bi-metal strip to bend (see illustration 14.5). Such movement is used in many ways to switch current or operate hydraulic valves in various branches of engineering, and in this case is used to switch turn signal lamps on and off at a pre-determined rate.

**6** The physical layout of illustration 14.6 shows two bi-metal strips clamped at the lower ends and with a contact on each, normally apart, at the upper tips. Of the two coils, wound in heating resistance wire, the voltage coil has more turns and higher resistance than the current coil which has few turns and carries the full lamp currents.

**7** Illustration 14.7a shows the circuit with the turn signal switch in the OFF position. Note that the contacts are apart and that the voltage coil connects straight to the battery.

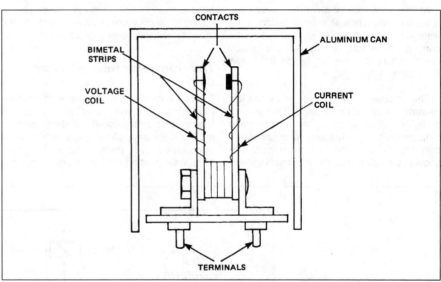

**14.6 Bi-metal turn signal relay (flasher unit)**

When the switch is operated, the voltage coil carries a current through the turn signal lamps which do not, however, light because of the high resistance of the voltage coil. However, enough current flows to bend the left bi-metal strip towards the right (see illustration 14.7b).

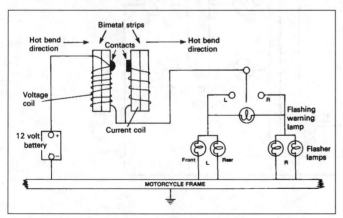

**14.7a Turn signal circuit diagram with bi-metal relay**

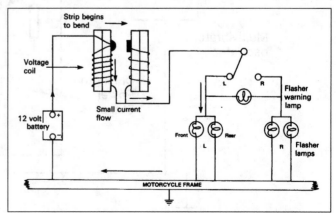

**14.7b Bi-metal relay turn signal circuit with switch closed – left-hand strip begins to bend**

**14**

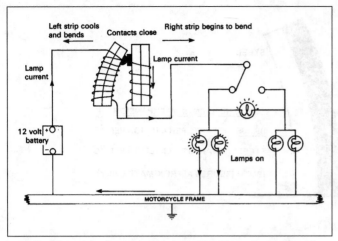

**14.7c Bi-metal relay turn signal circuit with contacts closed – current coil carries lamp current**

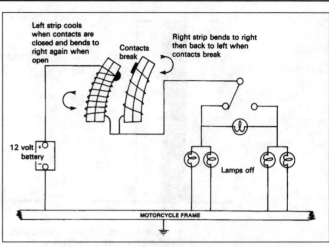

**14.7d Bi-metal relay turn signal circuit with contacts breaking – cycle repeats**

At the point when the contacts close, the lamp current increases sharply because the voltage coil is now almost shorted out by the current coil which, remember, is of much lower resistance: the left lamps light (see illustration 14.7c).

The voltage coil no longer heats the left bi-metal strip which cools and begins to straighten. Simultaneously the right bi-metal strip bends to the right and so the contacts part rapidly and the lamps go out. The sequence continues as the left strip begins to bend to the right again and the right strip, now having no current coil heating, returns to the upright position (see illustration 14.7d).

### The transistor relay (flasher unit)

8 Using a multivibrator oscillator to produce ON-OFF square wave pulses, this type of flasher unit has become widely used in motorcycles and cars. There are several advantages over thermal types including constant repetition rate, provision of audible or visual warning of bulb failure (which is signalled by a doubling of flashing frequency) and the ability to give hazard light warning over a long period.

The output from a multivibrator is (nearly) a square wave voltage and this is passed to a Darlington pair power stage (see Chapter 2).

The load on the Darlington stage is an electrical relay which switches the turn indicator lights on and off (see illustration 14.8a).

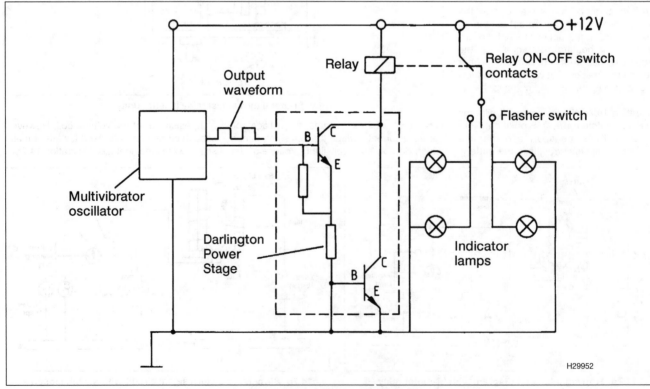

**14.8a Transistor relay flasher unit**

**14.8b All-electronic transistor flasher unit (Denso)**

A power transistor *could* be used to drive the turn indicator lamps instead of a relay but would result in a loss of about one volt and it is also susceptible to spike voltages when switching. A modern all-electronic alternative is to drive the lamps directly by a power field-effect transistor, eliminating the need for a relay (see illustration 14.8b).

Inevitably, the use of separate components has given way to an integrated circuit form of electronic flasher relay but the principles of operation are the same.

## 15 Self-cancelling turn signals

1 For many years the majority of automobiles have been equipped with self-cancelling turn signals. These are controlled by a cam attached to the steering column; as the steering wheel returns to the straightahead position after negotiating the turning, the turn signal control is tripped back to the OFF position.

2 Unfortunately, the simple cam-operated arrangement used on cars cannot be implemented on a motorcycle because the steering stem moves surprisingly little during normal riding. The obvious approach is to employ some sort of timer circuit to cancel the turn signals after a predetermined amount of time has elapsed. This works fine for overtaking, or for turns where it is not necessary to wait for traffic, but if the rider is obliged to wait, it would result in the system switching off prematurely.

To get round this problem a second control is added which measures the distance travelled (see illustration 15.2). This takes the form of a distance sensor built into the speedometer head and working in the same way as the pickup coil in an electronic ignition system. The signal pulses are 'counted' by the timer circuit, which will keep the turn signals operating until the specified time and distance have been covered.

In this way, when overtaking on a straight road, the distance will have been covered way before the timer has elapsed. Conversely, when waiting at a road junction the timer will rest, leaving the system running until the correct distance has elapsed. In addition, the rider has the option to override the self-cancelling system and switch the turn signals off manually.

## 16 Horns

1 Today motorcycle horns are nearly all of the electro-magnetic vibrating diaphragm type. With the exception of the air horn, vibratory motion of the diaphragm is on a similar principle to that of the electric bell, in which an iron armature is attracted by a current

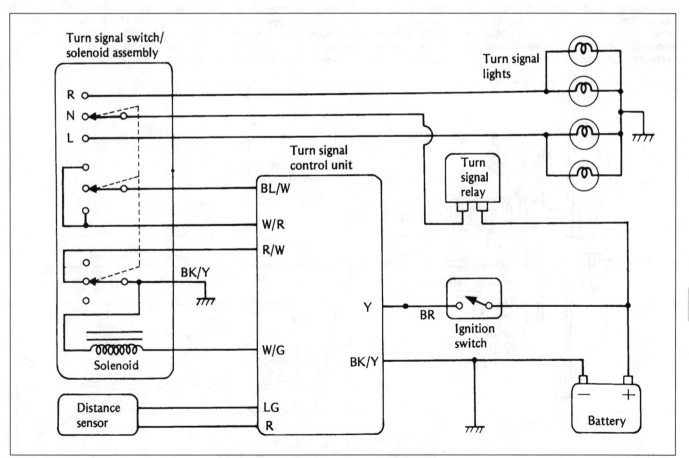

**15.2 Self-cancelling turn signal circuit diagram**

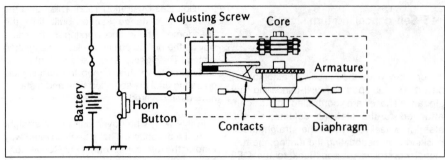

**16.1 Schematic of horn showing the electro-magnetic vibrator principle**

carrying coil; the movement of the armature breaks a pair of contacts thus cutting off the current to the coil, the armature returns under spring pressure and the cycle repeats (see illustration 16.1).

The armature is connected to a diaphragm which pushes air back and forth at a frequency high enough to be audible.

**2** Most motorcycles are fitted with a horn which works on the vibrator principle, but there are two vibrator sound sources from the diaphragm and also from a tone disc. The diaphragm oscillates back and forth at a relatively low frequency, say 300 vibrations per second, and the attached tone disc at about 2000 vibrations per second. The low notes have the particular property of distance penetration while the high frequency notes will be heard easily over traffic roar.

Illustration 16.2 shows the principle of operation; when the horn button is pressed the coil energises the electromagnet and the armature is attracted to it and hits it. The movement breaks the contacts and so the armature releases, the contacts close, and the process repeats so long as the button is pressed. The mechanical shock of armature/magnet impact makes the tone disc 'ring'. The tone disc vibrates at an overtone frequency of the diaphragm (ie at an exact multiple) and the resulting combined tone produces an effective penetrating sound which is (hopefully) not too harsh.

**3** Wind tone horns are sometimes fitted to motorcycles and operate on the same principle, except that a sea-shell-shaped horn produces an acceptable note, but in order to obtain both distance and penetration they should work ideally in pairs. The current drain

is high and would be a very heavy battery load. Where they are used, a relay will avoid the need for thick wires to the horn button.

**4** Although horns are frequently subjected to engine heat and the weather, they are remarkably reliable, but after long use the contact points may roughen with the effects of quality and volume loss. In this case adjustment may be made via the adjuster on the rear of the unit until satisfactory performance is restored. After adjustment lock the adjuster with lacquer. Little else can be done to horns and the only other likely cause of trouble is corrosion in the horn button which should be taken apart and cleaned or replaced. Illustration 16.4 shows the typical loudness and current consumption of a simple horn of the electro-magnetic vibrating diaphragm type.

**5** Air horns are simple in principle. Air or gas is pumped in under pressure to a chamber which is closed at one end by a diaphragm; against the diaphragm pressure the annular end of the horn prevents escape of air/gas. When the pressure is high enough the diaphragm is pushed to the left (see illustration 16.5) and the air/gas is released up the horn mouth. The diaphragm closes and the cycle repeats. To obtain the necessary gas pressure an electric pump is operated by the horn button. It is possible to run a horn by a special aerosol can with a trigger control but these are not in common use.

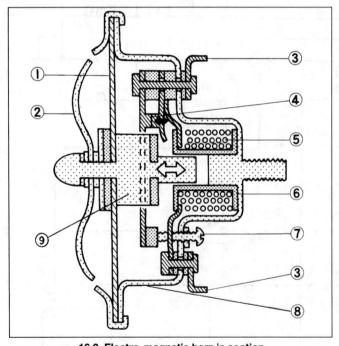

**16.2 Electro-magnetic horn in section**

| | | |
|---|---|---|
| 1 Diaphragm | 4 Contacts | 7 Sound adjuster |
| 2 Tone disc | 5 Coil | 8 Horn body |
| 3 Wire terminal | 6 Insulator | 9 Armature |

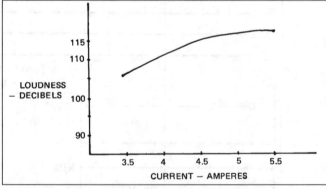

**16.4 Horn current and loudness graph**

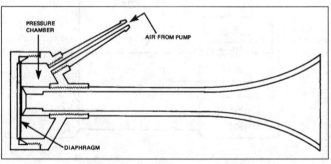

**16.5 Simple air horn construction**

# Chapter 15
# Starter motors

# Contents

## 1  Introduction

**1** Electric starter motors are commonplace on motorcycles of all sizes from the smallest machines up to superbikes, and undoubtedly the attraction of push-button starting is now so great that it has become standard specification on almost all motorcycles and scooters.

**2** The principle of operation of the starter motor is closely related to that of the generator. Basically, the only real difference is that in the case of the generator the input is mechanical torque to turn the rotor, the output being electrical energy, whereas in the starter motor electrical energy is put in and mechanical torque taken out at the shaft. Indeed, all dc generators can be made to run as motors simply by supplying direct current, and conversely all dc motors can be made to act as generators.

**3** For the production of torque at the driveshaft it is necessary to supply direct current to an armature situated in a magnetic field. The simple motor (see illustration 1.3)

shows the main field from N to S, an armature loop and a commutator which ensures that the armature current switches so that it always flows in the same direction as it passes under a particular pole (see also Chapter 2 for electric motor principles).

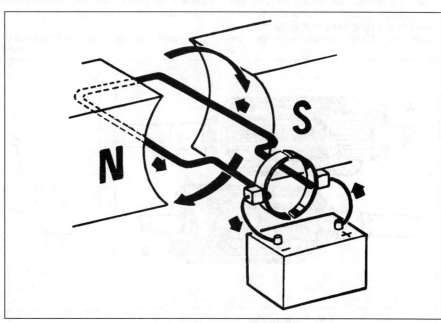

**1.3  An elementary dc motor**

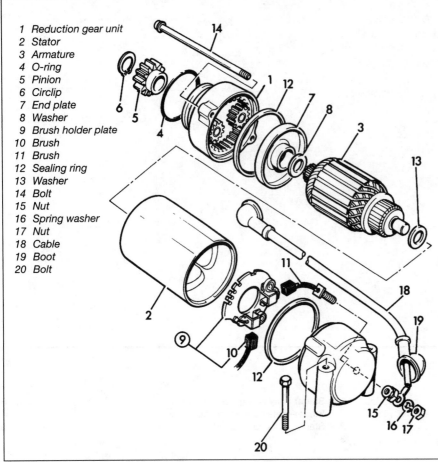

1 Reduction gear unit
2 Stator
3 Armature
4 O-ring
5 Pinion
6 Circlip
7 End plate
8 Washer
9 Brush holder plate
10 Brush
11 Brush
12 Sealing ring
13 Washer
14 Bolt
15 Nut
16 Spring washer
17 Nut
18 Cable
19 Boot
20 Bolt

**1.4a Exploded view of a typical 2-brush starter motor**

**4** The practical armature has a series of coils which are connected to a multi-segment commutator giving a practically uniform torque over a complete armature rotation (see illustration 1.4a). Armature coils are embedded in slots of the iron frame used to make the iron path for the magnetic flux of the main field.

The commutator is supplied with current by two or four copper/carbon brushes which are small shaped blocks in contact with the commutator bars under light spring pressure. Contact with the brushes is made by a drum or face type commutator (see illustration 1.4b). The face type commutator is not common but may appear in possible future designs.

The armature frame is made up of iron laminations pressed tightly together but insulated one from another, the reason being to prevent the flow of induced eddy currents in the iron, which would cause heating losses.

**5** The magnetic field may be produced by permanent magnets attached to the starter motor frame (stator); this is the PERMANENT MAGNET MOTOR. Alternatively the magnetic field may be obtained by winding field coils round the pole pieces. The field coils are wound in heavy gauge wire and connected in series with the armature; for this reason, this type is called a SERIES MOTOR (see illustration 1.5). The series motor has an ideal characteristic for turning over an engine from standstill. At switch-on, the armature is stationary and has no back emf to limit the current which is, therefore, high. This current flows through the series field winding also and the high magnetic field it produces reacts with the high current in the armature conductors giving maximum torque at standstill. This is just what is required to turn over a cold engine.

**6** Note that a characteristic of the series motor is that it will race up to high speeds on no-load. Do not therefore leave a series motor running light for long or the armature may be damaged due to windings flying out of place due to centrifugal force. A sectioned series motor is shown in illustration 1.6.

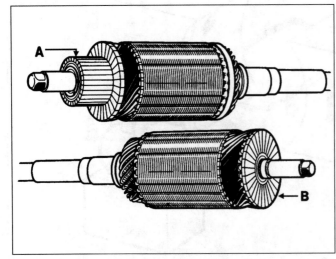

**1.4b Commutator types**

A  Drum commutator     B  Face commutator

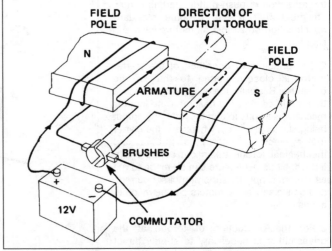

**1.5 Direct current series motor**

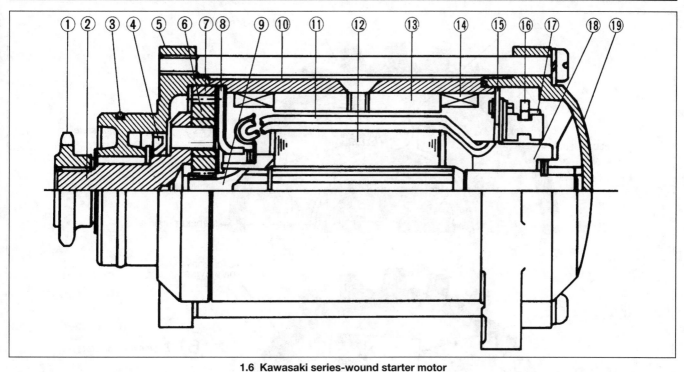

**1.6 Kawasaki series-wound starter motor**

| | | | | | |
|---|---|---|---|---|---|
| 1 | Starter motor sprocket | 8 | End plate | 12 | Armature |
| 2 | Output shaft | 9 | Sun gear | 13 | Field coil |
| 3 | O-ring | 10 | Yoke assembly | 14 | Core |
| 4 | Oil seal | 11 | Armature winding | 15 | Brushplate |
| 5 | End cover | | | 16 | Spring |
| 6 | Planet pinion | | | 17 | Carbon brush |
| 7 | Internal gear | | | 18 | Commutator |
| | | | | 19 | End cover |

## 2  Starter motor – operation

**1** Considerable gearing down is necessary for a starter motor (series type) to turn over a motorcycle engine, a ratio of about 14:1 being average. Reference to illustration 2.1 shows a Honda motor; at the end of the armature, the pinion drives two planet gears which drive an inner gear and the chain sprocket.

**2** When the engine fires it is necessary to disconnect the mechanical drive between the starter motor and crankshaft. In most motorcycles this is by means of a roller-type clutch. Illustration 2.2 shows starter motor clutch operation. The clutch body is driven by the crankshaft. When the starter clutch sprocket rotates in the direction of the arrow (Part A) the roller is in the narrow space between the sprocket hub and the clutch body and so drive is transmitted.

**3** As soon as the engine fires, the clutch body runs faster than the clutch sprocket, so the

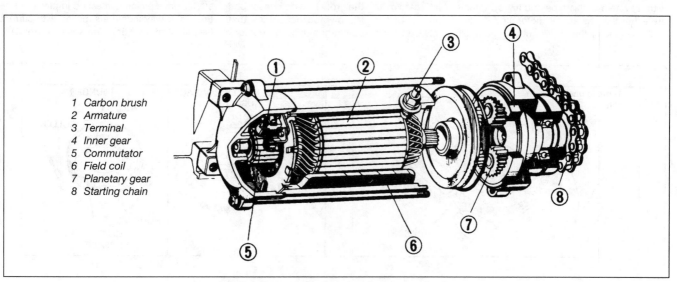

1 Carbon brush
2 Armature
3 Terminal
4 Inner gear
5 Commutator
6 Field coil
7 Planetary gear
8 Starting chain

**2.1  Honda starter motor showing gear reduction**

**15**

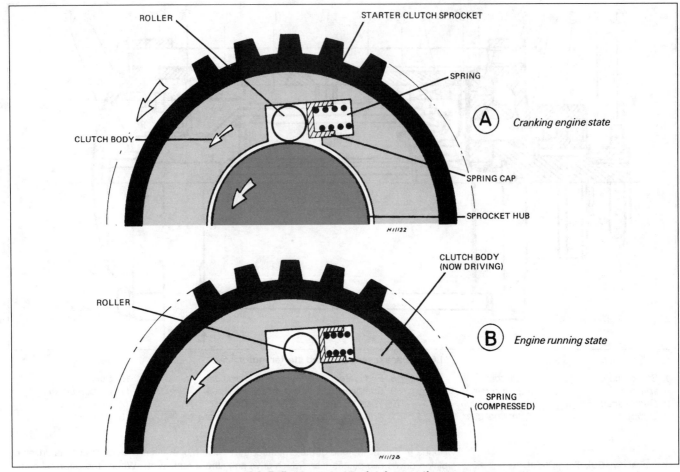

**2.2  Roller-type starter clutch operation**

*A  Cranking engine state        B  Engine running state*

roller drops back against spring pressure to the right (see illustration 2.2, Part B) and drive between starter motor and engine is broken. Clearly wear is bound to take place eventually with a system of this type and the symptoms are either that the starter motor stays locked to the engine or that it will not engage at all.

Another view of a Honda clutch is shown in illustration 2.3.

**4** Sometimes a sprag clutch is used as an alternative to the roller type described above. Sprags are pivoted eccentrics that release transmission in one direction but lock up in the opposite direction (see illustration 2.4).

**5** The pre-engaged starter has been used by BMW and Moto-Guzzi and in this type the starter drive pinion is meshed in place before the motor windings are supplied with current (see illustration 2.5a). The solenoid (relay) is

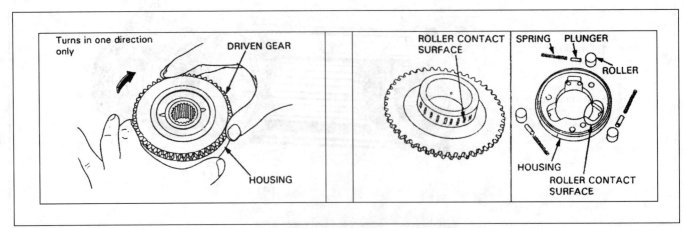

**2.3  Honda roller-type starter clutch assembly**

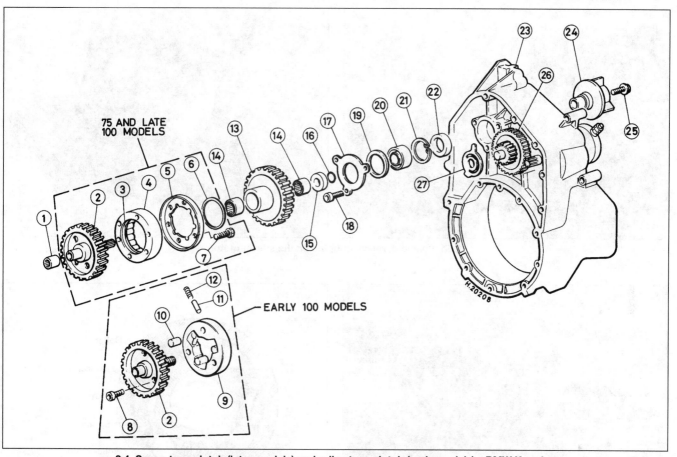

**2.4 Sprag-type clutch (later models) and roller-type clutch (early models) – BMW K-series**

1  Bearing
2  Auxiliary drive shaft
3  Cage
4  Sprag-type starter clutch
5  End cover
6  Conical spring washer
7  Bolts
8  Screws
9  Roller-type starter clutch
10  Rollers
11  Plungers
12  Springs
13  Starter clutch gear pinion
14  Bearing
15  Thrust washer
16  O-ring
17  Retainer plate
18  Allen bolts
19  Conical spring washer
20  Bearing
21  Circlip
22  Oil seal
23  Bellhousing
24  Alternator drive flange
25  Bolt
26  Starter idler shaft
27  Spring (where fitted)

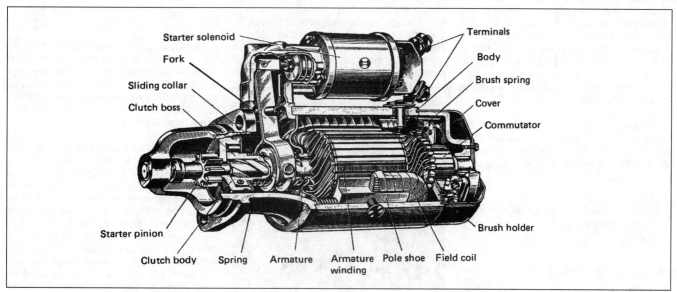

**2.5a Pre-engaged starter motor**

15

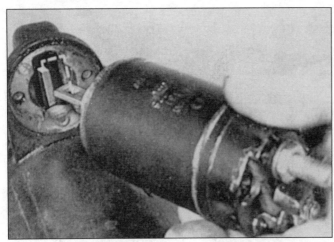

**2.5b Solenoid (relay) mounted on the starter motor**

**2.5c Over-running clutch**

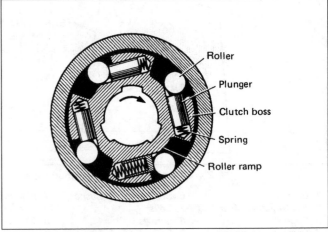

Roller

Plunger

Clutch boss

Spring

Roller ramp

**2.5d Over-running clutch detail**

mounted on top of the starter frame (see illustration 2.5b) and when the starter button is pressed a laminated iron plunger is pulled into the solenoid centre. By a fork arrangement the starter pinion is driven into mesh with the engine flywheel; as the plunger completes its travel it closes a heavy duty switch which connects the motor windings straight to the battery.

For armature protection an over-running clutch is used (see illustrations 2.5c and 2.5d) and this is usually of the roller type, not dissimilar to the type already described.

## 3  Starter motor – brush gear and commutator

### Brushes and springs

**1** Brushes must be of low resistance in order to maximise the current through the motor, so they are made of copper and graphite. Care should be taken to replace brushes with genuine types since they vary according to the type of starter motor, rated output and voltage. When worn down to the limit specified by the manufacturer they must be renewed (see illustration 3.1). Regular

**3.1 Checking brush length**

inspection is advisable since severe damage can be done to a commutator by a worn out brush

**2** Brush springs sometimes are jammed in the holder or faulty with the result that pressure on the brush is insufficient to pass the large operating currents involved; doubts about spring pressure can easily be checked with a spring balance – about 500 gram or 1 lbf is normal (see illustration 3.2).

**3** Starter motors frequently have 4 poles and can have up to 4 brushes, although it is possible to have only 2 brushes which will, in that case, be more heavily loaded. Inspection of the commutator is called for if the motor shows poor performance and bad sparking at the brushes (although most dc motors normally have a small amount of sparking). It may be possible to clean up the commutator with a fine grade of *clean* sandpaper (see illustration 3.3); do not use emery because the hard particles become embedded in the commutator surface.

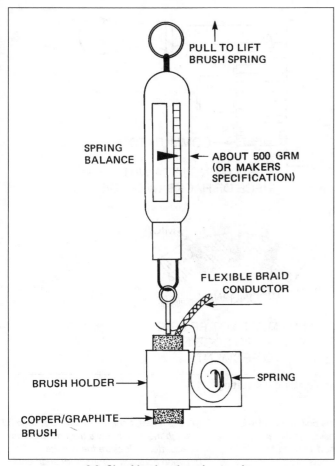

3.2 Checking brush spring tension

3.3 Commutator clean-up using sandpaper strip

3.4 Checking the commutator diameter

After using abrasive paper it is important to clean away the last traces of residue or the brushes will be damaged. Some manufacturers do not approve of any abrasive being used and, in those cases, clean the commutator with methylated spirits (stoddard solvent) and a clean rag. It is worth trying an ink eraser to burnish the segments so as to remove any surface oxide before installing the brushes.

3.5a Undercutting mica insulation

## Commutator

4 Burning or grooving of the commutator calls for skimming true on a lathe, but note that each manufacturer will specify a minimum diameter – if truing up takes the commutator below this limit, the armature must be renewed (see illustration 3.4).

5 Skimming of the commutator will necessitate undercutting of the mica insulation between the commutator bar segments. A thin saw blade is required (see illustration 3.5a), together with patience and great care; after undercutting to about 0.6 mm (0.02 in) take the burr off the commutator segments or the soft brushes will be quickly ruined. Make sure that the undercutting is square as shown in illustration 3.5b and to ease the start, a fine Swiss three-cornered file may be used at the segment edges. The saw used must have very fine teeth.

6 Bad burning at the commutator should be investigated. Using an ohmmeter or multimeter, make the following checks:

(a) Check the resistance between adjacent commutator bars on the R x 1 ohms

**15**

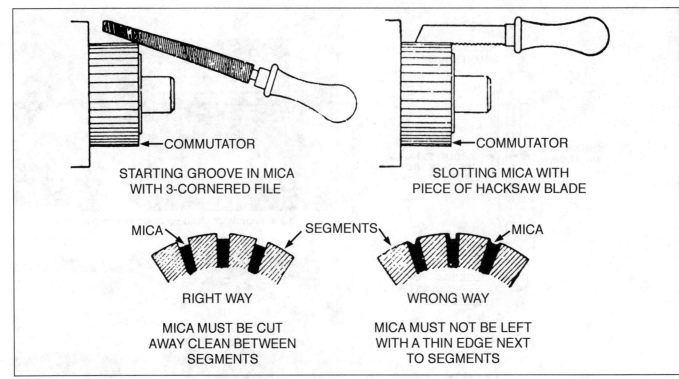

COMMUTATOR

STARTING GROOVE IN MICA
WITH 3-CORNERED FILE

COMMUTATOR

SLOTTING MICA WITH
PIECE OF HACKSAW BLADE

MICA          SEGMENTS          MICA

RIGHT WAY

MICA MUST BE CUT
AWAY CLEAN BETWEEN
SEGMENTS

WRONG WAY

MICA MUST NOT BE LEFT
WITH A THIN EDGE NEXT
TO SEGMENTS

**3.5b  Correct method of commutator undercutting**

range. All should read the same; if one pair gives a very high reading this indicates an open-circuit (see illustration 3.6a).

(b) Check the insulation between any commutator bar and the shaft (see illustration 3.6b). Using the highest ohmmeter range, measure the resistance – any reading below full scale indicates a short circuit or partial short.

(c) To locate a short circuited coil in an armature a growler is used (see illustration 3.6c). This consists of a coil wound on an iron core with a gap in which the starter

armature is placed. The coil of the growler is connected to the mains electrical supply. If there is a short-circuited coil in the starter armature it acts like a short-circuited secondary winding of a transformer and a large current is induced in it. Holding a thin strip of steel or a hacksaw blade over the point of the short-circuit a loud buzzing takes place. However, if a short-circuit is located it normally means a replacement, although for machines long out of production there are specialists who will rewind an armature. An alternative to the growler is

to pass a direct current of say 10 amperes through the armature via the brushes from a car battery. Measure the voltage between adjacent commutator segments using a multimeter with pointed probes. Any variation indicates short circuited coils connected to the two commutator segments.

In all cases it is unlikely that repairs can be effected. Whilst the starter motor is stripped down, it is worth checking with an ohmmeter that the field coils are continuous and that the insulation to the frame is very high.

**3.6a  Check for equal resistance between adjacent commutator segments**

**3.6b  Insulation test between commutator and shaft**

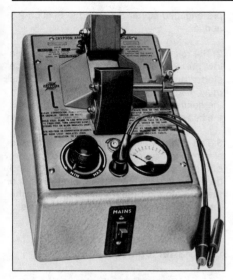

**3.6c The Growler**

*Courtesy FKI Crypton*

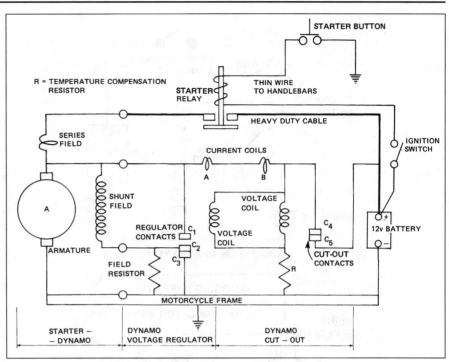

**4.2a Starter-dynamo and associated circuits**

## 4 Starter-dynamo – description

**1** As the name implies, the starter dynamo performs the function of starter motor and dc generator. This combined unit is normally coupled to the crankshaft by direct drive with no gear reduction, and for this reason it is confined to smaller motorcycles up to about 200 cc. It is no longer used in production but enjoyed success on the Yamaha RD200 in the 1970s and 1980s.

**2** The starter-dynamo fitted to the RD200 has a stator, an armature, contact breakers and a centrifugal ignition advance unit. The voltage regulator, cut-out and magnetic switch (ie relay) are mounted elsewhere on the motorcycle frame (see illustrations 4.2a and 4.2b). Note the relatively large diameter of the armature.

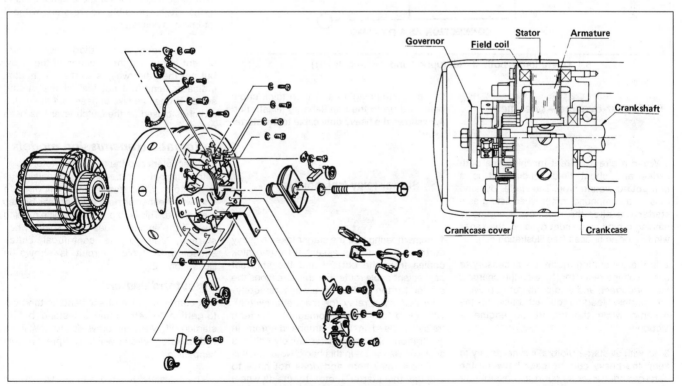

**4.2b Yamaha RD200 starter-dynamo assembly**

**15**

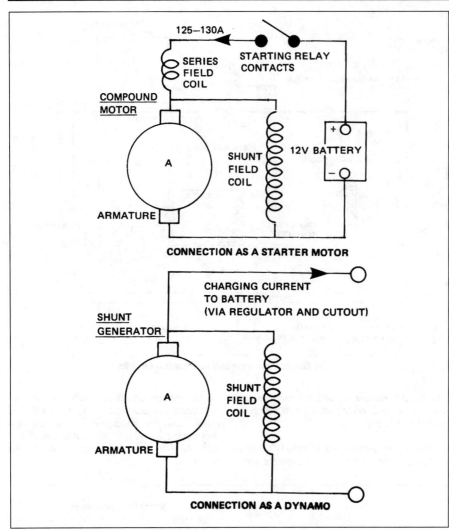

**5.1 Operation as both starter (upper) and dynamo (lower)**

## 5  Starter-dynamo – operation

1  When a direct current machine has both series and shunt field windings it is a **compound**-wound type. The starter-dynamo runs as a compound motor when acting as a starter but after the motorcycle engine is running it runs as a shunt dynamo, the series winding being unused (see illustration 5.1).

2  In the generating mode it is necessary to use a voltage regulator, to keep the charging current correct, and also a cut-out to prevent the battery feeding current back to the dynamo when the motorcycle engine is stopped.

3  As with all starter motors, it is necessary to keep the heavy current leads between the battery and starter as short as possible for minimum volt drop; a starter relay is used for

this purpose (imagine a ¼ inch thick cable being led up to the handlebars!). Illustration 4.2a shows the heavy duty cable to the starter relay.

## 6  Starter relay (solenoid)

1  Remembering that the starter takes a heavy current on load, it is essential to use thick cables from the battery and the shortest convenient cable route. For these reasons the starter button switch is always remotely-operated by a relay (or magnetic switch), which is a form of electromagnet. The term 'relay' is used in the Yamaha diagram in illustration 4.2a and is alternatively called a solenoid elsewhere in this book. Note that it is a simple relay here and does not have to engage the starter motor to the flywheel mechanically as in the case of the

pre-engaged starter described in Section 2.5 above.

2  The relay coil (see illustration 4.2a) takes a low current which is easily handled by the starter button switch on the handlebar. The relay magnetic field pulls the iron plunger to the centre of the coil, and in so doing closes the heavy duty contacts of the starter switch.

3  The starter-dynamo and the associated electromagnetic control unit and now dated, but the idea of a combined starter and generator is useful for small motorcycles and the combination may well reappear in the future with some form of electronic controls.

## 7  Starter lock-out circuits

### *Manual transmission models*

1  Illustration 7.1 shows the arrangement of the clutch, neutral and starter button switches in the starter circuit.

If the starter button switch is pressed, battery current will pass through the starter relay coil and reach earth (ground) if either or both the clutch switch or neutral switch are on (closed). The clutch switch closes when the rider pulls the clutch lever in and the neutral switch closes when the gearbox is in the neutral position. Thus if the engine stalls in traffic, it is possible to re-start without returning to neutral.

The purpose of the diode (which lets current through in the direction of the arrow but not the other way) is so that the neutral indicator lamp will not light if the neutral switch is open (ie bike in gear), but the clutch switch is closed (ie the clutch lever has been pulled).

### *Automatic transmission models*

2  On scooters and the few other motorcycles with automatic transmission, provision is made so that the starter motor will operate only when either or both front or rear brakes are applied. This is to prevent the bike running away if the engine surges up in speed when starting, due to the centrifugal clutch engaging. A typical circuit is shown in illustration 7.2.

### *Sidestand switch*

3  A common cause of accidents is the rider forgetting to retract the sidestand before starting off. Many motorcycles are now fitted with a safety circuit which will prevent this happening.

The sidestand is fitted with a rotary switch or a plunger-operated switch, which, unless

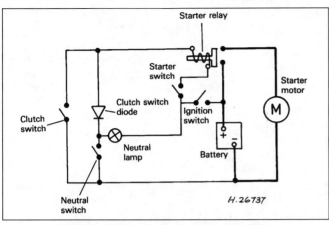

**7.1 Starter lockout circuit – manual gearbox**

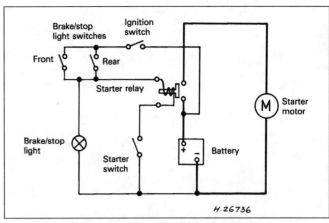

**7.2 Starter lockout circuit – automatic transmission**

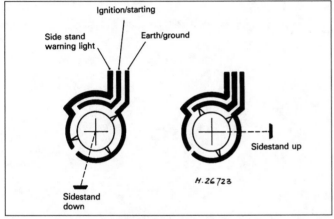

**7.3 Sidestand rotary switch**

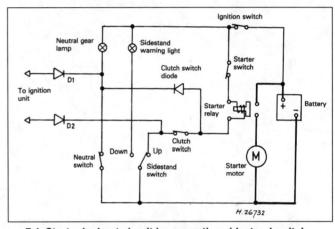

**7.4 Starter lockout circuit incorporating sidestand switch – manual gearbox**

the stand is retracted (up) will prevent the starter motor from operating and/or the ignition from working. Sidestand switches are located at the top of the sidestand.

Illustration 7.3 shows the rotary sidestand switch in the down and up positions. When in the down position, the sidestand warning light will illuminate (if fitted) and the starter/ignition circuit will be broken. In the retracted (up) position, the sidestand warning light will

extinguish and the starter/ignition circuit will be on.

**4** Illustration 7.4 shows a motorcycle starter circuit (with manual transmission) incorporating a sidestand switch. When the ignition switch is ON and the starter button switch is pushed, battery voltage reaches the starter relay coil.

The coil is not connected to earth (ground)

to allow the starter motor to operate unless the neutral switch is ON (transmission actually in neutral), causing the current to flow through the clutch switch diode to earth (ground), or both the clutch switch and sidestand switch are ON (lever pulled in and sidestand retracted).

**5** The ignition circuit may also be inhibited by taking a connection from the neutral switch and from the clutch switch to the ignition unit, where the circuit is disabled without a path to earth (ground) through diodes D1 or D2.

Under these circumstances ignition is not possible if the sidestand is down or the transmission is in gear. Only when the ignition unit has an electrical path to earth (ground) can ignition firing take place.

**6** The table shown in illustration 7.6 is of a typical starter lockout system which applies to many motorcycles.

| Side stand position | | Transmission | Clutch lever | Ignition | Starting |
|---|---|---|---|---|---|
| Lowered | | Neutral | Pulled In | Possible | Possible |
| | | | Released | Possible | Possible |
| | | In Gear | Pulled In | Not Possible | Not Possible |
| | | | Released | Not Possible | Not Possible |
| Retracted | | Neutral | Pulled In | Possible | Possible |
| | | | Released | Possible | Possible |
| | | In Gear | Pulled In | Possible | Possible |
| | | | Released | Possible | Not Possible |

**7.6 Typical starter lockout arrangement**

**15**

**Notes**

# Chapter 16
# Circuits and system components

## Contents

# Part A: Wiring

## 1 Wiring

**1** The supply cable to an electrical component is the *feed wire* and the *return wire* conveys the current back to complete the circuit. Most often the return is the motorcycle frame. Wires and cables are usually made of copper because of the property of low resistance and, to make the cable sufficiently flexible, strands of bare copper wire are twisted in a slow spiral rather than using one thick wire of copper. Wire strands are often tinned and this assists in making soldered connections if necessary. However the tinning process was also necessary in the days of rubber insulation to avoid chemical reaction but now that PVC cable covering has superseded rubber the need has gone in this respect.

Cables are covered with insulation which is generally PVC plastic and, in the USA, polythene is also used. For higher temperatures PVC polymers have been introduced which will withstand temperatures up to 100°C approximately, some 30° higher than the maximum working temperature of ordinary PVC.

**2** Cables are bound together in a loom (or harness) to give protection and the loom is clipped to the frame at certain points so that there are no sharp bends or interference with other moving parts of the bike such as handlebars. The individual cable only emerges from the loom near the point of connection in order to give maximum protection. If rewiring is carried out be sure to mount the cable loom correctly (see illustration 1.2a) and keep the loom or cable away from hot areas such as the exhaust. If wires or harnesses must come into contact with a sharp edge or corner then cover them with at least two extra layers of tape (see illustration 1.2b).

**1.2a  Correct cable loom support is important**

*Secure wires and harnesses to the frame with wire bands at the designated locations. Install the bands so that only the insulated surfaces contact the wires or wire harnesses*

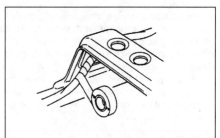

**1.2b  Give extra protection to the loom at sharp edges**

*Protect wires and harnesses with at least two layers of electrical tape, or with electrical harness tubes, if they contact a sharp edge of corner*

**16**

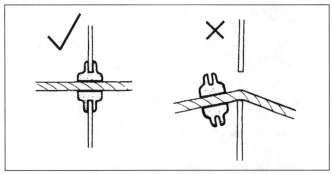

**1.3a  Seat grommets in their holes properly**

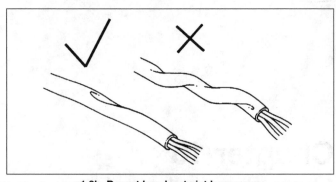

**1.3b  Do not bend or twist harnesses**

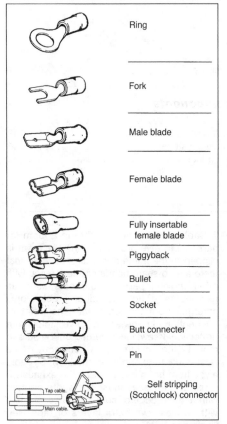

Ring

Fork

Male blade

Female blade

Fully insertable
female blade

Piggyback

Bullet

Socket

Butt connecter

Pin

Self stripping
(Scotchlock) connector

Tap cable.

Main cable.

**1.4  Commonly used pre-insulated
connectors**

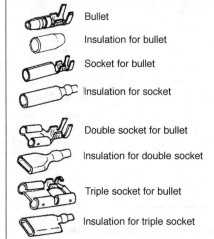

Bullet

Insulation for bullet

Socket for bullet

Insulation for socket

Double socket for bullet

Insulation for double socket

Triple socket for bullet

Insulation for triple socket

**1.5a  Japanese 3.9 mm connectors for
cables up to 2 mm²**

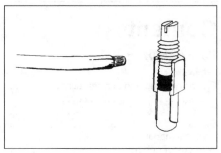

**1.5b  Post connector**

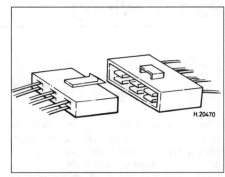

H.20470

**1.6  Multi-pin connector with
security latch**

**3** Cables and wires are often taken through a hole in the component or the frame. It is essential that the correct grommet is used which is the right size for the job and that it is mounted properly (see illustration 1.3a). Avoid twisting or distorting a refitted loom as mechanical stress can give rise to future fracturing of one or more wires in the loom (see illustration 1.3b).

**4** Wires emerging from the loom will be cut to the required lengths to reach the component for which current is to be provided. The wires will be terminated or joined with some form of connector – a blade or blade socket, eyelet, bullet connector or self-stripping (Scotchlok)

type connector being common (see illustration 1.4). Connectors may come as pre-insulated or non-insulated. For the non-insulated types there are blade insulation sleeves which slip over the blade male or female connector.

The pre-insulated types are less trouble but where extra insulation against the weather is needed then the 'Heatseal' pre- insulated terminals are effective. After crimping the wire to the connector heat is applied to the shrinkable polyamide sleeve and the hot melt adhesive round the crimp metal barrel.

**5** Japanese 3.9 mm connectors (see illustration 1.5a) are used extensively and will not match the older British 4.7 mm type. The Lucar type blades are now rare except for some add-on applications and more advanced connector methods are in use. Now because electronic equipment is so common on motorcycles some circuits may work at only a few milliamperes and leakage currents cannot be tolerated. This requires connectors to electronic components to have the highest quality often with gold-plated pins. Bare wires are occasionally terminated by a post connector which may be a moulded-in part of an item of equipment (see illustration 1.5b).

**6** Multi-pin connectors are used at a major junction of several wires and are moulded in two parts designed to fit one way only (see illustration 1.6). A locking latch is usually provided. To prevent corrosion the pins of a multiconnector could be lightly smeared with silicone grease specially made for electrical work but *note that ordinary grease must not be used*. Particular care must be taken with connectors that go to an ECU or other electronic component and the instructions of the manufacturer must be followed with regard to maintenance.

**7** The importance of good clean electrical connections on a motorcycle cannot be overstressed due to their exposure to the weather. It is true to say that most electrical problems turn out to be trouble with contacts and electrical connections.

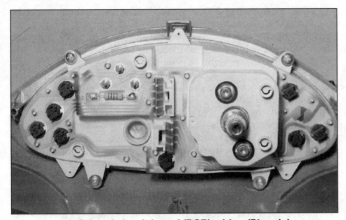

1.8 Printed circuit board (PCB) wiring (Piaggio)

1.9 CBR900RRW Fireblade instrument panel (22 mm thick!)

Things to look for are corroded battery terminals, poor earth (ground) connections to the frame and wire insulation that chafes due to the motion of the machine; it is always good practice to clip wiring in place and make use of the cable ties and clamps provided by the manufacturer. Remember that the object of the cable is to convey current to the point where it will be used with minimum voltage drop.

For example, a poor connection between a battery terminal and its cable attachment can result in a loss of voltage, and when a large current is required, such as when the starter button is pressed, the connection may go temporarily open-circuit – every technician seems to meet this phenomenon at some time!

**8** Instrument panel wiring is now frequently in the form of a printed circuit board (PCB). The PCB is a sheet of insulating board (usually glass fibre) which has a thin copper foil sheet bonded to both sides. The 'wire routes' are drawn out by photographic means and the unwanted copper stripped away by etching or other means, leaving only the required conducting paths. It is possible to join points on the back and front of the board by through-pins, which are then soldered. Connectors specially designed to grip and make contact on the board result in a much cheaper method of making the instrument panel connections. Care must be taken to ensure that no current overload occurs on a PCB, because the copper foil quickly blows, like a fuse (see illustration 1.8).

**9** Connections can be troublesome, and it is worth checking the PCB plug and socket if intermittent faults occur. Sometimes capless bulbs are used in the board as indicator lamps, and special attention should be given to ensuring good connections.

Should a copper foil strip be damaged and broken, it is possible to bridge a gap with thin tinned fuse wire using the minimum amount of soldering iron heat. The result of using a thin flat PCB for all the wiring results in a very compact unit and the instrument panel of the Honda CBR900RRW Fireblade shown in illustration 1.9 is a good example. This panel houses all the indicator lamps, speedometer and rev-counter and yet is only 22 mm thick!

## 2 Cable sizes

**1** It is important that the cross-sectional area of the copper wire is large enough to carry the current without overheating. Additionally, the volt-drop in the wire must be low enough to ensure correct operation of the equipment to which it is connected. For all this, on the grounds of cost, the manufacturer will use the minimum size of cable which is consistent with the above requirements.

**2** Both metric and inch measurements are in use, depending upon the country of origin, but the principles of choosing the correct size are the same. As said above, the manufacturer will use a cable which is the minimum size to do the job (a thought to bear in mind when adding accessories), the criteria being as follows:

(a) The volt-drop on full-load must not be too great (especially in the headlight circuit).
(b) The cable heating must be within specified limits.

**3** In order to carry current to meet condition (a) the copper cross-sectional area must be sufficient; cable heating (b) will also depend on the cross-sectional area, but additionally, the factor of the cable's ability to get rid of the heat is important. A single cable exposed to air can be used to carry a much higher current than if it were bunched up with other cables as a part of a loom. Cables that carry current for only a short time (eg the starter motor) can be worked at a higher current density, but

here the permitted volt-drop is the important consideration.

**4** Wires are graded by denoting the number of strands and the diameter of a single strand; for example, 14/0.01 (inch) has 14 strands, each of which has a diameter of 0.01 inch. In the case of metric cables the same idea is used so 14/0.3 (metric) indicates 14 strands, each of diameter 0.3 mm. Metric dimensions are now in widespread use and will be referred to in the following Sections.

Wires are graded differently in the US, see Section 3.

## 3 Cable volt-drop and current ratings

**1** The list of popular size cables given below will meet the needs of most motorcycle applications. They have been worked out on the basis of amperes of current per unit area of wire cross-section. What that figure is has been found by experiment to give a reasonable volt drop and heat dissipation.

In the accompanying table, it is assumed that the current density is 8.525 amperes per square millimetre (A/mm$^2$) of copper for cables up to 44/0.3 metric and 6.975 A/mm$^2$ for larger sizes.

| Metric cable size (mm) | Current rating (amperes) | Volt-drop (volts per metre per ampere) |
| --- | --- | --- |
| 9/0.3 | 5.5 | 0.0271 |
| 14/0.3 | 8.75 | 0.01742 |
| 28/0.3 | 17.5 | 0.00871 |
| 44/0.3 | 25.5 | 0.00554 |
| 65/0.3 | 35.0 | 0.00375 |
| 84/0.3 | 42.0 | 0.00290 |
| 97/0.3 | 50.0 | 0.00251 |
| 120/0.3 | 60.0 | 0.00203 |

*The current ratings shown may be reduced to 60% for cables run in the interior of a loom.*

**16**

**2 Applications:** For any item of equipment with low current loading use 9/0.3 size cable. Size 14/0.3 cable would be satisfactory for general applications on the motorcycle such as parking and tail lamps, turn signals, etc, and 28/0.3 size for headlights, horns and any other added high current loads. For large alternators a heavy cable will be required and it is best to work out the size as follows.

**3** For example, a 180 watt alternator on full-load will give 180/12 amperes approximately – that is 15 amperes (remember volts x amperes = watts). For this loading, a 28/0.3 cable would *just* do, but choosing a larger size would be better, say 44/0.3 or 65/0.3, to keep the volt-drop from the alternator to battery to a minimum.

**4** In the United States, cables are rated according to the number of circular mils of cross-section in the cable wire. A mil is 0.001 inch and a circular mil is the square of the mil figure. For example, an 18 AWG wire that has a diameter of 0.0403 inch has a circular mil area of:

Area of cross-section = 40.3 x 40.3 = 1624 circular mils

A rule for equipment design might be to choose a current density of 230 circular mils per ampere according to how the wire is used. From this the 18 AWG wire could run at 7 amperes. In a wiring loom this would be just adequate but it is always better to use a thicker wire if possible, particularly in a 6 volt system where a cable volt drop is more significant than in a 12 volt system. In practice, tables are used to select a wire for a particular current load like the one shown above.

**5** The American Wire Gage (AWG) and the British Standard Wire Gauge (SWG) have a near equivalence as shown in the table below:

| Metric size (sq mm) | AWG | SWG (nearest) | Amperes* |
|---|---|---|---|
| 0.205 | 24 | 25 | 1.76 |
| 0.326 | 22 | 23 | 2.79 |
| 0.518 | 20 | 21 | 4.4 |
| 0.823 | 18 | 19 | 7.0 |
| 1.310 | 16 | 18 | 11.2 |
| 2.080 | 14 | 16 | 17.9 |
| 3.310 | 12 | 14 | 28.4 |
| 5.260 | 10 | 12 | 45.2 |

* Based on current density of 230 circular mils per ampere.

## 4 Fuses

**1** Many electrical circuits have protective devices so that in the event of a short-circuit, the battery is isolated. The battery is capable of driving a high current into an accidental short-circuit and this may be sufficient to burn the insulation off cables, damage sensitive electronic components, possibly buckle the battery plates, or cause a fire – **a fuse is used for such protection**.

**2** A fuse consists of a cartridge with contacts on each end and a strip of soft metal or length of tinned wire connected between them. When an overload occurs the fuse wire or strip will melt, breaking the circuit. The fuse must be renewed but it is first necessary to trace and rectify the fault otherwise the new fuse will also melt.

On small motorcycles and mopeds a single fuse is fitted, often of the 'in-line' type and located near the battery. On larger motorcycles fuses are used for the separate circuits; these may be located in a fusebox either behind a sidepanel, on the steering head or under the seat, or may be part of a central junction box shared by relays.

**3** Four types of fuse are presently in use on motorcycles (see illustration 4.3a).

(a) Flat-bladed fuses.
(b) Glass tubular fuses.
(c) Ceramic fuses.
(d) Fusible links or ribbon fuses.

Note that glass fuses are normally rated at the fusing value, but ceramic fuses are rated at the maximum continuous current that they can carry, being half of the fusing value.

**Flat-bladed fuses** are now common on motorcycles and consist of a coloured plastic holder with two flat projecting blades which plug into a fuse socket (see illustration 4.3b). The fuse wire spans the two blades internally (see illustration 4.3c). These fuses are fast acting and are consistent in the fusing current (to 'blow' them) so may be sized more accurately to the circuit being protected.

## FUSES (Flat Bladed)

| Identification | Rating |
|---|---|
| Purple | 3 |
| Pink | 4 |
| Orange | 5 |
| Brown | 7.5 |
| Red | 10 |
| Blue | 15 |
| Yellow | 20 |
| White | 25 |
| Green | 30 |

## FUSES (glass cartridge)

cone end        flat end

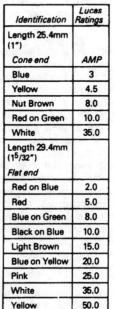

| Identification | Lucas Ratings |
|---|---|
| Length 25.4mm (1") | |
| Cone end | AMP |
| Blue | 3 |
| Yellow | 4.5 |
| Nut Brown | 8.0 |
| Red on Green | 10.0 |
| White | 35.0 |
| Length 29.4mm (1⁵/₃₂") | |
| Flat end | |
| Red on Blue | 2.0 |
| Red | 5.0 |
| Blue on Green | 8.0 |
| Black on Blue | 10.0 |
| Light Brown | 15.0 |
| Blue on Yellow | 20.0 |
| Pink | 25.0 |
| White | 35.0 |
| Yellow | 50.0 |

## FUSES (ceramic type)

| Identification | BSS Ratings |
|---|---|
| Length 25mm | AMP |
| Yellow | 5 |
| White | 8 |
| Red | 16 |
| Blue | 25 |

## FUSIBLE LINK (ribbon fuse)

4.3a  Fuse types and ratings

**4.3b Flat-blade fuses are a plug-in fitting**

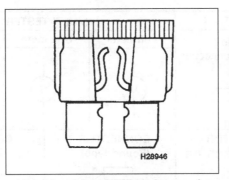

**4.3c A break in a flat-blade fuse can be easily detected**

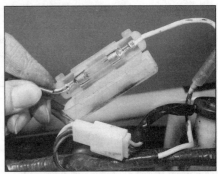

**4.3d A glass tubular fuse in an in-line holder**

**Glass tubular fuses** come in two types, the flat end and the cone end (note that they have different lengths as shown in illustration 4.3a). Glass tubular fuses are often used as the main fuse on small capacity motorcycles (see illustration 4.3d).

**Ceramic fuses** have a coloured ceramic body with a one-piece fuse strip and end caps (see illustration 4.3e). They do not have a glass shield and are open to the air. This type of fuse appears on motorcycles of European manufacture, although has now been superseded by the flat-blade fuse type. The whole fuse is clipped between spring terminals.

**Fusible links (or ribbon fuses)** are not common but may be found on a few models. The soft fuse element is held at each end by a screw and is designed to protect main circuits.

**4** Following automobile practice, the thermal **circuit breaker** may be met on the motorcycle. The advantage is that a circuit breaker may be reset after a fault has been cleared (see illustration 4.3f).

Breakers are of the bi-metal strip type in which the heat generated in the strip by the short-circuit current causes it to bend. This opens a pair of contacts which may be closed by push button after the unit has cooled down. A circuit fault must, of course, be found and corrected before re-setting the breaker.

## 5 Relays

**1** The idea of the relay is to save running heavy gauge cables round the motorcycle. Instead, the heavy cable follows the shortest route from the battery supply to the load, typically a starter motor. The starter is switched on by the heavy contacts in the relay and these are pulled in by a coil which takes a low current only. By

**4.3e Ceramic type fuses**

connecting the coil to the starter button the rider can switch in the starter current using only light gauge cables to the relay coil. For more details on relay operation see Chapter 2.

**2** In modern motorcycles the use of the relay is extensive and goes beyond just switching the starter motor. For example in the BMW R850 and 1100 Twins the bank of relays located under the rider's seat control the following:

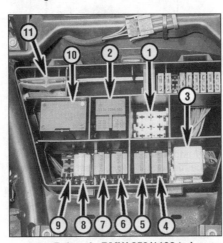

**5.2a Relays in BMW 850/1100 twins**
*See text for relay identification*

**4.3f Circuit breaker with reset button (arrowed)**

1 Encoding plug for Motronic and catalytic converter
2 Fuel level damping unit
3 Starter motor relay
4 Load relief relay
5 Horn relay
6 Fuel pump relay
7 Motronic relay
8 ABS warning relay
9 Blank
10 Turn signal relay
11 Relay removal tool

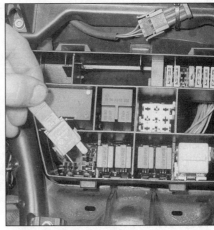

**5.2b Use the tool provided or needle nose pliers to remove plug-in relays**

**16**

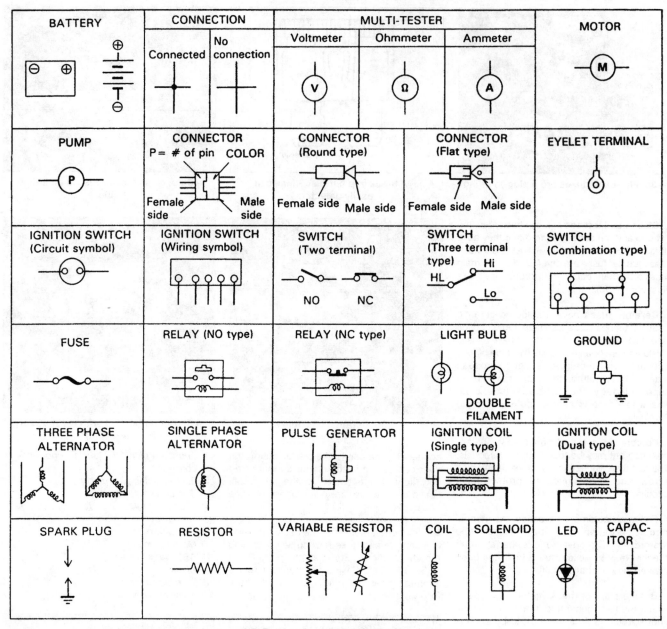

**6.2 Range of symbols used by Honda**

## 6  Wiring diagrams and symbols

1 An understanding of circuit diagrams is important for fault finding in a motorcycle electrical system. In order to follow manufacturers' wiring diagrams it is necessary to know most of the symbols used to indicate components, but these unfortunately have not been standardised throughout the world.

2 Japanese wiring diagrams use symbols which are sometimes pictorial in that they sometimes look like what they represent (see illustration 6.2). In addition, the component name is sometimes printed alongside.

3 On Continental European motorcycles (eg BMW and MuZ) the German DIN standards will be met and in these cases the diagrams are not so clear, being less pictorial, but have the advantage that manufacturers stick closely to DIN without introducing many variations of their own (see illustration 6.3). Circuits can be followed more easily in the DIN system because code numbers are used (see para 4 below).

Only some of the more common symbols in use on motorcycles are given and it will be seen that, in general, where coils are drawn to look like coils in Japanese diagrams, the DIN standard may use an alternative in the form of a black solid bar.

For a full treatment of DIN symbols see the Bosch booklet *Graphical Symbols and Circuit Diagrams for Automotive Electrics* (Available in the UK from Delta Press Ltd. 01442 877794).

4 Circuits bear numbers in the DIN system and these can be useful in cable route tracing.

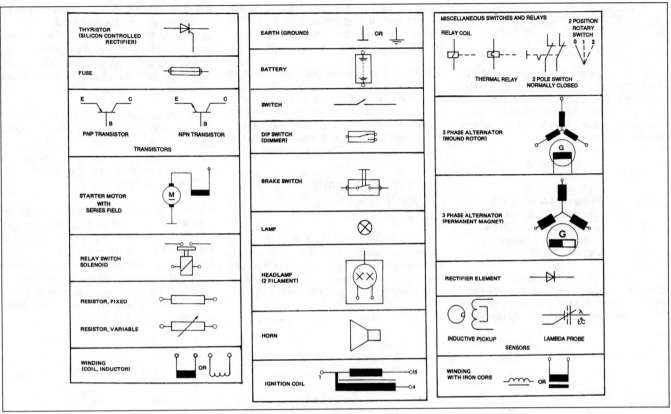

**6.3 DIN circuit symbols**

## DIN component and terminal key

| Terminal number | Wire leading from | To |
|---|---|---|
| 1 | Ignition coil | Contact breaker or ignition control unit |
| 2 | Magneto | Ignition switch (shorting switch) |
| 4 | Ignition coil | HT Spark plug |
| 15 | Ignition switch | Ignition coil |
| 15a | CDI pulse coil | CDI trigger terminal |
| 15/54 | Main switch or ignition switch | Coil, warning light, fuse for daylight current consumers (brake lights, horn, turn signals, etc) |
| 30 | Battery + | Starter, ignition switch |
| 31 | Battery – | Earth (ground) |
| 31b | Switch | Earth (ground) |
| 49 | Ignition switch | Flasher unit |
| 49a | Flasher unit | Turn signal switch |
| 50 | Starter button switch | Starter relay (solenoid) |
| 51 | Alternator or generator regulator | Battery, starter button or main switch |
| 54 | See 15/54 | - |
| L54 | Turn signal switch | Left turn signal light |
| R54 | Turn signal switch | Right turn signal light |
| 56 | Lighting switch | Dip (dimmer) switch |
| 56a | Dip (dimmer) switch | Headlight main beam and warning light |
| 56b | Dip (dimmer) switch | Headlight dipped beam |
| 57 | Lighting switch | Parking light |
| 58 | Lighting switch | Tail light, licence plate light, side light (side car) |
| 59 | Charging coil of flywheel magneto | Rectifier |
| 61 | Alternator or generator regulator | Charge warning light |
| B+ | Battery positive | - |
| B- | Battery negative | - |
| D+ | Generator + | Regulator |
| DF | Generator exciter winding | Regulator |
| L | Turn signal switch | Left turn signal light |
| R | Turn signal switch | Right turn signal light |
| UVW | Individual phase terminals | 3-phase rectifier pack |

**16**

## 7 Terminal markings

1 When confronted with a component such as a voltage regulator which may have several screw or brass tag terminals, it is helpful if they are marked for identification. Some manufacturers use letters for coding, such as the following:

| D | Dynamo armature |
| F (or DF) | Dynamo field |
| E | Earth (or ground) |
| CB | Ignition coil terminal to be connected to contact breaker |
| SW | Ignition coil terminal to be connected to ignition switch, etc |

2 An advantage of this system is that the letters usually give an indication of what they are intended for, but this cannot be said of the DIN system, which mostly uses numbers. For those working on European motorcycles it pays to learn at least the most common code numbers; it should be noted that there are a few exceptions where letters are used.

3 Certain code numbers are most important for it is seen that any terminal marked 30 is always live without a switch being operated (an accessory could be connected here): 31 represents an earth (ground) terminal and 31b is used when an electrical load is operated by a switch in the return circuit to earth (ground).

## 8 Wire colour coding

1 Colour coding of cables is most helpful in identifying leads on the motorcycle. Unfortunately, standardisation has not fully taken place and reference must be made to the colour key provided by the manufacturer.

2 Older British bikes used the Lucas coding and their diagrams (see illustration 8.2) show the colours with a letter code; the majority of cables are two colour – the main colour shown by a letter followed by another letter for the trace (ie a spiral of colour superimposed). Thus BW indicates a black cable with a white trace.

3 The DIN standard lays down rules for cable colours, and circuit diagrams show the code which not only gives colour, but the cross-sectional area of the cable. Illustration 8.3 shows a wiring diagram of the 8-valve BMW K100 models to illustrate this.

4 British Standard AU7a Colour Code for Vehicle Wiring should be consulted for those wishing to use UK wiring colours. A suitable extract is to be found in the Lucas booklet *Cable and Cable Products*. For comparison of styles, the reader should consult wiring diagrams issued by various manufacturers from which it may be seen that wide differences in practice occur.

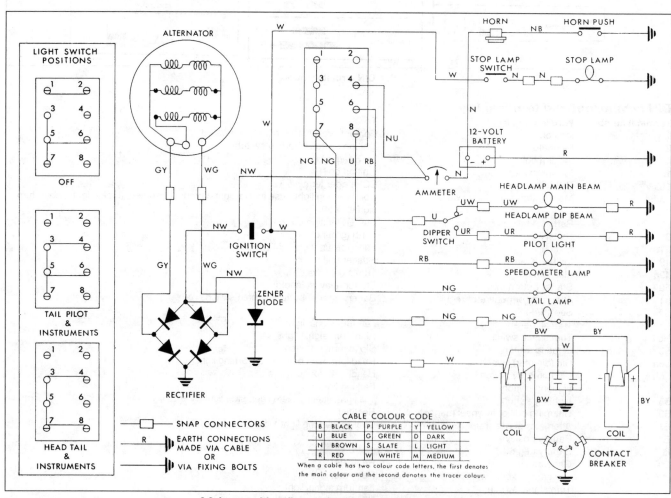

**8.2 Lucas wiring diagram layout showing colour coding**

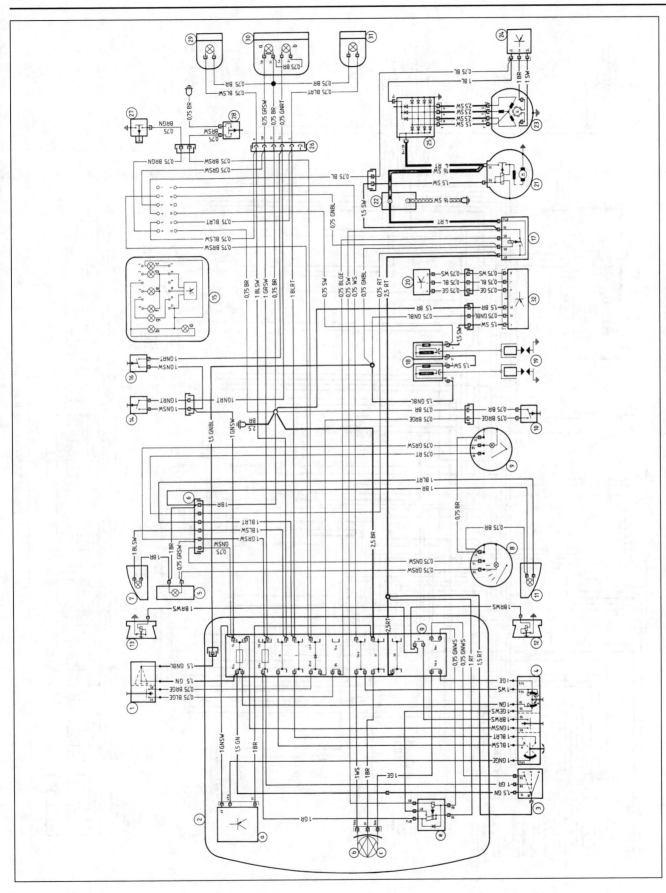

8.3 BMW R100RS/RT colour codes, DIN symbols and cable sizes

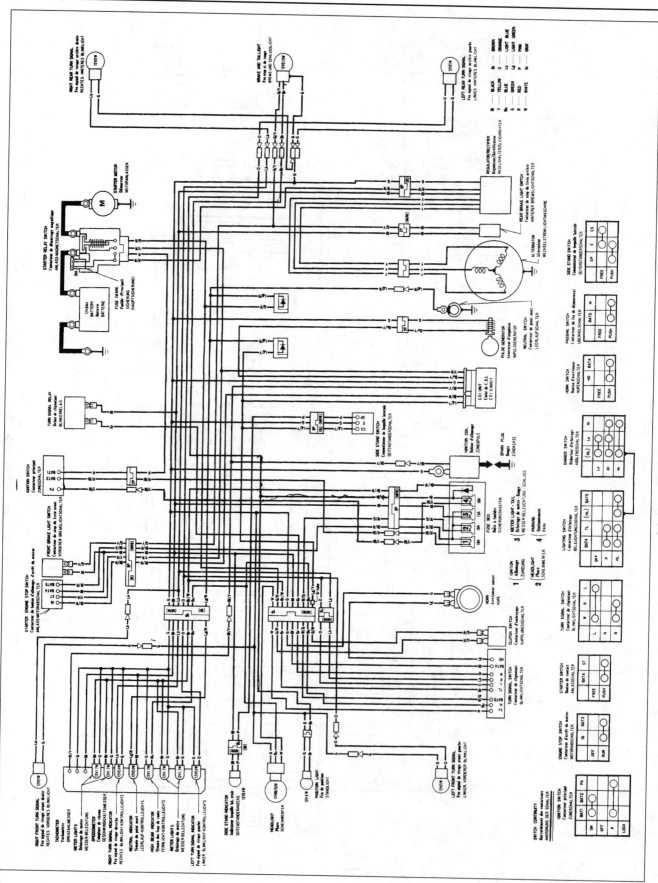

9.2 Honda NX500 wiring diagram

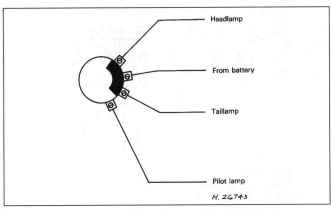

**10.3 Wiping contact rotary switch**

*The central rotor is a three position distributor which links up to three terminals. In the position shown, the head and tail lights are on. Further rotation clockwise gives tail and pilot lights on, then all off.*

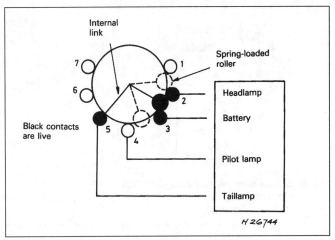

**10.4 Seven-contact Lucas switch used on many post-war British motorcycles**

## 9 Wiring diagram layout

**1** As the complexity of electrical equipment has increased so has that of the corresponding circuit diagram. The simplicity of the early Lucas diagrams (see illustration 8.2) was good but could not remain so with the motorcycles of today.

Automobile wiring diagrams are split into separate circuits and it is probable that this idea will spread to motorcycle diagrams. For example BMW now illustrate their motorcycle wiring as separate circuits for ignition/charging/starting, lighting/signalling and ABS.

**2** As an illustration of complete wiring diagrams, illustration 8.3 shows the wiring of the BMW R100RS/RT. Note the use of DIN symbols.

The Honda NX500 wiring diagram (see illustration 9.2) shows a contrasting style. What it comes down to is that wiring diagrams are unfortunately not standardised and each manufacturer has a different way of drawing.

**3** Although diagrams may look complicated when shown in entirety, do not be daunted by them. Each individual item breaks down to a supply wire coming from, or to, the battery, then to the load item concerned. The motorcycle frame forms the return 'wire' in many cases and it is important that good earth (ground) connections are made to the frame. All the separate circuits are in parallel and the currents taken by them add up to the total load current. This should not exceed the wattage rating of the alternator (or dynamo) – the starter motor current is not included because it is a short term load.

## 10 Switches

**1** The term 'switch' covers everything from a simple horn button up to complex multi-switches, and could even include the heavy current starter relay which is really an electrically-operated switch.

**2** Contact resistance within a switch is very low when it is in good condition, but after long use corrosion or wear may occur. Then trouble can show up as an intermittent contact or a total break. Another effect is loss of voltage across the switch due to high resistance between the switch contacts.

**3** Older British motorcycles used Miller, Wipac and Lucas switches and some could be dismantled, but with risk of flying apart in the process. Spring-loaded roller

**10.6a Handlebar switches are usually clamped around the handlebars**

switches bridged two connector terminals per roller, while others used wiping contacts. A wiping-contact Miller switch is shown in illustration 10.3. The brass strip rotor is turned by the switch knob and connects in head and tail lights, pilot and tail, or switches all off.

**4** The seven terminal Lucas switch (see illustration 10.4) distributes current by a moving spring-loaded rotor contact which presses onto the terminals. In this example, the rotor is permanently connected by a brass strip to No. 5 terminal which supplies tail lights and any other auxiliaries required. The rotor contact is shown bridging the headlight and battery terminals. Turning another clickstop clockwise would turn off the headlight and connect the pilot light.

**5** Maintenance is confined to keeping switches clean and making sure that no strands of connecting wire stick out of one terminal and accidentally touch another. If the switch can be taken apart the contacts may be cleaned and treated with an aerosol electrical contact cleaner.

**6** Modern machines (with the regrettable exception of some Italian types) have excellent switches which have a long trouble-free life. It is not always easy or possible to take them apart and replacement is usually essential, but it is worth trying to revive a switch with a spray of contact cleaner or water dispersant fluid.

Handlebar switches are usually in two halves clamped around the handlebar (see illustration 10.6a). Before stripping down to investigate a suspected fault, carry out a continuity check with an ohmmeter or multimeter to confirm this. By disconnecting the wire connectors from the switch, a

**16**

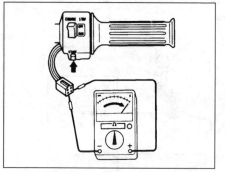

10.6b Simple continuity checks can often save unnecessary dismantling of the switch

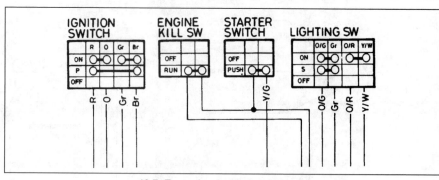

10.7 Example of switch grid layout

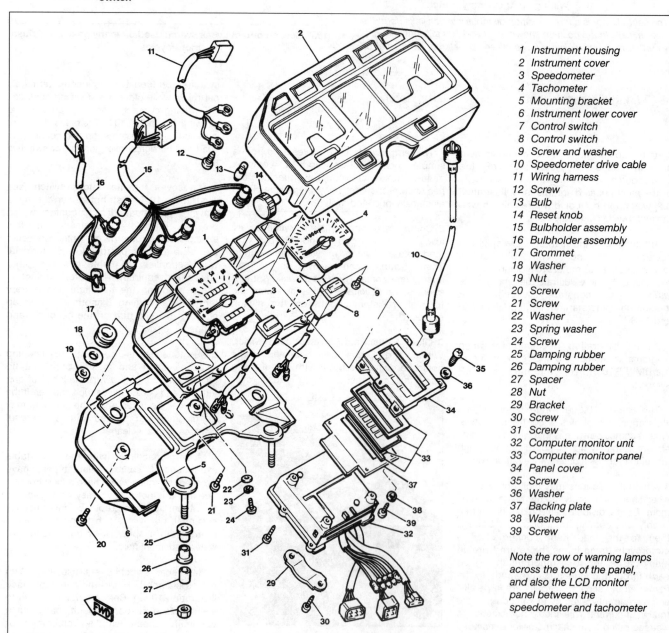

1 Instrument housing
2 Instrument cover
3 Speedometer
4 Tachometer
5 Mounting bracket
6 Instrument lower cover
7 Control switch
8 Control switch
9 Screw and washer
10 Speedometer drive cable
11 Wiring harness
12 Screw
13 Bulb
14 Reset knob
15 Bulbholder assembly
16 Bulbholder assembly
17 Grommet
18 Washer
19 Nut
20 Screw
21 Screw
22 Washer
23 Spring washer
24 Screw
25 Damping rubber
26 Damping rubber
27 Spacer
28 Nut
29 Bracket
30 Screw
31 Screw
32 Computer monitor unit
33 Computer monitor panel
34 Panel cover
35 Screw
36 Washer
37 Backing plate
38 Washer
39 Screw

Note the row of warning lamps across the top of the panel, and also the LCD monitor panel between the speedometer and tachometer

10.9 Instrument console fitted to the Yamaha XJ750

continuity check can be made in accordance with the switch connections shown on the machine's wiring diagram (see illustration 10.6b).

**7** Representation of switch connections on circuit diagrams was most frustrating on early Lucas diagrams, since wires were shown connected to numbered terminals, but with no indication on how they were connected together inside the switch. Later diagrams (see illustration 8.2) corrected this by showing connections in side panels.

Switch connection diagrams on today's machines are usually illustrated on a grid diagram (see illustration 10.7). Owners of early motorcycles would be well advised to check their main switches with a multimeter and draw up for themselves a grid diagram.

**8** When switching the main-to-dip beam of a direct lighting system, care has to be taken not to break the main contact before connection is made to the dip beam contact. A momentary cutting off of the load could

send the generated voltage up so high that the tail light would probably blow. Switches of this type are called make-before-break switches. It is important not to substitute an ordinary switch because this will lead to blowing of bulbs when switching over.

**9** Switches are often the heart of warning lamp circuits, and appear also on an instrumentation panel in the nacelle (see illustration 10.9). This XJ750 exploded diagram shows many switches and connectors discussed here.

# Part B: System components

## 11 Instrumentation and warning systems

**1** Like almost every aspect of motorcycle design, instruments have become increasingly sophisticated in recent years. The basic mechanical speedometer has been supplemented by a variety of extra instruments, usually electronically-operated. These include tachometers, coolant gauges, gear position indicators, clocks and fuel gauges. The array of warning lamps has also grown over the years and most current models are fitted with a comprehensive display indicating the status and general condition of the machine.

**2** The level of sophistication is, naturally enough, dependent on the type of machine. At one extreme there are simple mopeds with only a speedometer and one or two warning lamps, whilst some of the larger capacity

machines are equipped with complicated microprocessor-based instrument systems.

**3** In some of the latter arrangements, the instruments are interconnected via a central 'black box' which monitors all aspects of the engine and electrical functions while the machine is being ridden, and carries out a comprehensive self-checking sequence each time the engine is started. Information is gathered from a variety of switches and sensors and any fault is displayed by warning lamps or, in some cases, on a Liquid Crystal Display (LCD) panel and/or a meter built into the instrument console.

**4** As might be expected, the more complex systems use a number of sealed units, which are difficult to deal with in the event of a fault. The usual approach in these cases is to substitute new components for those that are suspect until the fault is isolated, though the construction of the control circuits is invariably such that repair is impracticable. The Fireblade panel shown in illustration 1.9 is an example of

a first class engineering design but the chance of carrying out repairs on it is virtually nil.

More typical, but still an engineering masterpiece, is the instrument panel of the Honda ST1100 shown in illustration 11.4.

**5** Another problem that besets the professional and home mechanic alike is the wide variation in monitoring systems, even between similar models from one manufacturer. As an example, the Yamaha XJ650 and 750 range featured a wide variety of instruments and warning systems on the various models; illustration 10.9 shows one of the more complex assemblies and it shows many of the switches, plugs and sockets that have been described in this Chapter.

## 12 Switches, sensors and sundries

**1** A wide variety of switches and sensors are employed to check the status or condition of the various parts of the engine and electrical system, and also to control safety features like starter lockout circuits. The type of sensor varies according to its function, but most are little more than switches. We have come across various ignition timing sensors in earlier Chapters but here are some of the other types which go to make up the modern motorcycle.

***Starter lockout switches (neutral, clutch and sidestand)***

**2** Refer to Chapter 15.

***Brake light switches***

**3** Refer to Chapter 14.

***Battery level switch***

**4** Where fitted, these are normally used in conjunction with a computer monitor circuit to warn of low electrolyte level in the battery, and are particularly useful where the battery is awkwardly located and thus difficult to check visually.

Headlight relay ⟶

**11.4 Instrument panel wiring (Honda ST1100)**

**16**

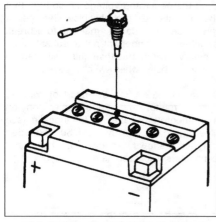

**12.4 Battery electrolyte level sensor**

A lead electrode is fitted to one of the battery cells, and when in contact with the electrolyte produces a reference supply of about 9 volts (see illustration 12.4). As long as this voltage is detected by the microprocessor, the warning lamp remains off, but if the level drops below the bottom of the electrode, the warning lamp comes on to indicate that topping up is required. Note that this is not fitted to many motorcycles.

### Coolant temperature senders

5 Most liquid-cooled machines are equipped with coolant temperature gauges which warn the rider when the coolant temperature reaches a dangerous level. The sender unit is a thermistor which has a resistance that varies according to its temperature. The sender is connected to a meter mechanism which indicates the temperature on the instrument panel (see illustration 12.5).

6 A fan switch operating on coolant temperature is used on liquid-cooled motorcycles, following automobile practice (see illustration 12.6).

### Fuel, oil and brake fluid level switches

7 These are float-type switches designed to warn of low fuel, oil or hydraulic fluid level by lighting the appropriate warning lamp in the instrument panel. The switch has one fixed contact and a moving contact fitted to the base of the float. As the level drops, the contacts close, earthing (grounding) the warning lamp (see also Chapter 18).

Many motorcycles are now fitted with a fuel level warning light (or gauge, or sometimes both) and an oil level warning light is common fitment on oil-injection two-strokes (see illustration 12.7). Brake fluid level switches are not common on motorcycles.

### Fuel gauge circuit

8 A float-operated sender unit is used in conjunction with a fuel gauge to give a good, but not precise indication of the amount of fuel remaining in the tank. A float is attached to the end of a wire arm and moves up and down with the fuel level.

As the float position changes in accordance with the fuel level it operates a variable resistance (a rheostat), comprising a number of turns of resistance wire wound round a flat former. The moving contact blade sweeps along the windings, thus determining the overall resistance in the circuit. This resistance is measured by the gauge meter mechanism which can then be calibrated to show the corresponding fuel level (see illustration 12.8). This is the most basic type and in some models the stabilisation is carried out electronically.

### Bank angle sensor

9 Sometimes known as a 'roll over sensor' this seismic device contains moving weights which will detect when the motorcycle is moving at less than walking pace **and** is banked over at more than 49° to the vertical. Given that both conditions are met it will cut off the ignition. This is a useful safety feature if the rider drops the bike or is involved in an accident. Illustration 12.9a shows the sensor fitted to the Honda ST1100 and illustration 12.9b shows its location on the right-hand side of the headlight.

### Carburettor heater

10 For cold starting and running, the carburettor heater shown is replicated for all four carburettors in this example of the

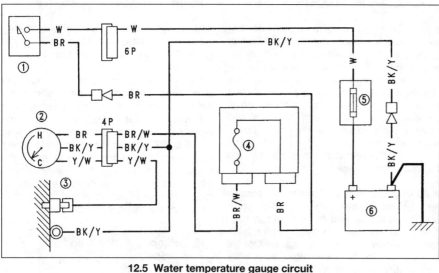

**12.5 Water temperature gauge circuit**

| 1 | Ignition switch | 3 | Temperature sender | 4 | Circuit fuse |
| 2 | Temperature gauge | | (thermistor) | 5 | Main fuse |
| | | | | 6 | Battery |

**12.6 Cooling fan motor and fan switch circuit**

| 1 | Fan motor | 3 | Circuit fuse | 5 | Battery |
| 2 | Fan switch in radiator | 4 | Main fuse | | |

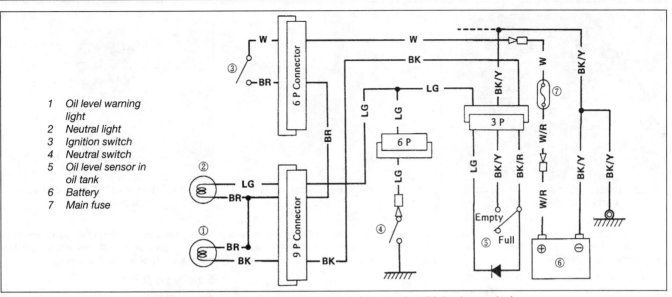

1   Oil level warning
    light
2   Neutral light
3   Ignition switch
4   Neutral switch
5   Oil level sensor in
    oil tank
6   Battery
7   Main fuse

**12.7  Engine oil level warning light circuit (two-stroke oil injection engine)**

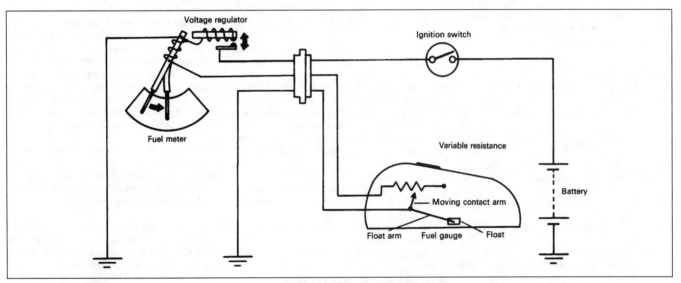

**12.8  Typical fuel gauge circuit**

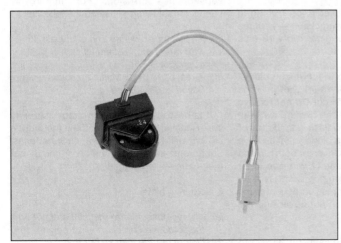

**12.9a  Bank angle sensor (Honda ST1100)**

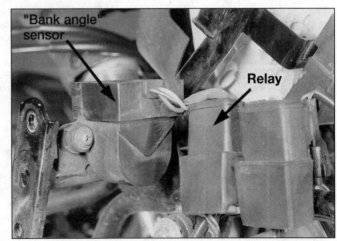

**12.9b  Bank angle sensor and relay location (Honda ST1100)**

**16**

**12.10a  Carburettor heater (one for each carb) (Yamaha XJ900S)**

**12.10b  Carburettor heater capsule**

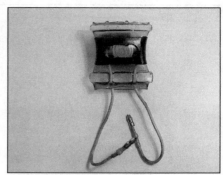

**12.10c  Thermoswitch for carburettor heater control**

Yamaha XJ900S (see illustration 12.10a). The heater capsule is screwed into the body of the carburettor (see illustration 12.10b).

For temperature detection a thermo-switch (see illustration 12.10c) is connected in series to the battery via the ignition switch. The thermo switch is designed to be closed as the temperature rises from a cold level, opening at 23°C. When the temperature falls from a high level it will close again at 12°C.

## 13 Electrical tool kit

**1** It is advantageous to keep a set of special tools just for electrical work, since there must be no possibility of oily tools being used anywhere on motorcycle circuitry. Here follows a list to meet most needs.

*Pocket knife (for scraping connections clean)*
*Spark plug spanner with rubber insert for plug tops*
*Electrician's screwdriver set*
*Cross-head screwdriver (chubby and 4 inch)*
*Engineer's combination pliers*
*HT cable pliers (optional)*
*Side-cutting pliers*
*Snipe-nosed pliers*
*Needle nosed pliers*
*Circlip (snap ring) pliers*
*Impact driver*
*Adjustable wire stripper*
*Crimping tool, with box of assorted connectors*
*Sets of Allen keys (Metric and Imperial)*
*Ignition spanners (for magneto adjustment)*
*Flat file for dressing contact points*
*Feeler gauges (plastic and steel types)*
*Jump leads with heavy crocodile clips*
*Grommet kit*
*Battery acid hydrometer*
*Soldering iron (45 watt for small work, 65 watt upwards for heavy jobs)*
*De-soldering pump (for printed circuit work)*
*Electrical contact spray*
*Multicore solder*

Test instruments are dealt with later but it is good to have a favourite compact multimeter in your portable kit at all times.

## 14 Electrical connections

**1** Motorcycle wiring suffers from a harsh environment and where connections are made care must be taken to ensure weatherproofing. Fitting any add-on electrical equipment may involve connecting into existing wiring; good electrical and physically strong connections are important. A sudden failure of lighting, ignition or an alarm system can be dangerous, especially at speed or in a fast lane.

**2** Three types of connection are used for most add-on or changes to motorcycle wiring.

(a) *Self stripping (Scotchlok) connectors.*
(b) *Soldered joints.*
(c) *Crimped joints.*

### Self stripping (Scotchlok) connectors

**3** These may be used for wiring-in accessories into an existing circuit without the need for cutting the original run-wire (see illustration 14.3).

Slot the run-wire into the through channel and push the accessory (tap) wire into the blind hole as far as it will go. **Do not** remove any insulation. Squeeze the blade down with engineer's pliers until it is flush with the top of the Scotchlok body. The blade will then have sheared through the insulation of both run and tap wires and be in contact with the inner copper conductors. A firm grip is achieved by the unique spring compression action of the blade. Snap over the hinged cover and the connection is complete.

Scotchloks come in several sizes to accommodate different cable diameters.

Make sure you use the right one or you may find the connector will shear through too many strands of wire in the cable.

### Soldered joints

**4** The soldered joint is reliable when made properly and is the surest way of making an electrical connection. Solder is an alloy of tin and lead. When melted between two metals to be joined, it will wet both surfaces and form a solder joint when cooled below the solidifying temperature of about 183°C (360°F), depending on the type of solder chosen. The solder forms an alloy with the metal parts to be joined and gives a good stable low resistance joint, providing the following conditions are achieved.

(a) *The joint metal surfaces are clean of dirt and oxide.*
(b) *The temperature of both metals to be joined is high enough for the solder to flow freely and wet the surfaces.*

**5** Final cleaning of the surfaces is achieved by the use of soldering flux which, for light electrical work, is already in the solder wire in the form of a rosin-based core. **Never** use acid flux (Bakers fluid) with electrical equipment because of the danger of subsequent corrosion. For motorcycle connector soldering you need the following:

(a) *An electric soldering iron of at least 45 watt rating with a stand as shown (see illustration 14.5).*
(b) *A reel of 18 SWG Multicore solder – either Savbit or 60/40 type.*

It is best to use a mains voltage soldering iron. Running a 12 volt iron off the motorcycle battery will quickly run down small batteries. Such irons are used by the car fraternity but their batteries are bigger!

**6** Soldering hints:

(a) *Always put solder to the joint and not on the soldering iron bit.*
(b) *Do not get the joint so hot that the wire insulation melts!*

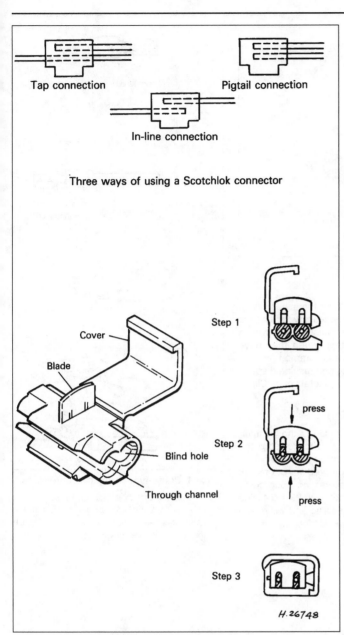

**Three ways of using a Scotchlok connector**

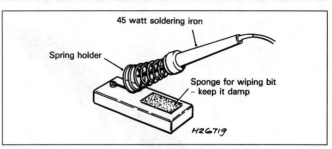

**14.5 A soldering iron is essential (shown complete with stand)**

*For larger jobs use a 60 watt iron (or larger)*

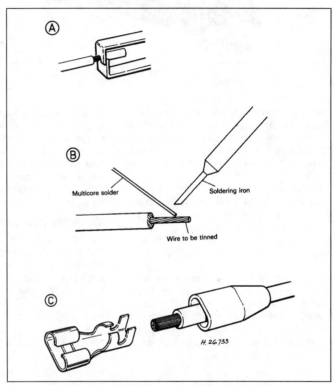

**14.7 Making a soldered connector joint**

A    Use wire strippers to remove insulation – be careful not to cut any
     wire strands
B    Put solder on the work – not on the iron
C    Connector prepared for soldering

**14.3 How to fit a Scotchlok connector**

**7** Illustration 14.7 shows the procedure for soldering a female blade connector onto a cable. First, make sure the soldering bit is tinned with solder and remember to wipe it occasionally on a damp sponge.

Slide the insulating cover on the cable. Strip off about ¼ inch (6.4 mm) of insulation from the wires to be joined by the connector (14.7 part A).This may be done with a pair of wire strippers or carefully with a penknife. Clean the exposed wires with a penknife or abrasive paper and tin lightly with solder (14.7 part B). Make sure the connector solder area is clean, scrape clean if necessary and then tin the channel in which the wire will lie. Lay the wire in place and reheat the joint, flooding wire and

tag with solder so that it flows. (Tinning means putting down a thin layer of solder.)

Do not use any more solder than is necessary so that the connector wing grips can be bent over the soldered area. If the connector has grips for the insulation like the one shown, bend them over with pliers and slide on the insulating cover (14.7 part C).

**Crimped connections**

**8** A quick and widely used method of joining wires to connectors, crimping consists of pressing the connector sleeve (or wings) down onto the wire by a simple hand tool. This method achieves the same result as soldering but with lower reliability. Note that

when fitting alarms which disable ignition, it is better to use soldered joints because of the small chance of accidental circuit failure due to corrosion.

**9** Making a satisfactory crimped joint depends on cleanliness of wires and connectors. It is essential to remove oxide film and dirt by scraping both the wire and the connector until bright, abrasive paper or a penknife being the usual means involved.

**10** Blade connectors are available in both insulated and non-insulated types and it is important to use the correct crimping tool. Crimping tools are available from auto accessory dealers, and are usually for

**16**

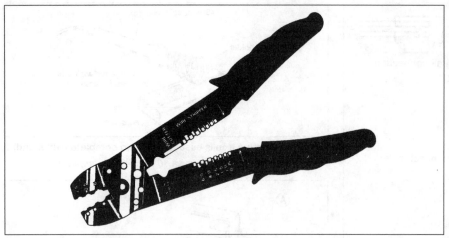

**14.10 Crimping tool**

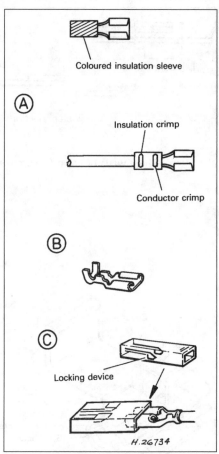

**14.11 Blade-type crimping connectors**

A   Insulated blade connector (female)
B   Non-insulated blade connector (female)
C   Clikfit sleeve – insulates full range of ¼ in (6.4 mm) connectors crimped or soldered.

insulated connectors (see illustration 14.10). Tools for non-insulated connectors have different teeth for compressing the tags. Crimp tools also have a useful wire insulation stripper which can be seen in the illustration.

**11** The crimping method is shown in illustration 14.11. Pre-insulated terminal connectors require that 6 mm (about ¼ inch) of wire insulation be stripped back. Crimp firmly over the wire and then over the insulation as shown.

Non-insulated spade connectors will have two pairs of wings, one for gripping the wires and the other for the wire insulation (part B). Do not forget to slide a PVC cover over the wire *before* the crimping operation. Using the correct part of the tool, crimp down the wings over the wire and then over the insulation. In this operation it may be necessary to bend the wings over separately, finishing off with a squeeze over both wings when they have been correctly located. It is common practice to use the PVC cover for non-insulated spade terminals but there is also a total cover 'Clikfit' type (part C).

## Weather protection

**12** Where joints are exposed to the weather, additional protection is afforded by the application of silicone-based grease. This applies to crimped, soldered or Scotchlok joints. 3M, the makers of Scotchlok connectors, also supply Scotch 23 self-fusing tape which is moisture sealing and will mould to the shape of the protected object – in this case one of the joints described above.

# Chapter 17
# Braking and traction control (ABS and TCS)

## Contents

### 1  Anti-lock Braking System (ABS)

**1** The purpose of the Anti-lock Braking System (ABS) is to provide maximum braking when required, but also to prevent wheel skid. Maximum braking force between the road surface and tyre will be present just short of the point of skidding; when a tyre skids across a surface the rider loses directional control because turning requires a sideways (lateral) force between tyre and road surface – this is not present when skidding. The almost inevitable result is that the rider will come off and add to the accident statistics.

**2** The single-track vehicle (ie motorcycle or bicycle) is not balanced in itself and only remains stable at low speeds due to the force exerted by the rider on the handlebars, and at higher speeds due to the gyroscopic effect of the two wheels – especially the front wheel. Whenever the wheels stop turning for more than 0.5 seconds, the motorcycle will suddenly become unstable.

**3** Most riders instinctively know that when the front and the rear brakes are applied there is a proper proportion of braking to achieve the correct total amount of braking in all situations. *Those who do not learn this quickly are at risk!*

It is known that one in ten riders falls off due to overbraking, but that many accidents (statistics unknown) are due to insufficient braking in an emergency. It is estimated that only about 70% of maximum possible braking is used by most riders on the straight and 60% when cornering.

**4** ABS braking allows the rider to apply the brakes as hard as he can without risking either wheel locking up – **providing** he is riding straightahead. On treacherous road surfaces with low frictional coefficients, eg wet roads, gravel, sand or diesel oil, ABS has a far superior performance than the most skilled rider. Additionally, traversing a change from a dry to wet surface requires a sudden but precise alteration of brake pressure – ABS achieves this, but many riders do not.

Cornering is a different matter and even with ABS full application of brakes is not possible. When the bike and rider lean in round a corner, the tyre contact point with the road moves over, away from the tyre centre line. If the rider brakes in this situation, the motorcycle automatically moves upwards from its inclined position and tries to run straightahead. Given these circumstances, full braking is impossible.

### 2  Principles of ABS braking

**1** All systems have toothed wheels on both front and back axles, sometimes attached to brake discs. A fixed sensor on each assembly counts the teeth passing and the sensor voltages are fed into an Electronic Control Unit (ECU).

**2** Usually when reaching the skidding point during braking, one of the wheels will have a different rotational speed from the other. The ECU reads the difference in rotational speed of front and back wheels; when there is no speed difference, the ECU takes no action.

Where a difference of more than 30% occurs, the ECU activates one of two pressure modulator units which are hydraulically connected to the braking system. The pressure modulator reduces the hydraulic brake pressure on the wheel just going into the skid condition until there is no further sign of wheel locking, then increases the pressure again up to locking point.

This process repeats 3 – 8 times per second for as long as the rider maintains the brake lever pressure and the speed does not fall below a certain point (4 km/h or 2.5 mph in the case of BMW) (see illustrations 2.2a and 2.2b).

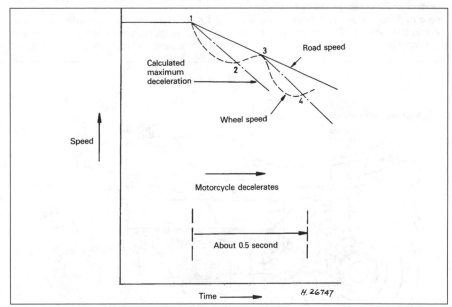

**2.2a  Overbraking sequence with ABS – speed diagram**

*1  Skid imminent – wheel speed falls below calculated maximum possible deceleration rate. Pressure on brake reduces and wheel speeds up*
*2  At point 2 wheel speed corresponds to maximum deceleration and pressure modulator de-activates*
*3  If the rider continues to overbrake cycle repeats*

**17**

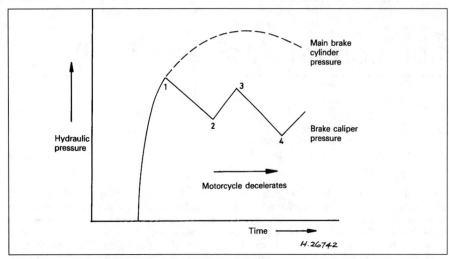

**2.2b Overbraking sequence with ABS – hydraulic pressures**

1    Skid detected – modulator reduces pressure
2    Modulator de-activates – wheel speed deceleration ideal
3    If applied brake pressure is too high, slip (skid) may re-occur – the process is repeated at a
     rate of 3 to 8 cycles per second depending on frictional value of road surface (ie
     slipperiness)

**3** Another, less common, condition may arise where the rider applies both brakes evenly so that both wheels go into the skid (lock-up) state simultaneously. To meet this state the ECU road memory has a programme for the maximum deceleration short of skidding. When the wheels slow down quicker than this figure due to locking-up action, ABS is applied to both wheels.

**4** Automobiles with ABS can exhibit a vibration which is felt on the footbrake pedal. Some motorcycle systems have a one-way valve in the hydraulic system which prevents this sensation.

**5** Different manufacturers' designs vary but the essential feature is the same. When the rider manually applies enough brake pressure to take a wheel up to the skidding point, the pressure modulator will reduce the braking force at the brake disc. It will then re-apply it up to skid point, reduce it again, etc, until the motorcycle is brought down to the speed required (often this is standstill). This produces the maximum possible deceleration and removes the danger of skidding.

**6** Correct tyre sizes and inflation pressures are important on any motorcycle fitted with ABS. The front and rear wheel sensors detect wheel speed difference and if, for example, one tyre had very low pressure, this could give a false reading to the ECU.

## 3  Current designs

**1** At the time of writing, ABS has appeared on the BMW R and K-series, the Honda ST1100 ABS-TCS, the Kawasaki GPZ1100S and the Yamaha FJ1200A and GTS1000A.

**2** ABS braking was first fitted on production cars as far back as 1978, and soon motorcycle design engineers began experimental work to see if the benefits could be applied to two-wheeled vehicles. The first working system based on hydraulic/mechanical principles was developed in Britain.

German work followed later using electronic/hydraulic units developed by BMW, FAG and Hella and known as the FAG-Kugelfischer system. This system first appeared on BMW K-series motorcycles in 1988 and is undergoing constant development (see illustration 3.2).

Japanese systems have subsequently been introduced, and have appeared on the models listed in paragraph 1.

## 4  BMW ABS

**Note:** The following is a description of BMW's ABS I system. All current BMWs are equipped with the ABS II system which uses a single pressure modulator.

### ABS components

**1** The ABS operating circuit is shown in illustration 4.1a and the electrical circuit in illustration 4.1b.

**2** Wheel speed sensors, mounted on extensions of the brake calipers, continually monitor individual wheel speeds and transmit this information to the ABS control unit. The sensors must be set up carefully if disturbed to ensure that the airgap between the sensor tip and toothed ring is as specified by BMW.

**3** Separate modulator units mounted low in the frame, just above the rider's footrests, control brake fluid pressure. Each unit weighs 3.8 kg (8.4 lb). The modulators are activated by the ABS control unit housed in the tail fairing.

**4** The control unit has a self-check facility which automatically checks the system components and voltage; if a fault is detected rendering the system inoperative, this is brought to the rider's attention by warning

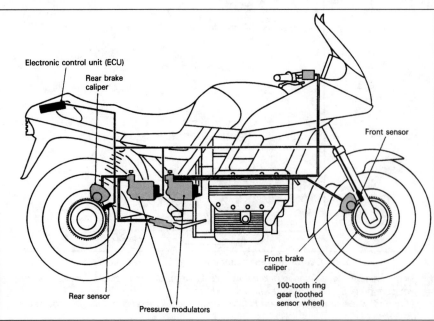

**3.2 BMW K-series with ABS braking**

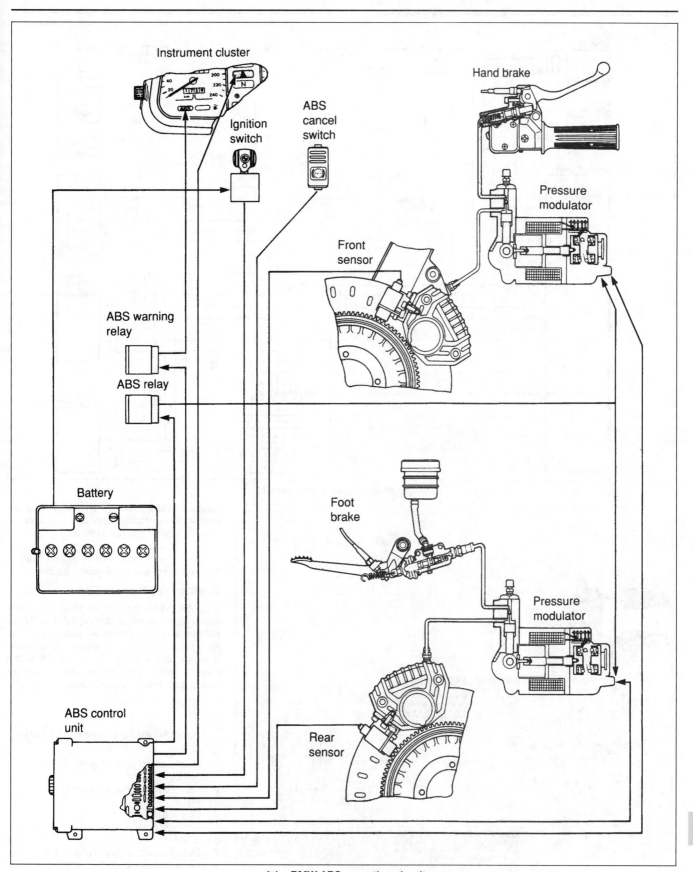

**4.1a  BMW ABS operating circuit**

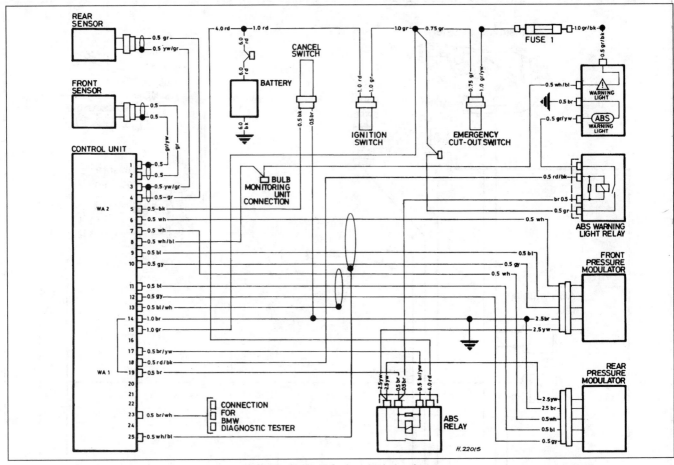

**4.1b BMW ABS electrical circuit**

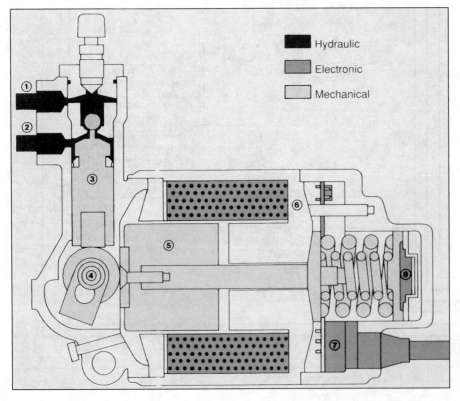

Hydraulic

Electronic

Mechanical

lamps in the instrument cluster. Faults are held in the unit's memory and can only be read by a BMW diagnostic tester.

5 ABS can be switched off by a cancel switch to revert the system to normal rider-braking.

### Control unit operation

6 Switching on the ignition produces a self checking sequence of flashing lights which go out when the motorcycle exceeds a low speed of 4 km/h or 2.5 mph (depending on the model) if all is in order. At the same time the control unit switches on the pressure modulators through the ABS relay.

**4.8a BMW ABS pressure modulator in section**

1   Fluid connection from brake master cylinder
2   Fluid connection to brake caliper
3   Piston
4   Idler rollers
5   Solenoid core
6   Solenoid
7   Output powerstage of control unit
8   Piezo element (detecting pressure of springs)

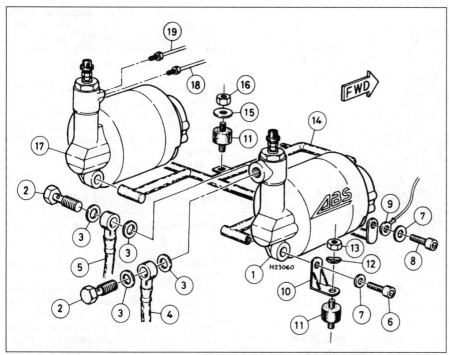

**4.8b BMW ABS pressure modulators (see Note at beginning of Section 4)**

| | | |
|---|---|---|
| 1 Rear brake modulator | 7 Washer | 14 Mounting bracket |
| 2 Union bolt | 8 Allen screw | 15 Washer |
| 3 Sealing washer | 9 Earth lead | 16 Nut |
| 4 Hose to rear master cylinder | 10 Rear bracket | 17 Front brake modulator |
| 5 Hose to rear caliper | 11 Rubber mounting | 18 Pipe to front master cylinder |
| 6 Allen screw | 12 Lock washer | 19 Pipe to front caliper |
| | 13 Nut | |

**7** The inductive wheel speed sensors do not have permanent magnets so as to avoid picking up magnetic particles, but carry a direct current through the sensor coil to produce the same effect. When the teeth pass close to the sensor the direct current has an added ac wave superimposed, corresponding to the rate at which the teeth pass the sensor.

The frequency (the rate at which the teeth pass the sensor) of both sensor outputs is compared in the ABS control unit. Any sudden difference corresponding to skid condition causes the control unit to activate the pressure modulators as explained in Section 2.

### Pressure modulator operation

**8** The pressure modulator (modulator means 'to change') is shown in illustrations 4.8a and 4.8b. The system operation is described using illustration 4.8a; under normal use the flow of brake fluid from the master cylinder (1) to brake caliper (2) is unhindered through the ball valve, so long as this is held open by the pressure pin of piston (3).

**9** Referring to illustration 4.8a, note that when skid conditions are detected by the sensors, the output power stage (7) receives signals from the control unit and switches on current through solenoid (6). The core (5) moves axially (like the core of a starter solenoid) to the right, against spring pressure. The idling rollers (4) move to the right and the piston (3) moves down, closing the ball valve. This removes any subsequent pressure pulsation through the brake lever.

**10** As the piston moves down, the volume applied to the brake caliper (2) increases, reducing the pressure. The drop in pressure allows the wheel to accelerate again at a rate determined by the tyre's grip on the road surface. Increase of wheel speed is notified by the wheel sensor to the control unit which switches off the modulator solenoid (6). The coil springs force the solenoid core (5) to the left, lifting piston (3) to the original position. If the applied brake pressure by the rider is still too high, the action repeats.

**11** Piezo element (8) is a quartz crystal which produces a voltage proportional to pressure. The signals generated by spring pressure on the piezo crystal check that the solenoid is working and contribute to the self checking of the system.

## 5 Yamaha ABS

### ABS components

**1** The location of ABS components is shown in illustration 5.1 and, in common with other systems, the heavier components are fitted roughly midway between the front and rear wheel.

**2** Hall effect sensors and toothed rotors (termed 'sensor rings') are located within the

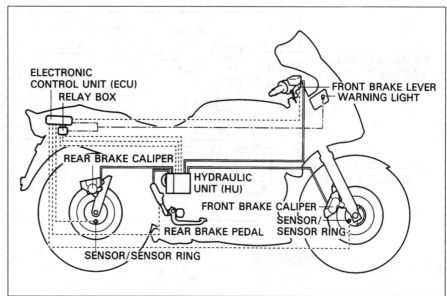

**5.1 ABS component location on the Yamaha FJ1200A (GTS1000A similar)**

**17**

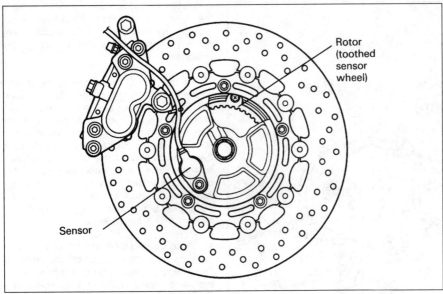

**5.2 Yamaha ABS sensor and rotor units**

hubs (see illustration 5.2). When refitting a wheel it is not necessary to check the sensor to sensor ring gap since these will not have been disturbed.

**3** Brake fluid pressure is modulated by an hydraulic unit (HU) which contains a motor driving two pumps, one for the front brake lever circuit and one for the rear brake pedal circuit (see illustration 5.3).

A buffer chamber is incorporated in the front and rear circuits of the hydraulic system;

these chambers store brake fluid from the brake calipers when pressure is released. The fluid is then returned to the brake line.

### ECU operation

**4** The ECU checks first that the system is working correctly. Coded flashing signals are given to indicate all correct, or any one of several fault conditions. Its second function is to determine the running state of the motorcycle. Memory in the ECU can store information on faults which can be retrieved when the system is connected to a diagnostic tester.

The final function is to determine whether braking force should be increased or decreased, a task carried out continuously whether the rider is applying the brakes or not.

**5** If when braking, the front and rear wheel speed differs from the optimum pre-determined braking speed programmed into the ECU, the ECU activates the hydraulic unit to regulate the brake fluid pressure at the calipers. Decisions on this are made by the ECU every 8 milliseconds.

### Hydraulic Unit (HU) operation

**6** During normal braking, the master cylinder pressurises the brake caliper directly (see illustration 5.6).

**7** When ABS operates, the solenoid valve opens releasing brake fluid to the buffer chamber. The flow control valve is sucked over to the right because of the pressure difference on either side of the orifice. The flow control valve cuts off the caliper passage on the left side of the orifice and, as the movement continues, the passage to the right of the orifice opens, so depressurising the caliper (see illustration 5.7).

**8** When the danger of skid is past, pressure is re-applied to the caliper at a graduated rate. The ECU switches off the current to the solenoid valve, shutting off the buffer chamber, the contents being circulated by the pump. The flow control valve moves over to the left, re-pressurising to a specified amount by the metering edge (see illustration 5.8).

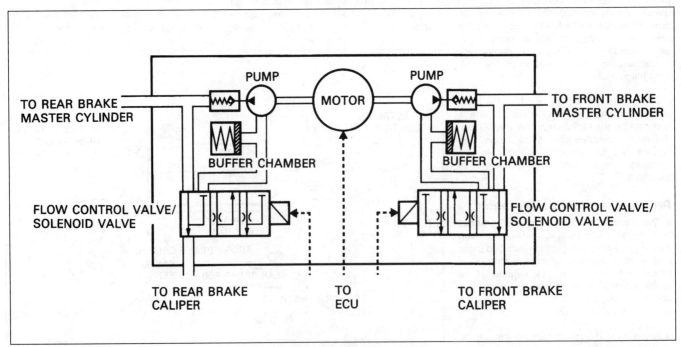

**5.3 Yamaha ABS hydraulic unit (HU)**

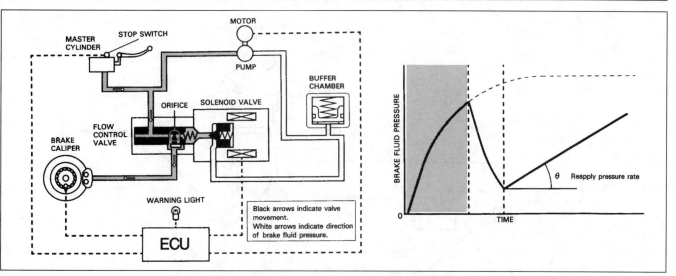

5.6  Yamaha ABS – normal braking (ABS on standby)

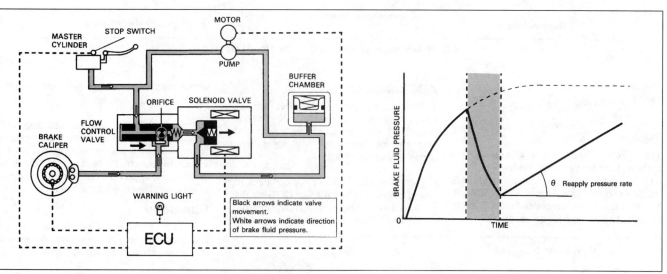

5.7  Yamaha ABS – skid onset (pressure reduced)

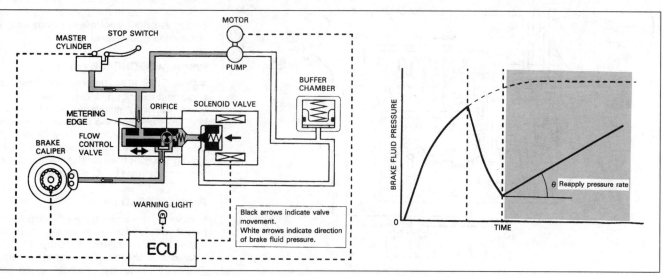

5.8  Yamaha ABS – pressure reapplied at graduated rate

17

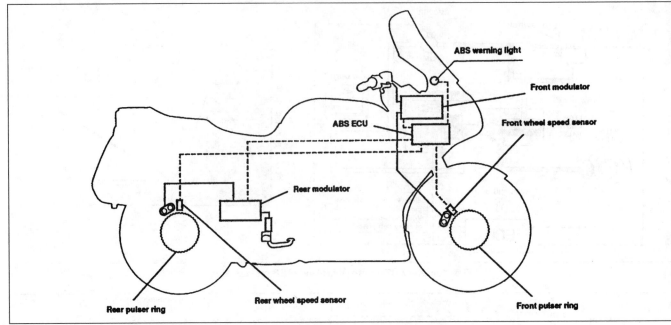

6.2  ABS component locations on the Honda ST1100

## 6  Honda ABS

**1** The only Honda model featuring this system at the time of writing is the ST1100. It has a combined ABS braking and TCS traction control system, known as ABS-TCS. The ABS function is described in this Section, but refer to Section 7 for details of TCS.

### ABS components

**2** The Honda system employs an ECU controlling two separate, self-contained, pressure modulators which are maintenance-free. The location of the ABS equipment is shown in illustration 6.2.

Each modulator features two compact, high speed solenoid valves (IN and OUT) for quick and precise hydraulic pressure control. A pump and motor pressurise the modulator with a fluid which is kept separate from the brake fluid in the calipers.

At start-up the ECU carries out a diagnostic hydraulic pressure check; errors are signalled to the rider by a coded flashing lamp in the instrument cluster. There is fail-safe provision in the event of pump failure which is referred to in Honda literature as the 'back-up' mode.

### Operation

**3** Other systems work on the principle of pressure decrease and pressure increase to the brake caliper of a slipping wheel.

On standby mode (see illustration 6.3) the master cylinder is connected directly to the brake caliper. Up to the onset of skidding the brakes are rider controlled. Honda use 3-stage working, described as follows.

### Pressure DECREASE mode

**4** When the ECU detects the onset of skidding it reduces hydraulic pressure to the brake caliper by simultaneously closing the inlet valve and opening the outlet valve (see illustration 6.4). Loss of pressure on the right side of the cylinder valve moves it to the right, closing the cut-off valve. This de-pressurises the pressure in the brake caliper line.

### Pressure HOLD mode

**5** Following a pre-determined decompression period the outlet valve closes and the hydraulic pressure remains steady but lower than that pressure which causes skidding. This allows recovery of wheel speed (see illustration 6.5).

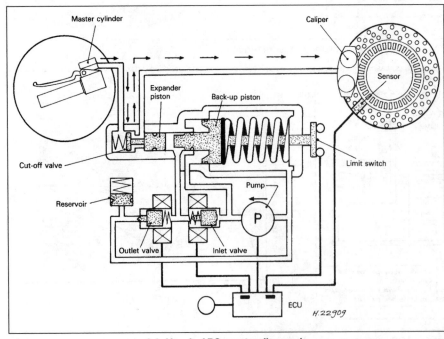

6.3  Honda ABS on standby mode

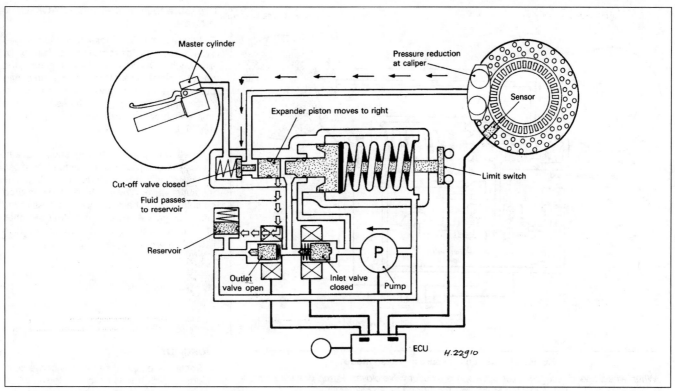

**6.4 Honda ABS on pressure decrease mode (skidding threshold)**

*Outlet valve opens – expander piston moves to the right – pressure to caliper reduces – cut-off valve closes – master cylinder isolated from caliper*

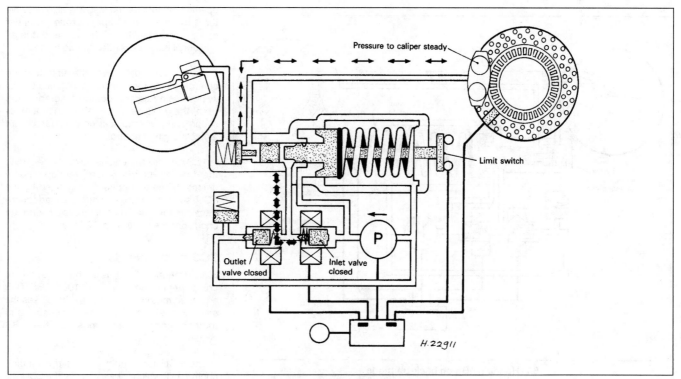

**6.5 Honda ABS on hold mode**

*Both valves closed holding caliper pressure steady*

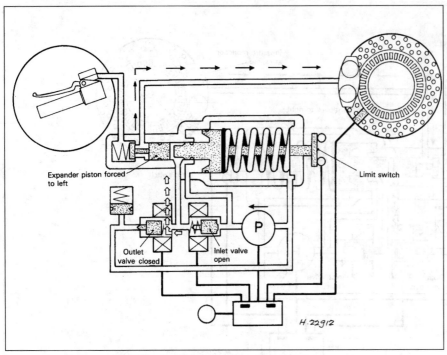

**6.6 Honda ABS on pressure increase mode**

*When wheel speed recovers, inlet valve opens – outlet valve closes. Pump pressure forces expander piston to left, re-pressurising brake caliper line*

### Pressure INCREASE mode

**6** The ECU will detect the recovery of wheel speed and once this is attained, it signals the opening of the inlet valve and closing of the outlet valve. Pump pressure forces the expander valve to the left, so re-pressurising the brake caliper line (see illustration 6.6).

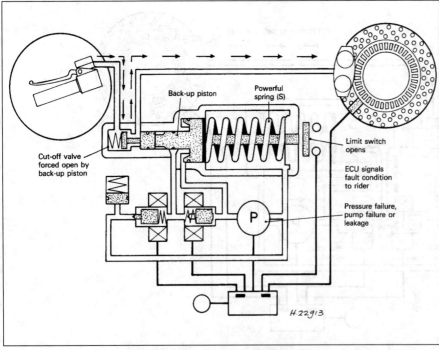

**6.7 Honda's ABS on back-up mode**

*If pump pressure fails, the back up piston is forced left by springs. The back up piston pushes the expander piston to the left, thus opening the cut-off valve – rider has control of braking*

### Pressure loss protection – BACK-UP mode

**7** If there is a loss of pressure in the pumped system due to leakage, pump failure, or simply when the rider switches off ignition, the back-up piston under force of a strong spring pushes the cut-off valve open and normal rider-operated braking now takes place. The limit switch opens, signalling this condition to the ECU.

When the rider starts the engine again, unless the pump pressure builds up to close the switch within 5 seconds, the ECU opens the outlet valve, allowing the pressure to drop completely. The back-up piston moves to the left, opening the cut-off valve. ABS switches off and a warning light comes on (see illustration 6.7).

## 7 Honda TCS

### Description

**1** Traction slip is, in a sense, the converse of skidding. With traction slip the driving wheel will accelerate faster than the friction between tyre and road surface can cope with. The result is wheel spin without appreciable movement of the motorcycle.

While this may be caused by a rider opening the throttle too fast, it is also possible for it to occur on a slippery road. In either case, riding stability is affected and it is an additional hazard the rider can do without.

**2** Honda have produced the first traction control system for a motorcycle. It is a simple system using certain common components from the ABS and has the main aim of suppressing tyre slip, leaving the rider with an ample margin of control.

TCS reduces the engine power by retarding the ignition timing when traction slip is detected. The retardation is regulated by the ECU so that the rear wheel has adequate traction for the particular road surface condition (see illustration 7.2).

### TCS components

**3** Illustration 7.3 shows the location of components on the ST1100 ABS-TCS equipped motorcycle. Note that TCS uses the same Hall-effect wheel speed sensors and toothed rings (pulser rings) as the ABS system.

The ECU is combined with the ignition control unit, which is logical since the ECU will put ignition retard signals into the ignition control unit when wheel spin is detected.

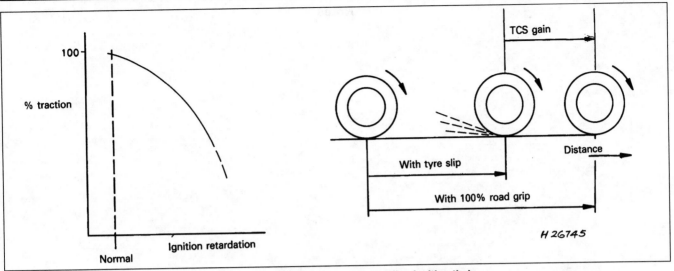

**7.2 TCS reduces engine power by retarding ignition timing**

Repetition sampling rate is approximately 100 operations per second. The ECU calculates rear tyre slip and the engine running condition to determine how much ignition retardation is required. The result is the correct control of engine torque to keep tyre slip within the desired limits.

**4** A 'TCS-ON' light in the instrument panel comes on when ECU is applying retardation. It may be regarded as a hint to the rider to adjust his acceleration level.

### Developments

**5** While no fundamental developments have taken place in the basic operation of ABS/TCS in the last few years, Honda have combined the two systems into one.

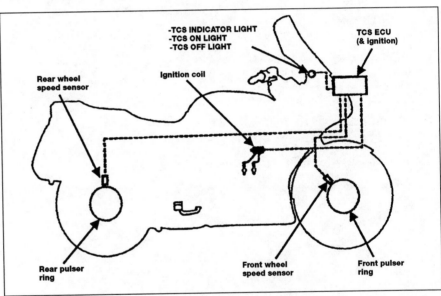

**7.3 TCS component location on the Honda ST1100**

**17**

**Notes**

# Chapter 18
## Testing and fault finding

## Contents

# Part A: Basic meters and tests

## 1 Continuity testers

**1** Checking for electrical continuity (that is – not a break) in a circuit is probably the most common test carried out. Continuity can be checked with an ohmmeter, a multimeter or a continuity tester.

Continuity testers have a battery and a bulb or a buzzer. When the probes touch a continuous path, say both ends of a cable, the bulb lights up or the buzzer operates (see illustrations 1.1a, b and c).

Some testers are cheap to buy and can even be made up with flashlamp battery and a bulb. However, this is an inconvenient arrangement and it is far better to have a purpose-made tester in the electrical toolkit.

**2** Since all the above have a built-in battery they must not be used on live circuits. The ignition must be switched OFF and preferably the battery negative lead disconnected. Take care also not to use a battery continuity tester on electronic equipment because the battery supply could ruin circuit components.

## 2 Test lights and buzzers

**1** These differ from continuity testers by having no built-in battery. The test light shown in illustration 2.1a has a sharp probe with a safety cover; the purpose of the probe is to touch on the point to be tested but also it may be used carefully to penetrate insulation on a covered wire or cable to check if it is live. This must be done only on ordinary wiring cables and never on wiring associated with electronic equipment such as the ECU.

**2** An alternative to the test light is the buzzer which again has no internal supply voltage but will buzz when it senses the voltage of the

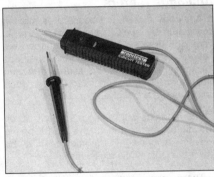
**1.1a Battery-powered continuity tester**

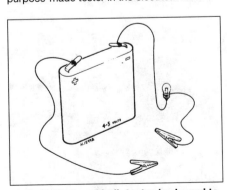
**1.1b Battery and bulb tester (awkward to use – buy a proper one!)**

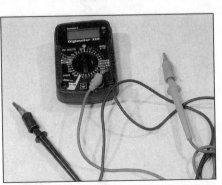
**1.1c Digital multimeter with built-in buzzer**

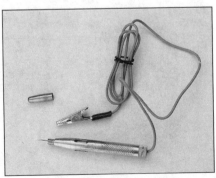
**2.1a Test light with sharp probe**

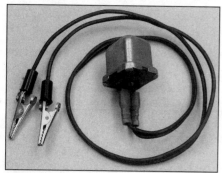

2.1b A buzzer is useful for voltage checks

3.2 Simple analogue general purpose meter

3.5a Pocketmeter 1 – good yet inexpensive

motorcycle system (see illustration 2.1b). The test light and buzzer are used with the battery supply connected, unlike the continuity tester.

## 3 Multimeters

1 It is inconvenient to have separate meters for amperes, volts and ohms. For general testing work the multimeter is widely used and every technician should invest in one. The decision to be made is whether to buy an analogue meter or a digital meter. Analogue meters are those with a pointer and the digital type reads out in figures, but apart from the type of readout there are other things to consider.

### Analogue meters

2 Analogue meters are based on a moving coil instrument (see Chapter 2) and are fragile. They do not stand up to being dropped but nevertheless have been used in workshops for many years like the simple meter in illustration 3.2. If kept carefully a good analogue meter will give good service.

The readings will be more steady than on the digital meter due to the inertia of the movement, but again the accuracy may be lower than that of the digital meter.

There are now many other good inexpensive analogue meters available.

Although cheap meters look tempting, do get the best you can afford. Cheaper types are often insensitive to small currents and cannot be repaired if spares are required.

3 Analogue meters need special care when switching from one range to another. The rotary switch may pass through current ranges (amperes) before reaching the desired voltage range. On 'ampere' positions the meter presents a low resistance to the external circuit and if the test leads are left in position while switching ranges on a live circuit, this can mean the end of an expensive instrument. *Always disconnect the test leads before changing ranges.*

Digital meters often have a protective circuit to guard against accidental overload but it is best practice *always* to disconnect the leads from the circuit before range switching, whether or not the meter is analogue or digital.

### Digital meters

4 Digital meters have come down in cost and now are more popular than the analogue type. In general they are more accurate but as with all instruments the reading should not be relied upon as being 100% accurate. *All instruments have an error* and it is really a matter of how big the errors are!

One important advantage over the analogue meter is the higher input resistance

(usually greater than 10 megohms) and this means that when a voltage measurement is made on electronic equipment there will be less effect due to the voltmeter.

5 Ideal for motorcycle general purpose testing and at low cost is the Gunson Pocketmeter 1 which has amps, ohms and volts facilities; it will measure up to 10 amperes dc and can test diodes and transistors (see illustration 3.5a).

For good value and comprehensive specification the Gunsons Digimeter 320 is worth considering. It has ranges for amps, volts and ohms together with 250 volts ac, frequency, period, pulse width and dwell (see illustration 3.5b).

The Clarke CDM 20 is another value instrument with most of the usual facilities plus ranges of 1000 volts dc and 700 volts ac (see illustration 3.5c).

6 Of unusual interest is the Draper ac/dc clamp meter (see illustration 3.6). The feature of it is the clamp which opens up and clamps round

3.5b The Digimeter 320 – ideal for motorcycle work

3.5c Another useful meter with high voltage scales

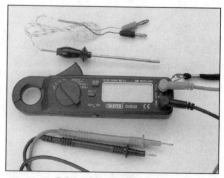

3.6 ac/dc clamp meter

the cable to give a current reading. Normally to measure current by an ammeter means disconnecting the cable, which is inconvenient. The meter will read up to 200 amps dc and ac and so is ideal for checking starter motor and alternator charging currents. It has also scales for 600 volts dc and ac, plus a thermocouple for engine temperature measurements, and is one of a wide range of useful test equipment by Draper.

## 4  General testing

### Switch checks

**1** If a switch is at fault, trace its wiring up to the wiring connectors. Separate the wire connectors and inspect them for security and condition. A build up of dirt or corrosion here is likely be the cause of the problem – clean up and apply a water dispersant such as WD40. Switch contacts may wear with prolonged use and eventually give rise to high resistance or even an open circuit.

**2** If using a test meter, set the meter to the ohms x 10 scale and connect the meter probes across the wires from the switch (see illustration 4.2). Simple ON/OFF switches such as brake light switches have only two wires whereas combination switches like the ignition switch have many internal links.

Study the wiring diagram to ensure that you are connecting across the correct pair of wires. Continuity (low or zero ohms) should be indicated with the switch ON and no continuity (high or infinity) with the switch OFF.

The polarity of the test probes is of no importance for continuity checks but if you are testing a diode or other electronic component then it may be relevant.

Surprisingly, the polarity of the voltage appearing at the test prods of an *analogue* meter on the ohms range is opposite to what might be expected.

The prods and the sockets they come from are usually marked in red and black or + and -.

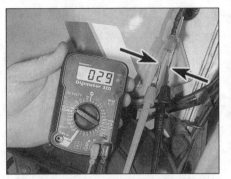

**4.2  Continuity check of brake light switch using a meter – note split pins used to access connector terminals**

The internal battery of the ohmmeter in fact gives a negative polarity at the red (+) lead and a positive polarity at the negative (-) lead!

**3** A continuity tester or a simple battery and bulb may be used in the same way. Connect the probes across the switch wires as in the last paragraph. The bulb will light when there is continuity (ON) and will not light in the OFF position (see illustration 4.3). Remember to switch off the ignition while testing or disconnect the negative battery lead.

### Wiring checks

**4** Many electrical faults are caused by damaged wiring, often due to incorrect routing or chafing on the frame. Loose, wet or corroded cable connectors are frequent causes of electrical problems especially in exposed locations.

A continuity check can be made across a single length of wire by disconnecting it at both ends and connecting a continuity tester across the ends (see illustration 4.4).

Continuity is OK if the resistance is low (or the bulb lights) but if there is no continuity you have a break in the wire somewhere along it. One solution to this is to cut a length of wire of the same gauge and tape it firmly to the outside of the loom and use it in place of the faulty section.

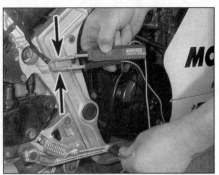

**4.3  Continuity check of rear brake light switch using a continuity tester**

### Checking for voltage

**5** A voltage check will tell if the supply is reaching a component. If the supply voltage is there, then the component and not the wiring is at fault. Voltage can be checked with a voltmeter (set to the dc voltage range), a test light or a buzzer (see illustration 4.5a and b).

A voltmeter has the advantage of not only checking for the presence of voltage but also the actual value.

Voltage testing should be carried out with the ignition ON in most cases. Set the voltmeter to dc volts and the scale which will suit the bike voltage of 12 volts (or 6 volts for some older machines).

**6** Identify the wiring circuit by reference to the circuit diagram. Note that sometimes other components work off the same supply line and if they are working but the item under test is not, this tells you that up to the point of the circuit dividing all is well.

To test, connect the negative lead of the multimeter to a good earth point on the frame (or directly to the battery negative terminal) and test with the other probe. The same goes if you are using a test light or a buzzer.

Switch the ignition ON and test at the component, for example a rear light bulb. If no voltage is indicated work back until voltage

**4.4  Continuity check of front brake light switch sub-harness**

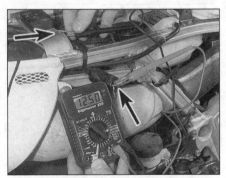

**4.5a  Checking for voltage at a component using a meter**

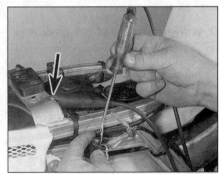

**4.5b  Checking for voltage at a component using a test light**

once again appears. This tells you that the fault is between this point and the last one to be checked.

### Checking the earth (ground)

**7** Earth connections are made either directly to the engine or frame. For example, devices like lights, starter motors etc. have one feed wire or cable and the current returns to the battery via the frame earth. Sometimes a component will have an earth wire or strip connected to the motorcycle frame.

A large number of electrical faults occur due to corrosion causing a bad earth. The classic case is in lighting when, for example, the rear light goes out when the rear brake light comes on. This points immediately to a bad earth and the remedy is to take the earth connection apart and scrape it clean and also the point of connection on the frame. After reassembly, smear a touch of petroleum jelly over the new earth joint and all should be well.

**8** Another common case of poor earthing is when corrosion inside a bulbholder prevents the bulb current from returning to earth. Look inside the bulbholder and there will be the characteristic grey film and possibly water which may have caused the problem. Clean the inner surface up with a fine abrasive paper and also the outer shell of the bulb, spray the holder lightly with WD40 or an electrical contact aerosol. Make sure the lamp weatherproof sealing is good and reassemble.

**9** For other cases of poor earthing check that the negative battery lead is making good earth contact and also the main earthing point of the wiring harness. If corrosion is suspected, dismantle the connection, clean all surfaces back to the bare metal, reassemble and cover with a protective film of grease, petroleum jelly or WD40 spray.

**10** To check the earth on a component use an insulated jumper wire to bypass the earth connection (see illustration 4.10).

Connect one end of the jumper wire to the component body and the other to a good earthing point on the frame. Switch on the offending component. If it now works, the original earth is faulty. Clean up and protect the earth point as above.

### Tracing a wiring short-circuit

**11** A wiring short circuit means that current is going to earth before it reaches the component it is supposed to feed. A short circuit in wiring is usually due to insulation failure possibly due to chafing on a sharp metal edge. It invariably blows a fuse and the circuit goes dead.

With the component (eg a headlamp) switched off, remove the circuit fuse and connect across the fuseholder terminals a multimeter on the dc volts range. A testlight or a buzzer could be used instead.

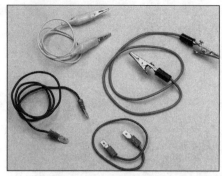

**4.10 A selection of jumper wires for making earth (ground) checks**

If there is a voltage shown or the light/buzzer operates, the short circuit is confirmed. Wiggle the cable or loom along it's length and there should come a point where the voltage disappears perhaps momentarily. That is the short circuit location and it will often show burned insulation (but not always).

**12** The same test can be used on all parts of the circuit, even the switch. Cure the fault as seems appropriate but it is best not to use burned cable again. If there is any doubt put in a substitute wire running along the same route as the faulty wire and tape it firmly in place.

### 5 Ignition spark testing

**1** Simple testing for sparking may be carried out without difficulty by use of a spark gap in place of a plug.

**2** The Gunson Flashtest has a pair of electrodes one of which is pressed onto an earth point such as the engine block and the other has the spark plug HT lead connected (see illustration 5.2). By opening out the scissors the gap can be increased to the point where the spark is no longer regular and this gives an idea of the reserve in the ignition system. The scale indicates if the ignition circuit is satisfactory.

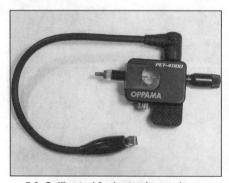

**5.3 Calibrated 3-electrode spark gap tester**

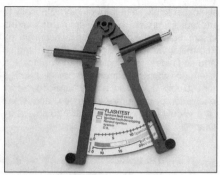

**5.2 Gunson flashtest**

**3** More sophisticated is the Oppama calibrated gap used by Yamaha (see illustration 5.3). This has a variable gap and there is a third insulated electrode. This creates the correct electric field round the sparking electrode and has a similarity to the magneto test gap shown in Chapter 5, illustration 4.8.

The HT is connected and the spark will be seen in the window. The gap is widened by the adjuster and if the spark is maintained without faltering at a 6 mm gap then the ignition system is satisfactory.

**4** There are limitations to this form of measurement because a plug may work in air but may not in the high pressure and hostile environment in a working cylinder. The ideal instrument would measure the spark voltage and the spark current (see Section 6).

**5** A useful indicator which can display the spark without having to hold anything in the hand is the Draper In-line HT ignition tester (see illustration 5.5); HT means high tension or high voltage.

It is one thing to have the spark voltage available but only the knowledge that a spark current is passing under working conditions can prove that the whole circuit is working satisfactorily. Such an instrument is the IgnitionMate used for peak voltage measurements.

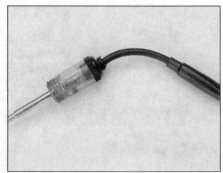

**5.5 In-line HT ignition tester**

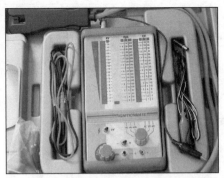

**6.1  The IgnitionMate peak voltage tester**

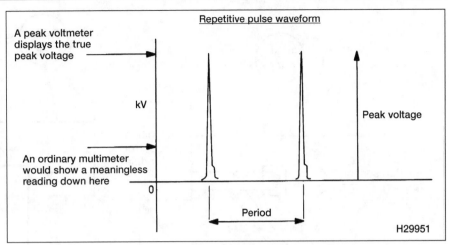

**6.2a  Pulse waveforms are measured by a peak voltmeter**

## 6  Peak voltage testing

**1** The IgnitionMate displays peak voltages on illuminated strips (see illustration 6.1). The dual display can show simultaneously, for example, the spark voltage while monitoring another related function such as the pulser coil, charge coil, battery voltage etc.

What singles it out from a normal multimeter is that it can read both steady voltages and peak voltages on scales ranging from 4 to 40,000 volts.

**2** First let us see why a multimeter will not read pulse voltages:

Multimeters are calibrated on the assumption that all alternating voltages are sinusoidal and read the root-mean-square (rms) of an alternating current or voltage. For *sine* waves the rms value is 0.707 x peak value. However, applying a multimeter to a pulse waveform such as those in ignition systems would give a totally meaningless result.

**3** Illustration 6.2a shows the dramatic difference in the readings of a multimeter and peak voltage meter when applied to a pulse waveform.

The input circuit to a meter designed specially to measure the peak value of a pulse waveform will have a capacitor and resistor in parallel as in the simple version shown in illustration 6.2b. The capacitor will charge up to the peak height of the input voltage and if the CR time constant of the two components is long compared with the time between pulses, then the capacitor voltage will be approximately that of the peak voltage input since the charge could not leak away very much before the next pulse came along (see Chapter 2 for meaning of *time constant*). In early versions of this type of meter, a multimeter set to the dc voltage range would measure the capacitor voltage. This simple version would be able to measure low voltages such as those from sensors but extra components would be needed for high voltage work. The trend now is away from direct contact with the spark plug leads and to use an inductive clamp round the cable.

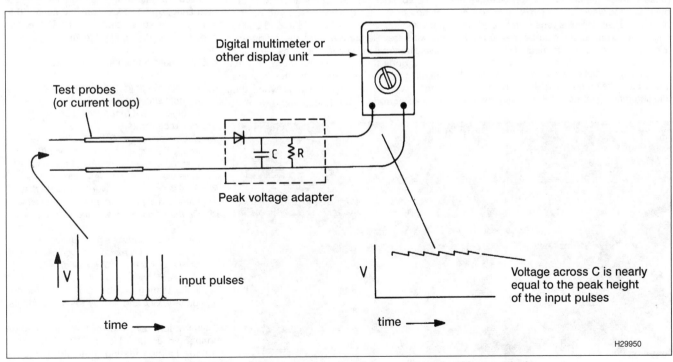

**6.2b  Peak voltage adapter converts pulses into a constant dc with some ripple**

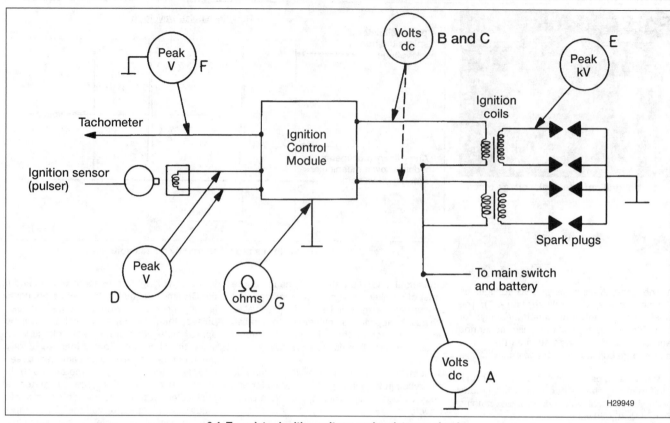

**6.4 Transistor ignition voltage and resistance checks**

**4** Illustration 6.4 shows the application of a peak voltage meter such as the IgnitionMate to a transistor ignition system. The ignition pulse voltage generator (sensor) will give a pulse voltage waveform which will rise both in peak value and in pulse repetition rate as the engine speed rises. It would be measured on a low voltage range of the meter (D).

Typically the pulser signal voltage would be 1.0 to 5.0 volts on cranking, 4.0 to 12 volts on idle and running up from 1000 to 6000 rev/min

should give 10 to 35 volts (guide figures only.)

**5** The voltages on the secondary side of the ignition coils (E) would be measured on the peak kilovolt ranges. A double ended coil is shown here. Remember that the plugs will have different firing voltage because the spark current goes through one the 'correct' way but will then pass through the other one the 'wrong' way. The correct way is when the centre electrode of the plug is negative with

respect to earth (ground) (see Chapter 7 on the wasted spark principle).

Guidance voltage figures might be: With the plug firing, 6 to 15kV at cranking speed, 6 to 14kV at idle speed and 6 to 13kV over the speed range 1000 to 6000 rev/min.

**6** Other measurements possible are:

(a) Direct voltage (dc) at A at the ignition module should be equal to the battery voltage except that a fall on cranking would be expected.
(b) Direct voltages at B and C should be about the same as at A. This would show that the primary windings of the ignition coils are continuous, ie no break in them.
(c) A peak voltage at F would indicate that there is a signal on the tachometer wire.
(d) On the ohms range at G there should be zero or very low resistance if the earthing of the ignition module is good. Note the measurement is made between the module case and a good earth (ground) point.

Similar testing can be carried out for coil and battery, CDI and energy transfer systems.

**7** Illustration 6.7 shows the IgnitionMate connected up to a Honda CB250 for peak voltage ignition testing: note the inductive pickup clamp round the ignition HT cable.

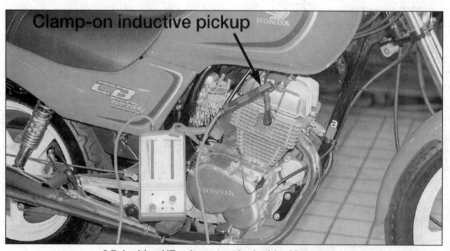

**6.7 Ignition HT voltage test by IgnitionMate meter**

# Part B: Fault finding

## 7 Fault finding – general

**1** This being a book on general electrical work and non specific for any particular models, it is possible only to give a broad treatment of fault finding. The main thing is to track down faults logically and one of the ways of doing this is to follow a chart as we shall do in looking at ignition faults. With experience much of this can be shortened and the problem area found more quickly.

**2** It is important to use the wiring diagram to trace faults and is far better than dabbling. Sometimes a list of typical symptoms is useful although they never seem quite to fit *your* problem!

## 8 Ignition – CDI (Capacitor Discharge Ignition)

**1** The flow chart shown in the illustration 8.1 applies to most CDI circuits but must be adapted to the model and system of the motorcycle worked on. Note the abbreviation ICU which means ignition control unit. The

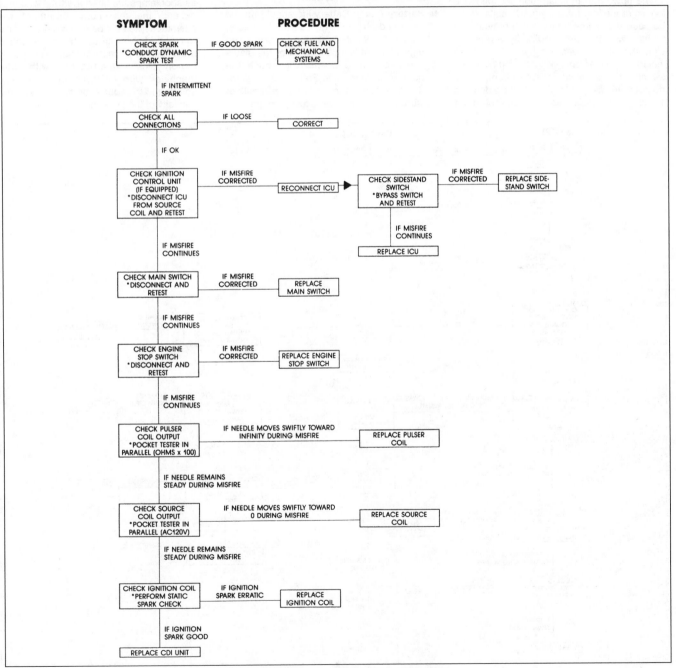

**8.1 CDI ignition fault finding chart (Yamaha)**

units have many different terms such as electronic control unit ECU, spark unit, igniter unit etc.

**2** Repairs to electronic items found to be faulty are not normally possible and there is no alternative but to replace faulty parts.

## 9 Ignition – TCI (Transistor Controlled ignition)

**1** The flow chart in illustration 9.1 follows a logical procedure for tracing TCI faults. It will be seen that some faults which prevent the ignition working are not directly connected with the spark generating circuits. These include the sidestand switch and the neutral switch, both of which are safety items. They do not normally give trouble but the sidestand switch is in a hostile area and is subject to wet

and mud thrown up from the road. Sidestand switches are described in Chapter 15 where they control the starter operation (starter lockout circuits). There are also sidestand and neutral switch safety circuits which inhibit the ignition operation (see below).

## 10 General electrical problems

### Battery dead or weak

● **Battery faulty:** Battery life should not be expected to exceed 3 to 4 years, particularly where a starter motor is used regularly. Gradual sulphation of the plates and sediment deposits will reduce the battery performance. Plate and insulator damage can often occur as a result of vibration. Complete power failure, or

intermittent failure, may be due to a broken battery terminal. Lack of electrolyte will prevent the battery maintaining charge. See Chapter 13 for full information on batteries and testing.

● **Battery leads making poor contact:** Remove the battery leads and clean them and the battery terminals removing all traces of corrosion and tarnish. Reconnect the leads and apply a coating of petroleum jelly to the terminals.

● **Load excessive:** If additional items such as spot lamps are fitted the total load may exceed the maximum output of the alternator. Then the battery will not be able to remain fully charged; this is a situation most likely to be met with smaller capacity motorcycles and often met with older machines with dc dynamos. The only solution is to reduce the load to suit the capacity of the generator.

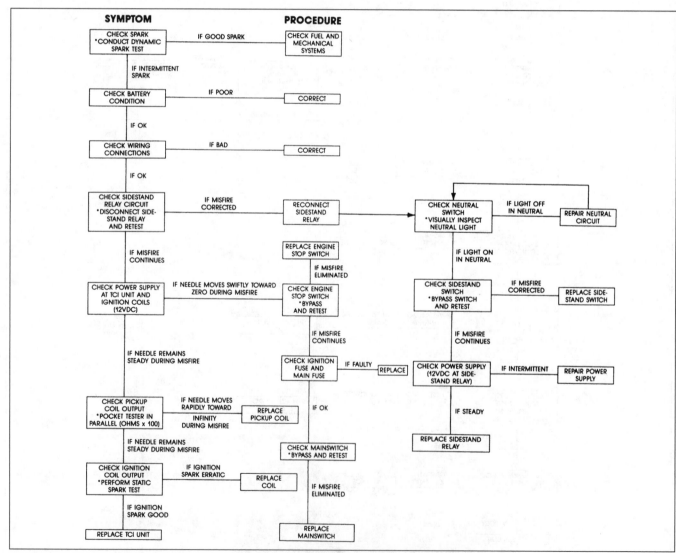

**9.1 Transistor Ignition fault finding chart (Yamaha)**

- **Regulator or rectifier failure:** It is not uncommon for a regulator to fail and testing by voltage measurements is the best indicator of what is wrong. Similarly, one or more elements of the rectifier may fail resulting in no charge or low charge. See Chapter 12 for details on circuits and testing.

- **Alternator failure:** Usually this can be traced to faulty armature or field windings (Chapter 12). Occasionally worn brushes on the rotor slip rings may give trouble and can be easily corrected. See also Section 6.

- **Charging path showing short circuit or open circuit:** This can happen if the wiring is frayed or there is a cable break due to vibration. Other causes can be corroded connectors or a faulty ignition switch. Wiring faults should be traced logically as explained in paragraphs above.

## Battery overcharged

- **Regulator or rectifier faulty:** Overcharging is indicated if the battery becomes hot or the electrolyte level falls repeatedly between checks. In serious cases the battery may boil causing corrosive gases and battery acid to escape through the vent pipe. This is one reason why it is important to ensure that the vent pipe is in place, not crushed and not full of dust. Tests on batteries, rectifiers and regulators are described in Chapters 12 and 13.

- **The battery may be too small for load it has to carry:** This will not be the case with original equipment but it has been known for an owner to fit a replacement battery which has too small an ampere-hour capacity for the work it has to do. Check with the handbook to see if the Ah capacity is correct.

## Total electrical failure

- **Fuse blown:** Check the main fuse; if it has blown then the fault must be traced before a new fuse is fitted. It is rare for a fuse to fail without good cause so the first move is to take out the blown fuse and put a buzzer or a bulb across the fuse holder terminals and follow the advice given in Section 4, Tracing a wiring short-circuit.

- **Faulty battery:** If a battery has developed a short circuit in one of the cells or has an internal break at the positive or negative terminal then it must be replaced. See Chapter 13 for detailed information on batteries.

- **Earth (ground) failure:** A problem can sometimes occur if the earth connection from the negative lead from the battery to the frame is poor. Take the connection bolt apart and clean the cable tag connector and the frame connection point and reassemble. Coat the reassembled joint with petroleum jelly.

- **Ignition switch failure:** Modern switches are complex and the ignition switch is continually used. It is inevitable that mechanical failures will occur and tracing the trouble is described in Section 4. Repairs cannot be made to switches except in rare circumstances and replacement is needed.

## Circuit failure

- **Wiring failure:** Most open circuit cable failures are due to the end connections being loose or corroded. Check in-line connectors carefully since they are sometimes subjected to flexing. In all cases when connectors are taken apart look for corrosion in pins and sockets. If the connectors are in order then look for a break in a cable or wire. See Section 4.

- **Switch failures:** All switches should be checked for continuity in each switch position. Refer to the circuit diagram and often the internal connections between the switch terminals are shown in a box diagram. Switch failure may be due to mechanical breakage, corrosion or ingress of water. See the Section above on continuity checking.

## Bulbs blowing repeatedly

- **Vibration failure:** This is often a design fault related to the natural vibration characteristics of the engine and frame. It is difficult to resolve. In such cases it may help to modify the lamp mounting to reduce vibration and unfortunately each individual case is different. Trial and error is the only way.

- **Intermittent earth (ground):** Repeated failure of one bulb can be due to a poor earth somewhere in the lamp circuit. Use earth checking techniques in Section 4.

- **Reduced voltage:** Quartz halogen bulbs need to be supplied with the rated voltage in order to maintain the internal temperature for proper working (see Chapter 14). Overloading the electrical system with additional equipment will reduce the working voltage as will poor connections to the quartz lamp(s). Reminder: do not touch the quartz glass with the fingers and if you do, then clean the quartz glass with a spirit such as methylated spirit and let it dry.

## 11 Starter motors

**Note:** *For further information on starters and associated equipment see Chapter 15.*

### Starter motor turns slowly

- Low specific gravity in battery (or dead battery).
- Poorly connected battery.
- Poorly connected starter motor cable.
- Faulty starter motor.
- Poorly connected battery earth (ground) connection.

### Starter relay clicks but engine does not turn over

- Crankshaft does not turn due to engine problems.
- Excessive reduction gear friction.
- Faulty starter pinion engagement.

### Starter motor turns but engine does not turn

Starter motor is running backwards because:
- (a) Brushes are assembled improperly.
- (b) Case assembled improperly.
- (c) Terminals connected wrongly.
- Faulty starter clutch.
- Damaged or faulty starter pinion.
- Damaged idler gear or reduction gear.
- Broken starter motor drive chain.
- Faulty starter clutch.

### Starter motor will not turn

- Look for a blown main or sub fuse before proceeding.
- Check that the side stand is positioned and/or transmission is placed for engine starting on models which use the side stand ignition cut off switch.

### Fault tracing method

- Trace starter motor faults in a logical manner as shown in illustration 11.1 (overleaf).

## 12 Alternators

1 The Chapter on Alternators contains some information on fault finding/general testing and reference will be made back to avoid repetition.

### Flywheel and single-phase alternators

2 See Chapter 12, part A or B respectively, for fault finding and testing.

**18**

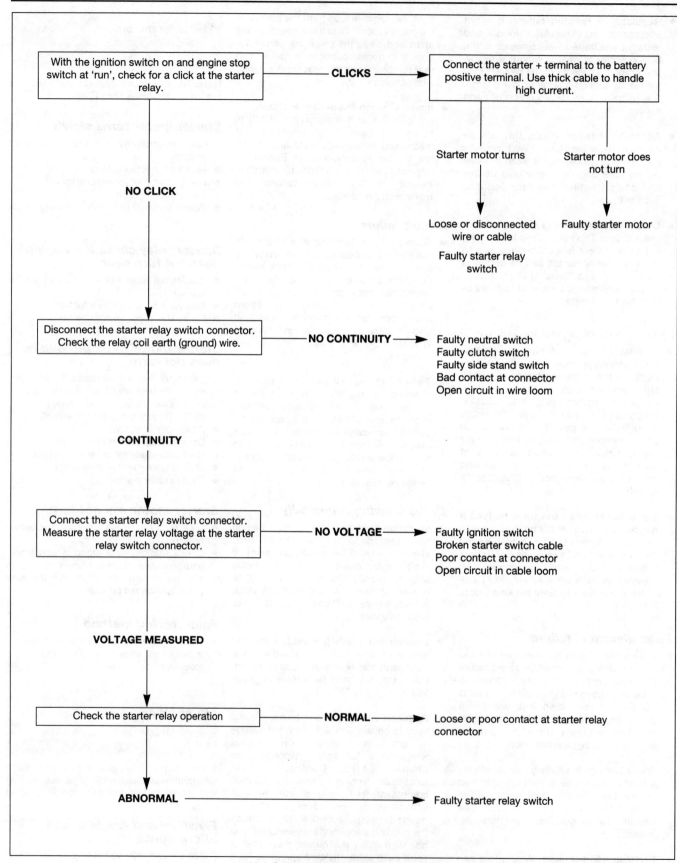

**11.1 Starter system fault finding chart**

## Three-phase alternators

**3** Common problems with three-phase alternators are shown in illustration 12.3. Refer also to Part C of Chapter 12 for testing details.

### 13 DC generators/dynamos

**1** Refer to Chapter 11 for information on testing and overhaul of dynamos and regulators.

### 14 Fuel injection

**1** Fuel injection systems are not designed for home workshop servicing and problems should be referred to the dealer who will have the specialised equipment for the task. Professional technicians will attend seminars on injection equipment as part of their training.

**2** The only work that can be carried out by the owner is to look for loose connections or to check the ohmic resistance of the injector windings if it is suspected that an injector is not working.

### 15 Engine management

**1** Peripherals such as sensors and ignition coils may be tested but the electronic control units (ECU) require specialist attention.

**2** There is normally no way of rectifying a problem with an ECU other than replacement. Fault finding on an ECU is often carried out with the aid of fault code readers which are plugged into the system and are the subject of specialised dealer training.

### 16 Horn, lamps and switches

#### Horn

**1 Horn does not sound:** Check horn button for continuity when pressed. If normal, disconnect the supply wire from the horn and check for voltage with the ignition switch on and the horn button pressed. If the voltage is reaching the horn, check the continuity of the earth (ground) wire to the frame. Look for

| Fault | Cause | Remedy |
|---|---|---|
| Flat battery | Often the first indication of an alternator fault. | Check battery. If OK check output of alternator Check diodes for leakage. |
| Alternator noise | Brushes squealing. Worn bearings. | Replace brushes and clean slip rings. Replace or exchange alternator. |
| Charge warning light* glows at idle speed | Poor contact in wiring. Faulty regulator. Worn brushes. Rectifier diode faulty. Rotor or stator shorting. | Check wiring connections. Check and replace. Replace. Replace. Check and replace. |
| Battery overcharging | Bad contact between regulator and alternator. Faulty regulator. | Check wiring. Check and replace. |
| Charge warning light* stays on | Faulty regulator. Wiring contact poor. Worn brushes. Faulty rotor winding. Poor rotor supply circuit contact. Faulty diodes. | Check and replace. Check wiring. Replace. Check and replace. Check wiring. Replace. |
| No warning light* with ignition on | Faulty bulb. Poor warning light connections. | Replace. Check wiring. |
| Complete electrical failure | Bad contact at battery terminals. Blown fuse. | Check and clean. Trace fault and replace fuse. |
| Dim lights and horn does not work or just squeaks | Flat battery. | Check alternator output. Test battery. Check rectifier diodes for leakage. |
| Bulbs blow frequently | Vibration. Poor contact. | Check that bulb holders are secure. Check bulb contacts and earthing. |

**Note:** * Charge warning lamps are not fitted to all three-phase charging circuits. Where they are in use (for example BMW) they give a useful indication of trouble.

**12.3 Three-phase alternator fault finding chart**

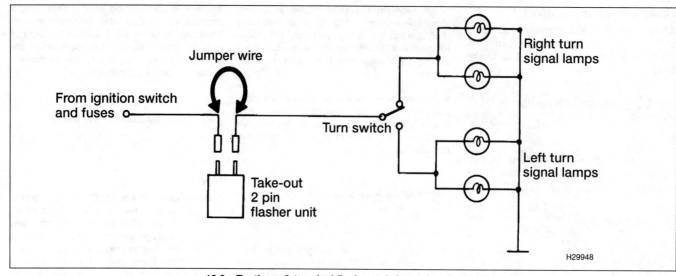

**16.2a Testing a 2-terminal flasher unit (turn signal relay)**

corrosion. If OK the horn is faulty. Older types can be adjusted but modern units cannot and must be replaced.

### Turn signal lamps

**2 Lights do not flash or flashing rate is high:** If the flashing rate is higher than normal this indicates a blown bulb. If there is no flashing check:

(a) Burned out bulbs?
(b) Fuses OK?
(c) Ignition switch and turn signal switches in order?

If normal, check a *two terminal* flasher unit (sometimes called a turn signal relay) by

disconnecting the plug from it. Bridge the plug terminals with a jumper wire. Switch on ignition and operate the turn switch. If the indicator lights come on the flasher unit is faulty or the connections are corroded (see illustration 16.2a). If the indicator lights do not illuminate there is a break in the supply voltage. Check cable for break.

If the flasher unit has three terminals, take off the plug and bridge the socket terminals that go to the supply and to the lamps (see illustration 16.2b). Switch on the ignition and operate the turn switch. If the lights come on then check the continuity of the third wire to earth. If there is continuity then the flasher unit

is faulty. If the lights do not come on there is a break in the wiring. This can be traced using the method given earlier in this Section.

### Neutral switch

**3** With the ignition switch on and the transmission in neutral, the neutral switch should turn the neutral light on. The neutral switch detects the gear position by the position of the shift drum and sends a signal to the indicator light. There are usually two possible faults:

● **Neutral light does not go off when in gear:** Disconnect the supply wire on the neutral switch. Turn the ignition on. If the

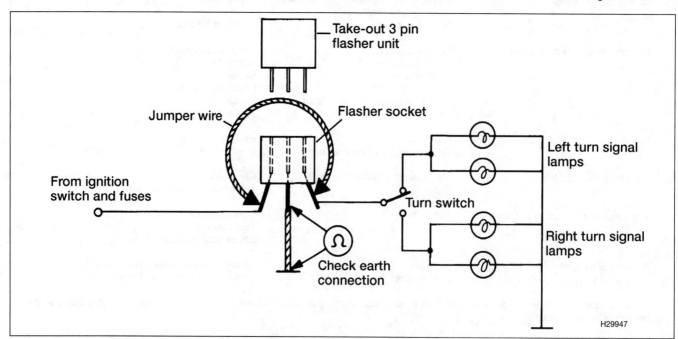

**16.2b Testing a 3-terminal flasher unit (turn signal relay)**

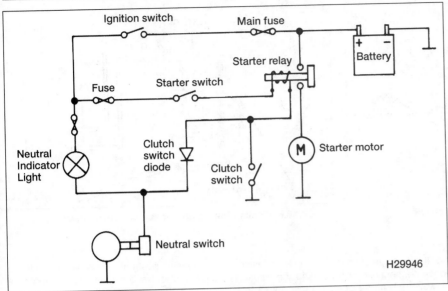

16.4a  Clutch switch circuit

light does not illuminate then there is a fault in the neutral switch. If the light does come on, there must be a short circuit to earth somewhere between the indicator light and the neutral switch.

- **Neutral light does not come on when in neutral:** Disconnect the supply wire at the neutral switch. Turn the ignition on and check if the battery voltage is reaching the wire. If voltage is there, then the neutral switch is faulty. If there is no voltage present then one of the following is the cause of the trouble:
  (a) Break in the wire between the indicator light and the neutral switch.
  (b) Blown bulb.
  (c) Sub fuse blown.
  (d) Bad connection at the fuse holder.

## Clutch switch

4 The clutch switch inhibits the starter motor operation when the transmission is in gear

(that is, not in neutral). For correct operation the starter should not be capable of operating with the clutch lever released, but should be operable with the clutch lever squeezed, if in gear (see illustration 16.4). To check the circuit and components:

- Disconnect the wire from the clutch switch and check for continuity between the switch terminals while pulling in the clutch lever (see illustration 16.4b). The resistance should be very low. If it is high or intermittent then there is a fault in the clutch switch. When the lever is released the resistance between the switch terminals should be very high (Infinite on the ohms scale).

- If the clutch switch is in order look for a shorted wire between the starter relay switch and the clutch switch. Also check the operation of the neutral switch as in the paragraph above.

- Check the clutch switch diode. The diode prevents reverse current flow from the neutral indicator to the clutch switch. The diode is ideally of zero resistance in one direction and very high resistance in the other depending on the polarity of the applied voltage. In practice there will be a small forward resistance and a measurable but very high resistance in the reverse direction. Think of it as a simple wire in the direction of the arrow but a break in the opposite direction. With a faulty diode, the neutral light may come on when the clutch is disengaged. If there are bad connections at the diode terminals then the starter motor will not work when the gearbox is in neutral. The diode may be checked by an ohmmeter or by the diode test position on a digital multimeter (see illustration 16.4c).

### Oil pressure switch

5 If the oil pressure warning light does not come on when the ignition switch is on with the engine not running, then follow this procedure to trace the fault:

(a) Disconnect the oil pressure switch wire from the switch by removing the tag or terminal screw.
(b) Turn the ignition on.
(c) Earth (ground) the oil pressure switch wire to the engine; the oil pressure warning light should come on.
(d) **If the light does not come on,** check the wiring for loose connections, look for a blown fuse or an open circuit.
(e) Check also for a burnt out bulb in the warning light fitting.
(f) **If the light does come on,** then replace the oil pressure switch.
(g) When replacing the pressure switch use a trace of sealing agent to the new switch thread.

6 If the problem is that the oil pressure warning light stays on while the engine is running, proceed as follows:

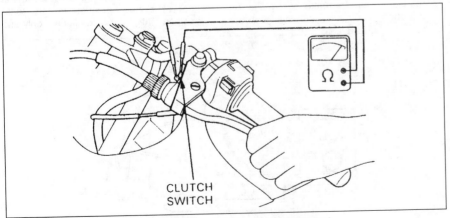

16.4b  Check the clutch switch for contact

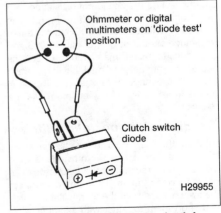

16.4c  Clutch switch diode: check for forward and reverse resistance

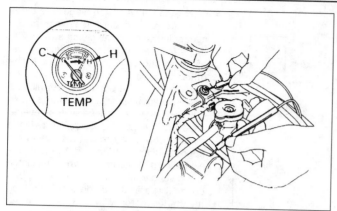

**16.7 Coolant temperature gauge check**

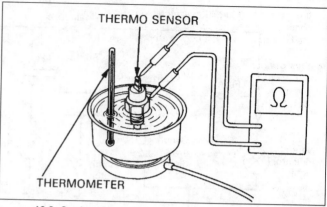

**16.8 Coolant temperature gauge thermosensor test**

(a) *The first thing to do is to check the oil level.*

(b) *Next disconnect the oil pressure switch wire from the unit and turn the ignition on.*

(c) *If the indicator lights then there must be a short-circuit to earth between the warning light and the pressure switch.*

(d) *If the light does not come on then there must be fault in the oil pressure switch or low oil pressure.*

## Coolant temperature gauge

**7 Gauge does not work:** Find the thermosensor and disconnect the sensor wire. With the ignition on, short the wire to earth (ground) (see illustration 16.7). The gauge pointer should go over to full scale deflection (Hot). Do not leave the short on for long as the gauge may become damaged. If it does not move, check the fuse in the circuit and the wiring for loose or corroded connections. If all is in order here then the gauge is faulty and must be replaced.

**8 Temperature thermosensor:** If the gauge and the circuit are in order then the temperature sensor must be faulty. To test it drain the coolant and remove the sensor. It may be tested by heating it up in an oil bath and measuring the change of resistance as it heats up (see illustration 16.8). Typically in one case (Honda CBR1000F) the sensor resistance should be 104 ohms at 60°C and should fall to 16.1 ohms at 120°C. Check the figures for your actual model, but in general if there is no change of resistance with rise in temperature then the sensor must be replaced.

## Fan motor thermostatic switch

**9** Where there is a cooling fan, the fan motor is switched on by a thermostatic switch located in the radiator. If the fan motor does not start when the engine is hot, disconnect the switch wires from the thermostatic switch and short them together with a jumper wire. Switch on the ignition. The motor fan should start (keep fingers clear).

**10** If it does not start, look for a blown fuse or loose connections or a break in the wires. If however the motor does run this points to a problem with the thermostatic switch.

**11** To test the thermostatic switch, suspend it in a pan of coolant mixture up to the thread. There should be no continuity at room temperature; gradually raise the temperature and connect an ohmmeter or a continuity tester across the terminals. The switch should close at a certain higher temperature. As a guide, for the CBR1000F, the thermostatic switch closing temperature should be 98 to 102°C. If it does not close (that is, zero resistance on the ohmmeter) then the switch is faulty and must be replaced.

## Brake light switches

**12** If the brake light does not come on with either front or rear brake applied, this points to a blown bulb and/or a fuse.

● **Front brake**. To check the operation of the front brake light switch, disconnect the connector and check for continuity between the switch terminals with an ohmmeter or a continuity tester. There should be low resistance (that is, good continuity) with the brake lever pulled on and open circuit when the lever is in the released position. There is normally no adjustment and a faulty switch must be replaced.

● **Rear brake**. The same procedure applies. Disconnect the rear brake light connector and check for continuity between the switch terminals with the rear brake on and off. There should be good continuity with the brake applied and zero continuity with the brake off. Check any adjustments and replace the switch if necessary.

## Fuel gauge and meter

**13** If the fuel gauge does not work at all, or reads incorrectly, remove the float and sensor from the fuel tank and test it as described below:

● **Sensor:** Connect an ohmmeter to the fuel sensor terminals (see illustration 16.13). Check the variation in resistance as the float arm is moved from top to bottom position. The change should be smooth without sudden jumps in the resistance as the arm is moved. Typically using our model of the Honda CBR1000F, the figures should be 4 to 10Ω with the float at the top (full tank) position, and 90 to 100Ω with the float at bottom position (empty tank) position. These are guide figures only and

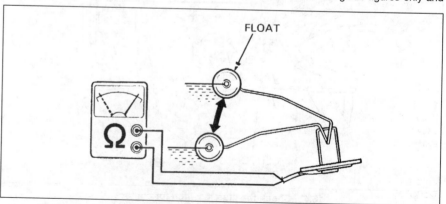

**16.13 Checking fuel level sensor resistance in the full and empty positions**

the main thing is to have a significant change from the full to empty position of the float arm and that it occurs smoothly.

- **Fuel gauge:** If the sensor is in order, put the connector back on. With the ignition on, move the arm from the full to empty position to check the fuel gauge pointer movement. If it does not move at all or reads incorrectly then check wiring for an open circuit or corroded or loose connectors. If all is in order replace the fuel gauge.

### Low-fuel warning light

**14** Here a thermistor is run in series with the indicator light (see illustration 16.14a). When the thermistor is immersed in the fuel, it is cooled and the resistance is high so the indicator does not light. When the fuel is low, the thermistor is no longer immersed and its resistance is low because it runs at a higher temperature. The bulb will then have sufficient current through it to light up. There are two possible fault conditions:

- Low fuel light does not go off. First check for the presence of voltage at the connector terminals (see illustration 16.14b). If the battery voltage is there then the thermistor is faulty or there are bad connections at the thermistor connector. If there is no battery voltage present then look for a shorted wire between the indicator light and the sensor.

- **Low fuel light does not come on.** Check for voltage at the connector terminals after it has been removed from the thermistor. If there is no battery voltage then check the voltage at the battery side of the indicator light (see illustration 16.14c). If there is battery voltage present then the fault is a blown bulb or a wire broken between the light and the thermistor. If there is no voltage present at the battery side of the light then it could be:

(a) a blown sub fuse.
(b) a faulty ignition switch, or
(c) a bad connection in the fuseholder.

### 17 Fuel pumps

### In-tank fuel pumps

**1** This type of submerged pump is located inside the tank and an example has been shown in Chapter 8. There the BMW Motronic system uses a high pressure roller cell pump with an output pressure of 2.5 bar (36 lbf/in²). Honda also utilise a high pressure tank pump on certain models and others with a lower working pressure for feeding carburettors. All these have a fuel pump relay and some models have additional control by a bank

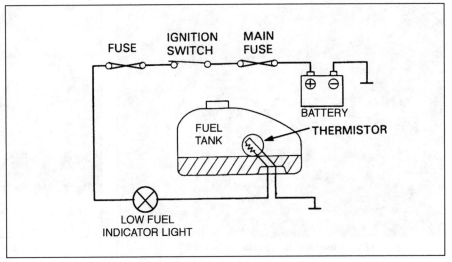

16.14a Low fuel indicator circuit

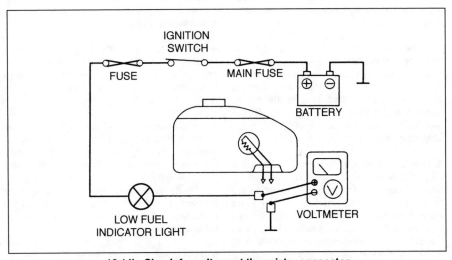

16.14b Check for voltage at thermistor connector

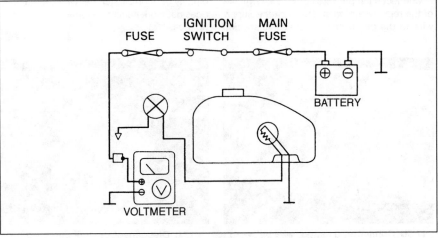

16.14c Check for voltage to indicator lamp

**18**

17.2 In-tank fuel pump (Honda ST1100)

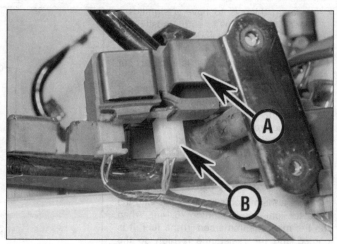

17.3a Fuel cut-off relay (A) and its wiring connector (B)

angle sensor (sometimes known as a lean angle sensor) for switching off the fuel supply in emergency.

**2** If the fuel pump is to be checked, the following test procedure will cover most types. Using the Honda Pan European ST1100 (see illustration 17.2) as a example, note that the fuel pump is controlled through the cut-off relay so that it runs whenever the ignition is switched on and the ignition is operative (ie, only when the engine is turning over).

**3** First switch on the ignition and start the engine if possible. It should be possible to hear the pump humming (it may be necessary to remove the seat to hear it). If there is no noise from the pump and the engine will not run, check the circuit fuse also the relay and pump for loose or corroded connections. If all these are in order, switch off the ignition and unplug the fuel pump relay (see illustration 17.3a).

Connect a jumper wire across the terminals of the relay wiring connector from the supply wire to the pump feed wire (see illustration 17.3b). Switch on the ignition; the pump should operate. If it does work then the relay or the wiring is faulty.

**4** Test the wiring by checking for full battery voltage at the relay supply terminal with the ignition switched on. If there is no voltage then there must be a wiring fault between the relay and the fuse.

**5** Disconnect the wiring connectors from the relay, fuel pump and the ignition control module. Check the harness continuity from the relay to the ignition control module and from the relay to the pump. Finally check the continuity from the (green) wire at the relay connector and earth. Continuity should be indicated in all the tests. Rectify any breaks or other faults found.

**6** If the pump still does not work then turn to the pump itself. Disconnect the wiring connectors at the tank (see illustration 17.6) and connect a 12 volt battery to the pump directly through two jumper wires. If the pump does not work it must be replaced (repairs are not possible).

**7** If the pump works and all the relevant wiring and connectors are good, then the relay is at fault. The only solution is to substitute a good relay. There is one last possibility and that is that the ignition control module is faulty.

**8** If the pump works but it is suspected of not giving enough output of fuel then it can be proved by running the pump with a jumper wire across the relay. Disconnect the fuel outlet hose from the tank side of the fuel filter and run fuel into a measuring beaker for 5 seconds then multiply the amount by 12 to give the pump output in cc per minute (see illustration 17.8).

In the case of the ST1100 it should be 640 cc per minute minimum, for a BMW R850/1100 it should be 1830 cc per minute. Bear in mind that the latter case refers to a fuel injection system where surplus fuel is returned to the tank.

### External fuel pumps

**9** The electromagnetic pump shown in illustration 17.9 produces a low pressure fuel input to carburettors.

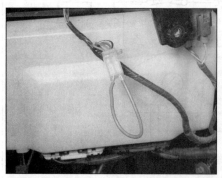

17.3b Connector a jumper wire between the specified terminals of the relay wiring connector

17.6 Disconnect the fuel pump wiring connectors

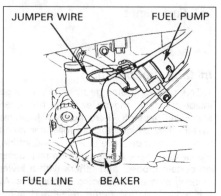

17.8 Fuel pump flow rate (output) test

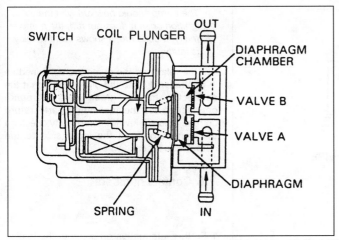

**17.9 Electromagnetic fuel pump**

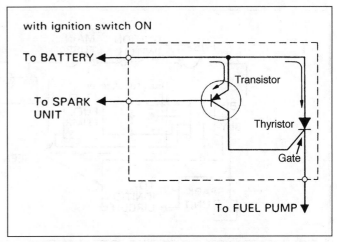

**17.13a Electronic fuel cut-off relay – ignition on but engine stopped**

When the engine turns over, the pump is switched on by the fuel cut-off relay. Current flows through the coil and the magnetic action on the plunger is to pull it towards the coil centre. The plunger is attached to a diaphragm which creates a vacuum as it moves to the left in the diagram, opening the valve A and sucking fuel into the diaphragm chamber.

The motion of the plunger also trips the switch contacts and the coil current is cut off. The magnetic field disappears and the spring returns the diaphragm back to the right. This pushes the fuel out through valve B and on to the carburettor.

Some versions of this pump have a built-in fuel cut-off relay and others have a relay which is separate from the pump.

**10** Generally trouble-free, this pump can, however, suffer from contacts sticking together. There are no spares available and the makers always state that a faulty pump

must be replaced. However it is sometimes possible after removing the end cover to separate the contacts and dress them clean with fine glasspaper (never emery paper) and to apply a touch of contact cleaner obtainable from electronics stores. Some readers may see the general similarity to the SU fuel pump used for many years on British cars.

### Fuel cut-off relay

**11** These come in two types, the electromagnetic relay and the electronic relay.

**12** Electromagnetic relays operate by the magnetic effect of a coil which serves to pull in a metal armature and so closing or opening contacts.

Testing consists of checking the coil for continuity and seeing that the contacts operate and do not have undue roughness or burning. Generally if an electromagnetic relay is giving trouble it is better to replace it for there is no technical information available.

**13** The electronic relay utilises the current switching capability of the thyristor (see Chapter 2). In illustration 17.13a, with the ignition on but the engine not yet running, there is no current flow through the thyristor because its gate is not supplied with current from the transistor. The transistor will operate only when receiving pulses from the spark unit (ECU or ignition control unit etc). Some variants of this type do have a timer function which sends a pump operating current through for a few seconds to fill the carburettor float chambers.

When the engine starts, pulses are sent from the spark unit to the ignition coil(s) and to the base of the relay transistor (illustration 17.13b). This now permits current flow from the emitter to the collector and onto the gate terminal of the thyristor, which switches on the pump current.

### Fault finding

**14** Using illustration 17.14a we see the fuel cut-off relay as a separate item from the pump

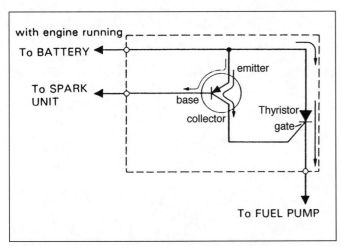

**17.13b Relay passes current to pump when ignition pulses are received**

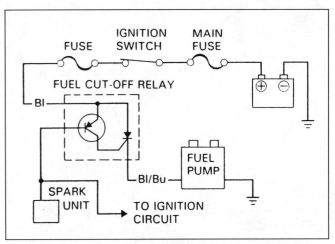

**17.14a Fuel cut-off relay circuit (separate relay and pump)**

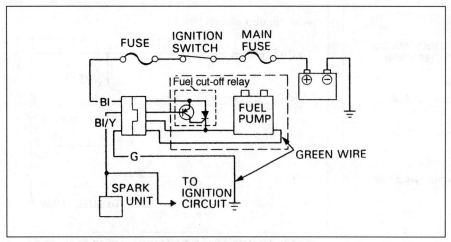

**17.14b  Combined pump and cut-off relay**

and a wire colour coding which will assist explanation. Note it may not correspond to colours in practice; these are given as an example only. If the pump does not work, carry out testing as follows:

(a) *Turn the ignition on. Check for battery voltage at the black wire (Bl) at the relay. If there is no voltage, check the fuse, look for a break in the black feed wire, check the ignition switch and look for a bad connection at the fuse holder connector.*

(b) *If battery voltage is present, turn the ignition off, then check continuity from black/blue (Bl/Bu) wire from the relay connector to the pump and check that there is a good earth connection (ground).*

(c) *Short-circuit the relay by connecting a jumper wire from the black wire at the relay connector to the black/blue wire.*

*The pump should now run with the ignition on. If it does not run, the pump is faulty: if does run, it shows that the relay is faulty.*

If the relay and the pump are combined as in illustration 17.14b the difference is that the connector has a green earth (ground) connection for the fuel pump earth return current. This will involve a continuity check on the connector from the input side to the output side for each wire.

## 18  Contact numbers

**1** Further information on some of the testing products described in this Chapter can be obtained from the following UK suppliers:

Draper Clamp meter and multimeters (Shadowfax Engineering), telephone: 01604 890995.

Gunson test equipment and meters, telephone: 0181 984 8855.

Clarke International meters, telephone: 01992 565 300.

IgnitionMate (Shadowfax Engineering), telephone: 01604 890995.

## About the MOT Test

In the UK, all vehicles more that three years old are subject to an annual test to ensure that they meet minimum safety requirements. A current test certificate must be issued before a machine can be used on public roads, and is required before a road fund licence can be issued. Riding without a current test certificate will also invalidate your insurance. The information on this page deals with the electrical aspect of the test only, the full MOT test also covers the brakes, suspension, steering, wheels, tyres, final drive and exhaust systems.

Note that there are certain exceptions which apply to machines under 50 cc, those without a lighting system and Classic bikes – if in doubt about any of the requirements listed, seek confirmation from an MOT testing station prior to submitting the motorcycle for the test.

It has only been possible to summarise the test requirements here, based on the regulations in force at the time of printing. More information about the MOT test can be obtained from the Stationary Office publications, *The MOT Inspection Manual for Motorcycle Testing*, and their book, *How Safe is your Motorcycle*.

# Electrical System

## Lights, turn signals, horn and reflector

✔ With the ignition on, check the operation of the following electrical components. **Note:** *The electrical components on certain small-capacity machines are powered by the generator, requiring that the engine is run for this check.*

a) Headlight and tail light. Check that both illuminate in the low and high beam switch positions.
b) Position lights. Check that the front position (or sidelight) and tail light illuminate in this switch position.
c) Turn signals. Check that all flash at the correct rate, and that the warning light(s) function correctly. Check that the turn signal switch works correctly.

**Headlight beam height checking equipment**

d) Hazard warning system (where fitted). Check that all four turn signals flash in this switch position.
e) Brake stop light. Check that the light comes on when the front and rear brakes are independently applied. Models first used on or after 1st April 1986 must have a brake light switch on each brake.
f) Horn. Check that the sound is continuous and of reasonable volume.

✔ Check that there is a red reflector on the rear of the machine, either mounted separately or as part of the tail light lens.
✔ Check the condition of the headlight, tail light and turn signal lenses.

## Headlight beam height

✔ The MOT tester will perform a headlight beam height check using specialised beam setting equipment **(see illustration 1)**. Details of this beam setting equipment will be found in the Stationary Office publication, *The MOT Inspection Manual for Motorcycle Testing*. If you suspect that the headlight is incorrectly set or may have been maladjusted in the past, yet specialised beam setting equipment is not available, you can perform a rough test as follows.
✔ Position the bike in a straight line facing a brick wall. The bike must be off its stand, upright and with a rider seated. Measure the height from the ground to the centre of the headlight and mark a horizontal line on the wall at this height. Position the motorcycle 3.8 metres from the wall and draw a vertical line up the wall central to the centreline of the motorcycle. Switch to dipped beam and check that the beam pattern falls slightly lower than the horizontal line and to the left of the vertical line **(see illustration 2)**.

**2**

3·8 m

90°

90°

H29003

**Home workshop beam alignment check**

# A

**ABS (Antilock braking system)** A system, usually electronically controlled, which senses incipient wheel lockup during braking and relieves hydraulic brake pressure at the wheel about to skid.

**AF** Audio frequency. That range of sound frequencies audible to the human ear.

**Aftermarket** Components suitable for the motorcycle but not on the machine when supplied.

**Air filter** Paper or foam element for trapping particles in the air intake.

**Alphanumerics** The use of seven segment displays to show numbers and letters.

**Alternating current (ac)** Electric current which flows *alternately* in one direction and then the other in an electrical circuit.

**Alternator** A mechanically driven generator for the production of alternating current.

**Ammeter** An instrument for measuring current flow (*Never* say ampmeter!)

**Amperage** A deprecated term. Use instead of *current* or *current rating*.

**Ampere-hour (Ah)** A measure of the capacity of a battery. For example, a 20 Ah battery should give an output of 2 amperes for 10 hours, or 5 amperes for 4 hours and so on. The hyphen means *multiply* so the capacity is always the amperes *multiplied* by the time in hours.

**Ampere (A)** Unit of electrical current. It is a rate of charge flow of one coulomb per second.

**Amplifier** A device that increases the voltage, current or power of an electrical signal.

**Analogue meter** An instrument that reads with a display using a pointer on a scale.

**Analogue to digital converter** A device that changes an analogue signal into a digital signal.

**Anode** The electrode of a device (such as a diode) to which electrons flow.

**Armature** In the dc dynamo and starter motor, the armature is the rotating member with current flow through the brushes and commutator. A relay armature is the moving arm operating switching contacts.

# B

**ATDC** After Top Dead Centre. See *BTDC*.

**Atom** Smallest particle of a chemical element that can exist alone or in combination with other atoms.

**ATU** Automatic timing unit. Attached to the contact breaker assembly, it provides ignition advance with increase of speed by centrifugal weight action.

**Backlash** The amount of movement between meshed components when one component is held still. Usually applies to gear teeth.

**Base** One of three electrodes of a bipolar transistor.

**BHP** Brake horse power. A measurement of output power (Now obsolete). The unit used for both mechanical and electrical power is now the kilowatt (kW). Both the PS and the horsepower (hp) are non-preferred units.

**Bi-metal strip** A flat strip made of two different metallic strips welded or riveted together. Due to the different rates of expansion with temperature, the composite strip will bend with change of temperature.

**Bias** The current or voltage which is applied to part of a circuit to make it function correctly.

**Bit (binary digit)** Either of the two numbers 0 and 1 which are the basic units of data in computers.

**BTDC** Before Top Dead Centre in terms of piston position. Ignition timing is often expressed in terms of degrees or millimetres BTDC.

# C

**Candela (cd)** The unit of luminous intensity.

**Candle power (cp)** Bulb rating sometimes used in US.

**Capacitor** A component which will store electric charge and give it out again when required.

**Carburettor** Device for mixing fuel and air in the correct proportions and for controlling engine speed.

**Catalytic converter** A device in the exhaust system of some motorcycles (and cars) which converts certain exhaust gas pollutants into less harmful substances.

**Cathode** The electrode of a device such as a diode, for example, from which electrons flow.

**CDI** Capacitor discharge ignition.

**Collector** One of the three electrodes of a bipolar transistor.

**Compression** Relating to engines, reduction in volume and increase in pressure and temperature of a gas caused by squeezing it into a smaller volume by the piston.

**Condenser** A term no longer used. Now called a capacitor.

**Contact breaker** An engine-driven switch which interrupts the primary current in an ignition coil.

**Continuity** A continuous path of low or zero resistance to the flow of electricity.

**Coulomb** Unit of electrical charge.

**Crankshaft** The main rotating member or shaft in an engine to which the connecting rods are attached.

**Crimping** The action of compressing a connector onto a wire or cable so as to make a good electrical joint.

**Current** The flow rate of electricity measured in amperes.

# D

**Darlington pair** A package containing two transistors often used as a power driver for ignition coils etc.

**Degree disc** Calibrated disc for measuring piston position in degrees relative to a fixed point.

**Detonation** Damaging explosion of fuel/air mixture in a cylinder instead of controlled burning.

**Digital meter** An instrument that reads out in numbers.

**Diode** An electrical component which permits current flow through it in one direction only.

**Direct current (dc)** An electric current which flows on average in one direction but not necessarily at a constant level.

**Dwell** The period over which the primary current of an ignition coil is switched on.

# E

**Earth return** The return path for a current using the motorcycle frame. (In the US it is known as *ground return*.)

**ECU** Electronic control unit for operation of an ignition system or ABS, as examples.

**EGO** Exhaust gas oxygen sensor. See *Lambda sensor.*

**Electrolytic capacitor** A capacitor which is polarised, that is, it must be connected correctly to positive and negative supply leads.

**Electromagnet** A block of soft iron, usually laminated, which produces a magnetic field when a surrounding coil carries current. The magnetic field virtually disappears when the current is switched off.

**Electron** Negatively charged particle forming part of the atom.

**EMF** Electromotive Force. The force driving current in a circuit, expressed in volts, usually produced by a generator, battery or sensor.

**Emitter** One of the three electrodes of a bipolar transistor.

**Engine management system** A system in which the ignition and fuelling are controlled by a digital computer

# F

**Farad** The unit of capacitance. Too large for engineering use; the millionth part, the microfarad μF, is used or the picofarad pF, which is one millionth part of a microfarad.

**Field** Can be a magnetic or an electric field in which magnetic or electric effects take place. Alternatively it can refer to the windings of a motor or generator which produce the main magnetic field in the machine.

**Firing order** The order in which the engine cylinders have a power stroke, starting with number one cylinder.

**Frequency** The number of times per second that a wave goes through a complete cycle expressed as Hertz (Hz), eg 50 cycles per second is 50 Hertz or 50Hz.

**ft-lbf** The Imperial unit of energy or work done (550 ft-lbf per second equals one horsepower).

**Fuel injection** A method of fuelling an engine by injecting fuel into intake air in the correct proportion.

**Fuse** A sacrificial protector against accidental circuit overload. It consists of a short strip of metal designed to melt at a certain current level known as the fusing current. Fuses are mounted in cartridges which clip into the sockets in a fuse box.

# H

**Hall sensor** A pulse generator which is derived from a silicon chip. A voltage pulse output is given when the chip is subjected to a changing magnetic field.

**Hertz (Hz)** The number of complete cycles per second of an alternating waveform.

**HT (high tension)** Meaning high voltage, this usually refers to the secondary circuit of the ignition coil(s), the spark plugs and the cables carrying the spark current to the plugs.

**Hydrometer** A float meter for measuring the specific gravity of battery acid.

# I

**Ignition coil** A transformer which provides the HT spark voltage to the spark plugs.

**Inductance** The property of a current-carrying coil which opposes any current change. The unit is the henry (plural, henrys).

**Integrated circuit (IC)** A circuit in which all components such as resistors, capacitors and transistors are formed on a single silicon chip.

# J

**Joule** The unit of energy (or work). One joule per second is a power of one watt.

# K

**kg (kilogramme)** The SI unit of mass. The force of attraction (weight) on a mass of one kg at the surface of the earth is 9.81 Newtons, but commercially we buy goods by the kg, the Newton being used mainly in engineering and science.

# L

**Lambda (λ) sensor** A sensor fitted in the exhaust system to measure the exhaust gas oxygen content in the form of an electrical signal. The signal is fed back to the ECU to make any necessary correction.

**lbf-ft** The Imperial unit of torque.

**lbf. (pounds force)** This is the gravitational force on a one pound mass at the earth's surface, otherwise known as *weight*. While the *mass* of one pound (lb) would be the same at the surface of the moon for instance, the *weight* in lbf. would be only one seventh of that on earth.

**LCD** Liquid crystal display.

**LED** Light emitting diode.

**Lumen (lm)** The unit of luminous flux (or light). The efficiency of a bulb is expressed as lumens per watt.

# M

**Magnetic field** A volume of space near a magnet or electromagnet in which magnetic effects are experienced.

**Magneto** An engine-driven generator providing the timed spark plug voltage.

**Meter** General term for an electrical instrument.

**Metre-Newton** The SI unit of energy or work done.

**MOSFET** Metal oxide silicon field effect transistor. An amplifying or switching semiconductor device.

# N

**Nm** Newton-metre (means Newtons x metres). The SI unit of torque.

# O

**Oblique stroke (/)** This reads as *per* and means *divide by*. For example m/sec reads metres per second. Not to be confused with a hyphen (-) which means *multiply*. Example: Newton-metres means Newtons *multiplied* by metres.

**Ohm's Law** In a constant resistance the current flow is proportional to the applied voltage. Usually written: Voltage (V) = Current (I) x Resistance (R), or V = IR

**Ohm (Ω)** Electrical unit of resistance to current flow.

**Operational amplifier (Op-Amp)** A very high gain amplifier which produces an output proportional to the difference between two input voltages.

# P

**Parallel connection** Electrical components connected so that all are subject to the same applied voltage. Often drawn as though geometrically parallel.

**Permanent magnet** A block of material (usually a special steel) which exhibits a magnetic field without external stimulation.

**Power** The rate of working or using energy. The unit is the watt. The kilowatt (kW) is 1000 watts and is now used for engine power output. One horsepower (hp) = 0.746 kW. The Continental unit is the PS = 0.736 kW.

**Proton** A constituent particle of an atom having a positive charge equal to that of the electron's negative charge. The proton has much higher mass than the electron.

# Q

**Quartz halogen bulb** A tungsten filament bulb with a halogen gas filling. Used for headlights because of the high efficiency in lumens per watt, long life and absence of blackening of the glass.

# R

**Rectifier** One or more diodes which convert alternating current into direct current.

**Regulator** A device for maintaining the charging voltage of an alternator or dynamo within a suitable range for battery charging.

**Relay** An electrical switch operated by an electromagnet which attracts an armature when the coil current is on, thus closing separate switch contacts.

# S

**Schmitt trigger** A snap-action electronic switch which turns on and off at two levels of input voltage. It is used to sharpen up slowly changing waveforms and to eliminate electrical noise from switches.

**SCR** see *Thyristor*.

**Sensor** A device which senses or measures a quantity such as pressure, rotational speed, exhaust oxygen, stress, strain in the form of an electrical signal.

**Series connection** Electrical components connected end-to-end in line.

**Silicon** Semiconductor material used for making electronic components such as transistors, diodes etc.

**Silicone** Semi-inorganic thermosetting plastic manufactured as fluids, greases, resins and rubbers

**Sine wave** A waveform plotted to a base of time or angle. The vertical height at any point on the base is the instantaneous value of the quantity being plotted.

**Solenoid** A form of electromagnet used for closing the heavy current switch contacts in a starter motor circuit.

**Starter motor** A dc motor for starting an internal combustion engine.

**Stoichiometric ratio** The ratio of air/fuel by weight in a petrol engine for complete burning of the fuel.
This figure is 14.7 and has a Lambda (λ) of 1.0 (see *Lambda sensor*).

**Sulphuric acid** The electrolyte used in lead acid batteries.

# T

**TCS** Traction control system which prevents wheel spin.

**TDC** Top dead centre.

**Tesla** The unit of magnetic flux density.

**Thermistor** A component made of a mixture of semiconductors. It has a marked change of resistance (usually negative) with a change in temperature. Used for temperature sensing.

**Thermocouple** A pair of wires of different materials joined to form a circuit. If the two junctions are at different temperatures an emf (voltage) will be generated. Measured by a meter, this gives a measure of the junction temperature difference. It is used as an electrical thermometer.

**Thyristor** A four layer pnpn device used for rapid switching. Also known as a silicon controlled rectifier.

**Timing light** A stroboscopic (flashing) lamp used for checking ignition timing with the engine running.

**Torque** The turning couple or moment of a force turning a shaft, screw, nut etc. Measured in Newton-metres (Nm) or in Imperial units poundsforce-feet (lbf-ft). *Not to be written the reverse way(ft-lbf ) since this is the unit of work or energy.*

**Turn signal relay** A 'flasher' unit. A switch which switches turn signal lamps on and off repetitively.

# V

**Volt (V)** Electrical unit of pressure.

**Voltage** The numerical value of electrical pressure expressed in volts.

**Voltmeter** An instrument or meter for measuring the voltage difference between two points of a circuit.

# W

**Watt (W)** Unit of mechanical or electrical power. It is the *rate* of using energy in joules per second. In mechanical terms it is the power exerted when a force of one Newton moves through a distance of one metre per second in the direction of the force. In electrical terms watts = volts x amperes, in a resistive circuit.

**Webers** Measurement of magnetic flux.

**Wiring harness or loom** The wires conveying power and signals on the motorcycle are taped together for convenience and protection. The taped bundle of wires is known as the loom or wiring harness.

# Z

**Zener diode** A special diode used as a voltage regulator.

# Haynes Motorcycle Manuals – The Complete List

| Title | Book No. |
|---|---|
| **BMW** | |
| BMW 2-valve Twins (70 - 96) | 0249 |
| BMW K100 & 75 2-valve Models (83 - 96) | 1373 |
| BMW R850 & R1100 4-valve Twins (93 - 97) | 3466 |
| **BSA** | |
| BSA Bantam (48 - 71) | 0117 |
| BSA Unit Singles (58 - 72) | 0127 |
| BSA Pre-unit Singles (54 - 61) | 0326 |
| BSA A7 & A10 Twins (47 - 62) | 0121 |
| BSA A50 & A65 Twins (62 - 73) | 0155 |
| **BULTACO** | |
| Bultaco Competition Bikes (72 - 75) | 0219 |
| **CZ** | |
| CZ 125 & 175 Singles (69 - 90) | ◇ 0185 |
| **DUCATI** | |
| **Ducati 600, 750 & 900 2-valve V-Twins (91 - 96)** | 3290 |
| **HARLEY-DAVIDSON** | |
| Harley-Davidson Sportsters (70 - 97) | 0702 |
| Harley-Davidson Big Twins (70 - 97) | 0703 |
| **HONDA** | |
| Honda SH50 City Express (84 - 89) | ◇ 1597 |
| Honda NB, ND, NP & NS50 Melody (81 - 85) | ◇ 0622 |
| Honda NE/NB50 Vision & SA50 Vision Met-in (85 - 95) | ◇ 1278 |
| Honda MB, MBX, MT & MTX50 (80 - 93) | 0731 |
| Honda C50, C70 & C90 (67 - 95) | 0324 |
| Honda ATC70, 90, 110, 185 & 200 (71 - 85) | 0565 |
| Honda CR80R & CR125R (86 - 97) | 2220 |
| Honda XR80R & XR100R (85 - 96) | 2218 |
| Honda XL/XR 80, 100, 125, 185 & 200 2-valve Models (78 - 87) | 0566 |
| Honda CB100N & CB125N (78 - 86) | ◇ 0569 |
| Honda H100 & H100S Singles (80 - 92) | ◇ 0734 |
| Honda CB/CD125T & CM125C Twins (77 - 88) | ◇ 0571 |
| Honda CG125 (76 - 94) | ◇ 0433 |
| Honda NS125 (86 - 93) | ◇ 3056 |
| Honda MBX/MTX125 & MTX200 (83 - 93) | ◇ 1132 |
| Honda CD/CM185 200T & CM250C 2-valve Twins (77 - 85) | 0572 |
| Honda XL/XR 250 & 500 (78 - 84) | 0567 |
| Honda XR250L, XR250R & XR400R (86 - 97) | 2219 |
| Honda CB250RS Singles (80 - 84) | ◇ 0732 |
| Honda CB250 & CB400N Super Dreams (78 - 84) | ◇ 0540 |
| Honda CR250R & CR500R (86 - 97) | 2222 |
| Honda Elsinore 250 (73 - 75) | 0217 |
| Honda TRX300 Shaft Drive ATVs (88 - 95) | 2125 |
| **Honda VFR400 & RVF400 V-Fours (89 - 98)** | 3496 |
| Honda CB400 & CB550 Fours (73 - 77) | 0262 |
| Honda CX/GL500 & 650 V-Twins (78 - 86) | 0442 |
| Honda CBX550 Four (82 - 86) | ◇ 0940 |
| Honda XL600R & XR600R (83 - 96) | 2183 |
| **Honda CBR600F1 & 1000F Fours (87 - 96)** | 1730 |
| **Honda CBR600F2 & F3 Fours (91 - 98)** | 2070 |
| Honda CB650 sohc Fours (78 - 84) | 0665 |
| **Honda NTV600 & 650 V-Twins (88 - 96)** | 3243 |
| Honda CB750 sohc Four (69 - 79) | 0131 |
| Honda V45/65 Sabre & Magna (82 - 88) | 0820 |
| **Honda VFR750 & 700 V-Fours (86 - 97)** | 2101 |
| Honda CB750 & CB900 dohc Fours (78 - 84) | 0535 |
| **Honda CBR900RR FireBlade (92 - 97)** | 2161 |
| **Honda ST1100 Pan European V-Fours (90 - 97)** | 3384 |
| Honda GL1000 Gold Wing (75 - 79) | 0309 |
| Honda GL1100 Gold Wing (79 - 81) | 0669 |

| Title | Book No. |
|---|---|
| Honda Gold Wing 1200 (USA) (84 - 87) | 2199 |
| Honda Gold Wing 1500 (USA) (88 - 98) | 2225 |
| **KAWASAKI** | |
| Kawasaki AE/AR 50 & 80 (81 - 95) | 1007 |
| Kawasaki KC, KE & KH100 (75 - 93) | 1371 |
| Kawasaki AR125 (82 - 94) | ◇ 1006 |
| Kawasaki KMX125 & 200 (86 - 96) | ◇ 3046 |
| Kawasaki 250, 350 & 400 Triples (72 - 79) | 0134 |
| Kawasaki 400 & 440 Twins (74 - 81) | 0281 |
| Kawasaki 400, 500 & 550 Fours (79 - 91) | 0910 |
| Kawasaki EN450 & 500 Twins (Ltd/Vulcan) (85 - 93) | 2053 |
| Kawasaki EX500 (GPZ500S) Twins (87 - 93) | 2052 |
| **Kawasaki ZX600 (Ninja ZX-6, ZZ-R600) Fours (90 - 97)** | 2146 |
| Kawasaki ZX600 (GPZ600R, GPX600R, Ninja 600R & RX) & ZX750 (GPX750R, Ninja 750R) Fours (85 - 97) | 1780 |
| Kawasaki 650 Four (76 - 78) | 0373 |
| Kawasaki 750 Air-cooled Fours (80 - 91) | 0574 |
| **Kawasaki ZR550 & 750 Zephyr Fours (90 - 97)** | 3382 |
| **Kawasaki ZX750 (Ninja ZX-7 & ZXR750) Fours (89 - 96)** | 2054 |
| Kawasaki 900 & 1000 Fours (73 - 77) | 0222 |
| **Kawasaki ZX900, 1000 & 1100 Liquid-cooled Fours (83 - 97)** | 1681 |
| **MOTO GUZZI** | |
| Moto Guzzi 750, 850 & 1000 V-Twins (74 - 78) | 0339 |

| Title | Book No. |
|---|---|
| **MZ** | |
| MZ TS125 (76 - 86) | ◇ 1270 |
| MZ ETZ Models (81 - 95) | ◇ 1680 |
| **NORTON** | |
| Norton 500, 600, 650 & 750 Twins (57 - 70) | 0187 |
| Norton Commando (68 - 77) | 0125 |
| **PIAGGIO** | |
| Piaggio (Vespa) Scooters (91 - 98) | 3492 |
| **SUZUKI** | |
| Suzuki FR50, 70 & 80 (74 - 87) | ◇ 0801 |
| Suzuki GT, ZR & TS50 (77 - 90) | ◇ 0799 |
| Suzuki TS50X (84 - 95) | ◇ 1599 |
| Suzuki 100, 125, 185 & 250 Air-cooled Trail bikes (79 - 89) | 0797 |
| Suzuki GP100 & 125 Singles (78 - 93) | ◇ 0576 |
| Suzuki GS & DR125 Singles (82 - 94) | ◇ 0888 |
| Suzuki 250 & 350 Twins (68 - 78) | 0120 |
| Suzuki GT250X7, GT200X5 & SB200 Twins (78 - 83) | ◇ 0469 |
| Suzuki GS/GSX250, 400 & 450 Twins (79 - 85) | 0736 |
| **Suzuki GS500E Twin (89 - 97)** | 3238 |
| Suzuki GS550 (77 - 82) & GS750 Fours (76 - 79) | 0363 |
| Suzuki GS/GSX550 4-valve Fours (83 - 88) | 1133 |
| **Suzuki GSF600 & 1200 Bandit Fours (95 - 97)** | 3367 |
| Suzuki GS850 Fours (78 - 88) | 0536 |

| Title | Book No. |
|---|---|
| Suzuki GS1000 Four (77 - 79) | 0484 |
| **Suzuki GSX-R750, GSX-R1100, GSX600F, GSX750F, GSX1100F (Katana) Fours (85 - 96)** | 2055 |
| Suzuki GS/GSX1000, 1100 & 1150 4-valve Fours (79 - 88) | 0737 |
| **TOMOS** | |
| Tomos A3K, A3M, A3MS & A3ML Mopeds (82 - 91) | ◇ 1062 |
| **TRIUMPH** | |
| Triumph Tiger Cub & Terrier (52 - 68) | 0414 |
| Triumph 350 & 500 Unit Twins (58 - 73) | 0137 |
| Triumph Pre-Unit Twins (47 - 62) | 0251 |
| Triumph 650 & 750 2-valve Unit Twins (63 - 83) | 0122 |
| Triumph Trident & BSA Rocket 3 (69 - 75) | 0136 |
| **Triumph Triples & Fours (91 - 95)** | 2162 |
| **VESPA** | |
| Vespa P/PX125, 150 & 200 Scooters (78 - 95) | 0707 |
| Vespa Scooters (59 - 78) | 0126 |
| **YAMAHA** | |
| Yamaha RD50 & 80 (78 - 89) | ◇ 1255 |
| Yamaha DT50 & 80 Trail Bikes (78 - 95) | ◇ 0800 |
| Yamaha T50 & 80 Townmate (83 - 95) | ◇ 1247 |
| Yamaha YT, YFM, YTM & YTZ ATVs (80 - 85) | 1154 |
| Yamaha YB100 Singles (73 - 91) | ◇ 0474 |
| Yamaha 100, 125 & 175 Trail bikes (71 - 85) | 0210 |
| Yamaha RS/RXS100 & 125 Singles (74 - 95) | 0331 |
| Yamaha RD & DT125LC (82 - 87) | ◇ 0887 |
| Yamaha TZR125 (87 - 93) & DT125R (88 - 95) | ◇ 1655 |
| Yamaha TY50, 80, 125 & 175 (74 - 84) | ◇ 0464 |
| Yamaha XT & SR125 (82 - 96) | 1021 |
| Yamaha 250 & 350 Twins (70 - 79) | 0040 |
| Yamaha XS250, 360 & 400 sohc Twins (75 - 84) | 0378 |
| Yamaha YBF250 Timberwolf ATV (92 - 96) | 2217 |
| Yamaha YFM350 Big Bear and ER ATVs (87 - 95) | 2126 |
| Yamaha RD250 & 350LC Twins (80 - 82) | 0803 |
| Yamaha RD350 YPVS Twins (83 - 95) | 1158 |
| Yamaha RD400 Twin (75 - 79) | 0333 |
| Yamaha XT, TT & SR500 Singles (75 - 83) | 0342 |
| Yamaha XZ550 Vision V-Twins (82 - 85) | 0821 |
| Yamaha FJ, FZ, XJ & YX600 Radian (84 - 92) | 2100 |
| Yamaha XJ600S (Seca II, Diversion) & XJ600N Fours (92 - 95 UK) (92 - 96 USA) | 2145 |
| Yamaha 650 Twins (70 - 83) | 0341 |
| Yamaha XJ650 & 750 Fours (80 - 84) | 0738 |
| Yamaha XS750 & 850 Triples (76 - 85) | 0340 |
| **Yamaha FZR600, 750 & 1000 Fours (87 - 96)** | 2056 |
| **Yamaha XV V-Twins (81 - 96)** | 0802 |
| **Yamaha XJ900F Fours (83 - 94)** | 3239 |
| **Yamaha FJ1100 & 1200 Fours (84 - 96)** | 2057 |
| **PRACTICAL MANUALS** | |
| Motorcycle Basics Manual | 1083 |
| Motorcycle Carburettor Manual | 0603 |
| **TECHBOOKS** | |
| ATV Basics | 10450 |
| Motorcycle Electrical Manual (3rd Edition) | 3471 |
| Motorcycle Workshop Practice Manual (2nd Edition) | 3470 |

◇ = not available in the USA    **Bold type** = Superbike

The manuals on this page are available through good motorcycle dealers and accessory shops. In case of difficulty, contact: **Haynes Publishing**
(UK) +44 1963 440635    (USA) +1 805 4986703
(FR) +33 1 47 78 50 50    (SV) +46 18 124016
(Australia/New Zealand) +61 3 9763 8100

MCL06.06/98

# Preserving Our Motoring Heritage

< The Model J Duesenberg Derham Tourster. Only eight of these magnificent cars were ever built – this is the only example to be found outside the United States of America

Almost every car you've ever loved, loathed or desired is gathered under one roof at the Haynes Motor Museum. Over 300 immaculately presented cars and motorbikes represent every aspect of our motoring heritage, from elegant reminders of bygone days, such as the superb Model J Duesenberg to curiosities like the bug-eyed BMW Isetta. There are also many old friends and flames. Perhaps you remember the 1959 Ford Popular that you did your courting in? The magnificent 'Red Collection' is a spectacle of classic sports cars including AC, Alfa Romeo, Austin Healey, Ferrari, Lamborghini, Maserati, MG, Riley, Porsche and Triumph.

## A Perfect Day Out

Each and every vehicle at the Haynes Motor Museum has played its part in the history and culture of Motoring. Today, they make a wonderful spectacle and a great day out for all the family. Bring the kids, bring Mum and Dad, but above all bring your camera to capture those golden memories for ever. You will also find an impressive array of motoring memorabilia, a comfortable 70 seat video cinema and one of the most extensive transport book shops in Britain. The Pit Stop Cafe serves everything from a cup of tea to wholesome, home-made meals or, if you prefer, you can enjoy the large picnic area nestled in the beautiful rural surroundings of Somerset.

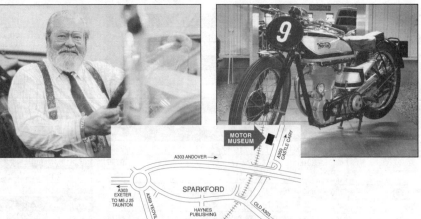

> John Haynes O.B.E., Founder and Chairman of the museum at the wheel of a Haynes Light 12.

< The 1936 490cc sohc-engined International Norton – well known for its racing success

The Museum is situated on the A359 Yeovil to Frome road at Sparkford, just off the A303 in Somerset. It is about 40 miles south of Bristol, and 25 minutes drive from the M5 intersection at Taunton.
Open 9.30am - 5.30pm (10.00am - 4.00pm Winter) 7 days a week, *except Christmas Day, Boxing Day and New Years Day*
Special rates available for schools, coach parties and outings  Charitable Trust No. 292048